de Gruyter Studies in Organization 61
Management of Knowledge-Intensive Companies

de Gruyter Studies in Organization

Organizational Theory and Research

This de Gruyter Series aims at publishing theoretical and methodological studies of organizations as well as research findings, which yield insight in and knowledge about organizations. The whole spectrum of perspectives will be considered: organizational analyses rooted in the sociological as well as the economic tradition, from a socio-psychological or a political science angle, mainstream as well as critical or ethnomethodological contributions. Equally, all kinds of organizations will be considered: firms, public agencies, non-profit institutions, voluntary associations, inter-organizational networks, supra-national organizations etc.

Emphasis is on publication of *new* contributions, or significant revisions of existing approaches. However, summaries or critical reflections on current thinking and research will also be considered.

This series represents an effort to advance the social scientific study of organizations across national boundaries and academic disciplines. An Advisory Board consisting of representatives of a variety of perspectives and from different cultural areas is responsible for achieving this task.

This series addresses organization researchers within and outside universities, but also practitioners who have an interest in grounding their work on recent social scientific knowledge and insights.

Editors:

Prof. Dr. Alfred Kieser, Universität Mannheim, Mannheim, Germany

Advisory Board:

Prof. Anna Grandori, CRORA, Università Commerciale Luigi Bocconi, Milano, Italy
Prof. Dr. Cornelis Lammers, FSW Rijksuniversiteit Leiden, The Netherlands
Prof. Dr. Marshall W. Meyer, The Wharton School, University of Pennsylvania, Philadelphia, U.S.A.
Prof. Jean-Claude Thoenig, Université de Paris I, Paris, France
Prof. Dr. Barry A. Turner, Middlesex Business School, London, GB
Prof. Mayer F. Zald, The University of Michigan, Ann Arbor, U.S.A.

Mats Alvesson

Management of Knowledge-Intensive Companies

Walter de Gruyter · Berlin · New York 1995

Mats Alvesson, PhD, Professor, Dept. of Business Administration, University of Lund, Sweden

With 4 tables and 20 figures

∞ Printed on acid-free paper which falls within the guidelines of the ANSI to ensure permanence and durability.

Library of Congress Cataloging-in-Publication Data

Alvesson, Mats, 1956–
    Management of knowledge-intensive companies / Mats Alvesson.
        p.   cm. – (De Gruyter studies in organization ; 61)
        Includes bibliographical references.
        ISBN 3-11-012865-9 (alk. paper)
        1. Consulting firms – Management. 2. Organizational behavior. 3. Enator AB – Management – Case studies.
    I. Title. II. Series.
    HD69.C6A48   1995
    001′.–dc20   94-37024
                                            CIP

Die Deutsche Bibliothek – Cataloging-in-Publication Data

Alvesson, Mats:
Management of knowledge intensive companies : [with 4 tables] / Mats Alvesson. – Berlin ; New York : de Gruyter, 1995
    (De Gruyter studies in organization ; 61 : Organizational theory and research)
    ISBN 3-11-012865-9
NE: GT

Typesetting: Converted by Knipp Satz und Bild digital, Dortmund – Printing: Gerike GmbH, Berlin. – Binding: D. Mikolai, Berlin. – Cover Design: Johannes Rother, Berlin. Printed in Germany.

Preface

I commenced the study which resulted in this book after having worked at a theoretical level for several years with symbolism and the cultural perspective in organization research. This background has influenced my work considerably, although the theoretical framework of this book encompasses several other perspectives and theories which can hardly be classified as organizational culture. The book looks at "knowledge intensive companies" and, in particular, focusses on a specific example in the form of Enator, a computer consultancy company. The book, too, combines an attempt to describe this type of company in general, and the case of Enator in particular, with a more theoretical aspiration of making a contribution to the development of cultural and symbolism theories in a corporate context. I have not been prepared to give one of these ambitions priority over the other.

I would like to express my gratitude to Enator's personnel, and in particular to Mr Rolf Thorsell, Enator's CEO at the time of my study, for doing everything possible to facilitate my work on this book. A great many colleagues have helped by reading and commenting on various drafts of the text. In particular, I would like to thank Yvonne Billing, Stan Deetz, Evert Gummesson, Gideon Kunda, Nelson Phillips, Anders Risling, Sven Erik Sjöstrand, Kaj Sköldberg and Rune Wigblad. I would also like to thank Ann McKinnon and Margareta Samuelsson at the University of Gothenburg for administrative assistance. This English version has been translated from Swedish by David Canter in Stockholm.

Parts of Chapter 6 have been previously published in *International Studies of Management & Organization* 1989/90, Vol. 19, No. 4 and Chapter 8 appeared in a slightly different version in *Organization Studies* 1992, Vol. 13, No. 2.

This book is part of a project financed by the Council for Research in the Humanities and Social Sciences.

June, 1994   Mats Alvesson

Table of Contents

1 Introduction

The starting point for this book is a case study of a young, rapidly-growing computer consulting company, Enator AB. Enator has attracted considerable attention in Sweden, both on the stock market (primarily in the mid 1980s) and in the mass media. In the latter case, this attention has been largely due to the company's somewhat spectacular characteristics: for example, its unique headquarters building and unusual corporate celebrations.

Enator is an example of a knowledge-intensive, professional business service company having the problem-solving competence of its employees at its core. This study examines Enator from a corporate perspective and from the perspective of managers and other employees. The study provides specific knowledge of Enator and a more general perspective on knowledge intensive firms.

From an organizational point of view, companies of this type are normally regarded as adhocracies, as the organization of work is set up in the form of temporary groupings in line with the varying nature of the tasks to be performed. An adhocracy is characterized by project organization as a working principle in contrast to traditional bureaucracies where the emphasis is on a more stable hierarchy, a clear division of labour, the specialization at tasks, and a clear distinction between task planning and execution. As a result, the adhocracy is a popular subject with many writers, and is claimed to be an increasingly common organizational form in business. The adhocracy deviates from conventional organizations in its management, its strategies and its working conditions. As a case study, Enator provides a basis for obtaining knowledge about an organizational form on which there has hitherto been relatively little systematic research.

Enator is interesting in itself, as a unique phenomenon and some of the aspects dealt with in this book concern circumstances which are specific for the Company. The purpose of this book is however, to illuminate broader phenomena. The company illustrates important trends in Swedish and international business, working life and management. Today, it would be almost banal to state that the service sector has expanded or that the number of companies and employees dealing with skilled semi-professional or professional services has increased. Sometimes such operations are spoken of as "knowledge-intensive" or "know-how" companies, and

this is supposed to indicate that there are considerable differences between them compared with traditional, mass production service companies. Naturally, there are major differences between a computer consultancy company and, for example, railway or airline corporations, McDonald's or other typical service companies. The service sector per se, even if
one is excluding professional services, is rather heterogeneous, despite
current ideas about "service management" and "service marketing" as
specific concepts.

Quite apart from this, the concept of corporate culture has, since 1980,
attracted attention as a somewhat diffuse but crucial phenomenon in organizations. Popular management books have described corporate culture as
a phenomenon which affects everything from management style, decision
making and collective awareness of corporate objectives, to job satisfaction and everyday priorities and social interactions. Closely related to corporate culture is what is sometimes referred to as "new forms of management". These new methods are based on the idea that the purpose of management is to create a feeling of shared community and identification between the company and its employees. This state of affairs is achieved by
means of soft personnel-oriented management methods which appeal to
the employee as a "whole person", rather than merely to the employee as
a wage earner. Management is increasingly used to state ideals and ideas
which lead to action, rather than to exercise concrete, detailed control
(Alvesson and Berg, 1992; Beckérus et al., 1988; Kunda, 1992). Many optimistic things have been said about this style of management, primarily by
management oriented consultants and academics (e.g. Deal and Kennedy,
1982; Peters and Waterman, 1982). It is scarcely surprising that sceptical
and critical comments have been made by union representatives (e.g.
Eriksson, 1986), by radical management theorists (Willmott, 1993), and by
working-life researchers (e.g. Sandberg, 1987).

However, there is still not much competent empirical research in this
area, at least not of a deeper nature as required by the subject – ethno-
graphic case studies. I will review the exceptions later in the book. Since
the case study object of this book constitutes a clear – and perhaps even
extreme – example of a company endowed with these "new management
philosophies", it follows that this case study may be able to throw some
light on this phenomenon. This book provides descriptions and interpretations of management and control structures and processes and their consequences for employees. While it primarily focusses on the case of Enator,
it also applies to other places of work with similar management and organizational conditions.

This case study focusses on a number of aspects of the company. Various themes are dealt with at a general level including socialization in the
workplace, organizational structure, corporate culture, organizational cli-

mate, management, leadership, working conditions, the business concept, strategies, and marketing. Perhaps this appears to be too many themes for a single book. However, as discussed here, the various facets of the company are closely related. This is true to a greater extent in a consultancy company than in many other types of firms, such as most manufacturing corporations. For instance, in a consultancy company, marketing and strategy cannot be clearly separated or distinguished from organizational and production activity. Almost all at Enator's employees interact with the employees of customer companies (the market). This contrasts with conditions in many other companies where, for example, marketing constitutes a specific, distinct function which does not necessarily concern the majority of personnel directly.

The use of culture theory and symbol theory as a framework for interpretation also serves to facilitate a broad approach, encompassing many different aspects and questions. I will be discussing this frame of reference in most of the chapters in this book, thus making it possible to handle and integrate in an acceptable manner the wide range of conditions which are discussed.

1.1   Theoretical Objectives

The objectives of this book may be usefully understood in terms of Glaser and Strauss' (1967) distinction between "substantial" and "formal" theory. Substantial theory is concerned with a given empirical area, while formal theory operates at a more general theoretical level.

The substantial area has been hinted at already. It involves contributions to the development of empirically oriented knowledge about management, organization, strategies and marketing in knowledge-intensive companies (primarily in the service sector), i.e. in a particular empirical area. The formal objective (i.e. at a more general theoretical level) involves, on the one hand, discussion and attempts to qualify some elements of organizational structure, leadership and strategy theory and, on the other hand, a contribution to organizational cultural research. The first of these two formal objectives, which is about different dimensions of the manner in which the company functions, is a matter of developing general knowledge about socialization processes, organizational structure, the way corporate culture is built up and its consequences, etc. The empirical case, for instance, provides a basis for discussion which is not confined to organizational structure in the type of company under consideration, but which is also concerned to some extent with how we can approach the subject in general terms which are independent of specific case study organization. It is thus not a question of attempting empirical generalization but rather of working with concepts, ideas, and dimensions which are of general interest. Contributions in a formal, theoretical sense make considerable demands on the researcher. I am well aware that in some sections of this book I have not succeeded in doing very much more than describe and interpret the specific case, even though this, in itself, may be of interest.

The second formal (theoretical) objective has been primarily to contribute to organization research from the perspective of culture and symbol theory. This theory is referred to in the next section, but is discussed more thoroughly in Chapter 3. At this stage, it suffices to say that this perspective constitutes a fundamental frame of reference which is intended to stimulate understanding both of the object of research in a substantial sense (Enator, knowledge-intensive companies) and of the theoretical themes which are dealt with. In this study, the theory of culture and symbols partly functions at a metatheoretical level. I hope to contribute to cultural research in a corporate context, primarily through showing the broad (wide) range of application of culture theory in management studies.

I will, instead of the conventional approach of developing/adapting one framework which guides the interpretation of the empirical material, sometimes alternate between culture theory and the more traditional management theories (see below) in relationship to interpretations of the case study. Culture theory also inspires re-interpretations of ideas in (conventional) management theories, e.g. on organizational structure and business concept. This means that I engage in a kind of "theory game" – going back and forth between culture theory and other (management) theories.

1.2   Theoretical Frames of Reference

Most of the literature and theories that I will be using in this book will be indicated and discussed in connection with the chapters dealing with the various themes. In other words, the discussion of the theory and the description of the empirical data from the case will alternate. (The only exception is in Chapter 3, where culture and symbol theory are reviewed. However, at this point I would like to focus briefly on the principal theoretical inspiration on which this book is based.)

First and foremost, the perspective adopted in this book grows out of theories of culture and symbols. Both anthropological and organizational culture and symbol theories are employed. The main point is that collective action presumes repetitive common meanings and symbols. A crucial aspect of social structures, action patterns, material objects, the language used, etc. is that they can function as collective symbols, in addition to purely technical, objective and rational aspects, and are given intersubjective meaning in the organization, thus providing a basis for coordinated action. Organization is thus basically defined in terms of shared meanings.

A second important source of inspiration is what could be described in rather approximate terms as a moderate version of non-rational organization theory.[1] By non-rational I mean ideas and arguments which focus on the contradictions, ambiguities, and discrepancies which exist in organizations and which point to the lack of clear, consistent and properly cohesive patterns of action. It is assumed that the social world is complicated and contradictory. Understanding companies and organizations does not only involve a search for systems, cohesive patterns, and well-arranged structures and functions but also the reverse: loose couplings between what is said and what is done, between different actions and structures, ambiguities, contradictions, confusion, etc. (cf. Brunsson, 1985; Calás and Smircich, 1987; Gray et al., 1985; Linstead and Grafton-Small, 1992; March and Olsen, 1976; Martin and Meyerson, 1988; Weick, 1976; Orton and Weick,1990; etc.)

In examining the organizational form and strategy of Enator, and of other organizations of a similar type, Mintzberg's ideas about organization structure and strategies in adhocracies are an important starting point (e.g. Mintzberg, 1983; Mintzberg and Waters, 1985). Giddens' (1979) theory of "structuration" and the organization research inspired by Giddens will also be dealt with (e.g. Ranson et al., 1980).

In the marketing area, general ideas about service sector marketing are of primary relevance (e.g. Grönroos; 1984, Normann, 1983). At the same time, there are significant differences between mass-produced services for consumers and the professional services, which may frequently be of a problem-solving nature, offered by Enator to industrial and other companies. In this case, the literature on industrial marketing is also of interest (e.g. Håkansson et al., 1981).

A certain inspiration provided by critical theory also surfaces occasionally in this book. This focuses attention on how different conceptions and forms of consciousness are spread and institutionalized. In other words, the natural, self-evident and taken-for-granted nature of some circumstances and arrangements are deeply anchored in the ideas and beliefs of a group. Attention is also focused on possible limitations on the freedom of thinking and action which certain ideas may involve. In other words, the ideology concept is regarded as important. Amongst other things, the concept of ideology indicates that certain definitions of social circumstances and certain ideals, which are considered worth striving for and which are therefore given priority, tend to supplant other definitions and ideals. Sometimes this occurs less as a result of careful reflection than as a result of the power-base of dominant groups and the dominant logic of society (which defines "common sense" and "rationality"). Critical theory empha-sizes that the encouragement of a reflective, critical approach to the domi-nant ideologies and definitions of social reality is an important function of the social sciences (Alvesson and Willmott, 1992, 1995; Deetz, 1992). However, I only make use of this tradition explicitly to a very small de-gree. Its influence on the book can be seen more in a general awareness of these aspects. It is hoped that this awareness permeates this book.

1.3   Knowledge-intensive Companies

The concept of the knowledge-intensive company has come to the fore in the late 1980s in both practical and academic circles in Sweden and to some extent in other countries. (In Sweden, people talk about knowledge companies, but the English concept which appears to be increasingly uti-lized is knowledge-intensive companies or firms.) There are different opinions about how to define this category. Sveiby and Risling (1986), for example, regard almost all companies which are concerned with sophisti-cated operations as knowledge-intensive companies, while others regard the category as more exclusive. Many writers (Gummesson, 1990; Hed-berg, 1990; Starbuck, 1992) consider that knowledge-intensive companies are characterized by factors such as:

- significant incidents of problem solving and non-standardized produc-tion;
- creativity on the part of the practitioner and the organizational environ-ment;
- heavy reliance on individuals (and less dependence on capital) and a high degree of independence on the part of practitioners.
- high educational levels and a high degree of professionalization on the part of most employees;
- traditional concrete (material) assets are not a central factor. The critical elements are in the minds of employees and in networks, customer rela-tionships, manuals and systems for supplying services;
- heavy dependence on the loyalty of key personnel and – this is the other side of the picture – considerable vulnerability when personnel leave the company.

There is an emphasis on knowledge-intensive operations, as opposed to labour-intensive or capital-intensive. Human capital is the dominant factor in knowledge-intensive firms.

One variation of this idea is to refer to knowledge-intensive operations as an overall category, subsequently making a sub-distinction between "pure" knowledge companies and high technology companies (Ekstedt, 1990). In both cases, personnel with a high degree of competence and experience may be central factors but, in high technology companies, knowledge and innovation are embodied in products and technology which transmit and incorporate the knowledge in question. In "pure" knowledge companies, individuals are the primary bearers of knowledge, even if this knowledge may be *partially* institutionalized and localized at the organizational level in the form of collective frames of reference (cultures), systematized methods of work, manuals, etc. (Bonora and Revang, 1993; Starbuck, 1992). For the most part, I employ the concept "knowledge-intensive company" in accordance with accepted usage, but I want to stress that my case study involves a company in which the focus is completely on human capital and, as a result, some discussions are centred on this (major) subgroup in the overall knowledge-intensive firm category. However, comparisons with research into more capital-intensive knowledge-intensive companies, i.e. companies with technology which requires greater capital resources (high-tech companies), indicate that in important aspects there are considerable similarities between the two categories (see in particular Chapter 14). Therefore, many of the ideas and results of this study thus have a broad relevance for a wide range of knowledge-intensive organizations.

One problem with the concept of the knowledge-intensive company is that considerable prestige is attached to the term. Sometimes I get the impression that almost every company wants to be seen as a knowledge-intensive company. This means that the term may often be employed because it sounds good rather than because it is a satisfactory means of describing important phenomena. The fact that it sounds good is probably a more important reason for the success of the concept of the knowledge-intensive firm (knowledge company) (in Scandinavia, at least) than its descriptive value. Of course this is a good (intellectual) reason for avoiding the concept. A related reason concerns the political implications of representing some companies and some work as knowledge-intensive, thereby implying that other companies and work are not knowledge-intensive. If knowledge workers are understood to be highly qualified individuals who belong to, or form a distinct component of a group of professional and managerial employees, a certain social division of labour is reproduced and legitimized in a way that "overlooks their common positioning as wage labour within a capitalist mode of production" (Knights et al., 1993, p 976). This problem can be handled by emphasizing partly that knowledge-intensive firms and workers are loose categories and that they do not necessarily encompass "more sophisticated" knowledge or more advanced or "sexy" operations than can be found in many other types of organizations and occupations. If we look at the "true" professions – medicine, dentistry, psychoanalysis, etc. – they are not normally particularly concerned with creative problem-solving; instead they are more likely to apply relatively standardized methods based on "science and proven experience" (cf. Mintzberg's professional bureaucracy). From the point of view of the criteria presented above, it is not clear whether organizations dominated by these professional groups can be automatically regarded as the best cases of knowledge-intensive companies. From the management aspect, many purely knowledge-intensive firms are rather small and thus less complicated to manage and organize than most companies with complicated technology and with multi-faceted production and distribution arrangements. Thus it would be a mistake to automatically associate knowledge-intensive firms with know-how and management arrangements which are regarded as the most prestigious in society. At least this is true at least if we give the concept of the knowledge-intensive firm a more limited definition, in line with the criteria above, and do not equate such firms with all types of knowledge-intensive operations.

The fact that knowledge is such a diffuse and all embracing concept is another problem (Alvesson, 1993c). Of course, all firms are based on some form of knowledge. The fact that knowledge, in knowledge-intensive firms, is primarily related to individuals rather than associated with organizations (routines, organized work processes) or built into machines and material technologies gives some indication of what is involved. Another clue is that a significant proportion of the personnel in such firms have advanced education and experience. A possible criterion of knowledge-intensive firms might be that half the employees should have university or equivalent education. (However, as is the case with a criterion of this type it should be used with the above characteristics, and with discretion.) One problem with this criterion is that it reflects social class factors. As Starbuck (1992) points out, higher education corresponds with upper middle-class interests as to what should be considered prestigious or regarded as expertise. Probably, many craftsmen might be regarded as more advanced in terms of knowledge than college graduates if an alternative approach to knowledge were to be applied. However, I will not enquire into the extent to which activities which are not based on higher formal education can be described vis-à-vis the activities of knowledge-intensive firms partly defined by the long formal education of the employees. Another open question is what talent-based activities – for example creative work in the advertising world or in theatres – fit into the concept of the knowledge-intensive firm.

Thus, as I am somewhat doubtful about the knowledge-intensive firm concept, I originally considered giving this book another title, which used the concept of a professional service company. The latter term is somewhat better demarcated but has a number of disadvantages, including the fact that it also has prestigious overtones. It is even more important to consider the problem of defining the professions and professional organizations. Computer consultancy is not really considered to be a traditional profession and it is difficult to determine the limits which distinguish an extended professional concept from occupations which lie beyond this limit. A term such as semi-professional is not helpful. However, there are certainly considerable differences between skilled services, such as computer consultancy and simpler services, such as cleaning and security services. (The difference becomes even more noticeable if we do not merely confine ourselves to producer services, but also examine the entire service area, including consumer services.) Nonetheless, the knowledge-intensive firm concept does indicate a distinction of this type in broad outline without going into detail regarding particular criteria of professions or semi-professions such as autonomy, restricted access to the work area (monopolization of a part of the labour market), specific education, professional associations, a code of ethics etc. (Alvesson, 1993c). These criteria are not very helpful for understanding most service work carried out by well educated and highly paid workers in business contexts. Yet another alternative might be to speak of consultancy companies, but here there are similar definitional problems in distinguishing between simple and complex services. In addition this term would result in a narrower focus than I intended in this book. Many of the topics covered are probably of much broader relevance than would be the case if we confined ourselves to the term consultancy companies. Many sections of this book, for example, are of considerable relevance for universities and high-tech companies. As already mentioned, many of the concepts and ideas discussed here are intended to provide more general contributions than those which are only relevant to understanding computer consultancy companies. Comparisons between my case and high-tech industries documented by Kanter (1983), Kunda (1992), Martin (1992) and others will clearly show this in the chapters that follow. (To a certain degree, I sacrifice empirical details for the benefit of broader theoretical arguments in this book.)

For these reasons, and in view of the fact that the term knowledge-intensive company and knowledge workers seems to be becoming more widely employed, I have chosen to refer to knowledge-intensive firms or companies, even if I am aware of the disadvantages of this concept. I shall try not to reinforce the prestigious aura which surrounds the concept. Rather than emphasizing the special nature of knowledge-intensiveness in relation to mass production companies and "professional bureaucracies", I will endeavour to apply a more subtle approach to themes of significance for understanding this type of organization, for example, ideas about the ad hoc character of (many) knowledge-intensive firms (see Chapter 6) and the significance of regulating images in the knowledge-intensive service sector (Chapter 10).

In this study I focus on a single company which probably represents a typical example of a knowledge-intensive firm, irrespective of exactly what definition among those expressed in the literature is employed. In fact, computer consultancy companies seem to be one of the most commonly utilized examples of this category. The case study attempts to focus on aspects and dimensions which are relevant for a broader understanding of such companies, but it should be said that different sections of this book vary as to the manner and the extent that they express ideas which have broad relevance. The generality of issues on marketing treated in this book are largely confined to consultancy companies, while issues related to corporate culture appear to be of significance also for many knowledge-intensive companies outside the service sector.

When conducting research into a specific knowledge-intensive firm -and this also applies to many other categories of organizations – it is important to note that it is generally difficult to focus on a single type of organization. This applies in the present case too; a case study also encompasses elements which are associated with the category but which cannot be reduced or equated with it. Often, for example, knowledge-intensive firms have an adhocratic form (Sveiby and Risling, 1986) but, as Chapter 6 indicates, other organizational forms may also be present or even be more salient. If the primary concern is to focus exclusively on understanding knowledge-intensive firms – if such an "purified" objective is at all possible – caution should be employed in equating knowledge-intensiveness with adhocracy. Knowledge-intensive firms are quite often characterized by rapid growth, success and a certain type of labour market, etc. At least, these characteristics have often characterized what have been termed knowledge-intensive firms in Sweden in the 1980s. This also applies in the present case. The extent to which this study and other studies describe knowledge-intensive companies "as such", or to which knowledge-intensive companies appear in a certain historical epoch and in certain specific development conditions (e.g. an expanding market and a certain lack of competent personnel) must be regarded as an open question. Clearly, this question can only be answered in a more extended historical perspective than that applied in current literature in this field, which has largely described this kind of organization in relatively favourable industries in the late 1980s.

In conclusion, I would like to point out that I have *not* consistently referred to knowledge-intensive firms in this study. The type of company which has been studied may very well be described in this manner, but my interest is not confined to describing precisely this type of firm. As already mentioned, this study also has broader theoretical interest. In addition, I will be dealing with phenomena which are of relevance in understanding at least a considerable range of knowledge-intensive firms (irrespective of exactly how this concept is defined), but which cannot be limited to or totally subordinated to or equated with this category. The great advantage of the term "knowledge-intensive" firm is that it draws attention to a loosely defined group of organizations. But it is not always as useful when looking more closely at specific management, organization and marketing problems as many of these may be salient in a number of companies of this type, but not necessarily be significant for all organizations in this (ambiguous) category or exclusive for it. In this study, therefore, I refrain from consistently emphasizing the concept of the knowledge-intensive firm and will be content, instead, to apply it in a looser manner.

1.4   Constraints

Although this book offers a broad description of the case-study company and raises a number of different theoretical themes, there are naturally a considerable number of factors which are not considered. The main emphasis is on general management, organization and marketing. Financial aspects of the company are hardly treated at all. Similarly, formal control associated with result requirements and follow-up are only dealt with at a marginal level. Naturally, traditional management is an important aspect of the operations of the company described in the case study. As in other companies, management is concerned with budgets, other forms of planning, supervision, coordination and control. I choose, however, not to look at these aspects to any great extent. This does not imply that these aspects are unimportant. However, in comparison with most other companies, normative forms of control – influencing ideas and feelings – are more prominent and, in combination with my theoretical interest in cultural aspects, I have therefore tended to ignore administrative and financial control.

In addition, I will refrain, for the most part, from considering purely production aspects or from describing the content of work, etc. Thus, technical computer questions and the conduct and management of projects are not considered here. I do examine working conditions to some extent but only in connection with the social situation of personnel, not in regard to the work content or the physical work environment.

Of course, it would have been preferable if I could have also studied these aspects and, no doubt, insights into themes which have been neglected would have contributed to an understanding of many of the phenomena dealt with in this study. But it would hardly have been possible to cover more than is already encompassed in this book, which is already quite voluminous.

1.5   The Structure of the Book

As already mentioned, most of the chapters in this book cover a theoretical theme, for example socialization, organization structure, etc. Specialized literature and theory within the field are discussed and relevant empirical documentation from the case study is presented. An attempt is then made on the basis of interpretations of this material and discussions of a more theoretical nature to say as much as possible about Enator as a typical example of a knowledge-intensive (professional service) company and then, about the theoretical theme itself. Cultural theory as a meta framework is invoked here to enrich the understanding of the empirical material as well as the theoretical theme of the various chapters. As the reader no doubt realizes, it is relatively easy to make pronouncements about Enator, but somewhat more difficult to say something more general about the type of company concerned, and even more difficult to provide new theoretical contributions of a general nature.

My presentation starts with a brief overall description of the object of my case study, that is to say Enator. This provides a skeleton structure for later chapters, in which various aspects are gradually built up. In case studies, it is often tempting to provide detailed descriptions of the object of research – which is easy – but my aim has been to subordinate empirical descriptions to ideas, arguments and conclusions of a more general nature. This means that I have attempted to limit the purely descriptive aspects of this book. It also means that there is no cohesive history of the firm, apart from an extremely sketchy outline in Chapter 2 and a strategy-focussed description in Chapter 11. Unfortunately, this makes it more difficult for the reader to interpret the case himself or herself.

Chapter 3 looks at organizational culture theory research. Chapter 4 discusses qualitative methods and questions of the philosophy of science. Some of the theoretical and methodological considerations which underlie this book are presented in these two chapters.

Chapters 5-12 take up various themes, the first of which is socialization. The reason for selecting this starting-point is that the socialization process also says a great deal about the company, its understanding of itself, etc. By presenting the company's picture of itself in a concentrated form – and by attempting to minimize the influence of my own interpretations – I hope that the reader may get a dynamic picture and an initial understanding of operations which are presented primarily in management terms. But obviously, in the book as a whole, the perspective is the author's, even though the meanings of the people that have been studied are taken seriously. Chapter 6 covers organization structure and design and a culture perspective on formal structure. Chapter 7 deals with corporate culture and organization climate, while Chapter 8 goes on to look at management and leadership. These three chapters treat management and organizational circumstances in a broad sense. Chapter 9 turns to the work situation of personnel, where, for example, I examine some potential problems faced by staff which are implicit in the types of management and social control which characterize Enator.

Subsequently, Chapters 10 and 11 discuss the company's business concept and strategy. In Chapter 12, the focus is on marketing – both external and internal. The result is that chapters 10-12 constitute a section in which the focus is on the business aspects of operations.

Finally, in Chapters 13 and 14, an attempt is made to weave various themes together employing the arguments and results covered in various previous chapters. In addition, a number of conclusions are formulated. Chapter 14 is an attempt to contribute to organizational symbolism theory as well as to summarize and further clarify some insights on knowledge-intensive companies.

This book is designed to permit independent, separate reading of most chapters, even if this may not be altogether straightforward. However, the two concluding chapters require prior reading of much of the rest of the book. For the most part, the reader is free to select chapters which are of particular interest and skip sections which appear less relevant. However, if the aim is to obtain a reasonably clear picture of Enator, Chapter 2 and the first half of Chapter 5 are required reading. Those who are not familiar with culture and symbol theory should also read Chapter 3, at any rate the two final sections, if they wish to understand the principal perspectives of this book.

Note

[1]   The fact that I make use of the concept non rational organization theory does not mean that I am rejecting the idea that (many) organizations function in a goal-rational manner at an overall level, i.e. they are mainly characterized by effective activity which leads to the realization, to a greater or lesser extent, of the objectives and goals for operations which the principal has established (see e.g. Abrahamsson, 1986). On the contrary, this is a reasonable idea which is not contradicted by my case study. Regarding the organization as predominantly an instrument, as in rationalistic organization theory, and

treating it as "a planned and established structure which is constructed by an individual, a group or class with the conscious and decided purpose of realizing the achievement of certain objectives which are in the interest of the principal" (Abrahammson 1986, p 53) means, however, that there is a focus on the more formal overall aspects. I am interested in a deeper penetrating analysis of the more "living" dimensions of the case company's "real" manner of working. Thus what I have termed non-rational organization theory does not contradict a rationalistic view such as Abrahamsson's. It is more a matter of a different level of questioning and analysis.

2 Description of Enator AB

I undertook my field-work at Enator AB during a six-month period in 1987 and the descriptions presented in this book date back to this period unless otherwise stated. For the most part, I have used the present tense (which then refers to conditions in the late 1980s. However, the past tense has been employed when dealing with circumstances which change rapidly (e.g. the number of employees). This chapter is mainly an attempt to present certain basic facts and a brief account of some general characteristics of the company.

2.1 Enator's History: 1977-87

The company was founded in 1977 by three people with experience in computers, management and consultancy. At that time, data processing was expanding rapidly and both programmers and people who could relate computers and overall corporate issues were in great demand. Enator defined its niche as the linking of computer and business (top management) operations. The three founders had an extensive social network and, in combination with an expanding market and an easy-to-sell business concept, this led to a rapid growth. Enator employed one hundred people by 1980, and by 1987 it had a staff of five hundred.

Enator originally concentrated entirely on administrative data-processing. A few years later, however, the company became more involved in technically oriented projects and began to provide customer companies with consultant services for the execution of computer application projects in industrial corporations. For example, Enator became involved in the development of industrial products in which mini or micro computers were components. While the administrative sections of Enator are concerned with the adaptation of computer systems to final users such as banks and transport companies, Enator's technical arm assists industrial companies in the computer and electronics industry.

Shortly after its formation, Enator's technical wing established its own subsidiary within Enator and called it Mikrotell. Right from the start, one of Enator's basic principles was to minimize the number of employees in each subsidiary, with a limit of not more than 50 individuals. When employees exceed this number within any Enator subsidiary, a new company is formed. Over the years, several new corporate branches have opened up within Enator. In 1980, a subsidiary was formed on the administrative side to concentrate on the maintenance of existing computer systems, while in 1983 a new company was created which specialized in mini and micro computers. On the technical side, Mikrotell subdivided on three occasions between 1983 and 1986 and formed new subsidiaries. Thus, when my study was carried out in 1987 there were three administrative and four technical companies.

A number of joint venture companies were also formed by Enator in the 1980s. These joint venture companies were formed to market computer systems which had been developed in cooperation with certain customers. All these subsidiaries are located in Stockholm.

As time passed, regionalization of operations occurred, in parallel with continuing expansion in the Stockholm region. Local companies were set up in Malmö and Gothenburg. At the same time as it was moving into the provinces in Sweden, Enator also set up operations on an international scale. Between 1981 and 1985 subsidiaries were established in Britain, Norway, West-Germany and Denmark, and subsequently in Switzerland and Finland. The two latter companies were joint ventures with Swiss and Finnish companies.

Enator was launched on the Swedish Stock Exchange in 1983, where it attracted considerable attention for a time thanks to a rapid rise in share prices. Utilizing its accumulated profits, Enator purchased the Prospektor Group which included a major consultancy in the construction industry (Skandiakonsult). Prospektor was much larger than Enator but had not been particularly successful for some years. This Group rapidly changed its name to Pronator, with Enator as one company among a group of subsidiaries within Pronator. Since Pronator subsequently acquired all the shares in Enator, Enator was withdrawn from the Stock Exchange in 1987. Enator's founders (owners) also dominate the Pronator Group.

Enator's three founding members made their mark on the company's operations, particularly in the first 6 to 8 years. However, one of the founders gradually bowed out in the mid-1980s and his shares were ultimately acquired by his two companions. One of the remaining founders was Managing Director of Enator until 1985, when he was promoted and became Managing Director of Pronator and was simultaneously Chairman of the Board at Enator. Enator's new Managing Director was recruited externally, having previously been MD at one of Enator's largest customers for a number of years. In 1987, when my case study was carried out, the third founder member was still partially involved in Enator.

In 1987 Enator celebrated its 10th anniversary. The company's 500 employees and a number of other guests flew to the island of Rhodes where Enator's success was commemorated for three, apparently highly memorable days.

2.2 Enator at the Time of the Case Study (1987)

Enator's product continues to be consultancy services in the computer area. Enator offers a comprehensive range within this field – everything from strategy studies to the implementation of computer projects on a large scale. There is a special emphasis on Enator's ability to manage projects, and to implement computer development projects in line with agreed time schedules and budgets.

In 1987, the Enator group consisted of some 20 subsidiaries each with 1 to 50 employees. Half of the total staff of 500 were working in the seven administrative and technical companies in Kista near Stockholm. Somewhat more than 50 were located in regional companies in Sweden, while approximately 150 were working in companies abroad. The remaining personnel were employed by the parent company, Swedish joint-venture companies, etc.

Much of the crucial data about Enator's financial status, personnel, etc. are presented in Figures 2.1 and 2.2, which also indicate developments in the period 1982-86 in terms of turnover, financial results, etc.

2.3 Something about Enator's Functioning and Management

The following is a brief outline of how the various corporate functions of Enator are related to each other. This will make it easier for the reader to understand how Enator functions "as a whole" and how the various aspects presented in Chapters 5-12 are related.

In companies like Enator the technological core is weak. Operations are not held together by a cohesive production process. Instead production takes the form of hundreds of projects each year which are carried out relatively independently of each other. Thus, compared with most manufacturing companies or mass-production service corporations, it would be misleading to represent Enator's organization as a machine in which different individuals or sections of the companies are cogs in the works. Instead, Enator consists of separate projects which are very loosely linked to each other.

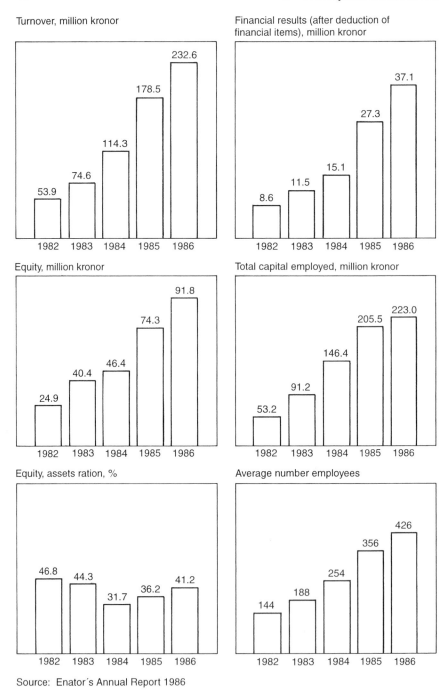

Source: Enator´s Annual Report 1986

Figure 2.1:   Data about Enator, 1982-86

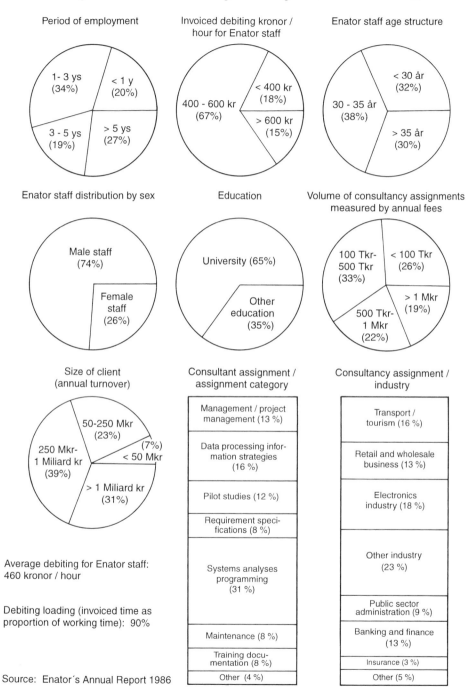

Figure 2.2:   Data about Enator, 1986

At the same time, Enator is also operating in a market which demands flexibility. For the most part, the planning horizon is brief and set-up times for consultancy projects are normally minimal. Technology is flexible, since it consists of the consultants' competence and know-how.

The nature of the consultancy assignments means that operative control is largely exercised by project managers and consultants in the field. Top and middle management have rather limited opportunities to exercise direct supervision and control. All they can do is to issue general guidelines for the methods to be employed and follow up the tasks by means of occasional talks with project managers and consultants. Since projects involve the solution of more or less unique tasks, control is often a matter of adapting to the particular assignment and to local circumstances.

The fact that projects mainly involve relatively sophisticated problem-solving and that almost Enator's entire labour force consists of well-trained consultants means that a traditional organization hierarchy can only function in a limited sense. Management can hardly be said to direct the work-process in any detail. Self-supervision is far more important than hierarchical control. In some contexts one might speak of competence hierarchies, which clearly deviate from the organization hierarchy. This means that people at low levels in formal terms may have competence and skills which are essential in dealing with a specific question and their influence may therefore be substantial.

These characteristics play a crucial role in the manner in which the company is run. The fact that the means of production are in fact identical with the competence of the personnel and that the production processes are heterogeneous and decentralized implies that traditional "structural" control can only be partially utilized. It also means that a centralized "top-down" formulation and implementation of strategy can only be applied to a limited extent.

In order to get the company to work as a whole – even if only as an entity with partially independent components – other means of control are required. Traditional and formal instruments are not sufficient. This applies internally at the organizational level, externally at the market level, and strategically with respect to long-term development. It is important that all members of the organization understand and accept certain fundamental guidelines for operation. It is not sufficient – as to some extent is the case in most traditional companies – for this to be understood exclusively by management and senior executives, with overall ideas, objectives and plans subsequently translated into concrete action by means of the allocation of resources, formal goals, standardization of tasks, etc. In organizations like Enator, the company's overall ideals, methods and exchange relations with its environment must be based on the decentralized functioning of its personnel. (Of course, this applies to many service companies and manufacturers of advanced products, as it does to some extent to all types of companies. In the case of knowledge-intensive companies, the need for a strong basis of support for overall ideas and guidelines for operations, running right through the organization, is particularly important.)

In organizational terms, structural arrangements and formal authority relationships are of somewhat lesser importance than in other companies. However, social ties, a common understanding of the nature of work, shared values and other "non-substantive" means of control and co-ordination of operations are all particularly crucial for this type of company. The ambition is to employ what is known as "corporate culture" as a means of control.

In marketing terms, traditional marketing methods play a relatively small part in building up and stabilizing exchange relationships with customer companies. It is difficult to demonstrate and sell professional services in advance either by marketing-mix strategies or by the use of special salesmen. In the professional services sector, consulting personnel, especially project managers, are themselves responsible for major aspects of marketing. As a result of their current and previous projects, such personnel have a long-standing and close contact with their customers. These contacts constitute an important base for sales and for the supplementary selling of new project assignments. Thus, the marketing function is partly built into the production function and integrated into the organization as a whole, rather than separately delineated and centralized in organizational terms.

Since a high proportion of consultancy assignments are undertaken at customers' places of work, in close cooperation with the customers' staff, most Enator personnel have close contact with the market and often have long-term interaction with customers. And since the personnel constitute Enator's total marketing offer, the manner in which they carry out their assignments and their ability to establish contacts and to transmit a picture of the company's methods and competence are of the greatest importance from a marketing point of view.

Thus, most personnel have an important marketing function and the crucial point here is that, as in the organizational context, what the company represents is well-based in the conceptual world of the employees. This is an important aspect of the identity. The interest and involvement of personnel in their work and their ability and willingness to transmit a good and cohesive picture of their company are thus central factors from a marketing perspective. Work performance that is only technically satisfactory is insufficient on its own, according to top management.

Major areas of the development and execution of the strategy are delegated to the consultants in operations of this type. Thus, it is not possible to regard consultants as simply the instruments for the realization of the objectives of top management. The personnel cannot be treated simply as foot-soldiers who are carrying out the general's plans. The consultants' network of contacts and their initiative is of critical strategic importance.

Strategic development and change in this type of organization are thus intimately linked with the way in which the organization and its personnel work as a whole, how employees define and redefine operations and their frameworks and also what initiatives and priorities employees take and apply. There is no doubt that top management functions as a central strategic actor and that a certain amount of strategic change takes place as a result of control exercised from the top down. But at the same time, major initiatives for strategic reorientation and general, collective tendencies for change coming from the bottom up may also be highly important.

In particular, I would like to emphasize how the three functional areas of organization, marketing and strategy are more closely linked than in traditional bureaucratic organizations. In business operations of this type, most of the company's personnel participate in intimate contact with the market. It might be said that the organization and the market are directly related to each other in several ways. Customer assignments determine how the work is organized so that Enator's organization overlaps with customer companies when projects are implemented in cooperation with customer personnel.[1]

As a result of the decentralized nature of operations, the project manager and other consultants have considerable market contact and can also demonstrate a considerable degree of freedom of action. The net result of this at subordinate levels within the company contributes significantly to determining the company's strategic development. Thus, the whole organization is involved, since, apart from corporate management, there are a considerable number of potential strategic centres. Attempts to give the entire company a common reorientation are also largely dependent on the extent to which certain central guidelines and ideas have been successfully anchored in the organization as a whole.

I have indicated several points which provide an overall perspective on the manner in which companies such as Enator work. Since this is a question of situationally adapted professional production of services, the pattern is markedly different from that in the dominant bureaucratic corporate form. Some aspects of my perspectives have been hinted at. As this book progresses, it is hoped that this will make it easier for the reader to form an overall picture, based on the various dimensions and themes which are covered. However, I would not wish to conceal that the breadth of the approach applied in this book, and also my attempts to link up with a broad range of general problems and theoretical orientations beyond the limits of the actual case study, mean that this book makes certain demands on a reader. Readers must be able to link up various lines of thought and form a total picture.

2.4   The Pronator Group

As already mentioned, Enator is part of the Pronator Group. Pronator's business concept is "to create, develop and run a knowledge-intensive service company" (Annual Report, 1985). At the time when my study was conducted, there were five operating companies: Enator, two technical consultancy companies and two financial services companies. In addition, Pronator has an "assets arm" which included properties and major share holdings in various companies. The reason for this relatively extensive aspect of total operations is to compensate for the consultancy companies' lack of physical assets in the form of stocks, machinery, plant, etc. Moreover, it may be noted that Pronator has made considerable profits on share holding and property dealings.

Pronator's strategy is to strengthen subsidiaries (sub-groups) by supplying business concepts and by endeavouring to achieve cooperation and synergy effects. In the long term, Pronator wishes to achieve a situation where 50% of its revenue comes from operations abroad. It has been stated that the parent company should be small.

Naturally Enator holds a special position in the Pronator Group since the Group's principal owner and Managing Director built Enator up and was an active participant in the company for many years. Enator's method of operation is regarded as a model for other parts of the Group. The Enator influence is reflected in Pronator's Board since three of the eleven directors in 1986 worked at Enator. Enator operates independently from the rest of the Group. Enator is treated in this book as an independent unit and I will only consider the Pronator Group as a marginal phenomenon in this context.

2.5   Market and Competitive Conditions

In Enator's line of business, there are a number of larger, and very many smaller, computer consultancy companies in Sweden. However, as far as Enator is concerned, the company is mainly competing with four other major companies: Programator, Cap Gemini, Data Logic and WM-data. In 1986, Enator and the three latter companies each had between 270 and 430 employees. Programator, on the other hand, had 2,400 employees, al-

though a considerable number were in areas other than computer consultancy. However, computer consultancy companies also compete with the
computer departments of customer companies. Pressure on consultancy
companies has increased as the supply of competent programmers has increased. Consultancies feel that the market has become tougher in 1986-
87. Growth has begun to slow down. Consultancies have to demonstrate
that they are so much more proficient in the execution of assignments than
their customers' own staff so that customers can justify the higher costs of
consultants.

There is a considerable market for consultancy services in this field. No
great degree of market differentiation is employed, either by Enator or by
its major colleagues. The service sold is flexible and the assignments vary.
The market is heterogeneous. Almost all organizations above a certain
minimum size are potential customers.

Note

[1]   Cf. Beckérus et al. (1988) who speak of assignment logic. Assignment logic
       differs from production logic and market logic which normally characterize
       the functioning of companies. Assignment logic denotes a certain perspective
       on the nature of operations which means that business is developed in close
       cooperation between the company and its customers: "In accordance with the
       assignment logic, products and services are defined in the actual interplay
       between the customer and the supplier. High quality in assignment activities
       depends on mutual confidence where joint ideas, beliefs and evaluations have
       considerable importance for decisions. This assumes an organizational and
       social competence to initiate, structure and deal with the interaction between
       the customer and various parts of the company's own organization" (p 56).

3　Culture Theory

In this chapter, I will review and discuss the culture concept and culture theory. Initially, the level of discussion is rather general and inspiration is derived from anthropology, ethnology and sociology. Subsequently, I will touch on some aspects of organizational culture and symbolism research.

I present culture theory in this early chapter since cultural and symbolic interpretations are a consistent theme throughout this book. Other theories are described and discussed in connection with the presentation of various themes such as socialization, organization structure, corporate strategy, marketing, etc. For the most part, my presentation of the literature, empirical description and interpretation of various themes are interwoven. In the various chapters, cultural interpretations supplement and provide deeper insights into conventional analysis of the different themes covered.

3.1　The Culture Concept and Theories about Culture

It is hard to define the culture concept in precise terms. There are many intermediate ways of using the concept between the two extremes of either equating culture with a form of life and thus including most social life in the cultural concept, or defining culture as a narrow sector of artistic activity. Two examples of intermediate forms might be culture as collective consciousness and culture as common values, ideals and norms.

The culture concept has an interesting history which provides an excellent illustration of the many different meanings of the term. Williams (1977) notes that terms such as society, the economy and culture have changed dramatically in meaning over the centuries, even if these terms are not particularly old. "Society" at one time denoted active companionship, social contacts and joint action. (Cf. another meaning of "society" in English is when it aspires to a form of association.) "Economy" represented the management of a household and later of a small township or community. Both concepts have, of course, subsequently come to represent a general system or order of comprehensive social circumstances or of production, distribution and exchanges. "Culture" originally denoted the growing and cultivation of plants and animals and, in a wider sense, the development of the human soul.

In the 18th century, "culture" was equated with "civilization". Attacks by Rousseau and the romantics on civilization as something superficial and artificial, helped to give the concept of culture an alternative meaning as an "inner" or "spiritual" process, contrasting with "external" development. Its meaning was then extended further to include both "inner" development and also all the various means and mechanisms which supported this development, that is to say religious, artistic, literary and other institutions and practices which involved meanings and evaluations. The latter are societal institutions, and the relationship between culture and society – whose changed meaning also contributed to the varying fates of the concept of culture – became problematical. However, the difficulties were to some extent surmounted since the social forms of culture were primarily linked with the "inner" life. As time passed, the religious aspect of culture diminished in importance. The further development of the culture concept meant that it became a social concept with varying sociological and anthropological meanings. The tension which arose between this meaning and the traditional idea of culture as an "inner" process (including art, etc.) has become crucially important. Williams summarizes this as follows:

The complexity of the concept of 'culture' is then remarkable. It became a noun of 'inner' process, specialized to its presumed configurations in 'whole ways of life'. ... In any modern theory of culture this complexity is a source of great difficulty (Williams, 1977, p 17).

As Williams points out, the relationship between "social" and "inner" life presents a problem in cultural analysis.

In anthropological culture theory, there are various approaches to the relationship between the social and cultural spheres. The cultural sphere is often understood as ideational, a matter of ideas and meanings. The following account is partly based on Keesing (1974).

The kind of definition of culture contained in an encyclopaedia might be presented as follows:

the integrated pattern of human behavior that includes thought, speech, action, and artifacts and depends on man's capacity for learning and transmitting knowledge to succeeding generations (Webster's New Collegiate Dictionary, quoted in Deal and Kennedy, 1982).

Definitions of this type are applied, especially in current corporate culture research, but according to many modern anthropologists they are far too broad and uninformative. A traditional, comprehensive meaning for culture should be restricted to cover less but reveal more. The question then is what culture should refer to – in other words what should be the focus of culture research. One approach is to start with the object of study (society or appropriate aspects of society – for example organizations) as sociostructural systems, and look at culture as permanently anchored in social conditions and manifested in a way of life, behavioural patterns and outcomes of action. It is assumed that there is a close and harmonious relationship between culture and social structure. Culture is viewed as a common functional mechanism for citizens in a society, which guarantees an integrated societal life, stability over time and adaptation to the physical environment. This approach is not so very different from the encyclopaedic definition quoted above. However, defining culture as a comprehensive control and integration mechanism is less all encompassing than "the integrated pattern of human behavior".

This intimate, well integrated relationship between the material world (the social structure) and its cultural equivalent means that both reflect one another. It is considered possible to deduce the cultural components in the sociocultural system on the basis of observations of patterns of behaviour and social institutions.

This rather broad view of culture has been common among anthropologists of an earlier epoch and it is still applied. It also appears to be popular amongst many who study the culture of organizations. There are two main orientations in anthropology – social anthropology and cultural anthropology. The former focuses on social structures and the latter on cultural patterns (Singer, 1968). Both social anthropology and cultural anthropology employ more specific and more narrowly defined concepts of culture than those cited above. Social anthropologists do not say much about culture explicitly, even if they employ an implicit culture concept in their descriptions and analysis. Instead, the focus is on the social structure, that is to say a network of systems of social relationships, social classes and roles which are of a relatively stable nature. Various types of social phenomena – moralities, laws, labels, ties of kinship, religions, upbringing, languages, customs, etc. – are not studied in the abstract or in isolation but, instead, in direct and indirect relation to the social structure. However, phenomena such as listed above are regarded as symbols and expressions of the social structure – and hence are considered to be links with the concept of culture (Singer, 1968).

Social anthropology is rather closely related to sociology but differs, for example, in that the object of study is primarily alien or exotic societies, particularly societies which are (or were) regarded as "primitive", "simple", demarcated and stable. (See e.g. Leach, 1982, for an introduction to social anthropology.) Although a great deal of traditional and more recent organization theory has clear points of contact with this anthropological approach (Allaire and Firsirotu, 1984a, Smircich, 1983a) there are relatively few explicit references to such links in organizational culture re-search. Normally, links are made with a somewhat imprecise sociocultural concept or cultural patterns are emphasized in the sense of *conceptual or ideational phenomena.*

In this book, I employ the latter approach, focusing on the ideational level, but not too strictly. This approach is dealt with in the remaining pages of this chapter.

In recent decades, increasing numbers of those studying culture seem to be employing a more limited cultural concept and are primarily becoming more interested in ideational phenomena when they speak of culture. One approach emphasizes the knowledge aspects of a culture. The most frequently quoted representative of this cognitive theory of culture is Goodenough, who states that:

A society's culture consists of whatever it is one has to know or believe in order to operate in a manner acceptable to its members. Culture is viewed as not a material phenomenon; it does not consist of things, people, behavior, or emotions. It is rather an organization of these things. It is the form of things that people have in mind, their models for perceiving, relating, and otherwise interpreting them. Culture ... consists of standards for deciding what is, ... for deciding what can be, ... for deciding what one feels about it, ... for deciding what to do about it, and ... for deciding how to go about doing it (quoted in Keesing, 1974, p 77).

According to Keesing, this approach has had only limited success, since it is too narrow to act as a guideline for anthropological studies conducted on a broad front. However, in organizational culture research there are a number of approaches which have points of contact with this cognitive anthropological school (see Alvesson and Berg, 1992, for an overview).

Another approach emphazises that cultures are symbolic systems. Culture is in this case defined as a system of common symbols and meanings. The central source of inspiration here is Geertz (1973). Like the cognitive anthropologists, culture is placed on a conceptual level but not, in this case, "inside" people's heads, but "between" their heads where symbols and meanings are general, collective phenomena. They can be seen in human patterns of action – at funerals, in cockfights, in Christmas festivities and in board meetings.

The following quotation illustrates 1) the ideational (conceptual) orientation, and 2) the difference between the symbol perspective and the cognitive perspective:

In attempting ... to reach ... a more exact image of man, I want to propose two ideas. The first of these is that culture is best seen not as complexes of concrete behavior patterns – customs, usages, traditions, habit clusters – as has, by and large, been the case up to now, but as a set of control mechanisms – plans, recipes, rules, instructions (what computer engineers call "programs") – for the governing of behavior (Geertz, 1973, p 44).

The "control mechanism" view of culture begins with the assumption that human thought is basically social and public – that its natural habitat is the house yard, the marketplace, and the town square. Thinking consists not of "happenings in the head" (though happenings there and elsewhere are necessary for it to occur) but of *a traffic in what have been called, by G. H. Mead and others, significant symbols* – words for the most part but also gestures, drawings, musical sounds, mechanical devices like clocks, or natural objects like jewels – anything, in fact, that is disengaged from its mere actuality and used to impose meaning upon experience (p 45).

Thus, Geertz considers that cultural patterns are organized systems of significant symbols and that the existence of such systems is a prerequisite for human existence. Without such systems, human behaviour would be incomprehensible, and only a meaningless and random cascade of actions and emotions. Meaningful and significant symbols and the cohesive relationships between various symbols correspond to human nature and are the basis of social life.

Geertz' culture concept means that culture governs the understanding of behaviour, social events, institutions or processes. Culture is the setting in which these phenomena become comprehensible and meaningful. In Geertz' view, good cultural analysis does not subordinate social conditions to cultural factors, nor does it regard culture as a reflection of an overall social structure, but instead it makes a clear analytical distinction between the social and the cultural system. The latter may be analysed in relation to the former, but clearly the culture researcher's primary task is to interpret culture.

The distinction between culture and social structure implies that the former is regarded as a cohesive system of meanings and symbols, in terms of which social interaction takes place, while the social structure is regarded as the patterns which the social interaction itself gives rise to. In the former case (culture), then, we have a frame of reference of beliefs, expressive symbols and values, by means of which individuals define their environment, express their feelings and make judgements. In the latter case – that is to say at the social level – we have a continuous process of interactions. As Geertz (1973, p 145) states, culture is the creation of meaning through which human beings interpret their experiences and guide their actions, while social structure is the form which action takes or the network of social relationships which actually exists.

This means that culture and social structure represent different abstractions of the same phenomenon. Culture describes social action as depending on the meaning this has for those involved, while social structure describes social action from the point of view of its consequences on the functioning of the social system. One advantage of this concept of culture is that, as pointed out above, it provides a more precise meaning and a better interpretive capacity than a situation where cultures are regarded as also including behaviour, etc. Another advantage is that it permits treatment of the tension arising between culture and social structure. A reasonable assumption is that culture and social structure are not necessarily in a well integrated and harmonic relationship with each other (i.e. not best defined or analysed in such a way). Discontinuity between social and cultural structures can occur, for example, when there is a change in social institutions which is not matched by a change in cultural patterns. (Geertz, 1973, and Chapter 6 of the present book, contain an illustration of this.)

Schneider (1976) takes a similar approach to culture. Like Geertz, he defines culture as a system of symbols and meanings. He also emphasizes that culture cannot be directly described on the basis of behaviour. Culture is a matter of meanings in social actions. Schneider makes an important distinction between culture and norms. The concepts denote different levels of abstraction. Otherwise, it is common in organizational culture research to define culture broadly as a set of norms along with other aspects (values, beliefs) which are closely associated with the norm concept (see for example Kilmann et al., 1985). Schneider defines norms as patterns of behaviour which are applied in a specific culturally-defined unit. The norm concept is quite close to the concept of behaviour. Culture is much more indirectly linked with behaviour, since it is a question of understanding social action itself.

Norms differ from culture, for example in regard to the range and the possibility of generalization for different social contexts. Norms are specific and limited, containing detailed rules for how human beings ought to act in various situations, while culture has a broader and more general coverage which, for example, influences the understanding of norms in various contexts. To the extent that what seem to be norms appear to have a far-reaching action-radius – for example "a boss should take responsibility for his subordinates" or "high productivity is important" – it is the cultural aspects of these norms which are general in that, in a far-reaching culture, people understand what is meant by "boss", "subordinate" and "productivity". However, when used as specific norms the above mentioned statements are not particularly widely accepted since the precise and prescriptive nature, which is characteristic of norms, is lacking.

Culture contrasts with norms in that norms are oriented to patterns for action, whereas culture constitutes a body of definitions, premises, statements, postulates, presumptions, propositions, and perceptions about the nature of the universe and man's place in it. Where norms tell the actor how to play the scene, culture tells the actor how the scene is set and what it all means. Where norms tell the actor how to behave in the presence of ghosts, gods, and human beings, culture tells the actors what ghosts, gods, and human beings are and what they are all about (Schneider, 1976, p 203).

Naturally, analysis of culture must be related to social conditions but, according to Schneider, analysis of culture does not need to cover an area which corresponds to a given social system. A purely cultural analysis can result in a picture of a cultural system which seems different when compared with a picture that emerges from a sociocultural study where it is assumed that cultural aspects are a pure reflection of a particular social institution. Schneider's idea also differs from current ideas in symbolic culture theory (e.g Geertz), where a specific social system (religion, politics, kinship/relationship, etc.) is first carved out and then the corresponding cultural system is analyzed (Keesing, 1974).

Despite the emphasis on culture as a purely conceptual phenomenon, given by Geertz and Schneider, culture analysis is, of course, not limited to purely idealistic aspects or to superstructural phenomena. Culture analysis may be applied to all forms of social action and all types of institutions, including the economy, technology and production. The point is that abstractions of a certain type, which involve meanings anchored and transmitted in a symbolic form, constitute the level of analysis which this form of culture research deals with.

This type of symbolic cultural research has had considerable impact in recent years, not only in anthropology but also on organizational culture research (cf. Alvesson and Berg, 1992, Smircich, 1983a). However, the problem specifically involves a question of what is excluded from the analysis. Naturally this applies both to the social aspects of "sociocultural phenomena", that is to say social institutions, social events, forms of life etc. and also to what is to be found in the consciousness of individuals – in their psychological world. Taking common symbols and their magic seriously, and penetrating their meaning and complexity, involves treating such symbols virtually as if they operated in a vacuum, and are thus loosely coupled to social, material and psychological circumstances (Keesing, 1974). A consistently implemented analysis of the symbols of cultures results in the risk that one might end up with "a spuriously autonomous and spuriously uniform world of cultural symbols freed from the constraints of the mind and the brain by which cultures are created and learned and through which they are realized" (Keesing, 1974, p 88).

Ehn and Löfgren (1982) employ a much broader and more eclectic view of the theory of culture than the above mentioned symbolically-oriented anthropologists, even if these authors have been inspired to some extent by the symbolic school. Ehn and Löfgren deliberately mix various cultural concepts. For example, they refer to culture as collective consciousness or as systems of meanings and symbols. This means that the experiences, ideas and values which human beings share and which they recreate and change in social action are the focus for study. The manner in which people are trained for and participate in the shared codes of a local community is also important. A second viewpoint is to regard culture as a medium – or a way in which experiences and knowledge are organized. Culture is then seen in terms of language, interpretation filters, cognitive categories and ordered systems. Culture presents the framework on which an understanding of reality can be built up. A third viewpoint regards culture as an instrument, as a means to power or as a defensive weapon. When used defensively culture is referred to as counter-culture. Struggle and antagonism between various groups are to some extent considered to have a cultural expression: a conflict is a question of the validity, the legitimacy and the dissemination of various competing pictures of reality. The word culture is employed, for example, to denote collective identity and social cohesiveness. Symbols, rites and signs are used as a means of persuasion and propaganda. They are loaded with various social and political implications.

By alternating between various cultural perspectives, Ehn and Löfgren consider that they can capture the multiplicity and rich shadings of reality. Another similar approach to culture is expressed in an anthology by Hannerz et al. (1982) in which cultural research is regarded as the study of collective consciousness and of the communications which support this consciousness.

Culture includes common knowledge, values, experience and cohesive patterns of thought. But it does not only exist in men's minds. Consciousness is common and shared only through communication, a shared language, the understanding of codes and messages and regarding the entire environment as loaded with meaning in a manner which is rather similar for everybody or at least for most people (Hannerz et al., 1982, p 10).

In the approach to culture employed by Ehn and Löfgren and by Hannerz et al., there are several important features which can also be found in the above mentioned cognitively and symbolically-oriented anthropologies. The point of Ehn and Löfgren's and Hannerz' et al. broad cultural concept is to attempt to depict culture from a broad range of perspectives. The approaches are somewhat less stringent and precise and more eclectic than those employed by the symbol and cognition researchers. Ehn and Löfgren (1982) themselves refer to their "loose, relaxed approach". Naturally there are risks involved in employing several different perspectives and definitions which are so broad that the continuing analysis and interpretation often do not fully correspond to the broad overall definition. They are then more a question of sub-units of a "total" definition. Amongst other things, the concept of culture can be too extensive and confusing shifts of meaning may occur. However, if one is fully aware of the perspectives and sub-definitions which are employed, these problems need not be serious, and approaches of the Ehn and Löfgren type may provide rich, multi-faceted and exciting results.

In terms of range, Ehn and Löfgren's approach to culture and cultural analysis is located somewhere between the socio cultural perspective – which in the cultural concept includes not only the world of ideas but also concrete social circumstances, forms of life, etc. – and the symbol school's (Geertz, Schneider) perspective which focuses on cultural symbols. However, Ehn and Löfgren and Hannerz et al. share Geertz and Schneider's restrictions on the world of ideas. Thus, they say culture is not a matter of behaviour but of meanings – it does not refer to the sociostructural world but to the context of culture to refer to shared symbolic meaning.

In this book I use the concept of culture in this ideational and conceptual sense. However, the study of my case (Enator) is also partly analyzed at a sociostructural level. I do not employ the culture concept in this particular analysis. Cultural interpretations supplement social analysis and in this case involve various organizational phenomena, exclusively in terms of symbolism and meaning.

3.2   Organizational Culture Research

In the field of organizational culture research, which has expanded dramatically since the late 1970s and today has become highly popular, there is a strange mixture of varying theories and approaches, some of which have derived inspiration from anthropology, while others are interested in "corporate culture" in a more or less "common sense" manner. At its worst, culture is regarded as a kind of balance item which can be employed to cover factors which are not dealt with by traditional business administration and organization theory concepts. In other words, culture is understood as the "soft" informal side of organizational culture.

The more reasoned view of culture, which is represented by the anthropologists, ethnologists, etc. referred to above, can be found in many examples of organizational culture research. I will come to these shortly. However, in large areas of cultural research into organizations, such awareness of the risk of using culture in an all-embracing way is lacking. This applies particularly to studies which discuss corporate culture rather than use the term organizational culture, (e.g. Deal and Kennedy, 1982; Kilmann et al., 1985). The problem here is that "corporate culture" is given a broad and imprecise meaning and that this diffuse, comprehensive concept is then used to explain everything – and nothing. It is frequently stated, for example, that corporate culture consists of the norms, philosophies, values, ideologies, symbols, etc., which are shared by and link members of the organization and that this culture controls the behaviour of members of the organization (see for example most of the articles in Kilmann et al., 1985). I have sharply criticized this view of culture in various contexts, but since I do not wish to repeat myself here, a short statement of my position will suffice. See for example Alvesson (1993a), Smircich and Calás (1987) for a more detailed critical examination of this question.

However, despite my scepticism at many applications of corporate culture when used as a scientific concept, this does not mean that corporate culture is lacking in practical value. For example, corporate culture can denote the values and norms which management and senior members of a company believe in and/or espouse and which they try to inculcate in a systematic manner into the employees in an organization. In this case, corporate culture denotes what is virtually a strategy for control and management (Ray, 1986). However, as an instrument, corporate culture is radically different from other variations which are more easily dealt with, such as organizational design, the formulation of objectives and management control. This is partly because corporate culture is difficult to employ in an effective and predictable manner and partly because the outcome of corporate culture to some extent pursues its own existence without being subject to effective influence and control by top management or other significant players. There is normally a considerable gap between intention and outcome in the case of corporate culture. For these reasons, it appears to be somewhat reductionistic to regard corporate culture as purely a management tool. The tool could prove somewhat intractable.

In my view, this approach to cultural phenomena in organizations leads to a drastic impoverishment of the culture concept. As a theoretical concept it is weak. On the other hand, it may be employed to illustrate crucial aspects of management, where it denotes the gap between corporate management of the "soft variables" and broader organic cultural phenomena (shared meanings, ideas and understanding). In contrast to corporate culture, "real" cultural phenomena are unified, deep, multifaceted phenomena, which have developed organically over time and which under normal circumstances are only amenable to modest influence from individual actors.

P. O. Berg and I have conducted an ambitious survey of the entire area of the type of organizational culture research which is most to my taste (Alvesson and Berg, 1992). We based our work on the conventions and perspectives which we feel that we can distinguish within a heterogeneous and rapidly expanding field of research which is, as a result, difficult to survey. This book also deals with the emergence of culture research, and current debates and lines of development within the area. Readers who are interested in such aspects are referred to Alvesson and Berg (1992), thus enabling me to minimize presentation and discussion of the theory of organizational culture in this chapter. See also, for example, Allaire and Firsirotu (1984a), Czarniawska-Joerges (1992), Hatch (1993) Jeffcut (1993), Martin and Meyerson (1988), Smircich (1983a) and Smircich and Calás (1987) for commendable attempts at an overview.

When studying organizational cultures, a fundamental distinction can be made between the view of culture as a variable and culture as a metaphor. Reference to culture as a metaphor involves the fundamental picture or comparison used to illustrate a phenomenon. (The metaphor concept is dealt with in somewhat more detail in the next chapter.) By looking at the organization *as if* it were a culture, the whole organization is studied by applying an anthropological or some other theoretical culture interpretation filter. If, on the other hand, organizational culture is regarded as a variable, the organization is seen as consisting of several different variables or sub-systems. Popular variables are power, administration, technology, social relationships, strategy and formal structure. Thus, culture is given the same status as these variables and is assumed to exist in principle alongside other organizational variables (Smircich, 1983a).

The distinction between culture as a metaphor, where it is assumed that an organization *is* (may be regarded as if it was) a culture, or culture as a variable, where it is assumed that each organization "has" its own more or less unique culture, is significant and denotes a decisive difference between various types of organizational culture research. The fact that a number of studies cannot be related unambiguously to one or other of these approaches in a pure form is quite another matter: several works within this area tend to adopt neither a strict metaphor nor the narrow variable approach.

Studies of the variable type relate culture to other central variables and sub-systems in organizations, for example the technical-economic and sociostructural sub-system (Pennings and Gresov, 1986). In this case, the relationship between sub-systems is of interest. Culture is isolated as a special factor which is assumed to have causal importance for behaviour, performances, etc. Culture is flattened out and given a narrow, "square-headed" meaning, to be regarded as a "competition variable" and is discussed in terms of whether culture is "useful", "unusual" or "difficult to imitate perfectly". These three dimensions are regarded as criteria which decide whether a corporate culture can achieve good financial results or not (Barney, 1986). For critical discussions, see Alvesson (1993a) and Siehl and Martin (1990).

As far as the metaphor researchers are concerned, this represents a reified view of the cultural concept. As in the case of the anthropological and ethnological cultural researchers (Geertz, Ehn and Löfgren, Hannerz et

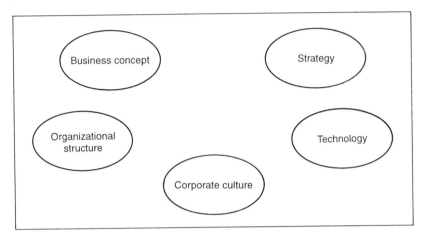

Figure 3.1:   Culture as a subsystem in an organization

al.), culture is a matter of symbolism, meaning, and consciousness as a fundamental dimension or level of analysis, which permeate various social actions, institutions, etc. There is no direct or causal relationship between culture and behaviour achievements. Nor can culture be defined as a kind of superstructure phenomenon which runs parallel with and is externally related to technological, economic and structural conditions. Instead, such conditions involve symbolism and meanings. Without meaning, no technology, economy or social structure.

Let me illustrate this in two diagrams. Figure 3.1 presents the variable view of culture. It shows that culture consists of several subsystems within the organization.

Figure 3.2. provides a picture of culture when it is based on the metaphor approach, in which culture constitutes a perspective on organizations. In other words it is a fundamental dimension of everything possible.

As the observant reader has seen, this book applies the metaphor approach to culture. In other words, as far as I am concerned culture constitutes a fundamental theoretical perspective which may assist in understanding various phenomena, in particular phenomena which may not be instantly recognized as "cultural".

There is an unfortunate tendency to associate culture with integration, harmony, clarity and consistency. As Martin (1992; Martin and Meyerson, 1988) points out, many authors define organizational culture in such a way. It is, however, fully possible to use a culture theory for investigating themes such as differentiation, conflict, domination, ambiguity and fragmentation as well (Alvesson, 1993a; Frost et al., 1991; Linstead and

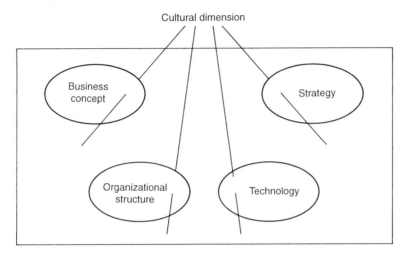

Figure 3.2:   Culture as a metaphor: a fundamental dimension which permeates
various "substystems"

Grafton-Small, 1992; Martin, 1992). Issues such as social conflict and organizational politics may, for example, be studied from a cultural perspective. Culture in the sense of shared meanings and understandings do not
guarantee consensus and harmony, nor is ambiguity ruled out.

   The cultural perspective on organizations may fruitfully emphasize the
central importance of symbolism in organizations. We can then refer to
organizational symbolism as a special variant of culture research. A few
words about the specific meaning of the concept of symbolism would appear to be justified.

3.3   Symbolism and Organizational Symbolism

A symbol refers to signs which express something more than their actual
objective, explicit content. A symbol represents a broader context of
meaning. While a sign is an objective representation of something, symbols are created subjectively or intersubjectively and are characterized by
the wider meaning which an individual or a collective gives to the symbol.

A symbol is a sign which denotes something much greater than itself, and which
calls for the association of certain conscious or unconscious ideas, in order for it to
be endowed with its full meaning and significance. A sign achieves the status of a
symbol when it is interpreted, not in terms of strict resemblance with what is signified, but when other patterns of suggestion and meaning are 'thrown upon' or 'put

together' with the signs to interpret it as part of a much wider symbolic whole (Morgan et al., 1983).

The difference between a sign and a symbol is often a question of degree. The density of meanings and the intensiveness of the emotional reaction determine whether it is fruitful to regard something as a symbol. Certainty and an indifferent reaction suggest that we are talking about a sign, while ambiguity and an affective reaction indicate that the phenomenon in question is best regarded as a symbol (Cohen, 1974).

Symbols may be simple or complex, conscious or unconscious, and may apply only to a single individual, may be shared by a group or may have universal application. Symbols may be of a verbal, action or material character (Dandridge et al., 1980). They may summarize the phenomenon in an emotionally effective manner or they may be elaborative in the sense that they can indicate the right way to act in a particular cultural situation (Ortner, 1973). Examination of the literature which deals with symbols and their significance, gives us the impression that practically anything can be treated as a symbol and that symbols can fulfil all types of functions, they can create cohesion and unity, generate conflict, stimulate change, operate in a stabilizing manner, increase the level of tension or reduce tension, etc.

Organizational symbolists consider that symbolism permeates every aspect of organizational life since human beings engage in symbolic processes and use them to give meaning to their world. Every possible aspect of a company or workplace involves a symbolic dimension. According to Leach: "Technique and ritual, profane and sacred, do not denote types of action but aspects of almost any kind of action" (quoted by Cohen, 1974, p 34) Organizations are regarded as symbolic fields in which the collective or collectives which inhabit the organization develop joint and similar approaches to the signs which characterize operations and convert them into symbols (Berg, 1985a, 1985b; Morgan et al., 1983). Some of these infinite varieties of symbols function as significant symbols (Duncan, 1968) or key symbols (Ortner, 1973). They are particularly significant for the collective, and the discovery and interpretation of them may be a central element in the research process.

A great deal more might be said about symbolism and organizational symbols at a general level. I would prefer, however, to briefly illustrate the approach with an example from organizational research.

The symbolic approach is illustrated by Feldman and March (1981) who describe how information in organizations may often be given highly symbolic meaning. They report findings indicating that organizations and individuals often collect and keep more information than they can reasonably expect to utilize in making decisions. At the same time, it seems as if people constantly require or request more information or that they complain about the inadequacy of such information. According to Feldman and March, there is a substantial basis for assuming that this is often the case in organizations, and not merely irrational and inefficient organizations but also in successful and well-adapted operations.

This phenomenon is closely linked with the symbolic nature of information and decision making. Information and how it is handled function as symbols for competence and social adequacy. A focus on information is a ritual confirmation of the central values in our type of society.

Because the acts of seeking and using information in decisions have important symbolic value to the actors and to the society, individuals and organizations will consistently gather more information than can be justified in conventional decision theory terms. Decisions are orchestrated so as to ensure that decision makers and observers come to believe that the decisions are reasonable – or even intelligent. Using information, asking for information, and justifying decisions in terms of information have all come to be significant ways in which we symbolize that the process is legitimate, that we are good decision makers, and that our organizations are well managed (Feldman and March, 1981, p 178).

An apparently exaggerated interest in information, from the point of view of a strictly instrumental or rational perspective on organizations, is thus associated with the use of and the demand for information. The justification of decisions in information terms is also a significant manner of indicating symbolically that decision making is taking place in an appropriate manner, that the decision makers are competent and that organizations are well managed.

3.4   Summary

In this chapter I have reviewed the culture and symbol concepts and described the theory of culture which I apply in this book (with some exception made for Chapter 7 on corporate culture, where a somewhat different perspective is applied to the cultural phenomenon).

In the main, my view of culture means that the meanings which a collective applies to a given phenomenon are emphasized. The phenomenon in question may be particular words and expressions, some aspect of formal corporate control, or a certain type of activity or action. Cultural analysis is largely based on major organizational symbols (key symbols). Key symbols are characterized by their importance for the organizational collective and they have a deep meaning which implies that they are ambiguous and complex and cannot be "read off" objectively. The researcher must pass through the conceptual world of the collective in order to be able to interpret them.

It is hardly possible to make a clear classification of symbols and non-symbols. The classification depends on how far one wishes to take the interpretation of symbols. In principle, everything may be regarded as a symbol. The fruitfulness of regarding an object as a symbol increases with greater density of various and to some extent disparate meanings which are given to this object and with the greater influence which this symbolism exerts. Cohen (1974), for example speaks of "symbolic potency" and ranks symbols on a scale which ranges from the least powerful symbols, which might just as well be treated as signs, to the most powerful symbols – key symbols – which have a strong symbolic loading and considerable significance for a collective.

Key symbols may be identified by applying the general criteria for regarding something, first, as a symbol (ambiguity etc.) and then by looking for indications that they are crucial for a collective's social cohesiveness and functioning or that they are essential guidelines for thinking and orientation in the environment and – indirectly – guidelines for action. Indications of key symbols may be that people often talk about them, that they are strongly loaded, that they appear in various contexts and that they are regarded as sacred, etc.

One risk in employing the culture perspective is that it is associated with what is a characteristically consensus view. Certain authors consider, for example, that unity and harmony are embedded in a common culture (e.g. Schein, 1985). But assumptions of this kind are problematical and certainly not an inherent aspect of culture. It is better to focus on the possibility that "structures of meaning are permeated by privileged interests" (Deetz, 1992, p 86), and that values, meanings and symbols may arbitrarily favour certain groups, while running counter to the interests of others. Thus, the fact that human beings accept certain values, ideals and viewpoints does not prevent us from questioning the origins of such values and ideals or stop us from wondering whether they really comply with the interests of people who espouse them. Another important dimension worth serious consideration is the ambiguity of cultural phenomena. Meanings and symbolism may include or provide consensus, consistency and clarity, but also dissensus, inconsistency and confusion in organizational life. Students of organizational culture must be open for discovering and interpreting different qualities in these respects (Alvesson, 1993a; Linstead and Grafton-Small, 1992; Martin, 1992).

4 Qualitative Research and Philosophy of Science

4.1 Interpretative Research

This chapter describes the methodology of this project and attempts to contribute to the discussion of qualitative, "non-objectivistic" research. In particular, the methodological problems which arise in culture research will be addressed. The chapter argues against dominating ideas about qualitative method and argues for a freer, more interpretative and less "data-fixated" approach.

Most of those who conduct culture research under the heading of organization theory consider a qualitative research approach to be both justified and necessary. However, one or two authors advocate "rigorous" methods. Pennings and Gresov (1986), for instance, note with regret that

'culture' is not yet manifestly amenable to rigorous quantification, advocates of qualitative approaches to organizations have understandably attempted to equate the topic itself with their cause (p 318).

However, there are quite a number of variations flying the "qualitative method" flag (Morgan and Smircich, 1980). We may, for example, make a distinction between qualitatively oriented authors with an "objectivistic" scientific approach and other authors who represent a research perspective in which the researcher's frames of reference (including theories, world view and values) and personal style are considered to be of crucial importance for the understanding of reality that results (Burrell and Morgan, 1979). I term the former group *data collectors* and the latter *interpreters*. The data collectors may be either qualitatively or quantitatively oriented. In the present case, only the qualitatively oriented group is of interest. Obviously, both data collection and interpretation form part of all research activities.

The difference between the two variations of qualitative research described above is seen in the relative emphasis placed on the collection of data or on its interpretation and the attitude adopted towards "data". Qualitative data collectors attempt to combine two sets of research concerns. On the one hand, they recognize the complexity of social reality, the inability of the quantitative approaches to produce new knowledge. On the other hand, they remain committed to scientific ideals regarding the clear presentation of methods of work and the generation of research results which are solidly based in empirical reality. Glaser and Strauss (1967) represent a salient example of this orientation. They advocate the development of theory on an explicitly empirical basis what they call a grounded theory approach.

In contrast with qualitative data collectors, interpreters are less concerned about procedural questions and the ambition of achieving exact compliance between empirical reality and research results. Research is regarded as an activity in which the researcher's "subjectivity" has an unavoidable impact. There is no such thing as ready-made data waiting to be collected up by the researcher's ingenious methods, whether in the form of responses to a questionnaire, semistructured interview topics or even open-ended interviews. The concept of data collection is peculiar and erroneous, since data is constructed by the researcher and is not merely collected (Arbnor et al., 1980). The researcher's frames of reference language and other elements in the prestructured understanding strongly affect that which he or she sees, how it is interpreted, and how it finally becomes a research text. The researcher's personality, experience, social situation, interests, vocabulary, theoretical knowledge, etc. are of considerable importance in this context. The development of knowledge is not merely regarded as a question of method and epistemology, but is dependent more or less on the researcher's ideological, political, ethical and moral views and opinions as well as on the textual, narrative style used to characterize the research process and the results achieved (Alvesson and Sköldberg, 1995; Deetz, 1985, 1992; Jackson and Willmott, 1987; Morgan, 1983a; etc.). While the data collectors consider that interpretation and theory are based on data, the interpreters assume that data, in the main, is the result of, and is principally determined by, interpretation and theory (Alvesson and Sköldberg, 1995).

This would appear to be the right point to define and clarify the concept of interpretation. Interpretation is the act of giving a phenomenon meaning or discovering (something of) its "inherent" purpose of significance. Interpretation describes underlying contexts or meaning, the not so obvious content of a word, sentence, action or event (Lindholm, 1981).

In Sweden, Asplund's essay entitled "Om undran inför samhället" (1970) (Reflections on Society) is often referred to by social scientists, although few researchers have been able to live up to its ideals. Asplund considers that the most interesting question concerning a given phenomenon, P, is not what causes P, what the consequences of P will be or how widespread P is, but that the real question which must be asked is "What does P mean?". This last question is fundamentally different from the others and represents a different scientific ideal. Stating the meaning of a social phenomenon means interpreting or deciphering its basic character.

According to Asplund, the social sciences involve developing ways of seeing (creatively discovering) aspects – the ability to conceptualize a phenomenon in an interesting and meaningful manner. According to this approach, verification, whether it is statistically processed or of a "qualitative" nature, cannot be considered to be of decisive significance in assessing the value of the research approach. Asplund refers with appreciation to Winch (1958), who states that understanding is the same as comprehending the meaning or the point of individual or social phenomena. This is far removed from the world of statistics or of causal laws.

Thus, there is a clear distinction between this standpoint and the use of qualitative research which distinguishes between, on one hand, research concerning the development of hypotheses and theories and, on the other hand, research aiming at testing and verifying hypotheses. A distinction is often made between "context of discovery" and "context of verification". Data collectors, in contrast to interpreters, often regard this distinction as fruitful and consider that verification is both possible and significant. Particularly, in the past the justification for qualitative approaches was presented in somewhat cowardly terms, by citing benefits in the generation of ideas, hypotheses and theories – while submitting the verification problem to more "rigorous" methods without really questioning it (see e.g. Glaser and Strauss, 1967). This opinion still dominates among advocates of qualitative method, but the present situation indicates considerable variation.

However inspiring Asplund's text may be, a few problems should be noted. One problem is a clear tendency to focus so intensely on creativity and originality in approaching social phenomena, thus making them so superior to other important virtues in social science research, that the ultimate purpose of research takes a back-seat. Whatever the purpose, whether it be problem-solving, cultural understanding, liberation from oppression or something else, the aim should be to encompass aspects and dimensions which may be felt to be linked to "the real and existing" social world. I consider it unrealistic to imagine that data which is skilfully derived from social reality in a quantitative or qualitative form is capable of unambiguously indicating yes/no to non-trivial hypotheses and interpretations. Interpretation is always built into the process which leads to the crystallization of the "data" and is just as much a question of the interpreter, the research design, the research project as a social process and the vocabulary chosen as of the "reality" which is studied (cf. Alvesson and Sköldberg, 1995; Clifford, 1986; Deetz, 1992; Steier, 1991). Nonetheless, the usefulness of a conceptualization or interpretation of a social phenomenon is to some extent in proportion to its "agreement" with the empirical material available. I say "to some extent" because, on the one hand, perfect agreement is unrealistic and, on the other hand, it is not really meaningful. One issue is presenting the hidden, original and creative aspects of a phenomenon. This is not the same thing as indicating the aspects that evaluators can easily confirm are in agreement with objective reality, that is the most obvious, simple, comprehensive and boring aspects of this phenomenon. As far as Asplund (1970) is concerned, however, it almost seems as if meaningfulness is decoupled from the ability of the interpretation to comply with all the empirical clues which may tell us something about the phenomenon which is in focus. Asplund refers appreciatively to Freud's analysis of Leonardo da Vinci, which was largely based on an erroneous translation of an important source. Asplund thinks that it was relatively unimportant that the premises for Freud's analysis were untenable and that the result was therefore not "true". Asplund seems to believe that the truth criterion is not the only factor and that it is not always a decisive factor in producing interesting social science. I agree that searching for absolute truths in social science research is a difficult if not hopeless endeavour which may often result in the study of trivialities. At the same time, efforts to achieve good compliance with social reality must be one important criterion amongst others in the social sciences. Interpretations should be well supported by empirical evidence but, at the same time, space must be allowed for other criteria that facilitate the development of new theoretical ideas.

One could say that good research is a matter of trying to achieve a reasonable outcome in two dimensions: interesting results (creative interpretations) and well verified agreement between interpretation and the underlying social reality (empirical grounding). However, like Asplund, I consider that it may be difficult to fully combine these two dimensions, even if interesting results require at least a certain amount of credible agreement between interpretation and intersubjective estimations of reality.

4.2   The Importance of Metaphors in Research

In recent organizational research, the aspect approach as a research ideal has had considerable impact. This has been expressed, for example, in a lively interest in metaphors and paradigms. (I will not discuss the paradigm dimension, however. The interested reader is referred to, for example, Burrell and Morgan, 1979; Guba and Lincoln, 1994.) The term metaphor refers to a comparison of one phenomenon (focal object) with another, a modifier, which helps to provide a clear picture. This comparison captures an interesting aspect of the focal phenomenon through the image created by the interaction with something which to some extent overlaps the phenomena but basically belongs to another frame of reference. A good metaphor has a satisfactory degree of overlap between what is to be illuminated and, at the same time, shows a clear difference between the modifier and the focal object (Alvesson, 1993b; Morgan, 1980). If there is too great a similarity between a phenomenon and the modifier, there will be no metaphor, or else there will be no point in the metaphor. If the difference is too great, no meaningful metaphor will emerge either, since the comparison will not be comprehensible. A useful metaphor does not equate fully with what it is supposed to illustrate. (If it did it would not be a metaphor.) On the contrary, the point of a metaphor is that something should be compared with something else.

The metaphor concept may be employed in different ways. In the broadest sense, the use of a metaphor means that a certain (non-trivial) phenomenon is always regarded from a certain point of view. This means that all knowledge is metaphoric, since all knowledge is dependent on a perspective in which we illuminate something explicitly or implicitly in terms of something else (Brown, 1976). In parallel with this view of the dependence of scientific and other knowledge on metaphors, the metaphor may be understood as a point of departure of a theoretical perspective. This means that a concept which normally fits into a certain frame of reference is used in another context and is then transferred into another frame of reference. One example in organization studies is reference to rites or political coalitions in organizations, which are concepts clearly borrowed from anthropology and politics. Creative research is very much a question of working with metaphors:

By transferring the ideas and associations of one system or level of discourse to another, metaphor allows each system to be perceived anew from the viewpoint of the other. Certain aspects of each are illuminated, others shadowed over (Brown, 1976, p 172).

In other words, the metaphor functions as an "amplifier" and "filter" in the research process. It can also be said to have a "refining" effect. In a complex, ambiguous social reality, the researcher becomes aware of certain objects which are perceived in a certain manner, while other possible objects are not perceived or are not taken seriously (Lindström, 1972). Thus, the idea of the decisive importance of metaphors in social science (and other) research is closely associated with the hermeneutic philosophy of science, where the focus is on the interpretation of phenomena which occur in the encounter between empirical reality (or the literary text – the difference is not necessarily great from a research point of view) and the researcher's application of the frames of reference which are his/her starting-point. Interpretation is based on more or less conscious filtering and amplification processes determined by the metaphors which the researcher has at his command or by the ideas which are captured by these metaphors.

In all structuring we must pay the price of coping with complexity, thus meaning must always involve some form of ignorance. The peculiarity of metaphoric structuring is the paradoxical nature of such understanding. 'Attention is at the same time distraction' (Jeffcutt, 1985, p 36).

As Brown (1976), Lakoff and Johnson (1980), Morgan (1980) et al. point out, metaphors permeate language and reality, both to the extent that fundamental metaphors ("root metaphors") appear as conceptual figures behind various views of reality, without necessarily presenting themselves as metaphors, and also to the extent that explicit metaphors are employed in everyday language. Attempts to eliminate metaphors from language as far as possible and to speak "in a straightforward manner" would result in a radical dilution of social and personal life. (Some examples of metaphors: "Things look bleak." "This office is a madhouse." "The organization is an instrument for the fulfilment of goals." "The innovatory climate is excellent." "He has a screw loose." "She got kicked upstairs and got a higher position.")

A metaphor can also be said to be a conceptual figure of speech which provides a fundamental representation of a given phenomenon by explicitly describing it at a more concrete, discursive level (Asplund, 1979). Such conceptual figures/metaphors also permeate organizational research and analysis. There is one metaphor (sometimes two or more), explicit or implicit, which describes an organization, and which lies behind every analysis of an organization, according to Morgan (1980, 1986). The metaphor employed constitutes the concretization of the overall paradigmatic assumptions on which the metaphor is based. If the metaphor(s) is are regarded as given, only puzzle-solving operations will occur, that is to say the guidelines and the frameworks of the analysis are established and research will normally be confined within these limits. Ambitious, creative work would require the further development of a metaphor or perhaps developing a new metaphor for the phenomenon in question. The organization, or part of it, is seen as something else. In other words, research becomes a matter of being interested in the question of what the organization "means" at the deepest levels.

Machines, instruments, bureaucracy, organisms and systems are, and have been, popular metaphors used in organization studies. In recent years, a number of new metaphors have emerged such as the political arena, theatre, psychic prison, text, etc. One of the most popular metaphors used is culture. When an organization is regarded as if it was a culture, this metaphor is then allowed to guide research, and we observe various organizational phenomena such as symbols, common meanings, etc. A meeting becomes a ritual, information becomes a symbol for reliability, a strategic plan is seen as a mantra, etc.

There are different opinions about metaphors and the overall perspective-controlling level which they represent. One view is that since metaphors are uncertain and ambiguous, they hinder rigorous research, the formulation and testing of hypotheses, and the accumulation of knowledge. Pinder and Bourgeois (1982; Bourgeois and Pinder, 1983), for example, argue that the use of metaphors as important concepts in organizational research should be avoided, or at any rate minimized. An alternative view is to regard research as primarily a question of creative approaches and of an awareness of the influence of frames of reference and theory on all research work – often in a way which the researcher cannot fully account for – and to regard metaphors as unavoidable and essential and fruitful in creative research (Brown, 1976; Morgan, 1980, 1983b).

The choice for sociology is not between scientific rigor as against poetic insight. The choice is rather between more or less fruitful metaphors, and between using metaphors or being their victims (Brown, 1976, p 178).

To return to my previous distinction between data collectors and interpreters as different "species" of qualitative researcher(s), it may be noted that qualitative data collectors, such as Glaser and Strauss (1967) tend to ignore or even totally neglect the importance of this metaphorical level, while (several) interpreter-researchers emphasize it.

Data collectors who want to develop theories regard the collection and classification of data – which has more or less problematically originated in empirical reality – as the basis for their activities. Compared with the traditional ("positivistic") scientific ideal, the importance of verification and generalizing is toned down, while development of concepts and theories is given high priority. However, it is still a question of a fundamentally empirical approach, and there are strong similarities between the qualitative data collectors and "hard-data" researchers[1]. Both orientations hold assumptions of an "objective reality out there" which determines the research result (at least if the research has been competently carried out). Data collectors frequently fluctuate between regarding representations of empirical reality and new theoretical approaches as their ideal. Glaser and Strauss (1967) argue for "the development of theory on an empirical basis" without observing the contradiction implicit in this idea. It is difficult if not impossible to produce advanced theories if your feet are firmly planted on stable, empirical foundations and your starting-point is "pure data". (As previously stated there is no "pure" data, as interpretation is needed for data to emerge. One may, however, try to "minimize" the element of interpretation.) The development of new theories requires ideas, impulses and the stimulus provided by concepts, perspectives and theories, etc. Research rooted in purely empirical foundations does not take you very far.

Brunsson (1982) goes somewhat further than Glaser and Strauss in his opinion of what is good research and thus winds up in the periphery of the data-collection ideal and closer to the interpretative approach which I favour. Brunsson rejects the traditional "ideal of representation" as a fruitful approach in societal research. Brunsson regards the verification of theories and generalization as not particularly important in research, or even as unrealistic. Instead, in Brunsson's view, the generation of theoretical ideas is of the highest value whereas empirical research only aims to cover a specific area of reality which is defined in terms of time and space as a result of the changing nature of most social phenomena. The researcher's most important task is the formation of language, that is to say the construction of new concepts and approaches to depict a reality. This means "that the researcher does not try to offer correct representations of reality, but rather options for language with which reality may be handled" (p 107).

This research ideal agrees rather well with the interpretative research approach. However, Brunsson gives priority to empirical work as the main route to the formation of language and this does not comply very well with the interpretative method:

There are many ways of creating language. What characterizes the method which research should employ is that language is developed by means of representation. Thus the language-formation perspective does not mean that representation is not relevant. On the contrary, representation is an extremely central research activity (Brunsson, 1982, p 108).

In the interpretative research ideal, language and what it expresses in the form of theories, approaches, etc. is a primary and determining factor in representation. (This does not mean that representational attempts are only a passive extension of frames of reference and language. Empirical "reality" cannot be reduced to just a researcher's image or perception – it also influences representation.) The formation of language cannot simply be a product of empirical studies, in which, in principle, the representation of reality plus skilled handling of reality produces theoretical and language development. By nature, such development is extremely complex and the importance of "pure data" is rather limited. The stronger the anchoring in systematic, "safe" empirical studies and unquestionable data, the poorer the linguistic and theoretical development. Theoretical development requires a freer stance and a somewhat weaker coupling with "pure" empirical facts. This does not mean that empirical studies are unimportant in this context. Apart from their considerable value in describing and mapping reality (at least partly interpreted through established theoretical and linguistic conventions), empirical studies may provide a good input for the development of language and theory. But this requires, on the one hand, theoretical frames of reference and well conceived perspectives and also stimulation from various quarters – literature, empirical observations, everyday life – where it is precisely the fusion of various sources of inspiration which is important. This has meant that the empirical "foundations" are constantly overlaid by theories, concepts, etc. which make them far from purely empirical. To repeat; theoretical development is not a pure reflection of empirical observations.

Representatives of interpretative research, such as Asplund, Brown, and Morgan, are highly tolerant of theoretical aims, the influence of the researcher as an individual, his/her subjectivity and of a research process which is based more on intuition, continuos interpretation, etc. than it is on explicit bureaucratic procedure and a clear account of the methods employed. For interpretative research the appearance of an external, empirical reality is always affected by the researcher's subjectivity and his or her theories, metaphors, paradigms, language, etc. with which he/she is more or less consciously permeated. Furthermore, from the perspective of interpretative research, the "data" is as much an artificial construction as it is a reflection of empirical reality.

Thus, competent empirical research, according to the position advocated here, is *not* a question of first working out a good plan, developing instruments for realizing it, and then collecting data of every possible description to make everything clear and to permit explicit presentation. Nor is it a matter of following the routes that data reveals, as grounded theory prescribes. Instead, qualified empirical research is primarily a case of being aware of theory and metatheory, continuously reflecting on the current position and future developments when reading and conducting empirical work, and being open to ideas and suggestions – often generated by a combination of literary inspiration, thought and what is read into the empirical "data". The sort of metaphor(s) used as a starting-point is just as important as the "data" obtained. Metaphors frame how reality is represented. Such ideas lead to the research process having a tendency of being loosely structured and there are limited opportunities for clearly describing the question of procedure, since complex frameworks and an endless number of interpretations, of which the researcher is only partially aware, cannot be described.

4.3   Avoiding the Objectivism and Relativism Traps

In interpretative research, it is clearly difficult to unambiguously demonstrate that the researcher has proceeded in a manner which is scientific and that the results obtained are "correct" (valid) or valuable. Certainly, verification and validity are not the sole decisive factors in interpretative research, at least not if these virtues are defined as proved correspondence with objective reality. (For a discussion of validity from an interpretative perspective, see Kvale, 1989.) Interpretative research is looking for meaning and insight and hence research results cannot be dismissed because of a lack of verification and validity. However, the problem cannot be ignored. Rule-guided, "positivistic" research, and studies which follow a definite procedure for qualitative research are superior to interpretative studies when it comes to formalized evaluation of empirical results. At the same time, the post-Kuhnian debate on the history and theory of science has questioned the value of clear, universal criteria for a scientific approach and of guidelines for carrying out good scientific work. Attempts to strictly subordinate all research to a given set of rules and bases for assessment appears, at any rate in a broad perspective, to be limited and to represent a barrier to theoretical development, rather than a guarantee for such development (Bernstein, 1983; Kuhn, 1970, etc.).

One possible conclusion has been to regard research as a fundamentally relativistic enterprise, in which all statements about the nature of the world and all criteria for scientific and theoretical value revolve around an individual's own views, or what is regarded as "true", "scientific", etc. by a particular group at a given time.

The relativist's essential claim is that there can be no higher appeal than to a given conceptual scheme, language game, set of social practices, or historical epoch. There is a non-reducible plurality of such schemes, paradigms, and practices; there is no substantive overarching framework in which radically different and alternative schemes are commensurable – no universal standards that somehow stand outside of and above these competing alternatives (Bernstein, 1983, pp 11-12).

While there was previously a widely-held concept of incommensurability (Burrell and Morgan, 1979; Kuhn, 1970) – i.e. the impossibility of translating different paradigms into each other and assessing results of different paradigms – there is a tendency to regard at least some debate and discussion between various proponents of paradigms as possible (see e.g. Bernstein, 1983; Gioia and Pitre, 1990; Reed, 1985; Rorty, 1992). Although there are no universal, unambiguous criteria for the evaluation of statements and results with scientific aspirations, we can have rational discussion in the research community, with critical debate and free conversation, in which in principle it is possible to arrive at what may be considered a good research-based understanding of what the subject is about on the basis of assessments, arguments and counter-arguments (Bernstein, 1983). Morgan (1983a) speaks of "reflective conversation" as an ideal which helps the researcher to arrive at self-realization and mutual understanding (within the research community) as regards the basis and value of the research approach. Of course, free and open debate does not always prevail in the research community and researchers may sometimes be more interested in protecting and advancing their own power, prestige and ego-positions than furthering progress in research. See Sloterdijk (1984) for a rather realistic and cynical discussion of this question. Another impediment to debate which discourages insight is the specific language employed. Even when writers with different frames of reference employ much the same words, these words often have different meanings depending on the theories employed (and their "metalanguage"). This impedes "reflective conversation" (Jackson and Willmott, 1987). The idea of a free exchange of ideas as a route to achieving greater rationality in the social sciences is thus far from unproblematic. But in principle, as a solution of the objectivism/relativism problem, critical debate provides space for strong arguments which determine the research results and positions that will be acceptable. This appears to be a considerably more attractive route than either a restricted locking-in of what is to be considered scientific through the development of methodological cookbooks or a fully liberated, subjectivist or relativistic "anything goes" approach, free from demands of justification or immune to critical scrutiny.

4.4   Research Texts which Stimulate Dialogue

Possible criteria for the choice of theory and assessments of the value of research results which can be used to facilitate a discussion of this kind in the research community might be, for example, reliability, consistency, range, simplicity and fruitfulness (Kuhn, 1977, quoted by Bernstein, 1983). The scoring of meaningful points and developing new lines of thinking might well be added to this list of rather abstract and ambiguous criteria (Alvesson and Sköldberg, 1995).

This approach means that research should be characterized by a style which facilitates dialogue. Generally speaking, social science texts vary considerably in terms of dialogue-opening or dialogue-blocking features. One example of a blocking feature is technical jargon, which is intended to lend the text an enhanced scientific aura but which also impedes understanding of the contents.

I will indicate some possible criteria for research texts which facilitate a dialogue with the reader and stimulate open and free discussion with the research community as well as with other readers:

1. *A personal style of writing.* A text – even a scientific text – has to be written by someone. This someone should be present in the text. The author's values, frames of reference, outlook, characteristics and idiosyncrasies influence the finished text. The literature which has been selected and the interpretations of this literature, the answers received in interviews and the interpretation of responses which are produced in an experiment are all coloured by the researcher's personality. Hiding this personality behind a pseudo-objectivistic style of writing and burying it in a bureaucratically laid-out research report does not favour a dialogue between the reader and the author. Presenting one's own values as clearly as possible does not solve the "objectivity problem", since this cannot be solved in the social sciences – at least not by the individual researcher – but it is nonetheless a significant step on the way (cf. Myrdal, 1968). (For an overview of styles of writing in cultural studies, see Jeffcutt, 1993, and Van Maanen, 1988.)

2. *Clearly presented frames of reference and repeated indications as to how frames of reference affect the presentation in various respects.* It is not enough to explicitly state the frames of reference initially and in the conclusions, and then deal with data collection and the processing in between as if they were divorced from the frames of reference. If a phenomenon is to appear as and be represented as data, a perspective is required and this perspective should be made explicit throughout the text. Instead of referring to systems, climates and other aspects of organizations as if they were objective attributes "out there", the writer should remind both him- or herself and the reader that these are metaphors and that it may be advantageous to regard the phenomenon concerned as if it was a system or a climate. Non-trivial statements about the research phenomenon should be consistently treated as aspects or outcomes of an interpretation process and heavily dependent on the perspective, not as unambiguous "data".

3. *Clearly indicated openness to the complex, transient and contradictory nature of social reality.* There is a definite tendency to look for, emphasize and perhaps exaggerate systems, patterns and non-ambiguous features in the social world. Everything else – exceptions to what is regarded as generally applicable – receives less attention. This also applies to ambiguities, which are often neglected. (See e.g. Calás and Smircich, 1987; Ehn and Löfgren, 1982; Martin and Meyerson, 1988.) In my opinion, good research should also deal with uncertainties, ambiguities and other aspects which are hard to capture in a clear and straight forward manner, e.g. point at variations and inconsistencies in interviewee's accounts of their social reality.

4. *Combinations of stringency and shifts in perspective.* Eclecticism – the mixing of various theoretical perspectives – is usually regarded as something negative. Personally, I do not find eclecticism particularly appealing either. Being able to generate ideas requires a perspective and a focus. At the same time, great demands on stringency give both empirical material and theoretical analysis an impression of unambiguity which, on the one hand, is not always or even normally fully backed-up (Alvesson, 1993b) and, on the other hand, tends to entrap the reader into either accepting or rejecting the discourse in question. A text which encourages dialogue must have a clear focus and stringency, but attempts to build up a watertight case may have the opposite effect. Watertight cases mean avoiding (hiding) contradictions and uncertainties in the analysis – something which is not always appropriate, perhaps, in a contradictory world.

Another ideal can be posed in opposition to the virtue of maximizing the stringency in an analysis – which in empirical work may result in the deletion of material which does not harmonize with the main thesis. This ideal is an awareness of the limitations of the central perspective and an ability to allow different perspectives to meet each other in a text. Of course, there should be an overall central perspective, but this does not necessarily exclude allowing for other perspectives, too. It is difficult to allow several theoretical perspectives, which are not totally on the same level, to form *the frame of a beautiful totality*, but attempts should not be discouraged. I feel that most of the texts which I have read in my time have an almost irritating predictability. If you read the first ten pages in a social science book, you know roughly what the rest will entail in terms of style, the author's preferences, etc. The author faithfully complies with a certain set of ideas and values and seldom offers any surprises.[2]

5. *The formulation of unanswered problems.* It can be an advantage to be able to formulate, consider and present questions which the author cannot answer, and riddles which cannot be solved. A partially overlapping technique is to indicate the limitations of one's own study and important areas and dimensions linked with the study which are *not* dealt with. What I am trying to get at here is something more ambitious than a description of objectives and what one is going to do (and not going to do). One must continuously remind the reader not only of what the author is dealing with, but also of what is *not* dealt with. Many issues are inevitably rejected and the *greater* the awareness conveyed by the text of the questions which are not answered in the study, the more the reader will be helped in assessing the text and the research area.

In organization-culture research, for example, there is an overwhelming range of cultures which can be studied – extending from western, national cultures to women's or group cultures at a given place of work (Alvesson, 1993a). Instead of choosing a culture (an object for cultural analysis, e.g.

an organization, division or a work group), as is customary, and concentrating interest solely on this culture, it would be better if the author also made it clear which cultures which are *not* studied. This does not merely mean a brief list of dutiful admissions about objectives and limitations. A statement of what has been ignored should accompany the presentation and the reader should be reminded of its existence here and there in the text. Naturally, this assumes that it is possible to do this in an effective manner. Of course, I do not recommend endless lists of what is clearly excluded from the study, but rather an indication of interesting and exciting problems, questions and dimensions which the author has been unable to, or not interested in, dealing with properly. The point is to open up the text to encourage a dialogue with the reader and to avoid presenting the reader of the text with a 'fait accompli'.

4.5   Culture Research

Something should now be said about the methodological aspects of research, particularly research about companies and work places. Pertinent and comprehensive points of view and also more precise opinions are presented, together with my own views.

The culture researchers referred to previously all adopt an interpretative approach and are not inclined to rely on following specific procedures as the route to knowledge. According to Geertz (1973), techniques and procedures do not define the project. Intellectual efforts give rise to "thick descriptions", that is to say the understanding of complex contexts of meaning. Research involves "constructing a reading" of an alien manuscript with many meanings. Ehn and Löfgren (1982) describe the essence of culture research as follows:

Every analytical cultural interpretation is a creation and, as such, the product of a number of different factors: thinking, reading, personal experience and interests, subjective ideas and cultural belonging. The research process is not different from other aspects of life – it feeds on life and often, in a more or less openly indicated manner, includes the processing of existential and moral questions which the researcher is personally involved in. The picture of reality which is finally conveyed is difficult to reconstruct as a systematic search for knowledge. Interpretations rarely involve a mechanical procedure in which steps are taken one at a time in accordance with agreed rules and conventions. In an effort to distinguish between science and art, books on method are written and lessons are given in research strategy – as if it were possible to arrive at scientific creativity through reading. This is not the case. Conducting studies and writing reports is certainly largely a matter of a craft which can be learnt, but each interpretation and each analytical argument is also coloured by personal qualities. Perhaps this applies in particular to culture research, which is dependent on such difficult-to-grasp and "unscientific" characteristics as imagination, involvement, understanding and the ability to depict contours (Ehn and Löfgren, 1982, p 105).

A number of ideas about methods in studies of organization culture have been published – most of them with a relatively strong interpretative focus (see e.g. Allaire and Firsirotu, 1984b; Czarniawska-Joerges, 1992; Louis, 1985; Rosen, 1991; Schwartzman, 1993; Smircich, 1983b). I agree with Allaire and Firsirotu (1984b) on the following considerations in the study of the culture of organizations.

The researcher must clearly decide which cultural concept he or she is using. In my opinion, a narrow and precise definition of culture is not essential. It is not at all necessary to refer very often to culture within the framework of a cultural approach, since the concept is so comprehensive (Pettigrew, 1979). In many cases it is better to use other concepts, such as meanings, values, forms of consciousness, symbolism, or whatever it is which is being aimed at. The theory of culture then functions primarily as a general frame of reference, while the other concepts are employed to capture concrete phenomena. However, it is important to decide clearly whether the starting-point is a holistic concept of culture which also includes forms of behaviour and life, or a more limited, ideational form. Personally, I confine myself to the latter.

The definition of culture as common meanings and symbols means that the cultural approach only covers certain aspects of organizations. In this book, some of the themes which are interpreted from a cultural perspective will be dealt with also from social and structural aspects. Corporate management, organizational structure and the business concept will thus be described in cultural and symbolic terms and on the basis of other, to some extent, more traditional concepts and perspectives in management and organization studies. I am thus not attempting to totalise a cultural approach, but I permit myself to indulge in a modest degree of eclecticism regarding the use of metaphors, perspectives and theories, with the object of comprehensively describing the organization phenomenon and avoiding the idealistic reductionist tendencies which may be present in a cultural approach (cf. Alvesson, 1993a; Alvesson and Sandkull, 1988).

Both diachronic and synchronic analyses of culture are required. Culture emerges over time, and is thus a historic phenomenon and must be understood as such. At the same time, culture operates in the present and is most easily accessible in this context. In my case, the company in question has a very brief background, stretching over a mere ten years. This makes it comparatively easy to describe, but, at the same time it is also doubtful if the organization has had time to establish and anchor a "genuine" culture (relatively stable patterns of shared meanings transmitted from an older to a younger generation) in the employee collective. This point is dealt with in detail at a later stage (Chapter 7).

The range of the study in terms of the empirical domain covered must be unambiguous. This is particularly important in culture research since it is easy to equate the organization with the culture and to assume that the members of the organization can always be regarded as members of the same culture. A great deal of culture research makes this assumption, but this gives rise to problems. The researcher must be aware of what is dealt with and what is not included and must make this clear to the reader. Is it a question of the entire organization, certain organizational units, a group within the company, or what? In this study, I am primarily discussing corporate management and aspects of Swedish operations which are based in Stockholm. In quantitative terms this covers approximately 60% of the total organization in terms of personnel. Of course, not all aspects of this 60% are covered, and I have also obtained some information about the foreign subsidiaries, but on the whole the study is concerned with management and the Swedish operations.

Another important limitation is that there is no particular explicit emphasis on societal cultural conditions. This is a significant deficiency, since companies are usually more a reflection of societal cultures than an independent culture (a distinct culture in relation to the society in its surroundings, Alvesson, 1993a). To some extent, this deficiency is due to the fact that the company studied demonstrates relatively extensive originality vis-à-vis the social conditions in its surroundings. More significant is that the incorporation of a societal focus would expand the study too far. The study covers enough themes already. As Jelinek et al. (1983) point out there is a shortage of good analyses of the modern company as a cultural form, seen in a broad societal perspective. Another theme that has not been covered more than marginally concerns gender relations. Like most culture studies, the gendered nature of organization is neglected.

Awareness of the use of the cultural concept as a metaphor is also important. The reader must be reminded of this fact all through the text and this gives the author an opportunity to remind him- or herself, too. Otherwise it is all too easy to slip into "objectivistic" forms of understanding, where one imagines that reality can be read off on its own terms and not via the frames of reference and metaphors which are utilized. At the same time, the use of other, non-cultural metaphors should be clarified as far as possible.

Finally we should be modest as to what can be understood with the aid of the culture concept in a company. It is tempting to allow everything to become a question of culture, to regard culture as an "all-embracing broom" which explains everything and describes all phenomena in cultural terms as rites, rituals, sagas, myths, heroes, etc. I consider that it is preferable to be somewhat cautious in this context and to primarily employ the culture concept and culture metaphors when there is a clear advantage in doing so. A genuine enthusiast would probably consider that this is always the case, but perhaps it only applies sometimes. There is no doubt that some meetings may be best understood and the descriptions made more exciting if meetings are compared with rites or rituals, while in other cases the idea of culture contributes nothing new compared with the options offered by traditional concepts (co-ordination, information, discussion of the facts, etc.).

4.6   The Method in the Present Study

Armed with inspiration gained from the literature quoted earlier in this chapter and from other sources (mentioned in Chapter 1) and with the methodological considerations of the preceding section in my mind, I then proceeded with my research.

I selected Enator on the basis of the criteria that I was interested in – a company which was young, expanding and which explicitly worked with culture as part of management and organizational operations. I was also interested in studying an organization which was open and where access could be arranged without too many problems and where it was possible to make observations. My wishes were amply fulfilled. A telephone call, an hour's meeting and discussion with a management representative, followed by confirmation of our agreement by a few senior executives and I was given the green light. Management thought it was a good idea that somebody would write about the company. There were no restrictions or pressures to ensure that my report would result in a public-relations oriented presentation. I was thus free to interview people and to attend certain meetings and other activities.

I interviewed about 35 individuals for an average of 1.5 hours each. I tried to achieve a coverage which would ensure that a number of people with different points of view would be included. This meant that my interviews ranged from one of the founder members and the first employee to staff who had just started to work for the company. My study included various corporate units and people at different levels in the company – from the managing director downwards. However, my efforts were concentrated to some extent on management and on people with considerable experience in the company. In some cases, these two groups converged, but I also talked to several veteran employees who had not received promotion above the rank of project manager. I interviewed male as well as female employees.

The topics which we talked about are all presented in this book. The interviews tended to be rather different. In fact, I introduced different themes, which resulted in moving into a greater depth in the course of the interview, depending on the informant's special knowledge and on my own interests which differed somewhat throughout the study as themes emerged and I felt satisfied with the amount of information/viewpoints I received regarding various issues. When talking to veteran employees, I asked about the company's development, with management I discussed strategy, business concepts, etc., and with more critical staff members I looked at the reverse side of the coin.

Discussion was largely a question of what I felt I could extract from my informants on the basis of their position, temperament, etc., especially in the case of the latter two-thirds of the interviews. In other words, I did not expose the interviewee to a list of questions determined in advance. This makes demands on the interviewer, requiring him or her to be flexible and to continuously interpret what might be interesting, or less interesting to pursue on the basis of what the interviewee is saying.

I also attended certain corporate activities as a participant observer. The results of these activities are presented in Chapters 5 and 7. The most important individual item in this context was participation in the company's course on project management philosophy, which all new employees, irrespective of status, had to attend. I felt this might give me a concentrated insight into the company and how cultural transfer takes place. (Cf. Ehn and Löfgren's view of cultural transitions as an appropriate focus, above.) I spent a week continuously in the company of Enator personnel, both Danish and Swedish, apart from the time I spent taking notes. I spoke to about 10 Enator staff about the course and about their opinions of the company, their work, etc.

In all, my empirical work consisted of approximately 35 interviews, about 15 brief conversations, some 3 weeks of participant observation and some additional studies of corporate documents. It is normal for qualitatively oriented researchers to attempt to focus considerable attention on quantitative information as to who was interviewed and the procedures employed in the empirical work. The idea is probably often to create an overall impression of "objectivity" and "rationality" and to counteract the uneasy feeling that the researcher's own individual personality and arbitrary moves permeates the results all too clearly.

However, the quality of the interviews and the researcher's interpretative ability is more interesting than the number of interviews and the researcher's method of producing, categorizing and classifying them. Amongst other things, quality is a matter of the interviewee's insights,

openness and honesty. Naturally, the interview material and the questionnaire responses are affected by the fact that the informants sometimes
wish to mislead the researcher, the fact that they do not know about important aspects and that a great deal is taken for granted and therefore
cannot be passed on to the interviewer. Van Maanen (1979) lists these as
important sources of error. They are particularly problematical because
many researchers do not seem to be aware of them, judging by the failure
of many authors to explicitly evaluate their sources.[3] It is therefore highly
important that the researcher tries to assess the quality of his or her material thoroughly. Different statements cannot be transformed into "data" of
equal weight on a routine basis without carefully attempting to determine
their quality on a basis of a total assessment of the person interviewed
(IP). What is the IP's vantage point? What current and previous experience does he/she have which may influence what she says today in the
interview? How coherent does the IP seem to be? Is the person in question largely positive or critical as regards circumstances in the company? Is
the IP reluctant to make negative judgements? Does the IP talk mainly
about superficial factual circumstances or does the interview convey the
results of the due consideration and processing of the IP's observations of
his or her place of work?

I asked myself questions of this kind in assessing my interviews, and I
have given different interviewees different weightings in my analyses on
this basis. Interviewees who seemed to me to be reflective, willing to share
problems or criticize without taking a fundamentally negative view of the
company, were seen as valuable informants. IP's who had many years of
experience of their place of work and who seemed to have a social network and/or duties which permitted the acquisition of a broad range of
information and overviews also played a relatively important part in my
analysis. On the whole, I have given less weight to interviews with employees with a "restricted" vantage point (e.g. new employees, even if they
sometimes expressed interesting opinions), to employees who provided a
picture of the company which scarcely deviated from the official line and
to employees who could not give me examples of thinking based on the
abstraction of everyday experience. The quality of interviews in terms of
the interviewees' willingness to supply sensitive information, their insights
into conditions and contexts and their ability to verbalize what may readily
be taken for granted are more important than the number of interviews
which have been conducted.

In my general approach to scientific research, the researcher's interpretative ability is more important than his/her capacity to follow procedures.
Interpretative ability depends on knowledge and insights at several levels,
ranging from the way to conduct the interview in a manner which combines contact/closeness and distancing/interpretation at a particular point

of time to awareness of the metatheoretical aspects of research (Alvesson and Sköldberg, 1995). Good interpretation makes considerable demands, most of which are difficult to put in writing.

One important aspect is reflection on what metatheoretical and theoretical frames of reference inform the practical work and interpretations. The metaphorical level is crucial in this context. Thinking through and making explicit the mental pictures which lie behind the study and also if they are not directly used in the study may improve the quality of interpretation.

Notes

[1] Strauss and Corbin (1990) emphasize that grounded theory is a scientific method "that meets the criteria for doing 'good science': significance, theory-observation compatibility, generalizability, reproductibility, precision, rigor, and verification" (p 27). Guba and Lincoln (1994) view this approach as "post-positivistic" – a sort of up-to-date version of positivism, that is open for the "rigorous" use of qualitative method – and compare it with a "constructivist" approach. The latter comes close to the position I am advocating here.

[2] Personally, I am probably no exception. However, in this book I have attempted to allow different perspectives to contrast with one another.

[3] Silverman (1985, 1989) draws attention to the fact that interviews are situations of complex social interaction, not only techniques for collecting valid information about "objective reality" or of their states of mind. He suggests that interviews, if conducted, are best treated as objects of study rather than as simple reflections of something external to the interview setting. I am not prepared to fully follow this route, but take the precaution of being careful and sceptical in evaluating interview statements seriously.

5 A Socialization Sequence: Course in Project Management Philosophy

Enator has a principle of letting all new employees – whether they are managers, consultants, salesmen or secretaries – participate in a course in "project management philosophy". This course is considered to be of vital importance in Enator's operations. Employees often refer to this course as highly significant. Its importance is emphasized by the fact that, when the project management philosophy course first took place in 1982 and for some years afterwards, two of the founders/owners (of whom one was also managing director of Enator) were teachers on the course. In this chapter, I shall be presenting a course of this type in which I myself participated for observational purposes.

The chapter provides a comprehensive picture of the company's (management's) self image, it's basic ideas and work principles. The chapter also indicates how the course functions as an element in the management of the corporation, not only as regards the concrete method of conducting projects but also as an instrument for coordination and management in the broadest possible sense, including the creation of involvement, interest and a community feeling among the employees. The contents of the course and the way in which the contents were transmitted, provide a basis for the analysis of other important themes in the company which are dealt with in later chapters, for example the corporate culture, business concept and internal marketing.

Another aim in this chapter is to use this course as an illustrative expression of the company's functioning and also as an important introduction to understanding the organization as a whole, particularly management attempts to control the values and ideas of Enator personnel. The course can be regarded as a culture-transmitting element and as a symbolic expression of the whole firm. Analysis of the course from the culture perspective contributes to a survey of certain cultural patterns in the company.

5.1   On Socialization in Organizations

The course which I will be describing may be regarded as a socialization process. All forms of social existence, including organizations, require socialization.

Organizational socialization ... refers to the process by which the employee is taught and learns 'the ropes' of a particular organizational role. In its most general sense, organizational socialization is the process by which an individual acquires the social knowledge and skills necessary to assure an organizational role (Van Maanen and Schein, 1979, p 211).

If an organization is to "survive", stability and continuity over time are required. Management and senior employees try to transmit the dominant social and cultural patterns of one generation in the organization to the next generation. There are often discontinuities, conflicts and crises between existing and new personnel which may lead to some systematic efforts to minimize such effects. New employees in organizations bring with them expectations, values and objectives which, initially, do not fully comply with conditions in their new workplace.

An organization's management and its experienced staff therefore train new employees in various ways so they accept the organization's fundamental requirements and conditions, thus teaching newcomers to regard and approach the organization's operations in approximately the same way as their more experienced colleagues. Naturally, excessive socialization may make it difficult for the organization to function if this means that all new employees adopt given patterns so completely that this results in conformism, and that no new ideas are contributed. Such a state of affairs is termed "oversocialization" and may ultimately lead to the petrification of the organization. However, a more common problem for management in most companies is probably the difficulty of achieving sufficiently effective socialization in organizations.

Socialization is intimately linked with culture. Socialization is the acquisition of culture – people adopt a culture and become cultural beings. Culture indicates the contents of and the results of socialization.

In a sense, socialization is a life-long process. It is only absent in a totally static situation. The life cycle at a workplace (and in existence in general) involves socialization. Here, socialization is most crucial in connection with changes regarding status, roles and social belonging. The most important form of socialization in an organizational context usually takes place in direct connection with the employee's job, at his/her workplace.

Socialization always involves collective circumstances such as rules, use of language, habits, norms and values, etc. which are applied by a social group. These collective attributes are represented in various ways depending on the specific role involved. For a new employee, it is a question of learning, on the one hand, about general collective circumstances and, on the other hand, of finding one's own specific role.

Van Maanen and Schein (1979) refer to three main dimensions of socialization processes. One dimension is concerned with *functions*, that is to say the areas of operation and the tasks which an individual works with. Is it a question of personnel, product B or G, technical development or maintenance, etc.? The second dimension is *hierarchies*. Individuals are promoted or allocated (perhaps informally) a more important role than previously. Sometimes they are demoted. Just like a change in type of occupation (function), hierarchical change in status is accompanied by a socialization process which may in some cases lead to a noticeable change of identity, both in relation to the organization and at a the individual level. The third significant dimension involves *inclusions*. Members of the organization may be peripheral or central in relation to the core of the organization. At one extreme, there are newcomers and at the other, central figures who, often after many years with the organization, are located in the middle of the sociocultural network, personifying the style, values, etc. of the organization.

The socialization process dealt with in this chapter only involves the inclusion dimension. The reason is that the course in question has the same contents for all personnel, irrespective of hierarchical status and function, and is intended to be a means of introducing new employees into the company. In terms of organizational-symbolic language it is thus a question of an "initiation rite" for new members (see e.g. Trice and Beyer, 1984).

5.2   The Project Management Philosophy Course from a Socialization Perspective

The course I attended consisted of twenty participants – plus three teachers who were also managers of Enator subsidiaries (with approximately 40 employees each). In addition, the manager of Enator Sweden also participated in the first three days of the seven day course, which took place in May on the island of Rhodes.

The twenty participants came from different subsidiaries. Four came from the Danish subsidiary, while the remainder, including the teachers, came from Swedish companies. Most of the participants were between 28 and 38 years old, 3 were women and 17 men. Most of the participants had been already employed for a few months in the company, except for one employee who was due to start work on the Monday after completion of the course, and another who had worked at Enator/Denmark for a year and a half but had not been able to participate in the course previously due to a heavy work load.

On the whole, the course participants were comfortably dressed. The four managers (i.e. leaders/teachers) wore shorts and T-shirts. In the conference room, the participants were seated on three sides of a square, with one end open. Grey files lay waiting for the participants when they entered the room. The Enator logo and the participant's name were engraved on the cover.

In the introductory presentations, which were initiated by the teachers, participants indicated their civil status, spare-time interests, and sometimes their age and current and previous jobs. The agenda then switched to describing the purpose of the course. It was indicated that participants were expected to

- understand Enator's business concept;
- accept and operate in accordance with this concept;
- be aware of the target group in accordance with the business concept;
- provide guidelines and create a common base for all Enator employees to enable them to realize the business concept.

The leader of the course commented that:

This seems simple, but very few companies achieve this kind of business concept. Some of Enator's success is because we have partially realized this concept.

It was also emphasized that the course was important. Participants were reminded that the course had not been sub-contracted to a professional training institution. This was not because such institutions were considered to be unsatisfactory, however. At Enator, representatives of top management, usually subsidiary managers, always ran courses themselves. Values were important in the Enator context and it was necessary for managers to participate and present their view, and the company's view, of what was involved. The first day's relaxed start, with only a few hours work, was followed by a few days with a tougher programme. The course started at 8.30 in the morning and continued after a couple of hours lunch break until 9 o'clock or 10 o'clock in the evening. On the second day, participants were greeted by the slogan "Be positive" on the blackboard and, for the most part, they were positive.

On one occasion, presentation techniques were on the agenda. One of the teachers spoke for an hour. Like his two colleagues he advanced well into the participants' horseshoe seating area. Participants were also urged to do the same when they presented their group-assignments – which everyone had to do on a couple of occasions in the course of the week. The

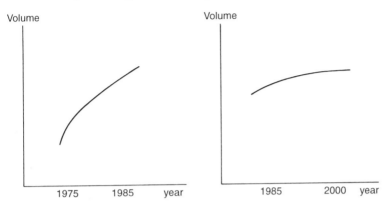

Figure 5.1:   The market for computer consultancy services in the mid and late
         1980s

teachers consistently employed active and persuasive pedagogic techniques rather than purely concentrating on supplying information. Participants were, of course, expected to emulate this approach. And the point of
the course was – quite specifically – that the participants were to absorb
and emulate Enator's ideas. Teachers walked around the inside of the
horseshoe, physically close to the participants, they spoke rather loudly,
looking into the eyes of participants and they employed body-language
with considerable forcefulness.

In the next few days, the teachers provided feedback, mostly in positive
and encouraging terms, on participants' group-assignment reports. The
participants were frequently encouraged to advance into the area around
which their listeners were sitting, turning their backs on some of the audience, and thus relinquishing the relative security of the overhead projector
(the "staff-transpirer"). In other words, participants were encouraged to
take risks: "How did it feel? You didn't advance into the square?" Most of
the people who made presentations advanced a few paces into the horseshoe and, on the whole, the teachers seemed to be satisfied with the results.

After this discussion of presentation techniques, the Managing Director
of Enator Sweden commented on Enator's business concept, market prerequisites and operational methods. Among other things, the participants
were told in clear terms that overall market conditions were now tougher
than when Enator was founded. This is illustrated in Figure 5.1.

Teachers informed participants that Enator's customers were top-level
decision makers, for example chief executive officers, R&D managers or
divisional managers in major companies. According to the Managing Director of Enator Sweden, if the customer's corporate management was not

involved in consultancy projects, Enator refused to take the assignment. He also mentioned that what distinguished Enator from other companies in the business was: our ability to continuously communicate with corporate management with the aim of solving corporate problems (i.e. to improve the customer's business). Looking at the course as a whole, it is clear that participants were expected to develop a mental preparedness for communication of this kind. The importance of a bird's eye ("helicopter") view was emphasized. This meant that the individual should have both an overview and an excellent vantage point from which to deal with details. A helicopter view was what consultants involved in a project needed in addition to their day-to-day systems and programming work in order to understand contexts to enable them to focus on the customer's position and needs and on additional opportunities for Enator assignments.

During the week many examples of people's unfortunate behaviour were mentioned. On one occasion the course leader talked about an episode which involved one of the company's many managers – using him as an example – "since we are talking about this question of presentations and distracting attention". The manager in question was apparently standing in the corridor at his office talking to a customer, when he discovered that his shirt had slipped up over his belt. He proceeded to rearrange his belt and his trouser zipper and began to tuck his shirt back in place, without turning a hair. The teacher said that it might be thought that the customer's attention was distracted from the real content of the conversation and added that the director in question was unconscious of behaving like this sometimes. The teacher said that the manager was aware that his behaviour was going to be mentioned in the course and that he did not object.

The Pronator Group was also mentioned in the course of the training week. It was specifically stated that Enator represented a model for much of what happened throughout the Group. Teachers also frequently referred to Enator's close relationship with SAS and its Managing Director, Jan Carlzon, who was also on the board of directors of both Enator and Pronator. As an example of the values expressed, teachers maintained that:

There is nothing wrong with making money. Money helps you to develop the company. You can also have conferences like this and we can afford to work fewer hours per week in the summer, etc.

Much of the course programme was devoted to group work. New groups were formed after every two group exercises. Group assignments dealt with various aspects of the company and its method of operation, the point being that as many people as possible were to get to know each other.

For the most part, reports on group assignments turned out to be relatively satisfactory and, as usual, the teachers were both positive and complimentary. Teachers subsequently pointed out that the customer's own business concept and broader perspectives must be included in the overall picture when conducting an AD (administrative development) plan or pilot study. It was emphasized that contacts were to be established with corporate management/decision makers. But people in this category were not interested in details: "Executives don't understand anything about bits, bytes and bands and all the rest", according to the course leader.

One of the teachers explained that Enator's aim in pilot studies and AD plans was not to make money – "you never do that with assignments of this kind" – but that the point was to utilize such pilot studies and plans as a basis for future marketing and sales, and to achieve direct contact with customer management. Assignments of this kind were important mainly because it was possible to make money later from subsequent large-scale development projects.

This particular teacher emphasized the message in his own personal style. He walked around, brandishing his fists in the air, radiating involvement, (positive) aggression and salesmanship. He clearly demonstrated that the message should be strong and convincing and he was clearly trying to convey two ideas at the same time. One was to get the participants to "buy" the concept, while the other was to transmit the overall style and behaviour that Enator employees should adopt vis-à-vis their customers.

Considerable time was devoted to talking about the strategic importance of information technology. Using computers was not just a question of cutting costs or passively achieving corporate goals and strategies. Several examples were given of industries in which information technology had now become strategically significant, and even a prerequisite for operations: airline corporations, banking and finance, wholesaling and tourism for example.

The course leaders then provided some examples of Enator projects, which illustrated the business concept (i.e. the integration of management and computers to achieve strategic objectives). "In order to show that this is not just talk" was the label applied to the demonstration projects chosen, which mainly involved large and well-known companies.

Half way through the course, the Managing Director of Enator Sweden departed in order to return to Sweden. He thanked the participants and received in return a (demonstrative?) collegial hug from the course leader. The Danish participants were astonished at this behaviour, which did not comply with their expectations of the manner in which Swedish top executives function. This occurrence was apparently meant to show the significance of friendship and informality in the company.

The question of quality was discussed at one of the sessions in the course. The first point was to consider what quality really means. The participants were interested in this topic and they enthusiastically repeated appropriate excerpts from the discussion earlier in the week. Taking the customer's business concept into consideration and the importance of aiming for the right technical level were emphasized ("if a customer needs a Volkswagen, you shouldn't sell him a Volvo").

It was also clearly established that quality was a subjective factor and that the focus should be on the customer's perception of quality. Abstract and intangible aspects were definitely important – not just technical and functional features. A good relationship with the customer, acceptance of the product by the customer's staff and customer satisfaction were considered to be crucial.

At this point – as on so many other occasions during this course – it was emphasized that although technical quality was important it was not a decisive factor. Technical issues were not the real problem. Apparently, the soft dimensions – project management and organization, customer interaction and linkages with the customer's business – were the most important aspects, even if they were difficult to achieve. A quality formula was then presented:

Technical quality x Functional quality x Acceptance = Customer perception of quality.

Technical quality indicated how well the job was carried out from a purely technical point of view. (Does it work, is it reliable, etc.?) Functional quality was related to the tasks and the functions which the system was expected to undertake and fulfil. (Was the system appropriate in relation to the customer's needs?) Acceptance was the degree to which customer and the customer's employees accepted the product. (Did they get what they had expected?) On the whole, in Enator's view these aspects constitute customer-perceived quality, involving all types of interaction between Enator employees and the customers, from technical problem solutions to interaction between Enator consultants and the customer's reception staff.

The course continued with further group work which was relatively specific, although there were stronger links with the organizational and marketing aspects than with technical problem-solving. As in other aspects of the group assignments, this group work was more a question of getting participants to consider market and customer-contact orientation and business aspects than of improving their knowledge of systems applications and programming – which is what most of them would be mainly dealing with in the future.

On the final day of the course, the flip-chart in the classroom announced "Look out for the opportunities!", followed by a picture of the sun. The final group assignment was concerned with reaching agreement with the customer, and, above all, understanding what new assignments might involve.

The group considered how additional sales of new projects were to occur on a continuous basis as a result of existing projects. Previous customers would often become new customers. The unique factors at Enator were reiterated: identification of the target group of decision makers (management) in the company and maintenance of contact at this level through-out the project.

The participants were also confronted with Peters and Waterman's "In Search of Excellence" (1982). Attention was first drawn to Peters and Waterman's criteria for unsuccessful companies – for example too much analysis and too much bureaucracy. The next stage was to list eight organizational principles which, according to Peters and Waterman, characterized successful companies. SAS and its Managing Director, Jan Carlzon, were mentioned in this context by the teachers. Enator was singled out on a couple of occasions, as a company which had a simple organization – in principle only managing directors and consultants. However, this was not accepted uncritically by the group. The Danes considered, for example, that they had functional managers at an intermediate level between ordinary consultants and the managing director. In addition, the existence of project managers and project leaders (a particular function intended to monitor and support the work of the project managers) was discussed.

Motivation was the next theme. Reference was made to both Maslow's and Herzberg's theories of motivation. I assume here that the reader is familiar with Maslow's pyramid of needs. Herzberg's theory of motivation mainly states that certain factors in the job situation may create dissatisfaction, but never satisfaction. He calls these hygiene factors. Thus, in the worst possible case, such factors may give rise to dissatisfaction, while at best they only lead to a neutral situation. Other factors determine whether real satisfaction and motivation occur. These are referred to as motivational factors. Examples of hygiene factors mentioned by Herzberg are the physical work environment, personnel policy and pay. Examples cited by Herzberg of satisfaction or motivational factors are responsibility, promotion prospects and a qualified work content. (See also Herzberg et al., 1959.)

It was also emphasized that self-realization and personal development opportunities at work are important in general level, but particularly at Enator. The relatively minor satisfactional value of a high salary was also emphasized. According to the leader of the course, pay should not be the most important reason for working at Enator. He never attempted to persuade people to start working at Enator by offering a salary increase, nor did he use such an incentive to make them refrain from resigning. Obviously, employees should have a reasonable salary. The principle was that: "No one should start working for Enator because of a high salary, but no one should resign due to poor pay".

The next phase was to present some of the guiding principles for Enator's method of operations. One feature was that people in the company should never shut themselves up in their offices. Rapid and direct interaction was important. In addition, every effort was made to avoid bureaucracy. Another detail mentioned in this context was that Enator's list of internal telephone numbers was being changed so that Christian names appeared before surnames and the Christian name constituted the search-word.

Participants were then present with a list of rules of thumb for personnel, to be used if they were to function properly in the organization. I present this list without any changes (and with minimal comment):

1. You have to give if you are going to get anything in return.
2. Listen to your colleagues ("Janne Carlzon and Hasse Larsson are excellent listeners").
3. Make sure that everyone feels they are important.
4. Create pride in the company.
5. Argue with feeling. (People certainly do not function purely on the basis of logic and reflection.)
6. Emphasize skill and authority, not controls and instructions.
7. Say it with flowers. ("Plus-minus-plus-method." If something is worth commenting on, it should be done so that things start on a positive note and finish with encouraging feed-back. Indications of what is less satisfactory and suggestions for changes should be made in between.)
8. Get everyone to become a problem-solver.
9. Encourage ideas.
10. Make things simple.
11. Justify your decisions.
12. Delegate decisions.
13. You can't win them all. (Everybody is unsuccessful sometimes. This is unavoidable.)
14. Be yourself.

In principle, this concluded the course. All that remained were certain ceremonial features. Enator's method handbook and a diploma were presented to participants and the ceremonial atmosphere was accentuated when some participants proposed that all three teachers should make their rounds and shake hands with all participants. The teachers did this, and some hugs were exchanged too. In some cases this was not surprising, but in other cases I was mildly surprised. Such behaviour seemed more artifi-

cial than natural since previous contacts between the persons concerned
did not appear to have been so close.

The course programme week ended with dinner and entertainment arranged by the course leaders/managers. On the next day, Sunday, everyone returned to Sweden or Denmark.

What did the participants think of the course? Everyone I talked to had
a positive attitude to what they had experienced in the course-week. Attitudes appear to have been balanced and positive, but were hardly permeated by an enthusiastic revival-meeting spirit. One participant said, for
example, that the course "was good, but not hallelujah". This could have
been a reaction to rumours that previous participants had reported that
the course was fantastic.

5.3   Course Objectives

The explicit purpose of the project management philosophy course was, as
already mentioned, that participants should understand and apply Enator's business concept, and that the course should provide similar guidelines for all Enator employees, irrespective of nationality, subsidiary company and type of work. Furthermore, employees in the different companies were supposed to get to know each other and to be trained to make
competent presentations.

In addition, it may be relevant to refer to implicit objectives, that is to
say objectives which the participants acquired but which were not explicit
and which course-management and teachers were not perhaps fully aware
of. This might be termed a "hidden course agenda" (cf. Broady, 1981). A
hidden agenda exists to a greater or lesser degree in all education. Even
the teachers are not necessarily aware of the contents of such implicit messages.

Time-scheduling discipline was an important element in the course. Participants learnt to be on time. All scheduling was indicated precisely and
sessions started "on the dot". Latecomers were not directly confronted
with their tardiness, but sometimes the course-leader asked the group
where the latecomer was. The idea appeared to be to (mildly) point out
that it was now time to start and that someone had not yet turned up. The
importance of maintaining the time-schedule was also discussed, more or
less directly, on a couple of occasions.

Another feature which was never clearly stated was the completion of
group tasks *on time*. To some extent, this overlapped with the time-
scheduling discipline. Performing group tasks on time was not, however,
primarily a question of turning up at an exact time, but more a matter of

planning and carrying out a task within a given time framework. One of Enator's slogans, and a crucial aim shared by other companies in the business, is to complete consultancy projects on time and within the budget. It was thus considered to be important to meet deadlines. Completion of group tasks required efficient time-keeping.

Another important course objective was to teach participants *flexibility* and adaptability. Group members were changed after each two group tasks were completed. This prepared participants for rapid adaptation to new work-groups. Actual consultancy projects usually follow a pattern in which project groups are assembled in accordance with the nature of the assignment. Once a project has started, consultants are expected to work together with new and perhaps unfamiliar people from their own and other Enator subsidiaries and from customer companies. Group assignments in the training programme reflected this situation.

A further and perhaps more significant objective was to teach new employees *the company spirit and style*, and the values and attitudes which should characterize company personnel. Informality, openness, and the avoidance of a narrow demarcation between work and private life were all examples of behaviour patterns transmitted in the course programme. Such items did not appear on the agenda, but they were expressed in the form of examples. Here are some illustrations:

- The "eminent director" at Enator who, unconsciously, pulled at his trousers and adjusted his shirt (and who knew that his colleagues were going to talk about this in the course).
- Teachers who discussed what it feels like to hold a presentation, both on the basis of their own experience and in relation to participants' achievements. On one occasion, a teacher asked another teacher how he coped and how matters worked out after his divorce.
- The course leader who gave the Managing Director of Enator/Sweden a hug when he departed to return to Sweden.

These examples were verbal respective action symbols (Dandridge et al., 1980) which, although somewhat superficial, transmitted a deeper and wider meaning than their explicit interpretation. The director who adjusted his shirt was not mentioned because participants should be aware of an unusual detail in his behaviour nor as a warning of inappropriate behaviour, nor (even) to give them a good laugh. Instead, this story made the point

- that personal and human characteristics are just as important as formal hierarchical status and that status should not be taken too seriously;
- that it is possible to be open and relaxed about relatively private matters;

- that it is neither extraordinary nor wrong to make a fool of yourself to some extent.

Apart from indicating appropriate personal behaviour, the course taught new employees the corporate ideology, that is to say the officially espoused and generally idealized formulation of overall ideas, norms and ways of thinking which characterize the company. This function was implied by the course title: Project Management Philosophy Course.

Enator's business concept, its strategy, competence and methods were described in general terms, and with positive overtones. This was an idealized model of how things worked, rather than a comprehensive description of how they might be in reality. Some participants did not really recognize their own short-term experience of the projects in which they were participating in the course leader's account of how Enator functioned. In fact, none of the participants I talked to had experienced projects which fully tied in with the picture which the course conveyed.

The principal message – that Enator is involved in relating computer issues to the customers' business concept – received considerable attention, but in a very superficial manner. There was a relatively brief presentation of the meaning of the term "business concept". Most participants had hardly heard of this concept before. However, they learnt that they were to always have the concept in mind when working on Enator projects and with customers. Mention of the business concept in presentations frequently gave rise to positive feedback from teachers. ("Very good", "champagne quality", they said.) However, the participants' use of the business concept and the parallels they drew with their own work and the customer's strategy, in the context of pilot studies, project implementation or project completion tended to be at a superficial level, on the whole. I find it difficult to believe that most of the participants understood what the business concept was in specific terms and how computer consultancy projects could be related to the business concept. Perhaps they were inspired to learn more about this ill-defined concept at a later stage, but the principal effect seems to have been to train the participants to use the term and to reinforce an image: that the company takes the customer's business situation seriously.

Thus, opportunities to apply the Enator business concept after the course seem to have been only partially realized. On the other hand, it seems as if the participants adopted the idea, per se. In presentations and discussions, they referred happily to Enator's uniqueness and competence, in accordance with the business concept. Thus, what the course seems to have achieved is to convey an idealized picture of the company and its methods and to achieve acceptance of this picture.

One function which was closely associated with the participants' acceptance of the corporate ideology was the establishment of pride and involvement. The satisfactory transmission of corporate ideology was obviously an important ingredient in creating pride in the company, but there were many other aspects of this process – for example Enator's excellent and close relationships with SAS and Jan Carlzon. Jan Carlzon was often mentioned in the course and the fact that he was on the board of directors of Enator and that SAS often utilized Enator's services clearly improved the corporate image, both externally and internally.

Another aspect of transmission of ideology was description of some of Enator's, major, successful projects. The projects discussed were not typical in the sense that they were statistically representative since they tended to be (described as) successful, prestige projects – major projects which were of strategic importance both to famous-name customer companies and to Enator. There was hardly any reference in the course to the very considerable number of small projects undertaken by Enator. (59% of Enator's total revenues in 1986 were derived from assignments with a turnover value of less than SEK 500,000. Less than 20% of revenues were derived from assignments worth more than SEK 1 million. SEK 1 million was at the time of the study equivalent to approximately GB£ 100,000 or US$ 150,000.)

A further feature which was probably designed to achieve a positive effect on participants' pride in the company, and which appeared successful in this respect, concerned Enator's organization and management style. Peters and Waterman's eight principles for top American companies were not emphasized directly as characteristics of the company, but it was implied that Enator fitted neatly into these patterns. Rapid decision making, simple organization, avoidance of bureaucracy, etc. were said to be characteristic of the company.

5.4   The Course as a Social-Integrative Management Instrument

At a higher level of abstraction, what has been stated above may be described in terms of viewing the course as a social-integrative management instrument. In using this concept, I am referring to endeavours to create a group of subsidiaries consisting of a multiplicity of loosely coupled units which link up and function as an entity by informal means. The links between the various subsidiaries and consultancy projects are not always particularly strong.

Regarding the course and the socialization process which it constitutes as a social-integrative management instrument means that the focus changes compared with the approach discussed above. Previous sections about the purposes of the course illustrated the personal characteristics and approaches which were encouraged on the part of personnel. There were also attempts to get participants to accept the overall corporate ideology, i.e. efforts to develop a particular kind of subjectivity.

What follows deals with the various managerial and personnel groups' approach to one another. Naturally, this is regulated by many different factors and the importance of the project management philosophy course in this context is limited. Nonetheless, it is worth noting. All the above mentioned points facilitate the total integration of operations. The encouragement of certain common personal attitudes and action patterns – ranging from good time keeping to an informal, free and personal style – and the encouragement of acceptance of, and involvement in, the business concept and the corporate ideology paved the way for cooperation between various subsidiaries and personnel groups. Obviously, pride in the company was also a source of mutual identification with Enator.

However, there are number of other important points in the socialization process discussed above which operate in a way that facilitates corporate integration. One such feature was that all new employees, irrespective of their function or rank, participated in the course on the same basis. This emphasized equality, while making the contradictory and normally more salient differentiation dimension less prominent in this context. The basis for participation in the course was employment at Enator rather than occupational status as a salesman, consultant, secretary or other type of employee in Enator/Denmark or in one of the technology subsidiaries in Kista, thus indicating an equality message which may be assumed to have had an integrative function which reinforced similarity and a shared social identity, associated with the company.[1]

Another point was that the course provided all employees with exactly the same experience. Other examples of this phenomenon were Enator's large-scale jubilees and anniversaries for hundreds of employees (see Chapter 7). Providing that they made the requisite impression, such common points of reference could facilitate cooperation, for example when a number of the individuals who did not know each other from various Enator companies, perhaps from various nations, were assembled together for a project, they were then expected to function, preferably within a short period, as an integrated working group.

One final point was the purpose of the project management philosophy course in getting personnel to accept certain fundamental ideas about the company and its operations. This was also part of the stated purpose of the course: to get personnel to accept and work in accordance with the Enator business concept.

One of the rules of thumb which was presented was that Enator "encourages ideas". Scarcely surprisingly, this was not followed up to any great extent in the course week. During the discussions, teachers were concerned to sell the current view of matters and new ideas were not encouraged. This was fully in line with the purpose of the course. The intention was socialization and not new approaches. New ideas did not figure on the agenda.

5.5   On the Processing of Social Information

To understand the effects of the socialization described above on the attitudes and approaches of new employees to the company and their future work, I will discuss Salancik and Pfeffer's (1978) theory about "social information processing". I will be returning to this theory later in this book. It is therefore reviewed in relative detail.

The theory of social information processing is a critical response to dominant lines of thought within organization theory and the psychology of work regarding the central importance of needs and the satisfaction of needs and how they affect the attitudes of individuals and their overall satisfaction at their workplace. Salancik and Pfeffer emphasize instead the manner in which the individual obtains information and interprets relationships on the basis of the social context. They consider that the immediate social environment affects individuals' attitudes and ideas about their needs in two ways. Firstly, this is achieved by presenting socially acceptable beliefs, attitudes and needs and acceptable reasons for behaviour, which lead to the preconstruction for the individual of certain meanings and definitions of reality. And secondly, the social environment channels the individual's attention towards certain conditions and certain types of information, thus creating specific expectations.

The importance of the social environment in determining how the individual perceives and approaches his/her work and his/her workplace is greatest in areas which are unclear and can be assessed in various ways. People are inclined to utilize social information when it applies to the development of ideas and attitudes about the meaningfulness, significance and degree of interest and variation in their work. Social information does not impinge much on the employee's ideas about tangible and unambiguous matters. If the physical work environment is hot and noisy, the employee notices this without needing to consult the social environment. (Obviously the social environment may also be relevant in this context, for example in determining whether the noise level is regarded as acceptable or unacceptable or to make a collectively based attempt to achieve change.)

Salancik and Pfeffer (1978) discuss four specific ways in which social influence can determine the attitude of individuals to their work. The first is the manner in which colleagues, managers and others exert an influence through direct statements. The individual is particularly receptive if the values and statements of others provide clues for the manner in which complex and ambiguous stimuli are to be interpreted. The statements made in the individual's social environment also influence him/her because they encourage agreement and compliance. Normally, individuals want to agree with what people in environment express, even if this is merely verbal. However, pressure for verbal agreement may also ultimately convince the individual of the correctness of what he or she is saying.

Another way in which social influence functions is through regulating the salience of the various aspects of the situation, i.e. influencing what dimensions which the individual is strongly aware of and aspects of the situation which attract relatively peripheral attention. For example, a job may be routine and boring, even if at the same time it may be socially important. And it is important for the individual's attitudes to his/her work to know whether it is the routine nature of the job or it is the considerable social importance of the job which is predominant in the comments he/she hears in his/her social environment.

A third aspect of social influence is the question of how clues in the environment are interpreted. For example, management or owners who apply tough methods may be regarded as exploiting the staff for their own narrow profit interests. But the same behaviour may also be regarded as an expression of a professional endeavour to ensure corporate growth and opportunities for development.

A fourth aspect discussed by Salancik and Pfeffer is the individual's sensitivity to the perceptions and needs of the social environment in terms of the understanding of his/her needs and wants. The individual does not interpret his/her needs and wishes in a social vacuum. If colleagues at the workplace regard taking time-off work to look after children as inconceivable for an upwardly mobile career-hungry person, it may be imagined that such a careerist does not feel any tangible longing to stay at home with his newly born child for a few months. Whereas if colleagues expressed the opinion that such a wish would be natural and important, he might react and feel differently. Self-awareness and the individual's own view of his/her needs is thus sensitive to the perception of his/her immediate environment, in Salancik and Pfeffer's view. (Similar ideas on the discursive constitution of subjectivity has also been expressed by poststructuralists, e.g. Deetz, 1992, Weedon, 1987.)

There are a number of interesting viewpoints raised by the perspective described here. One involves pay. If pay is generous and attracts considerable attention, this will mean that a number of other dimensions at work become less important in the individual's mental world. His/her attitude to work becomes strongly coloured by the high salary, that is to say an instrumental system of rewards. At the same time he/she will be less conscious of the content aspects of work. Salancik and Pfeffer consider that this explains the frequently reported observation that the introduction or reinforcement of instrumental rewards, e.g. high (higher) pay, in some cases leads to a deterioration in satisfaction with the work itself.

Another interesting implication of the "social information processing" approach in Salancik and Pfeffer's view is the manner in which the organizational climate should be defined, namely as

the shared perceptions of what attitudes and needs are appropriate, the shared definitions of jobs and work environments, and the definitions of how people should relate to the environment (Salancik and Pfeffer, 1978, p 240).

Salancik and Pfeffer predict that the influence of the organizational climate on the individual's approach and attitude in a given situation is determined by three circumstances: 1) how cohesive the common perceptions and beliefs which constitute this climate are, 2) how ambiguous and unclear the situation in question is, and 3) what other types of social information (i.e. "outside" the organizational climate i.e. not locally shared perceptions) exist in the contexts of which the individual is a part. The more there is of 1) and 2), and the less there is of 3), the more the organizational climate affects the individual's definition of and attitudes towards work. Here climate is given a meaning similar to a culture, as I and many other researchers define it. (I will deal with the relationship between climate and culture in Chapter 7.)

5.6   Comments on the Socialization Process from the Social Information Processing Perspective

Normally, a new employee in an organization finds himself/herself in an uncertain, perhaps anxiety-oriented situation. New employees want to reduce feelings of unease in this situation by meeting the functional and social demands and expectations placed on them as quickly as possible – both for social and cognitive reasons. The social factors are to do with feelings of belonging and the need to demonstrate their capability and to avoid making mistakes. From a cognitive point of view, the individual

wants to be able to understand and intellectually master his/her environment. As Van Maanen (1978) puts it:

The new employee's most urgent task is to develop a set of guidelines and interpretative rules to be able to explain the mass of activities which it is observed are going
on the organization and to experience these activities as meaningful (p 21).

The uncertainty and anxiety of the new employee increases his receptiveness to new social information about the workplace.

As already stated, the project management philosophy course contained
several (at least slightly) anxiety-generating elements for the participants.
Most of them were new employees. They came from different subsidiaries
which meant that most of them did not know each other. However, the
teachers concentrated on creating a friendly and positive atmosphere. For
example, they avoided increasing the level of stress by not being excessively critical. Critical comments from teachers were much less common
than positive comments.

The course supported frameworks and ideas on how to interpret the
various circumstances in the company, the work and in relationships with
customers. Opinions about the Enator business concept, its strategy, its
area of operations, Enator's organization, etc. expressed in the course and
also in a number of other contexts – ranging from day-to-day management
to the company general meeting (to be treated later in this book) – constituted social inputs for the participants' way of processing the information
they encountered in their work.

The course leaders' presentation naturally influenced what was considered to be sensible, correct and commendable. But it was equally important that all the participants themselves were allowed to say this in their
presentations. And people who were encouraged in a persuasive manner
to say that Enator was always concerned with customers' overall needs,
always tried to establish and maintain contacts with decision makers and
always looked for additional assignment opportunities, may be assumed to
accept this in their own outlook.

Conditions inside and outside the company which were primarily of an
ambiguous nature were partially perceived in accordance with the "instructions" of the project management philosophy course. The course provided broad guidelines for how to interpret reality. Take a complicated
question such as Enator's organization, for example. Is the organization
simple or complex? Hierarchical or unhierarchical? In this context, it is
sufficient to note that participants received information which strongly
drew attention to the simple and non-hierarchical features of the organization. As a result, these ideas predominated in newcomers' initial view of
the company, assuming that participants accepted the description and did
not then immediately encounter clear signs of conflicting circumstances.

An interesting detail regarding management's attempts to influence the individual's own understanding concerns the statement of the relatively unimportant status of pay in job satisfaction. This idea was established, both as a general phenomenon (according to Herzberg) and as a principle at Enator. In the course of my interviews with employees, I subsequently asked a number of individuals what their pay was. In their answers, many of them emphasized – without being specifically asked – that pay was not of any great importance to them.

However, the significance of the course in the processing of social information should not be exaggerated. The individual's own independent ideas, information on unambiguous matters, simple "objective" reality, and the different ideas and influences from various types of social groups, both inside and outside the company, help to ensure that links between what is transmitted in a socialization process of this kind and what are the future understandings and attitudes of the individuals concerned are not necessarily strong. Naturally, the social influence of management and the corporate culture on the individual's processing of information did not cease with the termination of the course. The idea of the course was that new employees were exposed, at a sensitive phase in their career with the company, to an influence process which laid crucial foundations for continuing influence on the employees' frames of reference and attitudes. This influence always takes place in organizations. Thus, the course appears to have had some importance, seen in this light.

5.7   Summary and Comments

This chapter has described the company's introductory course for new employees. Thus, an important feature of personnel socialization has been described and interpreted, and a picture of the company has also been built up.

The successful adaptation of a newcomer at a workplace also depends, apart from erroneous expectations about the job and the organization, on whether the new employee can make sense of strange and unexpected experiences and encounters. According to Louis (1980), entry into a new workplace is a process which involves surprises and different reactions to these surprises. The surprises may involve the employee's duties, the workplace, or the individual's personality in relation to the new job/workplace. Such surprises, many of which are negative, are inevitable. Entering an unknown scene means experiencing many things which may appear to be unexpected and incomprehensible. So the important factor for the outcome of the socialization process is precisely the ability to make such surprises comprehensible. Among other things, decisions such as whether to continue at a workplace or to resign after a time depend on how (negative) surprises are handled.

The course provided an interpretative programme for understanding Enator's methods of work and its "culture". It provided a background of information and knowledge which helped participants to bring order into their future experiences. But in less fortunate cases, this information may also have an opposite effect. Expectations about perfect or even reasonable compliance between what was taught in the course and what occurs in practice may create negative surprises and result in disappointments.

The course/socialization process involved three levels. At the first of these levels, the organization in question encouraged certain individual characteristics and approaches. There was both a disciplinary and a liberating element in this context. In the former case, we can see work discipline (respect for time schedules and norms), while in the latter case we can see employee liberation and relaxation (to be able to make fools of themselves and to be informal and relaxed). At the second, more abstract level, the purpose of the course was to get the individual to accept and identify with the company and its espoused business concept. The course aimed to influence new employees to adopt and ultimately internalize the corporate ideology. At a third level, the course and the socialization process had a social-integrative function. A feeling of cohesiveness, and a basis for cooperation and synergy were reinforced within a company which has relatively loose formal and structural links.

Finally, I would like to emphasize that the course only represented a very minor proportion of the socialization process for Enator personnel. Formal, planned socialization activities normally form only a small part of the entire socialization process. Day-to-day work, principally in the first few months of the new job, is a much more important aspect of the socialization process. Colleagues, of course, play an important part in this process. However, the project management philosophy course was significant since it transmitted concepts and ideas in a systematic and active manner. This appeared to have had an effect on later experiences and employee expectations. Many of the concepts presented in the course had significant perception-structuring potential, that is to say they strongly coloured the way in which the environment is regarded. The helicopter perspective, the business concept and the quality of performance from the customer viewpoint may be mentioned as examples. Naturally, continuous everyday socialization after completion of the course is largely outside management control – and is dependent on the projects, customer contacts, etc. which the new employee encounters. New employees who do not work at Enator's head office or are not involved in a major Enator project are naturally often exposed to random socialization processes. In such cases, the course-week described may be assumed to have exercised relatively limited influence. Employees, however, were regularly exposed to management messages similar to those expressed in the course, so this was seen as a vital element amongst many through which management "processed people".

As a rule, socialization processes can rarely be fully controlled and there are many elements of uncertainty. The only cases where individuals can be radically restructured in accordance with the organization's requirements are probably in totalitarian organizations (Goffman, 1960), for example military service, monastic orders, a mental hospital, etc. However, like most other companies, Enator is far from belonging to this category.

Note

[1]   Different social identities – organizational, occupational, informal, etc. – may be more or less salient for employees. From a management perspective, it is important to reinforce a social identity associated with membership in the company (see Ashforth and Mael, 1989).

6   A Flat Pyramid. A Symbolic Processing of Organizational Structure

This chapter discusses organizational structure and design. Special attention is paid to the corporate hierarchy and to management's attempt to control different representations of the hierarchy. This chapter starts by reminding the reader of the organizational structure concept as seen from a conventional, "objectivistic" perspective, but will later confront this perspective with a form of understanding which emphasizes the importance of "meaning patterns" and "interpretative schemes" for the understanding of social structures. In other words, the company's organizational form is discussed from a cultural perspective, where what is conventionally described as "the objective structures" are not regarded in such terms but rather as symbolic patterns whose meanings must be interpreted.

6.1   Organizational Structure

Traditionally, organizational structure has been thought to have exerted a decisive influence on the functioning of the organization. However, how the organizational structure should be understood is far from self-evident, as this case study illustrates.

Organizational structure is usually defined as the sum of the ways in which work tasks are distributed amongst different units and roles, and how tasks and roles are coordinated. In other words, organizational structure is a result of the division of labour and the formal authority hierarchy. The dimensions often considered to be of the greatest importance are vertical and horizontal division of labour (specialization), standardization and the formalization of work tasks, and the centralization of decision making.

In a "positivistic" spirit, many organizational researchers have tried to measure these variables and have attempted to study the degree of correlation between the variables and with other key dimensions (organizational size, corporate strategy, technology and the organizational environment – see e.g. Donaldson, 1985, and Veen, 1984, for overviews of the literature). On the whole, it may be noted that this research has not unambiguously succeeded in providing many interesting results. A not surprising result is that greater size tends to result in more hierarchical levels, increased functional specialization, formalization and decentralized decision making. Another "discovery" that appears to be generally accepted is that flexible, "organic" organizations, which emphasize the free flow of communications, participative decision making, and decentralization, are appropriate in situations characterized by uncertainty and rapid change.

One disadvantage of this type of strictly empiricist, law-seeking research is that it has not permitted itself to be guided by more general typologies. As Miller and Mintzberg claim (1983), the fundamental weakness of the analytical, variable-correlating research approach in organizational research, as in much other social scientific work, has been an excessive interest in testing simple, limited relationships rather than searching for or constructing rich patterns based on deeper insights.

Instead of studying various organizational variables that are isolated in relation to one another, Miller and Mintzberg propose that research should be based on the existence of configurations. That is, on clusters of attributes that are internally consistent and that correspond to actual organizational patterns. They argue that it is highly practical to operate with a limited number of configurations as a basis for research, and that such configurations exist in the real world.

Mintzberg's five configurations are the simple structure, the machine bureaucracy, the professional bureaucracy, the divisional organization, and the adhocracy (Mintzberg, 1983). The company I have studied fits the adhocracy configuration relatively well, although one might, with a little good will, also describe it in terms of the simple structure, the professional bureaucracy and the divisionalized structure. The characteristic feature of the adhocracy is that it combines personnel in different project teams with the objective of dealing with specific tasks in a given period. The personnel largely comprise specialists who supply innovative solutions. Project groups are formed and dissolved, depending on the nature of the task. It is normally almost impossible to formalize and standardize the work. Mutual adaptation between the members of the project groups, largely based on informal communication, is the main coordination mechanism. The adhocracy will be dealt with in more detail at a later stage in this chapter.

Are these configurations normally found in a more or less pure form or are mixtures of various types of organizational form common? Mintzberg (1983) considers that organizations often move towards a form of configuration in order to achieve a harmonious structure and form of operation. He considers that most organizations comply with one of the five configurations. Hybrids undoubtedly exist; they are sometimes dysfunctional and sometimes the logical result of forces which influence the organizations in one direction or the other. An additional possibility is that an organization utilizes different configurations in different sectors of its operations.

6.2   Enator's Organizational Structure

Enator has exploited the corporate subsidiary form to a considerable degree and is established as a corporate group with more than 20 subsidiaries, although some of these only employ one or a few persons. A principle is that each subsidiary has a maximum of 50 employees. This limit has been established as a compromise between two contradictory principles: market orientation and organizational/personnel orientation. From the marketing point of view it is probably not desirable to split up operations into a number of separate companies. Customers often work with several different areas of Enator's operations and they are not interested in dealing with several different subsidiaries. They prefer to deal with one Enator, which can give them everything they require. From a marketing point of view, it is also most fruitful to present Enator as one company, without complicating the picture with a myriad of subsidiaries, difficult for customers to remember. The marketing aspect thus favours a single large company.

On the other hand, personnel and organizational criteria tend to favour a small number of employees in each basic unit, according to Enator's management. Small scale operations facilitate a pleasant atmosphere, group loyalty, a feeling of common interests, and effective management without a hierarchical emphasis. The fewer the number of consultants involved, the easier it is for the subsidiary's managing director to provide support, coordination and personnel development. The relatively small groups that characterize the subsidiaries also facilitate flexibility and the acceptance of responsibility. Enator's owners and management regard the division into subsidiary companies as an important factor in the group's rapid growth and success.

In some respects, Enator is an extremely flat, unhierarchical organization with an informal hierarchy. One might say that there are only three hierarchical levels: managing director of Enator, subsidiary manager and consultant. Enator's management often emphasizes this in annual reports, interviews and introductory courses for new employees. As is the case with many other knowledge-intensive companies, including "high-tech" industries, there is a desire to preserve a certain degree of equality and downplay formal structure (cf. Kanter, 1983; Martin, 1992). But the situation is not quite so simple, in fact. Despite the apparent absence of formally appointed managers at other levels, such leadership functions actually exist. One subsidiary manager describes the situation as follows:

We don't really appoint managers. But of course we have an informal hierarchy. This is quite natural because otherwise things wouldn't work. But those who have quite a lot of authority have done so because they have created a position. They haven't been appointed by me. People have to create a 'platform'. You are not appointed to anything, you have to create it. We don't have any career paths in the consulting business traditionally. But of course there are careers which are based on authority and platforms.

As this subsidiary manager says, it is unavoidable that an informal hierarchy develops, both for reasons of competence – a competent individual with twenty years' experience is not on the same "platform" as someone who recently graduated – and for reasons of control and coordination – major projects require someone to take overall responsibility for the project and provide coordination. In professional organizations, formal position is often less important than the professional competence. This implies that influence and prestige are linked with competence in specific areas – and such competence by no means always follows formal organizational structures (Mills et al., 1983; Sveiby and Risling, 1986). However, it is worth noting that, nonetheless, organizational circumstances cannot always be adequately described on the basis of these two components, that is, a very low degree of formal hierarchy and an informal authority hierarchy based on competence. The subsidiary manager quoted above, who said that no formal superiors were appointed, said five minutes later in the interview that:

There is a management group in the company which is official. People know who's in the group. There isn't really any appointed deputy … . But actually there is. I have stated that X is the number two. There is a deputy managing director and a management group. But apart from that things are very flat.

In the larger subsidiaries (employing 20-50 persons), there is what is known as a "Number two" who holds overall responsibility together with the subsidiary's managing director. One or two other people are also included in the management group, perhaps a salesperson or someone with combined consulting and marketing responsibility.

Thus, the subsidiaries have a deputy manager *de facto*. Although he or she (some are women) may not have the title of deputy director, in practice a number of people meet expectations and act as if this was the case. They also have a wage corresponding to a managerial position.

It might be possible to treat Enator's emphasis on a flat organization and a lack of hierarchy as a purely rhetoric device, and to maintain that, in real terms, this is not strictly true. It might even be possible to regard such rhetoric as an attempt to deceive people. But a lack of formal positions and titles does indicate a certain deemphasis of the hierarchy in Enator subsidiaries, and it means that the "second person" cannot totally and formally represent his or her superiority in relationships with the staff.

The "real" organizational hierarchy can, therefore, best be described as more fully developed than what might be indicated by the description of a subsidiary managing director surrounded purely by consultants. However, the hierarchy is nonetheless less clearly indicated than what references to a deputy managing director and an intermediate level between the managing director and the consultants might imply. In fact, one might say that Enator companies have 2 1/2 hierarchical levels (within the subsidiary companies – in Enator as a whole there are a further one or two levels above the subsidiaries: Enator's managing director and for the Swedish companies Enator Sweden's managing director). The traditional organizational chart's attempt to restrict descriptions to categories clearly separated into levels, with an unambiguous superior/subordinate notation, is hardly appropriate for this type of organization – and probably not for many other organizations either.

However, the relatively limited number of formal hierarchical levels within these subsidiary companies does not mean that these units function in a unhierarchical manner. Enator's organizational construction also implies that the subsidiary managers have established positions clearly superior to those of other employees, but in a manner totally different from what would be the case if the subsidiaries were departments or units in a division, for example. A subsidiary manager describes the position as follows:

Each company can really only handle one true leader. That's in the nature of the structure. Managing director lunches and other conferences for managing directors are arranged. Those who are one rung lower on the ladder feel that they are not part of this privileged circle.

The same individual felt that his position before he became managing director of a subsidiary was as follows:

If you presented important ideas it was to your own managing director, and if he passed on these ideas they were virtually his ideas.

As Eriksson (1986) observes, it is not only the number of rungs on the organizational hierarchy that are significant, but also how far apart the rungs are placed. The Enator project organization – which is supposed to function in line with the fundamental model describing the company in terms of how projects are conducted – also means that the hierarchical dimension receives some additional emphasis. Apart from having project members and project managers, there is also in large projects a superior level that is termed the project head. (The subsidiary manager or the deputy subsidiary manager sometimes has this function.) This practice does not seem to be particularly common in other companies in the industry. While the project manager has technical responsibility for the project, the project head has some overall responsibility for quality control, customer contacts, etc. (The project head is only marginally involved in the project and only spends a limited amount of time on it, e.g. a few hours per week or month, in order to monitor the progress of a project.) Thus it could be argued that there are often three formal hierarchical levels in a project.

It is interesting to note that the project organizational form is not mentioned in comments on the company's organization (e.g. in the interviews and in official corporate descriptions, such as in the extensive and to some extent "qualitative" annual report). Nor do management representatives or consultants mention the project organization form, in interviews regarding organizational structure and hierarchy. But even if the projects are organized on a temporary basis – for several years in certain cases – the projects are of central importance for the company's organization and functioning.

Enator's history is relevant in order to better understand these contradictory characteristics and tendencies. An employee who has worked with Enator almost since the start disappointedly commented:

If you look at the corporate culture and think about what people said at the beginning and how things have turned out. ... They always said that we should have as low profile a hierarchy as possible. And in a way that's what's been achieved, since every subsidiary company has a managing director. But actually the real hierarchy doesn't look like that. The hierarchy is just as overpowering as in any other ordinary company, almost at least. You have a manager for Sweden, a foreign manager, a global manager, and a board. And the owners – they were three originally – they put some life into the whole operation. But nowadays it is not like that. Who the hell meets the owners today? You see a glimpse of them going past occasionally. You don't meet Enator's managing director particularly often either (Consultant).

The quotation serves to illustrate two points. One point is the importance of key persons in emphasizing or weakening hierarchies. The founders appear to have (had) some ability in deemphasizing the feeling of a formal hierarchy and distance between levels through their personal style of management. They were successful in persuading everyone to feel a sense of participation in operations and to see the company as a whole, by providing information about what was happening in different places and corners of the company. The founders were also successful in appearing to be relaxed in their positions, avoiding prestige and distance, etc. Nonetheless, decisions were undeniably taken by the founders, and their power position was not in question. The company's early successes can be seen, to a large extent, as a result of this ability to combine strong control with good cohesion.

Of course such a style of management is closely connected with the size of the organization, but it is not purely determined by size. Given a certain size and a certain formal structure, social circumstances can reinforce or

weaken the feeling of (formal) hierarchy. On the whole, corporate management and subsidiary managers also seem to have the ability to regulate
the relationship between hierarchy and cohesion and, in some way, to
deemphasize consistently the special status of the "Big Bosses". One way
of achieving this is by using such expressions ironically and by requiring
subsidiary managers to participate in different types of social activities
outside working hours. This encourages informality and reduces the hierarchical element at work as well (Ouchi, 1981). It is hardly possible to fill
the vacuum left at the heart of the organization after the departure of the
previous owners or to compensate for the increased size in maintaining
ideas about the flat organization.

The second point illustrated by the above quotation is the survival of
certain corporate ideological elements, despite changes in the reality of
the organizational structure in terms of social relations. It is hardly possible to realize in full the flat organizational form when the company has 500
employees, in comparison with a situation in which there are only a few
dozen staff. It would be going too far to say that ideals and reality are in
conflict – on the contrary, flatness is something that is aimed at and in
some respects exists – but it is easy to identify obvious deviations from the
original ideological purity. This is probably a general phenomena (cf. Martin, 1992).

6.3   The Organization of the Consultancy Projects

In most cases, the consulting project is organized within a particular subsidiary. This means that the project only employs staff from this company.
This normally applies to assignments involving only one person or where
only a limited number of consultants are concerned. The consultancy
project may employ only one person for a few days or weeks, or dozens of
staff may be involved for several years. Sometimes the subsidiary awarded
the assignment and responsible for project management employs consultants from other Enator companies. This may be because the subsidiary in
question requires a given specialist competence or lacks the capacity to
handle the assignment. Another reason might be that another subsidiary
has low capacity utilization (i.e. consultants have nothing to do) and that
this subsidiary needs work. In the case of major projects, staff from more
than one Enator subsidiary are often involved. This is primarily due to the
fact that a subsidiary with less than 50 employees often does not have
sufficient personnel to staff a project requiring 8-10 persons, since it has
other assignments to handle as well. Staff employed on the project are
then operatively subordinated to the "project" subsidiary (i.e. the unit that

signed a contract with the customer and that appoints the project manager and project head). Consultants may be employed by a subsidiary for which they do not work directly, when the project they are assigned to belongs to another subsidiary. (The names in the following refer to different subsidiaries in Enator.)

I started to work for the company 3 years ago (at Dynator). I'm an administrative type who works with planning systems and I've done similar administrative jobs previously. My first experience was that I was lent out to Mikrotell, which is a technology company. They sent me to a customer company in Södertälje. There I worked with a fellow and we both soldered. I haven't touched a soldering gun since I was a small boy – not really my field. That was the kind of job which I had for about six months. Then I returned to Dynator and was lent out to Scanator (according to the invoice in any case). Then I went over to Affärssystem. A fellow who has been with Dynator for 4-5 years has now transferred to Mikrotell. He has never actually worked for Dynator – only for Mikrotell.

Consultants employed by one subsidiary but working on a project for another have two bosses in principle: the manager of their own subsidiary and the project management of the subsidiary which has been awarded the project (which, in its turn, is subordinate to the manager of this subsidiary). Thus, we seem to be dealing with a matrix organization, (i.e. a "mixed" organizational form, in which a "normal" hierarchy is overlapped by another authority structure.

The matrix organization permits flexibility and balanced decision making. Flexibility is a result of the possibility of assembling and modifying work and project groups in accordance with temporary requirements, while balanced decision making is a consequence of the involvement of two or more units with superior status and with different competencies and perspectives on operations. The matrix also means that an effective allocation of resources can be achieved in terms of specialization. Specialists are employed where they can be most useful at any given point in time, without being tied down to a particular given unit. On the whole, the disadvantages of a matrix structure are considered to include potential confusion, anarchic tendencies and power struggles (Davis and Lawrence, 1978). For further examination and discussion of the matrix structure at the general level, see for example Knight (1976) and Robbins (1983). (For an in-depth study of a company with strong adhocratic features, see Kunda, 1992. Kunda does not, however, use or refer specifically to the concept of adhocracy.)

Matrix features are weak at Enator, however, since projects normally occur in a subsidiary which appoints project managers and the project members among its personnel. Sometimes consultants are brought in from another subsidiary throughout the project period or for parts of it, and in this case the consultant's "parent subsidiary" debits the subsidiary which is responsible for the project. While the project is in progress, the subsidiary manager to whom the consultant is normally responsible has a relatively peripheral role as the consultant's superior. This means that some of the features normally observed in a matrix structure, such as a chain of double-command, complicated information and communication problems and the risk of confusion and power struggles, become less important.

6.4   Enator in Terms of Mintzberg's Configurations

How should Enator, as an organization, be regarded in relation to Mintzberg's categorizations? Some authors automatically place organizations of this type to the adhocracy category (see e.g. Sveiby and Risling, 1986). However, I consider that there are important signs of not less than four of the five Mintzberg configurations at work in Enator – the simple structure, the professional bureaucracy, divisional structure and adhocracy.

The basic unit at Enator is the subsidiary company. In several respects, the subsidiary structure complies well with Mintzberg's simple structure. In this type of organization the administrative part (technostructure, support unit) is very small, the division of labour is not pronounced, there is limited differentiation between units and the management hierarchy is limited. The most important aspect of the organization is its strategic core (i.e. the top manager, who is often also the founder/owner) and supervision is the primary coordination mechanism, according to Mintzberg (1983, p 157 et sec).

Apart from the latter feature – the crucial importance of the top manager and of supervision – this fits the picture of the Enator subsidiaries well. The subsidiary manager and his personal leadership style are also important, but not so crucial as in Mintzberg's definition of the simple structure. In other respects, subsidiaries comply with this configuration of a simple, uncomplicated organization. The administrative side is extremely limited (subsidiary manager of a unit comprising 45 employees: "the only overheads here are myself and the accounts girl"). The division of labour varies with the assignment, there are no marked specialist careers and, apart from the subsidiary manager, the management hierarchy is not espoused. Thus, the subsidiary companies fulfil Mintzberg's criteria for a simple structure rather well.

This also applies to the professional bureaucracy.

The professional bureaucracy relies for coordination on the standardization of skills and its associated design parameter, training and indoctrination. It hires duly trained and indoctrinated specialists – professionals – for the operating core, and then gives them considerable control over their own work. ... Control over his own work means that the professional works relatively independently of his colleagues, but closely with the clients he serves (Mintzberg, 1983, p 190).

The decisive parameter for this type of organization is thus the professional competence of operative personnel. Employees work independently in relation of each other and of superior levels in the organization, which are partly controlled from below. The professional bureaucracy differs from an adhocracy because relatively standardized results have to be achieved on the basis of standardized competence (e.g. a hip joint operation, carried out by an orthopaedic surgeon applying all the skills at his/her disposal, or a university course led by a PhD covering the standard knowledge in his/her field of expertize). An adhocracy is supposed to develop something new and unique, i.e. to be innovative. (This does not mean that the innovations are necessarily very advanced and the operations very complicated.)

Major aspects of Enator's operations function in accordance with the professional bureaucracy model. Clients turn to Enator to get certain tasks carried out, for example programming or a study of future computer utilization. In several of these subsidiaries, consultants primarily work on their assignments alone, on the basis of considerable specialist competence. In certain subsidiaries and in many major projects, unique solutions for unique problems are called for, and this means that work is based on a certain degree of innovation. In such cases, operations go beyond the definition of professional bureaucracy. A considerable proportion of Enator's operations comply rather well with the professional bureaucracy definition, however.

The most prominent feature of the divisionalized organization form is that units form groups independently, with the upper intermediate level in the organizational hierarchy functioning as a basis for such groups. Units function on a quasi-independent basis, without direct supervision of operative activity by management. Control is based on the output achieved by the units (financial results in relation to the budget).

Enator's subsidiaries display this divisional character. The Kista subsidiaries, at least, might be expected to be more integrated with the corporate whole than other subsidiaries, but subsidiary managers tend to feel that they have freedom of action. ("The only form of control exercised is that you must stick to the budget.") However, in a number of other respects Enator does not comply fully with Mintzberg's view of the divisional form. It is only partially true, for example that divisionalization is based on the market. One of the important reasons for divisionalization at Enator is that small scale operations are preferred for reasons of personnel.

Attempts to structure the market are partly means of achieving this. Some subsidiaries are differentiated on the basis of the service they offer, rather than on market conditions. Market conditions are complex and difficult to grasp, but in view of the nature of Enator's operations, no far-reaching differentiation of the different parts of the company is required for market reasons. Flexibility can be achieved in any case.

Thus, Enator displays features of the three organizational configurations described above and this means that, so far, we can describe the company as a divisonalized professional bureaucracy with a simple structure. But, to complicate matters further as far as Mintzberg is concerned, Enator complies – to an even greater extent – with his description of an adhocracy. This is discussed in some detail in the next section.

6.5   Adhocracy

The adhocracy concept as a description of a certain type of organization has been launched by Mintzberg (1983) who, in his turn, has borrowed it from other authors. Adhocracy means that the different parts of an organization are temporarily assembled to meet the requirements and needs which apply at any particular point in time. In an attempt to describe a similar phenomenon, Mills et al. (1983) refer to "a flexiform-structure". The flexiform-structure, however, overlaps with the professional bureaucracy, and Mills et al do not distinguish between professional bureaucracy and adhocracy.

Mintzberg considers that adhocracy is characterized by an organic structure, a low degree of formalization, a high degree of horizontal work specialization based on formal training and specialist competence, a tendency to group specialized personnel in functional units to facilitate administration and personal development ("housekeeping purposes"), while employing them in small, market-based project groups in work operations. Coordination and management are characterized by decentralized decision making to a relatively high degree, and by mutual adaptation at the project group level, rather than by control from above.

As a concept, adhocracy is in fashion at the moment. There are different views about how extensive adhocracy is, or is becoming. In the 1960s, Bennis (1966) argued that traditional forms of organization which characterize mass production companies (i.e. planning, standardization of work tasks and hierarchic control) were in the process of being abandoned. This was due to rapid and unexpected changes in the environment, increased corporate size, greater diversification of know how and the competence of personnel, and changes in values and management style. Sveiby and Riesling

(1986) consider that in a knowledge society, which they think are in the process of entering, there will, no doubt, be many large companies which continue to produce goods and services with traditional forms of organization, but

Organizations in a knowledge-based society will, however, primarily have an adhocratic character, for example in solving technical or socially sophisticated problems. Such organizations are personnel-intensive with a high degree of skill and competence. Personnel must be continuously creative (p 145).

Robbins (1983) presents the opposite perspective. Robbins considers that professional bureaucracies have emerged as an answer to the greater degree of knowledge required and that a professional bureaucracy rather than an adhocracy is a normal response to the need for sophisticated problem solving. Robbins presents the following argument to explain why the adhocracy is not an expanding organizational form.

First, adhocracies are the dominant structure in only a small number of industries. Second, the form is used most popularly as an adjunct to bureaucracy. Finally, where adhocracy is found, it would be more accurate to conceive of it as a 'vehicle' propelling the organization toward bureaucracy or failure rather than as an ongoing structure (p 223).

Even if I am jumping ahead to my conclusions to some extent, I may say that I agree with Robbins that the adhocracy in its fully developed form is relatively uncommon, and that this state of affairs will probably continue. However, it may be assumed that adhocratic features and units which function in an adhocratic manner within organizations, but principally in another overall organizational form, are likely to become more common, and that this will also apply for a – still limited – number of companies with adhocracy as their primary form of organization.

There is a tendency for the exciting nature of the adhocracy to encourage emphasis and over-emphasis of its applicability and its actual extent. Who can resist the belief that one's own company or what one is writing about is characterized by dynamism, flexibility, creativity, innovation, etc.? Adhocracy may be readily described in a seductive manner:

An adhocracy is an organization for people who believe in democracy but not in bureaucracy. On the positive side, there is dynamism and flexibility, but on the other hand there is uncertainty and conflict (Sveiby and Risling, 1986, p 149).

On one hand, the adhocracy permits the independent solution of problems, flexibility and dynamic cooperative relationships while, on the other hand it ensures a long-term orientation, survival for a long period and justice (p 154).

One aim in this chapter is to contribute to a more balanced view. To follow up these general perspectives on an adhocratic organization, I will now turn to Enator in relation to this concept (as used primarily by Mintzberg). I will first describe some crucial features of the company which comply with the perspective on adhocracy.

The ability to adapt is important. Project groups are assembled on the basis of project tasks and their requirements. Personnel are well-trained and have considerable opportunities to influence their own work. Coordination largely takes the form of informal communication and mutual adaptation. Problems are solved by obtaining the services of various key individuals in the network constituted by the entire corporation (group), when their advice and hints and perhaps their active participation in the project are required. Flexibility is an important component in the offering made to clients:

What I sell is flexibility – the ability to absorb knowledge and to apply it. I can rapidly see patterns, analyse them, see the customer's problems and do something about them (Consultant).

Another crucial dimension is that projects take place in close cooperation with customer companies. Operations frequently take place completely within the framework of the customer's organization and this means that the consultant/project group has sometimes considerably closer contacts with the customer company than with their own organization.

After a year or two with the customer, we feel we know him better than Enator (Consultant).

The adaptive nature of operations and the professional character of the personnel mean a limited degree of formalization and rules.

One important reason why Enator cannot be simply regarded as an adhocracy is that aspects of its operations are of a professional bureaucracy character, as pointed out above. It is frequently difficult to make a clear distinction between adhocracy and a professional bureaucracy.

In fact, for every operating adhocracy, there is a corresponding professional bureaucracy, one that does a similar work but with a narrower orientation. Faced with a client problem, the operating adhocracy engages in creative effort to find a novel solution; the professional bureaucracy pigeonholes it into a known contingency to which it can apply a standard program. One engages in divergent thinking aimed at innovation; the other, in convergent thinking aimed at perfection (Mintzberg, 1983, p 257).

Operations at Enator may be best described as a mixture of these two types of activity. There are assignments with clearly innovative qualities and there are projects and one-man assignments which mean that competence is applied in a qualified manner, even if no major new thinking is involved. Some assignments are virtually of a routine character and are not particularly sophisticated. In such cases consultants are employed as "grey labour".

To contrast with the widely held view that computer consultancy companies are adhocracies which are purely involved in sophisticated problem solving and are characterized by "high tempo, a high level of anxiety, tough requirements, continual challenges, built-in conflicts, and the risk of

eliminating people who cannot cope" (Sveiby and Riesling, 1986, p 149),
one might also claim that

A great many assignments involve a considerable amount of rubbishy tasks
(Deputy manager).
Regarding the actual solving of problems, things can vary considerably (regarding
the innovative component in assignments). Sometimes we are into what we call the
bread and butter method. We do the same thing we have done before. And we do it
in almost the same way. Sometimes we help customers to evaluate and purchase a
ready-made package. We try to get the customer to adapt to this ready-made product. In this particular project (I am currently working with) we are involved with
new development and we are into something which is different from anything we
have done before. ... And then there really is a lot of creativity (Consultant).

It is important to note the variety of different projects and activities which
involve innovation in varying degrees, sophisticated professional standard
solutions and relatively unsophisticated routines. It is debatable whether
the dividing line between innovative and standard activities as a criterion
for drawing a distinction between adhocracy and professional bureaucracy
is an adequate basis for unambiguously categorizing different organizations in accordance with one model or the other. New solutions are based
to a large extent on existing knowledge and standard solutions. In many
cases the execution of a standard programme involves considerable modification of a more or less creative nature. In research for example – even if
most types of research can be categorized as "mainstream", and far reaching creativity is often not involved – there are usually, nonetheless, certain
ideas and outcomes which cannot be readily characterized either as innovations or as standardized results.

It also appears that purely creative activities in the projects of Enator
are becoming slightly less common. This is the result of increased personnel costs, stiffer competition in the market place and – perhaps – growing
corporate size and consequently better opportunities to utilize scale advantages.

It is no longer possible to do a job completely on your own from beginning to end.
It is too expensive. You have to use existing components and solutions as ingredi-
ents (Subsidiary manager).

The fact that Enator only partially functions as an adhocracy may help to
explain why many of the disadvantages which are considered to be associated with this form of organization are not salient. Common problems of
adhocracy include a high degree of uncertainty and conflict, ambiguity
regarding authority relationships and responsibility, social stress and psychological strain for personnel as result of continual changes in the work
situation and work place, and considerable time spent in meetings and
informal discussions, according to the literature in the field. (For further

descriptions of problems and weaknesses, see Mintzberg, 1983; Robbins, 1983; cf. also Davis and Lawrence, 1978).

These features may be noted at Enator as in most other organizations, but the question is whether they are more prominent at this company than elsewhere. There are some special stress factors, but on the whole personnel apparently did not seem to experience their job situation as particularly difficult or wearing. There was low personnel turnover – when my study was conducted – and morale was good. (I will be returning to the question of the work situation in Chapter 9.) The level of conflict was relatively low and problematic relationships between superiors and their staff were not particularly common, according to interviewees. To some extent the need for discussion and exchanges of opinion in various forms were considerable, but this too varied. "Productivity" must be regarded as extremely high, at any rate from Enator's perspective, in view of the guide-line stating that each consultant in average should have a 90% work load (i.e. be able to debit 90% of his time to clients). This target has normally achieved, at the time of my study. (The remaining 10% of the consultant's time was supposed to cover meetings and activities within the subsidiary, apart from those included in consultancy assignments, sickness, training and slack periods.)

There are a number of factors which contributed to the avoidance of the usual problems, or at least to their reduction. In particular successful efforts to create a particular workplace climate and the fact that Enator was a young and expansive company operating on a growing market facilitated positive and supportive social relations. I will be looking at these themes in Chapters 7 and 8. Additional factors might also be that the matrix organization played a relatively limited role and that activities were not purely of an adhocratic character but also involved a considerable amount of professional bureaucracy as well as more simple tasks.

6.6   Adhocracy: Conclusions

In this section, I will be trying to draw some more general conclusions about the adhocratic form of organization, but with the important reservation that the views expressed here are based on a single case study.

As Mintzberg (1983) points out, an adhocracy is a "new" form of organization, both in the "real world" and in organization theory. This means that our knowledge about adhocracies is limited. Mintzberg also considers that it is the most complex form of organization, and this does not make it any easier to understand. However, in general terms the alleged complexity of adhocracies might be questioned: there are probably many different types of adhocracy. (In addition, one can note that the meaning of complexity is far from self-evident.)

Apart from the fact that what is referred to as adhocracy is sometimes used to supplement another, more dominant organizational form, and frequently is of a temporary nature, it is claimed that the adhocracy primarily characterizes film companies, consultancies, and special organizations such as NASA. Somewhat more sporadically, we may find mention of TV companies, theatres, World War II task forces, and oil companies as examples of adhocracy (Mintzberg, 1983).

The examples indicate a certain degree of disparity, and this has probably inspired Mintzberg to make a distinction between operative adhocracy, where the main objective is service to clients, and administrative adhocracy, where the company in question exists in its own right to produce its own product. NASA and oil companies are examples of the latter type of adhocracy.

Perhaps the most typical and representative type of operation which complies with the adhocracy concept – not only in the operative form but also at a more general level – is the consultancy company. (NASA is a rather special example in the above list, oil companies do not fully fit the definition as they do not produce something novel, film projects and theatres do not employ very many people and are of somewhat limited economic significance.) Consultancy companies vary considerably, however. In the consultancy industry, Enator is probably close to the median level of professionality, the complexity of problems, the level of innovativeness, and unique problem solving which characterize operations.

In other words, Enator seems to be fairly representative of organizations which authors who described adhocracies are attempting to analyse. Sveiby and Risling (1986), for example, use computer consultancy companies to illustrate their arguments about adhocracies on several occasions. Enator, however, only in part complies with the characteristics commonly applied to adhocracy. Certainly, operations are based on projects and assignments, project groups are assembled to some extent for each individual project, some projects are unique and require complex problem solving ability and flexible, mutual adaptation between project members constitutes a primary mechanism for coordination. But Enator also contains significant elements from other organizational forms, major areas of operations consist of one-man assignments, advanced creative projects cannot be said to predominate, and personnel tend to have similar basic competencies rather than different specialist orientations. Many of my interviewees did not consider Enator personnel to be more technically qualified than the customer staff. (But on the other hand they considered that Enator is better at project management, which in itself may be regarded as a special competence.) Features of matrix organizations were also not particularly salient at Enator.

Furthermore, many of the disadvantages and problems which are considered to characterize adhocracies do not apply at Enator to any great extent. This may be because Enator was in a growth industry, had good management or it may be due to the company's youthfulness, etc. Another explanation could be that the company only partially displayed adhocratic features. It is, however, perhaps more reasonable to question the general idea of adhocracies (organizations matching this ideal type) being, for example, especially conflict ridden. The case study points to the need to modify certain ideas current in the literature in this field.

One problem which emerges in the specialist literature is that adhocracy is primarily described as antithetical to bureaucracy (see e.g. Mintzberg, 1983; Sveiby and Riesling, 1986). In view of the fact that I can only rely on a single case study and that there are only a very limited number of other case studies of similar organizations, I refrain from trying to formulate a new adhocracy theory. However, some suggestions as to how a more balanced characterization of adhocracy might be achieved will be presented. In the first place I will be looking at items which deviate from what is normally maintained in the literature in connection with adhocracies, on the basis of my study of Enator.

An adhocracy is based on operations which are organized in project form. Such operations commonly demonstrate considerable differences, both as regards uniqueness and degree of complexity. Certain projects involve cutting loose from established patterns and creating new solutions. Other projects mean building on the foundations of a more or less applicable know-how and on experience which has been established. Projects normally involve requirements regarding flexibility and learning on the basis of existing specialised knowledge and methodological know-how about project work. The nature of operations encompasses different things, ranging from sophisticated innovation to routine professional work. Personnel are normally well trained, but experience and specialist competence vary. A high degree of specialist competence on the part of personnel may be a major aspect of the organization but this is not necessarily as salient as parts of the literature suggests. General knowledge within the framework of a specific profession, in combination with the development of flexibility and the ability to come to grips with and deal with new, unknown situations, may be another corner stone in what the customer is offered. In other words, overall operations do not need to be particularly advanced.

The element of strain may take the form of overloading due to the difficult nature of the work, stress, lack of security due to changed conditions of work and new assignments whose content is hard to predict, or the obligations to repeatedly join or leave new work groups. But the opposite state of affairs may also lead to problems: routine assignments and assignments providing no opportunity for development, or a lack of variation resulting from project operations which continue for several years. (See also Chapter 9.)

A unified command structure is the basic principle at Enator – and possibly in many other adhocracies, as in other organizations, but it is applied rather loosely and selectively. Every project and every employee has a superior who functions as the primary manager. In addition there are sometimes other bosses (functional managers) who may also be superiors in formal terms, in accordance with a matrix structure, but they are normally of lesser importance during the project period. As a result, chains of command are not mixed, in many projects. The matrix element is thus not necessarily significant. The traditional hierarchical structure is to some extent broken as regards communication, interaction, etc. In this area, flows are relatively free within the organization and are largely replaced by informal communication and group decision making in project groups.

6.7   Organizational Structure in a Dynamic Perspective

As already pointed out, considerable research into organizational structures over the past 25 years has not provided any particularly clear or consistent results. Where correlations between environmental factors, organizational size, technology, corporate strategy and, on the other hand, various organizational structural variables can be demonstrated, this has often been achieved in a very narrow context.

... insofar as relationship can be demonstrated, they exist between component aspects of the various characteristics, under certain specified conditions (Veen, 1984, p 705).

The problem with the idea of regarding technology, the environment, organizational structure, etc. as distinct phenomena which can be treated in an unambiguous manner, quantified and correlated with one another appears to some extent to be influenced by the fact that these concepts only superficially denote anything "real", with an apparently unproblematical ontological status (i.e. real phenomena rather than abstract research constructions). This can be questioned if subjected to closer examination from a non-objectivist perspective. The ontology is not problematical within the framework of an objectivistic, functionalistic paradigm (Donaldson, 1985). The difficulties are more of a methodological nature, since concepts such as technology and structure are complex and encompass a considerable number of aspects. Focussing on different aspects provides different outcomes. It is assumed that the difficulties can be reduced by applying clearer concepts and a greater degree of consensus between researchers as regards methods of measurement or by introducing new variables into what is to be correlated – for example "uncertainty" (Veen, 1984). This expresses a rather narrow intra-paradigm perspective which mainly indicates itself rather than solves problems.

Another approach is to work with different types of organizations and to investigate them with a view to discovering correlations between different characteristics of a natural law character. This approach is advocated, for example, by Mintzberg (1983) and Miller and Mintzberg (1983). It represents a modest modification of the traditional position, but it confines itself well within the borders of an "objectivistic" paradigm. On the basis of my case study the fruitfulness of categorisation into configurations might – in all modesty – be questioned. A more drastic criticism might involve, however, questioning the assumption per se that "organizational structure" can be analyzed as an objective, measurable phenomenon which is in principle decoupled from the ideas and meanings which the individuals involved associate with this structure.

An extensive debate has taken place in the last decade about the opportunities and value of regarding organizational structure as a "super-individual" category, which is independent of the collective consciousness of the individuals involved. Critics have maintained that trying to capture the fundamental nature of the organization by means of measuring variables and correlating variables with each other is to reify and mystify organization (e.g. Burrell and Morgan, 1979; Ranson et al., 1980; Reed, 1985; Zey-Ferrell and Aiken, 1981. Donaldson, 1985, and Pugh, 1983, defend the traditional stand-point.) Critics of the traditional view of the organizational structure have proposed conceptualizations of structure that take the dynamic, processual and sometimes contradictory elements of the organizational structure into account (Fombrun, 1986). Furthermore, the structure's direct links with the individuals' ideas and experiences are emphasized (i.e. at the actor level) (Ranson et al., 1980). Simply expressed, it might be said that there is an attempt to bring the organizational structure "to life".

The starting point of Ranson et al. (1980) is that the structure is normally regarded either as a question of a formal configuration of roles, positions and procedures (i.e. as the frame of reference which has been prescribed for the organization – e.g. in the organizational chart), or as regular patterns and processes in social interaction. This analytical distinction is important, but it creates problems if it is taken too far, since it implies a division between structures in the sense of constraints (instructions for action) and regularity in actions (behaviour patterns).

Most structural researchers have adopted the first of these approaches, in spite of Weber's view of modern organization as a question of impersonal structures which control work tasks and authority. Mintzberg and the other structural researchers who have been touched on earlier in this chapter fit into this category. However, other researchers have been interested in the idea of the structural concept seen "from below", based on the actions and social processes of the actors. Some researchers have come to the conclusion that structure (equivalent to positions, etc.) and action are to some extent independent of each other (March and Olsen, 1976; Orton and Weick, 1990; Weick, 1976). Organizational structure and "real interaction" are loosely coupled.

However, Ranson et al. (1980) believe that action patterns and organizational structure can be related to each other within the framework of a theory of "structuring of the organizational structure". Organizational structures are defined and mediated in the structuring process. In a somewhat simplified form, three aspects are of central importance: 1) "provinces of meanings", created by members of the organization and including an interpretative framework, articulated values and other landmarks for orientation (cf. culture), 2) relations of power and domination, which regulate relations between, and the importance of different patterns of opinion, and 3) contextual constraints in the form of environmental and organizational circumstances which constitute the problems and handicaps which social existence faces.

The idea is to emphasize the importance of actors – both significant actors (in positions of power) and other actors – actions, social processes and ways of interpreting matters, without therefore denying the idea of relative stability and repetitive patterns in organizational life (structure). Ranson et al. imagine that an analysis of this type can permit us to include the ambiguities in organizations which March and Olsen as well as Weick, amongst others, have dealt with, in which frames of reference and interaction patterns appear to be incomprehensible from a structural perspective, in which structural positions, means and objectives, intentions and actions are loosely coupled and in which the relations between problems, solutions, individuals and questions are unclear and temporary. At the same time there are also patterns and stability in the form of common expectations and forms of understanding. In organizations, frames of reference are developed which mean that things can be taken for granted and where there is a relatively routine and predictable organizational existence (Ranson et al., 1980, pp 5-6).

The interpretation framework, and the power and dependence relationships which influence it, are normally taken for granted by members of the organization but can be changed. Change then effects the continuous structuring of the organization.

Fombrun (1986) proposes a similar approach, emphasizing the dynamic aspect of the structure. He considers that structure should be understood as an aspect of a dynamic structuring process which binds individual actions through a process which involves both convergence and conflicts at three levels: infrastructure, sociostructure and superstructure.

Infrastructure refers to fundamental dependency relationships faced by the organization, such as technology, competition and the market. The *social structure* includes both administrative structure and other different types of exchange relationships. Three dimensions are normally indicated: division of labour/differentiation, the formal control system intended to coordinate operations and the informal social relationships. *Superstructure* denotes the ideational aspects of organizations, the symbolic representations and interpretations of collective life which are widespread among the members of the organization (i.e. the organizational culture). Thus Fombrun employs a complex structural concept in which he assumes that:

the structure of any social collectivity could be said to consist of three layers of constraint on individual and organizational action: (1) an infrastructure of productive activities, to which is coupled (2) a sociostructure of exchange relationships, itself overlaid by (3) a superstructure of shared values. ... In this view, structure is understood to be a temporary configuration of infrastructure, sociostructure, and superstructure – an instance in a dynamic process of structuring that imbues action with meaning. Thus, within organizations, structure is an edifice resting on the infrastructural foundation of a technological solution to the production problem, framed by a sociostructure of interactions, around which crystallizes a set of superstructural norms and values (p 405).

Fombrun rejects orthodox organizational theory which assumes that convergence between the three dimensions is a normal state of affairs, in which order, stability and homeostasis between the three dimensions and the organization's environment exist. This is an impossible postulate in Fombrun's opinion. Instead, divergence, conflicts and change are equally common. The different elements in the structure are often in a state of tension in relation to each other and/or to the environment. Convergence and homeostasis and divergence and conflict are temporarily separate aspects of the continuous structuring process.

According to the works which have been referred to and other authors with similar orientations on the issue of structure (e.g. Benson, 1977; Brown, 1978; Giddens, 1982) the two following aspects are important in understanding organizational structural phenomena. Firstly, structure is produced and reproduced through human interactions and an organization's structural quality cannot be separated from the feelings, thoughts and experiences of its participant members. Secondly, the structure is characterized by process, dynamics and conflict just as much as by stability and homeostasis. It can therefore be concluded that organizational structure is a complex phenomenon – and as far as I am concerned more dimensions than is customary need to be taken into account in explaining Enator's organization.

This can be achieved most appropriately by employing theoretical cultural terminology. Ranson et al. and Fombrun emphasize the central importance of this aspect in this context.

6.8   Organizational Structure from the Cultural Perspective

From cultural and symbolic perspectives, organizational structure is not regarded as something unambiguous and stable – an "objective" phenomenon with virtually physical characteristics. Instead, it should be viewed as a symbolic system (Geertz, 1973; Smircich, 1983a). The organizational structure cannot be read off or measured in a simple and unproblematical manner, it must be interpreted.

For example, the status of subsidiary managing directors and the process of establishing subsidiary companies acquires a different meaning from a symbolic perspective than from a traditional structural one. According to the 1986 annual report, Enator had 22 managing directors altogether (all men), half of whom are only in charge of themselves or a handful of individuals. Understanding the significance of managing director's status is crucial in comprehending Enator's organizational hierarchy. Generally speaking, in Sweden the title "managing director" has several different meanings besides the strictly legal and formal implications: the title denotes authority, responsibility, independence, and superiority. It is also associated with status and prestige. Its status may also be regarded as a symbol of action: activity, the ability to take actions, initiative, involvement, and hard work. With a more restricted policy on creating subsidiaries and hence managing director positions, the titles that in many cases replaced "managing director", e.g. department manager, or sales manager, were clearly associated to a much less extent with the above characteristics.

The symbolic significance of managing directors is not identical internally and externally. Despite customers' interest in the provision of different services by a *single* Enator rather than by a set of companies with differing names or orientations, the managing director function is clearly considered to have benefits when dealing with external relations. It may have a door-opening function in the outside world and therefore the managing director title makes it easier for subsidiary managers to function as salesmen. The considerable number of managing directors at Enator is strongly emphasized in the professional, extensive, and expensive annual reports. In the 1985 edition, for example, photographs of all the managing directors were presented and they were interviewed about their company's situation, future, etc. In the 1986 annual report, on the other hand, only

Enator's managing director and the national managing directors (i.e. managing directors for foreign companies, plus the managing director for Enator Sweden) were given the opportunity to describe their operations and future prospects. These eight managing directors appeared in enlarged pictures, occupying a half large page per person. However, most of the managing directors plus a couple of representatives of the executive staff appeared on a large photograph at the end of the annual report – a charming colour photograph in which the gentlemen appeared in their winter coats against a snowy background. A helicopter and a dog team are shown behind the group. The text to the picture reads: "Some of the leading executives in the Enator-group meeting at the base of Kebnekaise mountain for free discussions about the company's orientation." Kebnekaise is Sweden's highest mountain.

The names of these leading executives appear alongside the picture, together with their dates of birth, titles, and corporate responsibilities. On the next page appear the addresses of all the Enator companies, and the title "managing director" next to the name of the subsidiary managers is clearly stated.

This emphasis on the external denotation of the managing directors does not comply fully with the internal requirements of low emphasis on the organizational hierarchy. The considerable number of managing directors seems to imply that the company is top-heavy and dominated by directors. But the significance of managing directorship in Enator differs somewhat from Swedish norms in general and also with respect to relationships with customers and external interested parties. Enator's informal and familiar tradition implies that the status of managing director and formal titles should not be taken too seriously in connection with social relationships within the organization.

Managerial functions in a traditional sense – planning, organization, control and direction of operations – are generally considered to have low emphasis in the company. The fact that these aspects of managerial authority in general tend to be less prominent than traditionally believed (e.g. see Mintzberg, 1975), does not preclude even further deviations by companies like Enator (i.e. adhocracies) from a "systematic-bureaucratic" management style. Many Enator employees refer to the managing director as a sparring partner, that is, someone who functions as a partner in high level discussions about projects and project problems. Apart from this, the subsidiary managers' most important function is probably to attract assignments – i.e. to be a salesperson. Since management and leadership are dealt with in Chapter 8, I will not discuss how the subsidiary managers function and act in concrete terms at this stage. It is sufficient to state that they often function more as discussion partners and as a socially integrating force than as "directors" in relation to their personnel.

The company's attempt to give managerial status a significance that complies with non-hierarchical requirements as to how an organization functions is illustrated by the fact that, in the company, management speaks somewhat ironically of "Big Bosses" ("Giant Managers"). The organizational symbolic significance of managing director status at Enator still has some of the traditional attributes mentioned above, however – it denotes superiority, independence, responsibility, initiative, etc. These attributes are deemphasized and supplemented – but not replaced – by concepts such as "discussion partner" and "one of the boys". Thus the position of managing director must be understood on the basis of various interpretative systems and structures of values, which are to some extent in conflict with one another. Internally, certain expectations and demands are placed on the managers, which is quite different from the emphasis on directorship that is expanded externally. The idea of "Big Bosses" is totally inappropriate in many situations, but in the latter case it is a key for establishing contacts with client executives who need to be approached in marketing and business exchanges. Internally, Enator's management must clarify how managing director status should be interpreted and evaluated in the framework of the corporate collective. Managing director status varies in accordance with the context, rather than being an object of coherent interpretations.[1] In social terms, the managing director is supposedly on friendly terms with his staff, but in financial and economic terms, he is nonetheless responsible and must take major decisions.

To link up directly with Ranson et al. (1980), the organizational structure in this respect is a question of a structuring process in which the interpretive system is developed, partly based on the influence of Enator's management, and partly on more random and extra-organizational conditions. The organizational design is just as much a question of establishing certain understandings and evaluations of positions and relationships between these (formal) organizational structures as a question of the construction and structuring of (formal) positions, units, roles, etc. and relationships among them.

Understanding the structure also requires consideration of contextual circumstances, such as broader values and meaning patterns. These contribute both to determining the purely formal elements in the organization, by creating external expectations and associations as to the symbolic value of managing director status, for example, and also by influencing the members of the organization's "cultural" preparedness to allocate a specific meaning to managing director status. Since Enator is also internally based on the symbolic values attributed to the managerial role in several respects (such as responsibility for financial results), while it is also in some respects in conflict with the corporate ideology (downplaying hierarchy), it appears logical that the company makes considerable efforts to influence exactly how the staff should interpret managerial status within the company in various situations. Thus, an important aspect of local culture (corporate culture) is understanding the meaning – or rather contextually shifting meanings – of managing-director status in the company.

Another fundamental aspect of the company's structure that cannot be understood without giving the organizational members' definitions a central role is the "flat hierarchy". We may, for example, use the following quotation, which is presented as objective and unambiguous: "(Enator is) a very 'flat' organization and is a company which is unusually informal. The pyramid has been broad and low, and the hierarchy is virtually non-existent" (Enator's managing director in the 1986 annual report, p 3).
An enumeration of hierarchical levels conducted from an external standpoint in accordance with differing measures provides, however, a much more ambiguous and complicated picture. One might just as well end up with twice as many hierarchical levels (i.e. consultant, project leader, project head, subsidiary managing director, Enator Sweden's managing director and Enator's managing director), and not the three basic hierarchical levels of consultant, subsidiary managing director, and Enator managing director. Neither of these two conclusions is "more true" than the other. The second statement says that the company's organization is flat, while the first is in conflict with this stand-point.

However, it is more interesting to regard the Enator phenomenon from a cultural perspective than to count hierarchical levels or to use the pyramid as a metaphor to reflect the corporate structure. This implies that the quantitative aspects of the structure is of limited interest and the physical connotation of the pyramid should be abandoned. In this context, it may be relevant to draw attention to the problematical nature of the pyramid metaphor: in many cases it is misleading to use the pyramid's unambiguous physical form as a concept which can capture social interaction patterns in organizations.

Thinking and acting in Enator complies, to a considerable degree, with the managing director's description quoted above – i.e. the organization is flat and unhierarchical. To the extent that this picture is widespread and established in the collective consciousness of the employees, it is an important definition of the organization's structure and function. Formal organizational structures attain their "real" consequences (implications for relations and action) via the interpretations and meanings the employees give them. If collective consciousness says that the organization is basically flat and unhierarchical, this means more for the "real" functioning of the organization than the fact that the number of formal levels is increasing or falling somewhat.

Thus, the idea of the flat organization may be regarded as of symbolic importance rather than having a literal meaning.[2] It indicates an attempt to achieve cohesion among personnel, to create a feeling of belonging and a "we-sense". Flatness symbolizes proximity, informality, and free communication. Hierarchy and the managerially-controlled organization represent the opposite. The top-steered organization provides a "misleading" map of the organizational reality that it should represent, according to Enator's founder, management, and personnel. This is why the flat, broad organization is systematically presented as a picture of how the company should be regarded. To the extent that this representation is widely and deeply anchored, operations (behaviour patterns) should live up to this idea, at least to some extent. An employee's relationship with the manager who is formally two rungs on the ladder higher up is quite different, depending on whether one's mental chart says that this is a company that respects formal hierarchies, or the "flatness of the company" is widely emphasized in the organization.

Naturally, the "cultural level" (i.e. the cohesive frame of reference of symbols and meanings) is not independent of formal structures and action patterns. Nor is the cultural level a mechanical reflection of the social level. The long-run, collective sharing of the idea that the company is a flat, unhierarchical organization is dependent on continuous social action that should harmonize with – or at least not clearly contradict – this idea. However, the relationship between the various structural aspects is far from harmonious, as proponents of dialectical and dynamic organizational theories have emphasized (Benson, 1977; Fombrun, 1986). Potential discrepancies and contradictions have been pointed out in the discussion of the corporate and managing director structure at Enator. With regard to the relationships between sociostructure and the cultural level, it is also possible to discuss to what extent there is convergence and equilibrium. As dialectically minded organizational researchers point out there is no reason to assume that convergence and harmony are "natural" and "normal", while regarding tendencies to divergence and contradiction as something strange. Divergence and contradiction must be regarded as something central since: "Equilibrium structures ... are at best fleeting moments in a dynamic process of structuring" (Fombrun, 1986, p 418).

It might be imagined that social structures at Enator – including the formal organizational hierarchy – will develop so that a clearer discrepancy or conflict between the social structures and the cultural level will characterize the company. This would be the case if the latter does not change in harmony with the former (a "culture lag"). Tendencies toward such a contradiction between the "actual" organizational structure (i.e. the action patterns and social practices) and how the organization is interpreted can be traced at Enator. The relationship between the sociostructural and the cultural elements is not without tension – anything else would be strange. "Small scale operations" as an organizational symbol can hardly be unaffected by a development that has caused the company to evolve from being a closely knit small Swedish company to an international corporate group with five times the staff in a mere five years. This is clearly illustrated by the quotation on p 88.

Despite the weakening of this values, "small scale" operations nonetheless function as a clear symbol for the organization, even if the meaning of "small scale" is probably subject to a process of continuous reinterpretation. As Enator continues to grow and acquire the character of a major international corporate group, dramatic changes are probably required to the cultural level of interpretation (the pattern of meaning, the superstructure), if clear conflicts between the small scale and the flat ideology, on the one hand, and infra- and sociostructures, on the other, are to be avoided.

6.9 Conclusion

One way of summarizing this analysis is to focus on the multidimensionality in the hierarchy of the company studied. But this is hardly unambiguous. Hierarchical levels can be counted in different ways – resulting in three or six levels – which emphasize the distance between different levels in different ways and also take note of the fact that the hierarchy looks different from different perspectives. A traditional structural concept captures certain aspects of the organization, but it only permits a somewhat limited understanding of the company's functioning from the hierarchical point of view. Mintzberg's (1983) adhocratic configuration permits a better picture of Enator, but it also restricts itself to an objectivistic form of understanding and does not seriously take into account that the organizational structure "in operation" primarily depends on the meaning that organizational members give it. Thus, organizational structure is, among other things, a question of "shared meanings".

Instead of an unambiguous, objective hierarchical concept, Enator's structure can only be understood in the sense that it shows different faces in different situations and to different groups. Subsidiary managing director status, the core of the corporate hierarchy, must also be understood from an organizational-symbolic perspective. Externally, in a marketing context involving customer contact, it is a question of emphasizing high status. Internally this aspect is given much less weight. The idea (to a large extent realized) is that free flows of communication between levels and considerable opportunities for competence-based influence that is independent of formal status should be favoured. This appears to be typical for professional/knowledge intensive organizations in general (see Chapter 14). However, the managing director's formal position undoubtedly has considerable importance, and the total corporate hierarchy is not simply "flat". In social contexts, the hierarchy is heavily deemphasized, and friendship between managers and colleagues is stressed instead. The different hierarchical elements are not totally divorced from each other, but interact as the formal hierarchy heavily overlaps the "real" (experienced) hierarchy. The ideology" and values that emphasize informality and a certain degree of equality, together with considerable efforts to establish a "fun atmosphere" and feelings of belonging, soften the consequences of the formal hierarchy.

Thus Enator's organizational hierarchy is extremely flexible. This flexibility is assisted by the efforts to manage the symbolism of the managing director title and function. Considerable managerial efforts to reproduce the dominating patterns of meanings and values regarding hierarchy equality and to maintain social practices that comply with them have not hindered the emergence of contradictions between this cultural level and the sociostructural level, which is partly an outcome of increased corporate size and hierarchical differentiation.

The shifting character of operations also contributes to counteracting strict hierarchical structures. A consequence of the adaptive nature of operations, the need for adjustment to the situation in the customer's organization, and the professional character of the personnel is that the opportunities for bureaucratization are limited.

Notes

[1]   One could argue, in a poststructuralist spirit, that cultural meanings are never fixed, but always pluralistic, ambiguous and fluid (e.g. Linstead and Grafton-Small, 1992). I have sympathy for this theoretical position, in the sense that I think we must be open for these qualities of meaning. I do not believe, however, that all empirical observations are best interpreted in this way – space should be allowed for empirical input stimulating variation concerning interpretations of phenomena in terms of their degree of ambiguity and fluidity. In many cases an emphasis on relatively consistent shared meanings makes sense and may provide a good understanding.

[2]   I realize the theoretical problem in making this distinction – one may argue that language and meaning are better understood as symbolic than literal – but I want here to make the point that talk about the flat organization is more significant in terms of constituting ideas and beliefs than in mirroring how the organization is functioning.

7 Corporate Culture and the Organizational Climate

In this chapter, I will deal with "corporate culture". As indicated in Chapter 3 on culture theory, I am somewhat sceptical about this concept and about large parts of the literature on the subject. In this book, culture is treated primarily as a theoretical perspective on various organizational phenomena, for example organizational structure, the business concept, etc., and not as a separate sub-system in the organization which can be seen as parallel to and separated from structure, the business concept, corporate strategy, etc.

However, it is difficult to avoid treating corporate culture as a separate organizational phenomenon when studying a company such as Enator. Corporate culture is an important aspect of the organization's understanding of itself (i.e. the organizational members' understanding of their workplace), and a number of actions, activities and ideas are associated with Enator's "culture". In other words, Enator's culture may be regarded as a comprehensive concept that summarizes certain orientations and practices which characterize major aspects of the organizational collective and which deals with ideals, values and norms, and the various activities which transmit them.

Thus, in this chapter, corporate culture will be treated primarily from the point of view of how the members of the organization understand "culture" in the corporate context. Corporate culture, in the present case, is primarily a question of a conscious aim on the part of management, and to some extent personnel, to create social integration and common forms of subjectivity and identity. In other words, corporate culture is seen as one aspect of the company's way of functioning – as a sub-system within the company. However, as a purely theoretical concept, that is to say where culture is utilized as a metaphor to assist in the interpretation of actions and phenomena, the term culture is used here with discretion.

The chapter starts with a systematic description of Enator's corporate culture, based on my interviews and observations. Later sections deal with climate, a phenomenon which is sometimes confused with culture but which should be kept separate.

7.1   Corporate Culture in General

When speaking of corporate culture, it is customary to refer to aspects which are not easy to describe in clear, unambiguous terms. In the broadest and most "common-sense" definition, corporate culture is a question of informal, non-rational matters, which cannot be presented in descriptions of structures, roles, competences, technology, strategy and other "traditional" organizational concepts. Corporate culture refers to an organization's specific style or special character. Somewhat more precisely, corporate culture is a question of how nuances of organizational life are perceived, how various phenomena are interpreted and how the frame of reference for thinking and action constituted by culture colours attitudes, priorities, action and, ultimately, the functioning of the organization. It is often assumed that this culture is shared by all or by most members of the organization (company, division) and that it binds them together.

Corporate culture is also normally regarded as representing the special patterns of behaviour which characterize a given organization. "The way we do things in this company", as Deal and Kennedy (1982) imprecisely summarize their view of the corporate culture concept.

This is the somewhat broad and unwieldy meaning which some authors associate with corporate culture. However, many writers try to define and specify the phenomenon in more precise terms. Schein (1985) defines culture as a pattern of basic assumptions about how problems involving adaptation to the external environment and integration within a group are handled. These basic assumptions are accompanied by values. At a concrete level, the culture is manifested in behaviours and other artefacts.

This approach indicates that culture may be interpreted at various levels in terms of (un)consciousness. Conventional action is at a visible and relatively easily understandable level, while assumptions are difficult to handle, both for members of a given culture and for external observers. Members of the culture take these assumptions for granted. Values are at an intermediate level as regards accessibility and consciousness. This multilevel approach to organizational culture has become increasingly popular (see e.g. Lundberg, 1985 and Schein, 1985). A problem is a difficulty in separating levels of values and assumptions in order to get to the latter.

Another approach regards corporate culture as consisting of both content and transmitting components which cannot be readily graded in terms of depth and level. An example of this point of view can be seen in Trice and Beyer (1984), who emphasize two fundamental aspects of organizational culture: 1) the culture's content in terms of beliefs, values and norms and 2) the culture's form, that is to say the situations and circumstances which transmit the contents of the culture often in a symbolic form. The culture is anchored and expressed in rites, rituals and ceremonies. These are all activities with a strong symbolic content. In line with this approach, the study of cultures becomes a question of studying rites and ceremonies (Trice and Beyer, 1984). Of course, rites and ceremonies mean action and action patterns, but primarily special actions which deviate from and are restricted in relation to more everyday and typical activities and behaviour patterns. Thus, it might be said that this view of culture takes little direct interest in everyday behaviour (Alvesson, 1993a).

A third approach to corporate culture quite simply emphasizes the norms, values, beliefs and ideals which are adopted by a group or a collective in an organization, and which are assumed to exercise a greater or lesser degree of influence on the attitudes and behaviour of the group (e.g. Kilmann, 1985).

These approaches to corporate culture largely adopt the variable or sub-system view of culture – which means that the culture is given a limited meaning and can be related to other organizational variables. This is in contrast to the metaphor approach, in which all organizational circumstances are in principle considered to encompass cultural dimensions and are regarded as potential objects for cultural-theoretical interpretation (see Chapter 3, Figure 3.2). While, in this book as a whole, I apply the latter concept of culture, the review contained in this chapter deals with corporate culture in the more conventional sense which the authors referred to above apply, that is to say as something which the organization in a sense "has" (cf. Figure 3.1). The difference between these two concepts of culture is not necessarily particularly clear in interpretations of cases such as the present one, but this analytical distinction should be borne in mind. This also applies to the slight shift in meaning in this chapter, compared with the rest of the book, regarding treatment of the organizational culture theme.

Obviously, the three versions of a subsystem approach outlined here are not necessarily mutually exclusive. It is more a question of emphasizing different weightings. However, the third variant – with a focus on norms and attitudes – tends to ignore the depth dimension, while the first variant treats this dimension (basic assumptions) as the most important factor. Thus, the question of the "depth" of culture presents us with an important point which can be discussed on the basis of the case study: What does the deep structure look like in a corporate culture such as Enator's? How "deep" is it?

Another question is concerned with cultural content in relation to form. On the basis of the cultural-theoretical perspective outlined in Chapter 3 *all* organizational phenomena should in principle be regarded as cultural, that is to say they involve collective symbolism and meaning. This is what the culture metaphor would indicate. In corporate culture research there is an attempt to define the cultural sub-system and, as a result, to consider cultural forms associated with rites, rituals, special stories, etc. The more exotic and striking features of the organization tend to be regarded as the form for its culture.

The social institutions in the company which most clearly denote the cultural "sub-system" will be dealt with in reviewing Enator from a corporate culture perspective. A couple of questions are worth raising at this point: How "significant" is the symbolic content in these sub-systems? What is the relationship between institutionalized situations, which may well be interpreted as culture-transmitting mechanisms (rites), and other aspects of operations?

Another type of question, which is quite natural in view of the literature on the subject, concerns the sense in which it is profitable to speak of Enator being characterized by a distinctive corporate culture. Opinions differ in the current debate as to whether organizations normally "have" more than one culture. Possibly, most organizations do not have any culture of their "own" at all; however, cultural patterns which crystallize in the organization may perhaps reflect instead the overall attitudes of society or industry, the professions and age groups which populate the organization, and other factors outside the organization?

The degree of depth and unity which characterizes the corporate culture at Enator (if it is possible to speak of a corporate culture at all) is linked to this question to some extent. (I am ambivalent as to whether Enator may be said to "have" a fully developed corporate culture, i.e. be said to be culturally unitary and unique but, for the time being, I assume that this is the case. Possible criteria for a corporate culture and the circumstances and mechanisms which facilitate or hinder the formation of a "genuine" corporate culture are discussed later in this chapter.) Mention is sometimes made of "strong" versus "weak" or – and this is preferable – distinct versus heterogeneous organizational cultural patterns. A strong or distinct organizational culture is characterized by a large measure of consensus between the great majority of members of the organization as regards the values, norms, beliefs and ideals which are professed. In a non-distinct or heterogeneous organizational culture – which actually hardly justifies the name – there is little or no cultural homogeneity.

I have now presented some aspects of the current debate and theory within the corporate culture research area and I have introduced some of the questions which will be dealt with in this and in subsequent chapters on the basis of the Enator case study. (Detailed presentations of the theory and debate in this area can be found in Alvesson, 1993a; Alvesson and Berg, 1992.)

7.2   Corporate Culture at Enator: Content

I will start by considering a number of central values which characterize the company and then continue by saying something about the norms and action principles which are associated with these values. Subsequently, I will be dealing with some of the situations which most clearly express and transmit corporate culture.

7.2.1   Values and Norms

Values refer to a feeling of what is good and what "should be" (cf. e.g. Schein, 1985). Values provide an approximate and general guideline for what is right and how the individual should act. Values are present at various levels of consciousness. Individuals are clearly conscious of certain values as well as being able to appreciate that others may have different values than their own. But people are less conscious of certain other values, which may be internalized and which are taken for granted without thinking about them or regarding them as values. They are part of the global picture and deviations from such values are not regarded as "different" values which can be respected but are, instead, thought of as directly reprehensible, or even crazy.

Norms refer to unwritten rules of behaviour and attitudes. Norms exercise a social pressure on individuals. They are determined by values and are more precise and situationally adapted expressions of values (Schneider, 1976). While values provide a general indication of what is good and desirable, norms provide guidelines for concrete action. The dividing line in this context may be fluid. Examples will be provided below.

7.2.2   Typical Values at Enator

My impression is that Enator's corporate culture can be illustrated by the following words: selective openness, positive basic attitudes, loyalty, generosity, informality, non-bureaucratic style, friendliness and social participation. Let us look more closely at what may be hidden behind these concepts.

Openness means that the individual is honest and direct with regard to what is happening in the company, and also at the personal level. However, there is less emphasis on the personal side – this is regarded as a matter for the individual concerned. At the corporate level, the openness displayed is in some respects striking, in my opinion. My account of the

Project Management Philosophy course (Chapter 5) illustrates this. Another good example is the ease with which I could enter the company and be given an opportunity to conduct this study.

One result of this relatively significant internal openness is that employees have become accustomed to receiving a great deal of information about the company and about what is going on. This was most salient a few years earlier in the company's history when the company was smaller and the founders/owners led operations. Until a few years before the date of my study, most consultants felt that they were located close to the business and organizational centre of events. This is how one person described the situation when she commenced employment at Enator in 1981-82:

People were extremely open. If there was anything exciting going on, people told you about it. They didn't keep anything under wraps. If it was a question of something sensitive, they said that it could not be discussed outside the room. Anyway, we got information down to a real grassroot level, for example about the company prospectus, acquisitions and the situation in general.

The company's dramatic expansion, its increased size and the shift of business development to the group level has somewhat diluted the "total" information flow which previously characterized the entire organization. However, openness is still a guiding light at Enator, although the dissemination of information is now to some extent concentrated at the subsidiary level, seen from the perspective of an individual consultant.

The crucial importance of openness in the organization and its "sacred" character – and some contradictions in this context – are confirmed by a couple of deviations from this principle. One example was a new subsidiary manager who was recruited externally. He was soon forced to resign, partly because the employees felt that he had given them insufficient information and that he was not "open". His unwillingness to provide correct information about a situation in which there were too few consultancy assignments, in combination with other problems, made employees react sharply and take the initiative to achieve his dismissal.

Another example came up in an interview when I asked someone to indicate the most negative experiences he had had at Enator. The answer was a lack of immediate information in connection with the "Norwegian affair". In this case, most of the employees in the Norwegian subsidiary resigned and formed their own consultancy firm under the management of the previous director of the subsidiary. According to my interviewee, there was some delay in informing the employees about what had happened. He remarked that "people found it rather hard to accept this lack of confidence in the personnel".

An informant noted that, prior to this incident, the Norwegian managing director was described as "extremely competent" by top management but was subsequently characterized as virtually incompetent. People did not believe that they had been given a "true picture" of what had happened. Their experience of a discrepancy between ideals and reality as regards openness and a display of confidence was probably justified and it is difficult to believe that openness is a value which has always been given top priority in the company. It is quite clear that deviations from this principle occur. However, to put this comment in perspective, it is worth noting that inadequate information in this case should be seen against a background of high expectations and the fact that openness was the norm. As the interviewee quoted above said: In other companies they don't care if you don't get to know so much, but here they do.

However, a balanced picture of the value structure at Enator justifies mention of the selective nature of openness. One example concerned internal relations within the group of owners, involving conflicts which had gone on for years and which employees were hardly aware of. Another exception is pay, which employees are not in the habit of revealing to their colleagues.

The positive style is another Enator characteristic. Being positive, friendly and optimistic is regarded as something good. "Be positive!" was one of the many messages transmitted by the Project Management Philosophy course. Naturally, the other side of the coin is that criticism and negative aspects are not readily taken up. People make every effort to find and emphasize points which can be regarded as positive. As one interviewee put it: If you are critical, you have to be prepared to have an alternative or to have an extremely good basis for your information.

Naturally, it is easier to be positive in a company which is successful and expanding, for example Enator at the time of my study. But, in addition, a positive attitude appeared to be, *per se*, an important value in the organization. This will be dealt with later in the section describing the spirit and climate of the organization.

Loyalty is another important value at Enator. A typical statement within Enator is that

the culture is based on a 'we-feeling' and loyalty. There is a strong group pressure here, to help out. ... Many employees felt that they could work a little harder at Enator.

"A negative" sign of the strong impact of loyalty was dislike of resignations by personnel:

People who hand in their cards are not popular. But things have been getting better. There is more tolerance today than there was two years ago ... . At that time it was extremely unpopular to resign. It spoilt the atmosphere of shared collegiality. 'How can he pack it in?' It raised questions for the employees who were still there. You didn't talk about people who had resigned. They were simply struck from the minutes. They just stopped coming to the morning meetings. They didn't always advertise the fact that somebody had resigned, or was about to do so.

As a result of Enator's rapid expansion and the increasing proportion of personnel who were taken on after the original "entrepreneurial phase", ties of loyalty tended to become weaker. But belongingness to the company still represented an important value for many employees.

Generosity was referred to by many people as a characteristic of Enator, at least with respect to events such as company parties of various kinds. Enator also invested money and energy in social arrangements for project groups, both in terms of promoting cohesiveness in the group at the beginning of a project and as a reward upon completion. The major festivities in connection with company birthdays are of course a striking feature. Enator also sponsors other types of social activities, such as courses and clubs for employees.

On the other hand, the company is not regarded as particularly generous in terms of pay and training. Some long-term employees consider that Enator is actually mean regarding further training. According to some interviewees, Enator does not pay particularly well – in the view of many consultants the pay is perhaps average or even low in relation to the prices debited to customers. Generosity is restricted to social activities.

Friendship is another Enator value. Naturally, most people regard friendship as something good. However, this is not always as clear in corporations. Excessively close relationships may disturb the business aspects, many people believe. But this is not how Enator regards the matter. At Enator, friendship is considered to be something to which priority should be attached. For example, one major purpose of conferences for managing directors is to reinforce social ties (within the subsidiary manager and executive group). Social criteria are a significant factor in recruitment. On the whole, a great deal is done to reinforce a spirit of "being mates", chiefly within Enator itself, but also with external contacts. One characteristic of Enator is considered to be treating everyone as "friends", not merely colleagues and customers, but also suppliers and other contacts. Overall, this type of value and ideal is probably difficult to achieve on a broad front. It can easily become a matter of superficial behaviour which, however, may to some extent facilitate interaction in work and business.

I can claim, with reasonable certainty, that certain values characterize Enator to a much greater extent than many other organizations in Sweden. If I were to mention additional values, these might include a high level of work morale, accepting colleagues making fools of themselves, social affinity and creativity. These virtues are espoused in the company, but they overlap with those which have been previously mentioned. For example, a high level of work morale may be difficult to separate from loyalty to the company, as a value, in relationship to measurable aspects such as low absenteeism and participation in corporate activities outside normal working hours.

Humility and the ability to listen are other elements in the value system which are somewhat different from the aspects already mentioned. Several interviewees mentioned these factors as characteristic of Enator. This was considered a question of being highly sensitive to the knowledge, problems and needs of others – colleagues, clients, etc. Humility is a matter of learning from others – the speaker asking: "How do you do it?" rather than indicating how he himself performs the task, as one interviewee put it. However, my impression is that there is more ambiguity as regards the extent and impact of these values than for the values mentioned previously. For example, the project management philosophy course tended to be characterized by statements by the course leaders to participants about work methods, organization, values, etc. at Enator, rather than by allowing any real scope for dialogue, and for listening on the part of management. Another somewhat paradoxical situation arose when an interviewee spoke of the importance of listening and being humble, although he himself was hardly modest about his own performance.

In one way, much of the corporate culture and self-understanding at Enator can be summarized in the slightly paradoxical formulation: "We are very good at being humble."

7.2.3   Example of Typical Norms in the Company

The above values are accompanied to a greater or lesser extent by various norms which control behaviour. Norms are more concrete and action-specific than values. Various norms were illustrated in the review of values. "Provide constructive alternatives if you criticize" and "have a good factual basis for your arguments and extremely good reasons if you are going to criticize" are examples of norms which result from the value of endeavouring to be positive. Without wishing to repeat myself, I will deal with a couple of norms which express the corporate culture in a slightly different manner.

One important norm is that the managing director should be accessible to consultants. This means that the subsidiary manager and/or his second-in-command can be reached by consultants without significant delay. The following quotation illustrates this:

Actually, I dislike sitting in meetings, shut-in. I hate it when my consultants are not able to get to me, and are met by a secretary who says 'give him a call on Friday' (Subsidiary manager).

I can personally confirm that this norm is widespread and that subsidiary managers act in accordance with it. On the whole, my interviews with subsidiary managers were "disturbed" by at least a couple of telephone conversations from consultants in the field or from other people. Sometimes, too, staff visited the manager's room to provide or obtain information, and they exchanged a few words. However, this was always a question of brief communication. Sometimes the manager and the person at the other end of the telephone/the visitor agreed to telephone/meet later. But the point is that my interview did not result in the manager disconnecting the telephone or cutting short his visitors. Accessibility was maintained.

Another norm involves being prepared to work overtime if this is required. Personnel are expected to be willing to work extra to a considerable extent in order to complete a consultancy project in the time-span allotted. This norm also means that private life must not be given priority if it conflicts with work. As far as Enator personnel are concerned, this norm can be seen clearly when they work on projects with the staff of customer companies:

There are different standards of work morals at customer companies and Enator. Customer employees go home at 5 o'clock, even when the schedule is under pressure. But we have learnt to do things differently.

This norm is probably relatively typical of people working on projects and in organizations characterized by project organization. Concentrated extra work is sometimes required and is important for the success of the project and, as a result, for the success of the company. Applying this norm is facilitated because many employees are young and have no children.

7.3　　Cultural Forms of Expression and Transmission

The cultural patterns outlined above permeate everyday behaviour in the organization to a greater or lesser extent. The social situations which most clearly denote cultural content are normally termed rites, rituals and ceremonies. It is not uncommon for these concepts to be treated as synonyms.

It is hard to find any clear demarcation line as regards what is to be considered a rite (and in the following, therefore, I allow the concept of the rite to also include the other two types of ritual behaviour). Disagreement about how concepts of rites (rituals) should be defined does not facilitate matters. As Leach (1968, p 526) says, "There is greatest possible lack of agreement as regards how the ritual concept should be applied and how the implementation of rituals should be understood."

In principle, all social meetings and activities which demonstrate certain repetitive patterns which contain symbolic and expressive elements qualify for definition as rites. (Cf. Trice and Beyer, 1984, who define rites as organized and planned activities with both practical and expressive consequences.) Activities are normally relatively developed, dramatic, and are an expression of the culture, taking place before an audience (or within a group of active participants).

It may be maintained that practically all social activity which is not temporary and unambiguously directed towards a specific objective may be classified as a rite: everything from drinking coffee and the way we greet one another to the execution of certain tasks in a work group. However, the advantage to be gained by identifying the ritual element in a social activity varies considerably. What are the criteria for choosing to regard something as a rite? The degree of expressive, symbolic, emotional and irrational content is one answer provided by Van Maanen and Kunda (1989). In other words, the more complex and culturally "rich" the patterns expressed, the greater reason there is to regard the social activity in question as a rite.

There is also a more pragmatic point of view. If the researcher needs to treat something as a rite he or she normally has to have an opportunity to observe the activity. If this is the case, it is a definite advantage if the activity is public, distinct and readily identifiable (preferably in advance). This is a rather important aspect of studies of rites – both in general and in the present instance. Therefore, rites are regarded as relatively extensive events, involving a (considerable) number of people and of a semi or fully public nature, at any rate within the organization. The rites discussed below are primarily of this type – social activities which are typical expressions of culture and which have strongly expressive and non-instrumental features.

On the other hand, the complexity of fundamental cultural patterns is not fully dealt with, and on the whole this also applies to the deeper, unconscious structures. Within the organization there are probably other (events that can be interpreted as) rites which are not treated here – which are more subtle, non-public and difficult for an outside researcher to penetrate. Perhaps rites which express "tacit knowledge" and social relations in direct connection with the execution of system and programming functions should be included in this category. There are hardly any examples of rites directly connected with work activities in the literature of corporate culture, but examples can be found in certain sociological and anthropological texts based on the researcher's prolonged participation and observation over the years in the form of employment on the factory floor, for example (see e.g. Burawoy, 1979).

I would thus like to say something about what is not covered in the following pages, and to make it clear that important aspects of organizational culture are not dealt with here. To some extent, this is because my study is primarily concerned with aspects of management.

Unfortunately, it is all too easy to define cultural research within the corporate area so that it only encompasses relatively striking social phenomena, thus convincing both the author and the reader that a comprehensive picture has been achieved. I hope that I can avoid contributing to this tendency to couple corporate culture with clearly discernible rites and explicit values by 1) indicating the importance of more subtle cultural patterns which characterize everyday life in the organization, and not just the most obvious rites, 2) stressing that in this chapter I am dealing with corporate culture as a limited "sub-system" rather than a comprehensive concept covering the entire organization in depth; and 3) proceeding in various parts of this book beyond the "sub-system" approach and referring to culture as a metaphor or a fundamental perspective. Although a bias in favour of clear and explicit rites and values is justified due to the management focus of the study, it is not fully satisfactory to primarily pay attention to the most obvious values and rites which are embraced by management. In this book as a whole, I try to present a complex picture of the cultural patterns which characterize the Enator organization.

7.4 Organizational Rites at Enator

On the basis of the discussion above, the following activities may be regarded as rites:

- the Project Management Philosophy course;
- morning meetings every other week at subsidiaries;
- quarterly conferences;
- five o'clock beer;
- company general meetings;
- Victoria and other Enator birthdays.

The first item on this list may be regarded as an initiation rite denoting entry into the company. Morning meetings and quarterly conferences can be seen as integration rites within subsidiaries, while the three latter variants are activities which are common to all Enator personnel and may be regarded as integration rites for the Enator Group. (For discussion of these types of rites, see Trice and Beyer, 1984, 1985.)

In addition, I would like to discuss one ritual activity that only involves managing directors and other top managers, the quarterly "Big-cof" (cof = coordination forum, although nobody uses the full expression).

The project management philosophy course was dealt with in Chapter 5 and therefore I shall not refer to it again here. The remaining activities will be dealt with in some detail, however.

7.4.1   Morning Meetings

For an hour or so every other week, each subsidiary holds morning meetings. This means that all, or at any rate most, of the company's employees normally meet together early in the morning. The objective is to provide information and to make social contact. Let me illustrate how this may work out.

One of the four technical subsidiaries is having a morning meeting. Approximately 25 people are present, two of whom are women. The group is sitting in a large meeting-room in Enator's original premises. The personnel are sitting in an open square with the subsidiary manager at a desk at the open side of the square.

The subsidiary manager starts by giving information about diverse matters: my presence as a researcher, information about a company which was previously a customer but which has now gone into bankruptcy and which is probably unable to pay, and about a new assignment which is in progress. This is mostly a question of one-way communication with an occasional question from consultants. However, people seem to be awake and interested, even though it is only 8 o'clock in the morning. Then it is the turn of the personnel representatives who have attended a meeting with "Janne" and "Roffe", that is to say the managing directors of Enator and Enator Sweden. The focus then switches to the Norway affair, that is to say the resignation of most of the personnel in Norway. The group is highly interested. Several people ask questions about events.

The next item on the agenda concerns the next quarterly conference. What is it going to be about? "Brainstorming" commences. The group becomes heavily involved. Several proposals are made for sailing and a boat trip. The subsidiary manager tries, somewhat humorously, to discuss potentially serious items. He clearly wants something work-related on the agenda for the "conference" besides the recreational elements. However, this leads to further joking and no one takes his comments seriously. There is considerable interest in the "conference" and a great deal of cheerful conversation.

My impression is that employees are interested, find it easy to talk and that the atmosphere is rather pleasant. The meeting is at its most lively when the conference is discussed, but the Norway affair and the business aspects also arouse interest. At the same time, it seems somewhat inadequate that the meeting provides almost the only contact with Enator for two weeks, in view of the fact that many consultants spend most of their time at customers' places of work.

The morning meetings constitute a forum in which the subsidiaries' communal spirit and links between Enator and the personnel are emphasized. The transmission of information in an instrumental sense is subordinate to the forum's significance for forming social ties. This is stressed by the fact that almost all the subsidiary employees are present and that there is considerable scope for jokes.

7.4.2   Quarterly Conferences

We now come to the second integration rite which characterizes subsidiary companies – the quarterly conference. Quarterly conferences take place every three months, usually on Fridays and Saturdays. Quarterly conferences primarily fulfil a social function. It is a question of having a good time and reinforcing the spirit of comradeship. In addition, there is often a more or less prominent factual know-how content, for example something to do with computer technology or interpersonnel relations (e.g. transaction analysis). Some subsidiaries alternate between an exclusively social and a work-related content in the programme for their quarterly conferences.

On the whole, Dynator – the Enator subsidiary which is responsible for maintenance – has conferences with a higher tempo than the other subsidiaries. Dynator's manager considers that maintenance work is difficult and is thought to be something of "a dirty job". Dealing with old, unstructured systems and sorting them out, for example when a computer run has gone wrong, is not considered as attractive as working on new designs and systems development. The content of the Dynator quarterly conference is supposed to reflect the somewhat tougher conditions of work which are considered to apply at Dynator.

A mountain-walking expedition which took place turned out to be even more physically demanding than had been intended. Afterwards, all the participants received berets with a silver owl badge – Dynator's symbol is an owl. (Sometimes the consultants must work at nights when a system has broken down and must be repaired immediately.) Some employees received a gold badge instead – an overweight smoker who had walked for 40 kilometres even though he had been pouting after 100 metres, and three people who spontaneously volunteered to act as organizers and to help the others.

Quarterly conferences are designed to give subsidiary personnel special experiences which they can share with their colleagues. With the possible exception of Dynator, I do not have any basis for claiming that quarterly conferences necessarily express any particularly distinctive symbolism (of a deeper nature) – they often seem to have a rather immediate, obvious social function.

7.4.3   Five o'clock Beer

The week finishes with a minor social activity on a regular basis for those who are interested, namely taking a beer on the ground floor of the company building. Between 20 and 50 people relax for 30 minutes or an hour before going off for the weekend. This detail of corporate social life is familiar in bestseller literature about corporate cultures (e.g. Deal and Kennedy, 1982). Enator seems to have started the tradition before this wisdom was widely disseminated.

Apart from having a generally agreeable time together, one point of this activity is said to be that "it deemphasizes the fact that there are top directors" (Subsidiary manager). Thus, the idea is that top management (i.e. above the subsidiary level) and ordinary consultants can mingle. It is perhaps rather doubtful if this really occurs (Trice and Beyer, 1985). Another idea is possibly to emphasize the high level of work morale in the company – thus, even on Fridays, personnel are expected to work until 5 o'clock.

7.4.4   The General Meeting

Enator's corporate general meeting and the accompanying festivities also involve similar clear socially-integrative functions. I attended the 1987 general meeting. Traditionally, the general meeting is followed by a large party at which personnel, the board, shareholders and some customers may participate. This makes the meeting more interesting for employees.

The general meeting takes place in the reception area at the centre of Enator's spectacular building, on the first floor. The room is full of people, mostly consultants, perhaps up to 300 guests, and food and drink are provided. People circulate and talk; that is how it starts. The shareholders – some 50 of them – then sit on chairs temporarily placed along the walls of the reception premises. Most of the personnel watch the proceedings from the floors where their own subsidiaries are located. This means that they have a "gallery" view, since the building is open in the centre from floor to roof, and the staff get a good view of the meeting itself. In my opinion, the atmosphere is more reminiscent of a football match than a corporate general meeting.

Enator's managing director, Jan Rudberg, steps forward. He takes the microphone, greets the audience, the shareholders, the personnel and others, says that everyone is very welcome and continues: "we usually try to run Enator's general meeting in a pleasant and agreeable manner, but a 10th anniversary justifies a flashback."

Jan Rudberg then asks Christer Jacobsson and Hasse Larsson, two (of the three) founders who are still working in the group and who are major shareholders, and Rolf Thorsell, the first of the company's employees and now managing director of Enator Sweden (umbrella for the Swedish subsidiaries), to step forward. These three gentlemen do as they are told and sit on bar stools alongside the managing director. There are no tables between them and the audience. The managing director then interviews his three guests, asking them questions about history and corporate milestones, the current situation and plans for the future. Among other things, the audience is told that the first milestone occurred when the company took on its twentieth employee. That signified that the company was seriously in business and could survive if a couple of people were away from work for some days. The next milestone was when Enator reached 100 employees. This meant that it had passed the frontier which distinguishes consultancy companies which concentrate on a limited niche from consultancies which have a broader focus and greater impact on the market. The third milestone was stock-market listing, while the fourth was the establishment of companies abroad. Christer Jacobsson comments that international growth was originally very much based on a boyish dream and that the process was largely guided by intuition.

The next item on the agenda is the current and future position of the company. Among other things Enator is going to invest in are the three "T"s, the managing director of Enator Sweden says, "Transport, tourism and ... ." But he has forgotten what the third "T" stands for. None of the others seem to remember either, but Hasse Larsson adds "... and something else". This makes the audience laugh. The three interviewees then disappear and it's time for the managing director himself to be interviewed.

The formal aspects of the meeting are dealt with rapidly. The only break in the flow is a brief objection from a representative of the Shareholders' Association, who nonetheless thanks the company for an agreeable general meeting. "It is refreshing to have an annual general meeting in such a relaxed setting. I have attended a great many general meetings, each one more gloomy than the other", he says.

The party gradually gets going on the top floor where the public now join in. Several rooms on the top floor have been especially prepared for the occasion. Guests are offered sandwiches, wine, beer, etc. There is a good atmosphere, which gets better as the evening progresses. More and more people move into an attractive room with a grand piano. Someone is playing, and a tightly packed group of over 50 people are singing enthusiastically and capably.

The general meeting is of a somewhat ceremonial nature. Those present are reminded of the rapid march of history and of the continuity and links between the past and the present. Two of the three founders and the first employee are still working in the group, and they are presented at the general meeting.

The personal and informal atmosphere which characterizes the company is also given expression. Corporate representatives are not hiding behind tables but are sitting like "entertainers" on bar stools directly facing their audience. They mention that international ambitions were based just as much on personal as on business motives.

7.4.5   Victoria

Enator celebrates its birthdays. In the first five years of the company's existence such festivities were called "Albert", the name being based on local slang. Subsequently such festivities were called "Victoria". When I was conducting my study, the company was celebrating its tenth anniversary. This took place on the island of Rhodes in May 1987 and continued for three days. All 500 Enator employees were invited and the subsidiaries were supposed to contribute their own entertainment for the benefit of the other participants. In preparation for "Victoria", the various Swedish and foreign subsidiaries were divided into ten groups. Each team was given the task of representing one year of Enator's history. A great deal of rehearsing took place prior to the anniversary celebrations. The assumption was that all these evenings of practice before the day meant that subsidiary personnel learnt to work together in an agreeable atmosphere. The idea was that a feeling of common purpose, cohesion and ability to cooperate would be reinforced.

It was claimed that the actual ceremony on Rhodes was highly successful. The location was kept secret (employees were only informed that they must have a passport and that they would be away for three days). Once the staff were in the plane, the subsidiary managers functioned as cabin personnel. Measures had been taken to virtually eliminate checking procedures at the airport and the hotel. Personnel were offered a programme with varying content once they were on the island. One feature of the programme was that a morning was to be devoted to group activity – with groups comprising people from different subsidiaries and of different nationalities. This involved collecting rubbish, thus contributing to keeping the streets and beaches of Rhodes clean.

Arguably, there are several advantages in giving company personnel the task of illustrating corporate history in a light-hearted manner. Firstly, it is important that the collective of employees understands and has a feeling for company history. Ceremonies such as anniversaries always contain elements of this kind, and this is particularly important in a company in which almost half the personnel have been employees for less than two years or so and which is developing rapidly. It is obviously positive, from a management point of view, if staff have at least some understanding of earlier developments. Formal historical presentations, such as lengthy speeches at parties, are often boring. It can be assumed that the method chosen to present corporate history generates energy and interest in the various events and milestones in the life of the company.

However, the employees are not only observers but also actors. Active participation often leads to strong involvement in the theme which is presented. The activity preceding the subsidiaries' performances at "Victoria" probably contained several flashbacks and perhaps some research into the company's history, background, various events, key figures on specific occasions, etc.

Formulated at a more theoretical level, it can be said that the task of illustrating the company's history involved collective symbolization describing Enator's development, in which everyone participated. It may be presumed that the creative activities involved in making presentations, in the rehearsals, in the actual performance at Victoria and in experiencing the highlights of ten years of the company's history in a personal manner, with group involvement, contribute to establishing collective identity and cohesion.

7.4.6   A Top Management Rite

Four times a year, top management and all the subsidiary managers are involved in a joint activity called "Big-cof". "Big-cof" usually consists of three components: the journey, social contacts and discussions about strategy, corporate culture and other management questions. The journey component is not always routine. In the period covered by my study, managers travelled by helicopter and dog-sled up to the Kebnekajse mountain in Northern Sweden.

Social contacts appear to be the most important component. At least one subsidiary manager felt that purely management questions take second place. The conference involves "very pleasant contacts with a lot of eating and drinking" (Subsidiary manager):

They are a cheerful crowd … . It is the social contacts which are the important thing. There is a special style (Subsidiary manager).

One manager said that the managing directors like singing together. As soon as someone starts off – when they are having their group photographs, or at a party, etc. – then everybody joins in. There are no trained singers but most of them know the songs. "Big-cofs" also deal with matters involving corporate control. At an annual conference, for example, the main topic is the budget. There is thus an instrumental function which involves pure coordination of operations. But this is not just a matter of techniques and finance – the basis for the whole occasion is social cohesiveness. "Big-cofs" express a feeling of community and comradeship. At "Big-cofs" managers confirm that they enjoy good relations with each other and feel that they all belong to the same company. "Big-cofs" are a source of shared, positive experience. This facilitates and encourages everyday contacts, communication and mutual support between subsidiary managers.

7.5   The Enator Building

The company's most eye-catching symbol is its headquarters, which was completed in late 1985 and attracted considerable attention in the mass media. The Enator building employs a unique architectural design and an even more distinctive interior format. It is located in Kista, the "Silicon Valley of Sweden", in an area dominated by high-tech computer companies, and has five floors. Externally it represents a hexagon cut in half (see Figure 7.1).

The visitor enters the building by ascending half a floor, which takes him to a central triangular open area, extending right up to the roof, which is glass-covered at this point. The relatively expansive open area in the centre dominates the entire building. The reception facilities are located on the ground floor and, from this point, the visitor can look up to all the other floors. On each floor, corridors run around the edge of this open area. Since there is only a protective balustrade between these corridors and the open triangle, there is an excellent view over much of the rest of the building. There is a lift made of glass at one end of the triangle. A ride in the lift provides another good view.

There are a number of rooms along the walls on the bottom floor, surrounding the central triangle. This is where corporate management and central administration are located. As in the rest of the building, the internal partition walls are made of glass, thus providing full visibility from the

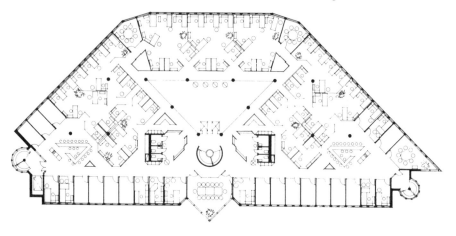

Figure 7.1:   Plan of the Enator building: floor for operative subsidiaries

outside. This also applies to many of the conference rooms on the ground and upper floors.

The various operative subsidiaries are located on the second, third and fourth floors. Office rooms and meeting rooms are located along the external walls. This is where the subsidiary managers, salesmen and secretaries have their offices. Consultants work in the central area alongside the triangle in open-plan offices. Their desks are close together, and in principle they only have a desk, a chair and not much else. The net floor working space per employee is only 6 square metres. There are glass partition walls here and there.

The design deliberately avoids right angles and long corridors. This applies to all floors. The visitor has to change direction several times to reach his/her destination. Since the various subsidiaries are not strictly separated and there are no signs or other indications which facilitate orientation, it is difficult to find the person you are looking for. This is a deliberate feature of the design. The idea is to encourage the visitor to find his own way by asking people.

There is a coffee room facility at both ends of each floor. These facilities are based on a triangular counter surrounded by bar stools. About 15 employees can sit down at the same time here.

Parts of the office premises and the interior design of the building appear appealing and inviting while other parts are impersonal. The building itself appears pleasant and welcoming, with nooks and corners, special lighting, and architecture which consistently avoids right angles and box-like shapes; the colouring is imaginative, with a painted clouds and sky design on the floor in the entrance. The conference rooms also make a pleasant impression. The rooms on the second, third and fourth floors are somewhat simpler, but they are nonetheless stylish and elegant. There are some more conventional conference rooms on the first floor, with high-backed armchairs. But there are no proper meeting room tables, just small triangular tables to put coffee cups on. This means that there are no tables to hide behind – you have a full-length view of your opposite number. The idea is that you can behave in a more personal manner and more freely, thus achieving better contact. There are only a few chairs in the room. Working groups are not supposed to meet here. This is the location for business conversations between Enator personnel and high level customer representatives.

While the whole of the "public" part of the building tends to give a warm and personal impression, despite a somewhat elegant and modernistic style, most of the offices and office landscapes are more impersonal, with functionalist fixtures and decoration and standardized equipment, often with very little on the walls and few personal items.

Thus, at Enator, we find an unusual situation, where the private areas have an impersonal touch, while the public facilities are original and appealing. However, these public areas have no trace of individuality or personal touch either – apart from those which are the product of the designer's imagination. Thus, individuals who inhabit the private and public areas in the Enator building do not set their personal stamp on the environment in which they operate.

The fifth floor is different from the other four. This consists of two departments: an entertainment/inspiration section and a conference area. In the board-room (which is called the Long Room) there is a long table surrounded by comfortable armchairs. A cliff face is painted on the surface of the table and the cliff descends into the sea. At one end of the room there is a triangular window. The door is of glass, but otherwise the interior walls are of non-transparent material. As is appropriate, the board-room breathes an atmosphere which is more elegant, formal and impersonal than other areas in the building.

There is also a dining-room on this floor, which is not intended for ordinary lunches but rather for somewhat more special occasions, and a large conference-room. There are attractive bathing facilities in Enator's "inspiration space", including a small swimming pool, a sauna, a changing room and space to relax, with comfortable basketwork furniture and a fireplace. Adjoining this area, there is a terrace with a barbecue grill, and alongside the terrace and the bathing facilities, there is a bar with a grand piano. The piano dominates this area, and is apparently considered to be an extremely good investment, for the entertainment of both personnel and guests.

In the Enator building, an attempt has been made to incorporate as much as possible of the corporate philosophy. One of the commonly es-

poused basic ideas is the importance of creativity for the company's operations and this is indicated by the absence of sharp angles and long corridors. Right angles and the rationalism which is associated with such forms
is avoided. The complicated passages and the lack of signs are supposed to
facilitate social contacts – the visitor has to ask people about guidance to
find his own way. Personnel going from point A to point B often have to
make a detour and are thus more likely to meet people. The idea is that
the unexpected gives birth to creativity in unplanned, spontaneous situations and encounters. This explains to some extent why the public facilities
in the building are given priority, at the expense of the office space and
other individual workplaces. Social interaction is intended to facilitate the
development of good ideas.

The public areas also express the importance of the purely social aspects
of the organization and the significance of a sense of community. This is
denoted by the bar, with its piano, and the emphasis on singing. There is a
rumour that when one of the founders outlined this idea when the building
was being designed, he started with the piano bar, gave it the key position
in the building and then went on to think about other functions.

Glass walls, the lack of intercoms, name-plates, etc. are all intended to
symbolize openness, informality, direct contacts and free, personal patterns of communication and interaction.

In the initial planning stage, the dominant concepts were the retention
of flexibility, the possibility of selling the building and its function as an
office. Advisers stressed the importance of the market value of the building – which meant that buyers with different requirements and tastes
could find it attractive. Gradually, as the planning process advanced, this
type of consideration became increasingly less important. Instead of regarding the project as an office building, it became more a question of
corporate development. Seen in this light, the building is primarily significant as a means of supporting operations and the business concept, and as
an internal and external showcase for the values which Enator represents.
Economic and financial considerations and the long-term net worth are
less important in this perspective.

This does not mean that the building was particularly expensive. Apparently, it did not cost more per work space than any other normal office
building. The explanation is partly that no luxurious and expensive materi-
als were employed, and partly that both the overall floor space and also
the net floor space are comparatively restricted per working space. I was
informed that the normal average gross area per office worker is 25 square
metres, whereas at Enator it is only 16 square metres. (This figure includes
also public space.) Possibly this may be regarded as an expression of the
fact that Enator's corporate philosophy does not give top priority to the
personal working environment of its staff. An alternative interpretation is

that management consider that there is positive value in working in close proximity. Another possibility is the idea that individual work spaces should not deviate much from the facilities available to consultants at customers' premises. As temporary, extra personnel, consultants may not always be given the best office space.

Obviously, corporate buildings and other material artefacts have always conveyed a cultural content. However, in the last decade there has been a tendency to exploit corporate architecture more consciously and consistently as a communicative tool in Western countries (Berg and Kreiner, 1990). Greater attention has been paid to a number of possible functions for corporate architecture, for example its significance in influencing the behaviour of individuals via the symbolism which architecture and design convey in denoting the corporate orientation and strategic profile.

Thus, the purely functional features of corporate architecture and interior decoration have taken second place to their expressive, symbolic and communicative functions. Enator is a good example of this development. Since Enator's product is extremely difficult to demonstrate – as is the case for most types of professional services – it is particularly fruitful for companies of this type to employ corporate architecture to compensate for the invisibility of the product by demonstrating to the market in a more or less tangible form what the company represents (see also Chapter 12).

In Østerberg's (1985) terminology, we might say that Enator's building and its interior are strongly characterized by signitivity. The corporate architecture is intended to say as much as possible to employees, customers, visitors and the general public, who are reached via the mass media. Neither the degree nor the content of this signitivity are unambiguous, however. The signitive dimension in the material is a question of attention, interest and the ability to interpret.

As Berg and Kreiner (1990) point out, corporate buildings seldom speak for themselves. Initially, they communicate nothing, but "are instead the theme in conversations which organizations participate in, both internally and with the outside world" (p 62). New or modified corporate buildings may illustrate a particular message. This message may be transmitted directly rather than in the form of ambiguous symbols constituted by corporate buildings and their interiors. This means that the social processes which surround corporate materiality are of crucial importance if its signitivity can be fully comprehended. The extent to which a framework of interpretation favoured by top management can be anchored in a given collective is decisive in determining the extent to which a non-trivial message can be indicated in the material. Enator's numerous nooks and corners and the lack of corridors and right-angled spaces may be taken as an example. The idea is, among other things, that this should denote creativity, partly as an inspiration and encouragement to employees and partly as an external communication of what the company represents vis-à-vis customers and others. But this meaning is not obvious to those who observe the corporate building. The individual may regard the Enator building as incomprehensible, as a refined way of separating different units from each other, as an expression of management or architectural ego trips. If the building is to be interpreted as a sign of creativity, at least three conditions must be fulfilled: that the material must give an expression of creativity, in other words it must comply with the interpretation that it is creative (or at least not contradict it); that the message must be soundly anchored in the collective, which can thus describe the building and what it denotes; and that corporate practice must comply relatively well with this message (or at least not too obviously deviate from it).

Generally speaking, corporate architecture tends to be heavily imbued with history. The material used is often an expression of values, actions and considerations which are a couple of decades old or more. In such a case, material aspects may mean inertia or sluggishness. They represent the restrictions of history in the form of both physical frameworks for behaviour and in the transmission of signs and messages. This also limits corporate management's control over material aspects. It is possible that such material considerations may point in a direction which management did not intend.

However, at Enator, management had virtually full control over the material aspects when the building was designed. The architecture is a relatively eloquent expression of management objectives. This is partly a result of the considerable effort and creativity devoted to the construction of the building, the high priority given to its significance as a communicative instrument and the fact that the building is new. However, it is also the result of a reasonable degree of consensus among employees as to what the company represents, and in their interpretation of the building and its interior. Obviously, this is not a static situation. In the course of time, the significance of the Enator building will probably be more ambiguous, and possibly in certain respects contradictory, in relation to what management wishes to communicate and to company practice. In contrast to the corporate building, the market and the social conditions within the company are not static. Presumably, in the long-term market, personnel and management circumstances will not comply perfectly with the building's present design. Perhaps it may then be time for a new major construction project, if corporate architecture at that point in time is still considered to constitute a fruitful way of achieving influence. Alternatively, perhaps, the material aspects may be reinterpreted. Signitivity can be modified to some extent so that the material features are regarded as harmonizing with social and cultural conditions other than those which applied when the material construction was created.

In saying this, I am not trying to speculate about the future but, instead, I am once again trying to link up with the convergence/divergence dimension (cf. Chapter 6). In a corporate context, consensus and discrepancy between corporate management and corporate material aspects may vary over time. When my study was conducted, there was good agreement between management and material circumstances. The building functioned as an effective signitive instrument primarily due to acceptance by the personnel, that is to say their ability to correctly interpret what the company and the building represented.

7.6   A Brief Flashback to the Development of Ritual Forms

Enator's brief history and its dynamic development mean that the ritual forms have not been stabilized and institutionalized in the same manner as in more traditional societies and organizations with a longer history. This becomes clear if we look back at the rites which have been described. These rites – morning meetings, the project management philosophy course, etc. – still continue in the same form as they did previously, but their content and degree of expressiveness seem to have changed with the passing of time, and to have become diluted, compared with their original significance.

Employees who were with the company for its initial five to six years feel, for example, that morning meetings no longer have quite the same character as they did in the past. Originally, consultants felt that they participated in central management issues, such as business developments. Today, they primarily receive information about their own subsidiary and its management. The dynamic, intensive atmosphere concerning what was happening and what top management was doing is no longer experienced to the same extent. This is virtually unavoidable in view of the company's increasing maturity and size.

The exchange of information which previously characterized morning meetings expressed a sense of community, closeness, confidence and affinity between the company, its owners and its staff. As Feldman and March (1981) put it, information may often function as a symbol, with both unconscious and conscious aspects. When the idealized and glorified heroic figures (that is to say the founders) provide inside information, in particular confidential information in a dramatized form, they involve the imagination of employees in the battle for the company's survival, success and ultimate triumph. Morning meetings in the first years of the company may be regarded as an arena or a stage which obliterated the dividing line between observers and participants, and in which observers felt that they were participants.

In recent years, the most important actors in the morning meetings have disappeared and the platform for their performances has shifted. The owners are dealing with business at a stage which is far removed from the everyday work of consultants and the sense of affinity which characterizes the subsidiaries. Morning meetings and similar opportunities for contacts are separated from corporate management and business development on a broader company-wide scale. Consultants still receive information but this is felt to be largely neutral items of more limited interest. As one interviewee with nine years of experience in the company put it:

> The founders pushed ahead with development. But the subsidiary Managing Directors seemed to be more interested in management and administration. If you remove someone with creative ideas who makes things happen, you lose a lot of information, of course. The next generation lack the same forcefulness. They just try to realize their own role. And the other aspects – the perspective for the future, wild ideas, etc. – are lacking. They too are just passive observers.

Developments suggest that institutionalized forms at Enator have changed in character slightly over time, which implies a shift in their social role and significance. In contrast with the rites and rituals which anthropologists speak of when they study relatively stable societies, the corresponding phenomena in organizations often demonstrate a more superficial and fluid character. The stability of the expressive content of Enator's forms of action which are of a ritual nature is rather weak. In the course of just a few years, the meaning and expressive content of a particular rite may be changed dramatically due to its heavy dependence on external social factors, the development status of the company and the presence of actors who set their stamp on the situation. As a result, the character of the cultural forms will be determined by the situation-specific circumstances to at least the same extent as it is by historical-cultural features which, over time, reproduce a specific symbolic content. In an organization with a historically developed, established distinct (local) culture the expressive-affective dimension is less situationally dependent. Rites, rituals, symbolism, etc. have an impact on the feelings and consciousness of the collective, which is relatively little affected by the presence of specific key individuals and which is not influenced by the company's specific external situation. In this case, the culture is more "self-propelling".

Quarterly conferences, morning meetings and other types of arrangements and activities have been institutionalized at Enator. However, the degree of institutionalization and reproduction differs as regards form and structure, and also content, meaning and social function. The forms for achieving good information, a sense of common interest and participation in the company remain, while the meaning and thus also the consequences of these forms have been partly changed. A morning meeting at Enator in 1987 seems to have a lower expressive content than it did in 1980, thus producing a lower degree of closeness, cohesiveness and participation.

It is no doubt unrealistic to attempt to achieve the same kind of climate which characterized the company in its initial years, and perhaps it would not be desirable either. An established, large-scale company cannot function in the same manner as a newly-established, dramatically expanding company in its entrepreneurial phase.

7.7   Comments on Rites and Other Symbolic Forms at Enator

The rites and other symbolic forms which have been described can be characterized in various ways. Two different types of categorization will be briefly summarized here. One simple way of illustrating symbols and their functions is to assume a dualistic perspective following Daft (1983). Here, it is imagined that symbols exist on a continuum where the instrumental-functional elements can be found at one extreme and the social-expressive at the other. The former is a question of symbols which serve to facilitate the performance of work tasks, while the latter represent emotional and social satisfaction and the social integration of activities.

We can therefore imagine Figure 7.2 depicting the rites described above and the other symbolic forms.

Naturally, it is not possible to determine the "correct" placement of the various symbolic forms in the diagram exactly. The boundary lines between socio-emotional and instrumental factors are fluid.

Some of the symbolic forms vary considerably in socio-emotional and instrumental content. For example, the managing director tries to control the contents of the Big-cof events in accordance with what he considers to be most desirable. Sometimes reinforcement of social ties is the aim; once a year the budget is discussed. Of course, the budget may also – like everything else – be seen as highly symbolic, but budget discussions seldom attain the same socio-emotional level as (successful) social events, engineered to foster a sense of community in the company.

Another way of describing rites is to assume a typology of various types of rites. Trice and Beyer (1984, 1985) propose six kinds of rites.

Rites of passage, experienced by people whose status changes, serve to facilitate adoption of the new role. Such rites occur, for example, when entering an organization, receiving a promotion or resigning.

Demotion rites occur when someone loses power and status. It may be supposed that this does not merely apply to individuals but also to groups,

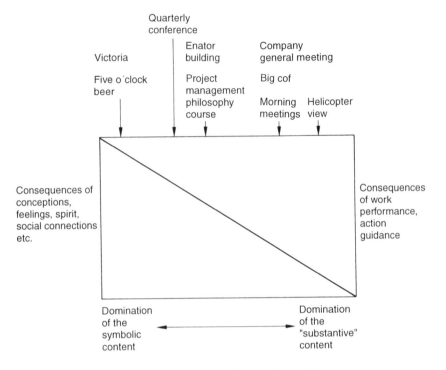

Figure 7.2:   Charting the cultural forms of expression at Enator

departments, projects, etc. Demotion rites can probably often be included under the rites of passage heading, since they denote a more or less drastic change in status.

Reinforcement rites are organized, expressively loaded activities which emphasize social identity and confirm members who have done something which is considered to be appropriate. Rewards of a public nature are one example.

Renewal rites involve ideas about the development of social structures and practices. This is not necessarily a question of real, deep change in material terms – if this were so, it would hardly be possible to talk in terms of rites – but it is primarily a case of social activity signalling renewal. Organizational development activities might be one example in this context.

Conflict reduction rites are a matter of handling conflicts and aggression. One illustration might be negotiations between management and trade unions.

Integration rites involve encouraging and maintaining common feelings, linking people together and maintaining adherence to a particular social system.

In parallel with these specific characteristics and functions which distinguish each type of rite, there are also fundamental common features and functions. Rites are organized and planned. They have an expressive content and are of a more or less public nature. Their function (to use a contested term) is to transmit and reinforce the values, beliefs and norms which characterize the culture, and to maintain cultural stability and cultural integration.

In the Enator case, the project management philosophy course provides a good example of a rite of passage, or more precisely an initiation rite. As far as newly appointed and internally recruited subsidiary managers are concerned, initiation into managing director activities, such as Big-cof, presumably also serves as a kind of rite of passage.

There is a notable absence of demotion rites in the company, at least in a strict sense. There are no instances of a sinner publicly handing over his belt and sweater with the Enator logo to his managing director in the reception area. When somebody is dismissed, this is done quietly and the circumstances and processes vary. I do not feel that it is meaningful to force the concept of rites to cover the cases which I am acquainted with.

None of the rites described above are principally reinforcement rites. However, particularly in Enator's initial years, there were clear examples of reinforcement rites. If someone achieved a particularly good performance, for example implemented a project on time and with appropriate expenditure, this was followed up by a demonstration of approval and rapid and effective publicity. Individuals were sometimes rewarded with the opening of a bottle of champagne relatively frequently. A positive and confirmative approach still applies within the company, but perhaps the strength of such reinforcement acts has been diminished.

The meaningfulness of referring to specific renewal rites at Enator may be discussed. In a company which is ten years old and rapidly expanding in a dynamic industry, renewal is of such a comprehensive nature that it exceeds the content of specific rites by a wide margin. Naturally, there are many rites connected with various new features, such as the inauguration of new offices, but in such cases renewal indicates the context of such rites (the reason for them), not merely their content. However, certain reorganizations and the burgeoning of new companies can be seen, to some extent, as symbolic expressions of renewal. New companies are regarded as an expression of vitality.

Conflict-reduction rites imply that a conflict has occurred or is emerging. So far, conflicts have been relatively unusual at Enator. There is no special institution in which conflict reduction has a prominent function –

such as co-determination or discussion groups in the health-care field. On the other hand, the managing directors meet staff representatives on a regular basis (there is no union at Enator). Within the company, certain types of regular meetings probably involve this type of feature – for example the control groups which are assigned to follow up and manage consultancy projects are composed of both Enator personnel and customer representatives, and there has been an attempt here to build in elements which counteract dissension and conflict. In certain circumstances, contracts, the minutes of meetings, regular reports on the current situation, joint social activities, etc. may be regarded as rites with conflict-reducing qualities.

Finally, Enator provides many and impressive examples of integration rites. Victoria, the quarterly conferences, the five o'clock beer ceremony, Big-cof and the general meeting may all be regarded as integration rites. The heavy emphasis on large-scale integration rites may be regarded as a reflection of the corporate structure and its methods of operation. Subdivision into a number of subsidiaries and projects which are loosely linked with other activities within the company involves disintegration tendencies. This means that integration rites are of particular importance.

7.8   The Depth of Symbolism

At the beginning of this chapter, I wondered about the complexity and depth of the organizational symbolism. What I am referring to here is the extent to which unambiguous, conscious, simple and readily comprehensible symbols are involved, where an actor with good insights has an excellent overview and some control over these symbols, or whether the symbolism is complex, more or less unconscious, hidden and difficult to handle in a "rational" manner for the collective which gives such symbolism its meaning.

In organizations, as with psychological and social life in general, there are different types of symbols and symbolism, either simple or complex (Morgan et al., 1983). In this chapter, I have introduced symbolism which may be said to be part of the corporate culture, as this concept is conventionally defined. This means that many of the most complicated and deep symbolic patterns are ignored. The focus is on company-specific systems of values, norms, beliefs and symbolic forms.

Enator is a young company. On the whole, control in terms of values, ideals, norms of behaviour, etc. has been straightforward and open. There has been a clear articulation of the corporate philosophy and the "culture" which the company has aimed at. The level of consciousness in this context tends to be relatively great. In my opinion, it cannot be claimed that the collective has incorporated these aspects of culture at any deeper, more or less subconscious level.

According to Schein (1985), the methods successfully employed to handle organizations' internal and external problems tend, over time, to give rise to values regarding what is good and ultimately to assume the character of basic assumptions about various key dimensions for operations. An extended historical process is normally required if central principles of operation are to give rise to such basic assumptions, which are stable, effective and which control values and actions. As far as Enator is concerned, the youthfulness of the company means that company-specific values and beliefs cannot be meaningfully described as basic assumptions in line with Schein's definition.[1]

In fact, a certain "superficiality" characterizes the rites and other symbolic forms which are dealt with in this chapter. This, too, is connected with the fact that social patterns of action and activities, and the physical symbolism contained in Enator's building, etc., reflect management's intentions and its control of operations. In contrast with the rites that anthropologists normally study, rites that have emerged over a long time period and that are loaded with religious and historical significance as part of a culturally relatively stable context that determines the world of ideas for the collective in question, the rites that I have discussed are specifically introduced to achieve deliberately thought-through, socially desirable purposes in an effective manner. In this context, it would be appropriate to refer to "rational rites", which differ from "organic" rites. "Rational rites" are deliberately controlled and are expected to provide desirable financial and organizational outcomes. Of course, intentions are not always realized in practice.

Thus the complexity of the symbolism is hardly a matter of layer upon layer of meanings, but is often more a question of simple meanings. In the long run, the complexity of this symbolism will probably increase. In the long term, too, there will tend to be more stable and more solid foundations for the symbols in the company as a collective, assuming that personnel turnover remains at a low level and that the general business situation of the company does not change too drastically.

Naturally, it is possible to interpret the symbols I have described in terms of a deeper symbolism than I have attempted to indicate in this chapter. For example, the general meeting may be interpreted as a rite in which, apart from appropriate recognition of possible company-specific characteristics, broader capitalist industrial "sacred" values in the form of growth, profits and financial security, the guardians of such values (managing directors and the board) receive confirmation and legitimacy. But such an interpretation would be some way from what is normally regarded as corporate culture and from those aspects of operations which are of central interest in understanding how corporate management operates and how organizations function at a corporate-specific level, where attention is *not* normally paid to more general and fundamental cultural patterns and symbols.

7.9   Does Enator Form a Distinct Corporate Culture?

This question may seem somewhat strange in view of the fact that I have devoted considerable space to the characterization of its corporate culture. However, I have also signalled my scepticism of this concept, both in general and in relation to Enator. One argument against the concept of corporate culture is that companies and other organizations are not normally sufficiently distinct in relation to their environment to make it fruitful to claim that they have their own culture – "unitary and unique" (Van Maanen and Barley, 1985). It might also be argued that different types of cultures penetrate a company when different groups – social classes, professions, sexes, etc. – that are active in a company, bring their cultural patterns with them to their place of work. (For further discussion, see for example Alvesson, 1993a; Alvesson and Sandkull, 1988; Martin, 1992; Van Maanen and Barley, 1984.)

It is probably difficult to answer the question of whether a given social system has its "own" culture or not on the basis of "objective" measurements. In this case, such measurements would lead to rather different results, depending on how culture is defined and operationalized. This is, of course, always the case in strict attempts to achieve empirical studies – empirical reality takes different forms depending on the language used to describe it – but the theoretical and conceptual sensitivity of the "data" is particularly acute when dealing with complex and elusive phenomena such as culture.

Rather than referring the determination of the question of the existence of corporate cultures to the "data", we should be asking instead: When is it justified and fruitful to refer to corporate cultures? And in what circumstances is it probable that organizations develop distinct cultural patterns which give them special cultural characteristics vis-à-vis the society which surrounds them and the different industrial, occupational and class cultures which characterize this society?

Wilkins and Ouchi (1983) discuss this question, arguing that a distinct, local culture can only be established if the organization in question is characterized by members who have served in it for several years, by frequent interaction between different types of activity, and by the lack of what they call institutionalized alternatives, which means different types of cultures which members are clearly exposed to and which have a powerful influence on members of the organization. Wilkins and Ouchi are primarily thinking of Japanese companies, and Western companies influenced by the Japanese, and also, what are known as "total institutions" (e.g. the army, psychiatric hospitals, etc.). Van Maanen and Barley (1985) also point to frequent social interaction as a prerequisite for the development of a common set of meanings or culture.

History is another important factor. If the concept is not to be devalued, culture requires a history of development and a depth in the collective to which it corresponds. A distinct culture can certainly not be formed overnight, and an individual recruited into a new culture will not fully adopt it in a short time. The period required varies, due amongst other things to the distance between the previous culture and the new, the degree of socialization which occurs (i.e. the power and effectiveness of cultural influence) and the depth with which the values, ideals, meanings and other cultural attributes of the culture which has been left behind were absorbed. If someone rapidly adopts a new culture, something must be wrong somewhere, perhaps not in the reality ("the data") but in the logic. This is because, in this case, it is *not* a question of "rapid adoption" of a "new" culture, but perhaps more a matter of a similar or even, in the main, identical culture. Alternatively perhaps, it may be a question of superficial adaptation rather than genuine adoption. By definition, the adoption of a new culture takes time. The rapid adoption of a new culture (a different value or meaning system) is a contradiction in terms.

The clarification of mechanisms reinforcing or weakening tendencies to the formation of a distinct set of local meanings in an organizational context is important if we are to be able to assess the depth of a corporate culture, and to understand its stability, and its impact on thinking and action.

An important argument which indicates the (meaningfulness of talking about the) existence of a specific local culture at Enator is that the company contains a relatively homogenous collection of human beings. Few organizations of this size would appear to have so little differentiation as regards the people working within it. The overwhelming majority of the employees are computer consultants. Thus, there is almost a total overlap in the company between the two social and cultural categories of the profession and the organization. In other contexts, it is common for professions to form sub-groups in relation to the organization as a whole, which then leads to internal differentiation in social and cultural respects (Van Maanen and Barley, 1984).

Age is another aspect of homogeneity (cf. Hofstede et al., 1990). The overwhelming majority of the employees are in the age-range 25 to 45. A third aspect is recruitment. Apart from recruiting people with similar education and professional background and in the same age-range, the company also endeavours to recruit people with certain personality characteristics. Employees should be flexible, extroverted and want to work in a team – lone wolves and narrowly focused experts are avoided. Although, in practice, different types of personalities are recruited, there is probably a tendency towards a certain standardization in the type of employee taken on.

A spirit of comradeship may also be regarded as a culture-generating mechanism. Cohesion is seen as good – employees mix socially to a great extent with colleagues. The dividing line between working life and leisure becomes indistinct. All these factors mean that the company becomes an important part of the employee's social identity.

Another aspect of this spirit of closeness is that hierarchical divisions are weaker than in many traditional places of work. This is partly because Enator is a knowledge-intensive service company which cannot be managed as a bureaucracy as regards hierarchical relationships, for example, and partly because of the youthfulness of the company, relatively young managers and the fact that the corporate philosophy encourages a spirit of comradeship rather than a patriarchic approach. It can thus be said that social links, both vertically and horizontally, are relatively common. Several joint activities contribute to this (Victoria, quarterly conferences, etc.).

In this context, Enator's minimal personnel turnover should also be noted. No statistics are available, but everyone claims that this figure is extremely low, perhaps approaching 5% in most years. A considerable number of people who started working for Enator soon after it was set up are still employed by the company. And those who have more than five years or so behind them in an activity with significant social influence are probably capable of being bearers and transmitters of a certain workplace culture.

The most important reason for speaking of a specific corporate culture is its relatively special characteristics vis-à-vis the environment. Naturally, the possibility of demonstrating such special characteristics is a prerequisite for discussing corporate culture. Many of the values, norms, beliefs and rites and other symbolic expressions of the culture differ from current practice in Swedish society and industry. Possibly Enator differs less from other young and expanding knowledge-intensive companies. Presumably the Enator culture and the "industry culture" overlap. There are, for example, many similarities between the points discussed in this chapter and the engineering division of a high-tech company studied by Kunda (1992)[2] even though this company is a very large, American and in manufacturing rather than consultancy. There are also similarities with other high-tech companies described in the literature and I will come back to this later in the book. Even though there are other similar companies, one can still say that there is some empirical "evidence" that Enator has, in a particular sense, a distinct corporate culture compared with companies in general. However, this does not constitute final proof since it is hard to determine the extent and the depth of these special characteristics. It must also be emphasized that the "data" is always constructed (an outcome of interpretation) and can be interpreted in different ways.

Thus, there are several good reasons for regarding Enator as a special and distinct, although not entirely unique, corporate culture. There are, however, also good reasons for arguing the contrary. One general counter-argument is that Enator, in common with other companies, does not have fixed boundaries with the environment. If we confine ourselves to the Swedish side of the company, this bears the rather clear imprint of Swedish culture, with its relative equality and softer style at work.[3] Personnel have also been socialized for 20-40 years before being employed at Enator, and this experience naturally leaves its mark on them and establishes limits for the "deflection of" values, beliefs, thinking, social contacts, etc. in a company-specific manner.

Although some employees have been with the company for a long time and may be assumed to have internalized the "corporate culture", this nonetheless only involves a small minority. Since Enator had an average of 250 employees in 1984 and some of these have no doubt resigned since then, this means that approximately 60% of those who were working in the company in 1987 had been there for less than three years.

However, the question of the fruitfulness of referring to a corporate culture is not solely dependent on the number of employees who accept this culture in a deeper sense. Culture is a comprehensive concept and its possible existence at the corporate level cannot be reduced simply to a question of the number of individuals. The extent to which this culture characterizes thinking and action in specific organizational contexts is equally important. Since many of the key figures in the company – for example many managers of major subsidiaries and the experienced project managers – have long experience of the company and may be regarded as bearers of company-specific values and beliefs, such individuals have greater weight and depth in the ideational world of the corporate collective. However, the considerable number of employees who have only worked for Enator for a couple of years makes use of the culture concept to describe the overall collective in terms of "deep meanings" somewhat debatable.

The fact that many of the employees in the company appear to adopt the style which characterizes the company relatively rapidly also indicates that some doubt should be expressed when speaking of a specific culture.

As I have already mentioned above, one measure of the degree of distinctiveness of a culture may be the time it takes for new entrants to the culture to become immersed in it, and in this respect Enator is not so different from other companies in the same area of operations from a cultural point of view. However, a standardized recruitment policy weakens this line of argument to some extent. People whose personalities are regarded as different from the company "culture" are not recruited.

Enator's dynamic expansion, with substantial numbers of new employees and the setting-up of an increasing number of subsidiaries also means that it is doubtful whether it is possible to speak of a corporate culture worthy of the name, that is to say, which is adopted by a majority of the total number of employees with a certain degree of depth and comprehensiveness as regards values, beliefs, etc. When Enator was a small company and the three founder members made their mark on operations, there was a powerful and homogenous influence on all employees. Constant interaction between everyone in the entire company paved the way at that time for a common approach and the development of joint values, but as operations expanded these patterns were presumably weakened.

The age of the company is not irrelevant either. The development of a culture which is firmly based in a collective and which has made its mark on the consciousness and ideas of organization members at a deeper level takes time. Rites and other forms of symbolism must function independently of individuals and situationally-specific circumstances. Traditions, and the weight and the sense of sacredness which may be transmitted by such traditions, hardly exist.

Finally, I would like to highlight the nature of consultancy work and the extremely open contacts with the environment which this involves. Most employees work with customers, spending as much time with customer personnel as with Enator staff. This means that Enator's cultural boundaries are fluid. Presumably, inputs in the form of ideas, values, approaches, thinking, styles, methods, etc. are as likely to come from the outside as they are from Enator. As far as Enator personnel are concerned, there is no shortage of "institutionalized alternatives" (Wilkins and Ouchi, 1983) and thus, this criterion for the formation of a distinct culture is not fulfilled at all at Enator.

Thus, there are several reasons which argue both for and against the idea of an "Enator corporate culture". I prefer not to follow the usual path of emphasizing one line of argument at the expense of the other. Instead, I would like to demonstrate the difficulties of employing the corporate culture concept and I want to indicate which aspects should be taken into account, before deciding whether or not to use the corporate culture concept.

In the case of Enator, I feel that it is possible to refer to a corporate
culture, although with some hesitation. In this case, it is rather a question
of a corporate culture in the making, with a set of values and norms and a
tradition of certain social forms which heavily characterize the core of the
company, primarily the oldest subsidiary, Affärssystem, and the more senior members of the organization. The majority of the organizational collective tend to identify with the ideas and values of corporation. There is
no doubt that corporate culture as a management strategy exists. This
strategy is systematic and effectively carried out, but an endeavour of this
kind hardly results in total "mastery" of the overall cultural pattern in the
company. This intention is only partially realized.

I also consider that there are better reasons for referring to a corporate
culture in the case of Enator than in most other companies. My impression
is that there is a greater incidence of common values and ideas, and symbolic forms which have a distinct character, in comparison with many
other organizations.

When I refer to Enator's corporate culture, I thus do so in full awareness of the fact that the ice under my feet is not very solid and that many
other writers who consider that companies have a culture of their own are
walking on even thinner ice. A more cautious and possibly more useful
concept in this context is that of "organizational climate". Let us examine
this concept and see what Enator looks like from this perspective.

7.10   Organizational Climate at Enator

It is not easy to employ the organizational climate concept – any more
than it is to use the cultural concept. There is also considerable disagreement and criticism between different authors in their manner of employing
the concept of climate (Ekvall, 1985). Sometimes, there is a tendency to
speak of climate in evaluative terms, which means that the concept overlaps with what is normally referred to as job satisfaction and enjoyment.
Sometimes the climatic concept is employed as if it were analogous with
culture. Payne (referred to by Ekvall, 1985, p 5) defines organizational
climate as "comprehensive concepts which reflect the content and force of
values, norms, attitudes, behaviour and feelings which characterize a social
system". Many organization-culture researchers characterize their objects
of study in this way nowadays. It is understandable that climate researchers may draw the conclusion that current writings about organization
culture are quite simply a repetition of the idea of an organizational climate. Ashforth (1985) notes that when the term "culture" became popular
in the 1980s, less was written about climate. However, there are good rea-

sons for distinguishing organizational culture and climate approaches, even if a certain overlap is probably unavoidable.

The cultural concept represents a deeper, more comprehensive and more total phenomenon, which grows over time and is relatively durable. Climate may also share these characteristics but its scope in terms of time, depth and comprehensiveness is more restricted. If a company experiences a drastic change, this may affect the climate relatively directly but will only influence the culture indirectly and gradually. Culture represents values, norms, meanings and symbolic forms, while climate denotes feelings and perceptions of organizational circumstances with affective connotations which are shared by a collective. The climate is close to experience, while culture underlies and contributes to the determination of experiences. Despite a certain inevitable overlap between the two concepts, one should be careful to avoid confusing them (Ashforth, 1985; Ekvall, 1986). A phenomenon which is superficially similar takes on a different aspect if it is regarded as a cultural or as a climatic phenomenon. Being "positive" may be a value or a norm and comes under the heading of culture. It can also be a denotation of climate, but is then an experienced realization of the culture. It can be imagined that the values and norms exist, but that various non-cultural circumstances, for example resource constraints, create a situation in which the climate, in this context, is not experienced as "positive".

Expressed in the most simple manner it might be said that climate is influenced by both culture and other circumstances. Ashforth (1985) claims, for example, that the work group, corporate culture, management and the physical environment determine climate. In addition, I consider that external circumstances such as the market situation may also be crucial. Corporate growth and success may, for example, contribute to the creation of a certain climate. This will be discussed further at a later stage. But first a few words about what especially characterizes the company spirit and the climate at Enator. (Company spirit and climate are employed analogously.)

The company spirit at Enator may be described as extremely good, on the whole, at least according to interviewees:

The spirit is rough but sincere. We have a fine spirit of working here (Subsidiary manager).
There is a relaxed style. People don't hesitate to laugh or make slightly sarcastic comments. At the same time, we are also nice to each other (Subsidiary manager).
We have a great team here at this company. We have a lot of fun together. I have some critical views about Enator but I really enjoy myself a lot. I would find it hard to imagine moving over to another job. It's a lot of fun here, both professionally and, as far as I am concerned, personally. I have made an enormous number of friends through Enator. I'm very happy here. But I don't believe that everyone has

as good a time as I do and I doubt if I will see things the same way in 5 years time, if I'm still here (Consultant).

The last sentence indicates that there are clear variations as regards attitudes and personalities among the employees and their degree of extroversion and social talents. There are also variations as regards the way their own interests fit in with the leisure activities organized by the company, which are an extremely important ingredient in the company spirit. Another difference is the individual's positioning as regards life cycles and also in relation to the company's development. As one consultant put it: "You get most out of Enator if you don't just devote your working time to the company, but also a considerable proportion of your spare time to the social activities." Enator is particularly attractive to single employees of both sexes.[4] And perhaps Enator finds single employees to be the most attractive employee category.

There is some difference in the climate between those who were with the company right from the start, that is to say the actual entrepreneurial phase until the early 1980s, and people who are relatively new employees. Recent recruits are not distributed evenly throughout the organization – many veterans are working in the older subsidiaries, particularly at Enator Affärssystem (Enator Business Systems).

The climate at Affärssystem and amongst many long-time employees is characterized by considerable loyalty, cohesion and a good company spirit, but it may also be noted that the degree of energy devoted to activities may have declined somewhat, and that there has been a loss of close contacts with the founder-managers and consequently a reduced sense of being at the centre of events. After the founders disappeared from the central focus at Enator, many individual employees felt slightly depressed:

The intensive spirit which existed when John, Christer and Hasse were there and kept the team together doesn't really exist any more (Consultant).
When Christer, John or Hasse were no longer managing directors at Affärssystem and somebody else came along, you started to lose your grasp of the whole operation. Something was missing. The original managing directors were important and they established the tone ... . Now we've got used to things. But it was damn hard work for a time, when things broke up, say in 1985-86. That was when John, Christer and Hasse began to sail away and disappear into the shadows out there (Consultant).

While the older generation of employees are characterized by a strong and deep feeling for the company and long-standing feelings of comradeship within the company, younger personnel have, according to interviewees, a more "egoistic" approach to Enator. They are primarily interested in getting something out of the company. Most of the employees who resign have only been with the company for a short time, which is normal, *per se*.

Obviously, it always takes time before strong loyalty to the company is developed, but the difference between the older and the newer generations is also a question of at which phase in the company's history they were recruited. Participating in the build-up phase – with its greater intensity and spirit of close comradeship – produces a form of collective identification which is different from that experienced by people who join when guidelines have already been laid down for some time and when the degree of emotional intensity is no longer so high.

Nonetheless, the organizational climate is characterized by social closeness, a feeling of comradeship, informality, enthusiasm and a go-ahead spirit. Conflicts appear to be extremely unusual, at least in relation to the normal state of affairs in companies and other organizations (Frost, 1987; Pfeffer, 1981b; Robbins, 1983; etc.).

If we compare things with my previous company, they used to solve every problem by restructuring things and putting in new people. ... And then they just let things happen and let the strongest man win. That's totally different from what happens here (Consultant).

The top-management group, in particular, is characterized by excellent cohesion and a low level of conflict.

There is an extremely strong feeling of belonging, extremely strong links between the managing directors. They constitute a fully merged team who look after each other and their interests. They don't all love each other 100%, however. They have their personal differences. And of course they have conflicting interests in business, but ... (Consultant).

These statements sound very positive. However, there is also a negative side to the picture – a tendency to be unwilling to accept criticism and possibly also new ideas. At least this is how some employees regard the situation. One manager referred to Enator's management as a "mutual admiration club":

People tell each other within a small group how good they are and fail to check how things are in their environment.

The same individual considered that it was difficult for new employees to get someone to listen to their ideas and suggestions:

I had the feeling that they didn't believe that people who came from the outside really could contribute anything.

Several people also mentioned the pressure to be positive, to avoid criticism and to express their enthusiasm. As one consultant put it:

Sometimes you can feel that Enator is so fantastic that you ought to be grateful for being allowed to work for the company. In my previous job, there was also a lot of social contact, but it wasn't pushed so hard.

Thus, the organizational climate is not purely a matter of "positive" features, but there are also elements which may be felt to be frustrating and which hamper criticism, re-examination and new approaches.

Naturally, the climate is imbued with the idea that this is a young, rapidly growing company, which is highly successful. One natural spin-off effect is enthusiasm, and also a tendency for reduced levels of conflict. There is not so much to argue about in a company which is financially successful in a growing market, compared with the situation in a restricted market with pressure on internal resources, requiring sharp elbow-work to stop colleagues from grabbing all the best pieces of the cake. It is an open question how the organizational climate and the level of conflict develop in a tougher market situation.

However, it would be a mistake to reduce the corporate culture and the organizational climate to a mere reflection of the fact that this is a newly-established company working in an expanding market. Other forces and factors of influence also enter into the picture.

7.11   What Determines the Corporate Culture and the Organizational Climate?

As I have indicated previously, it is difficult to fully separate corporate culture and organizational climate. However, the fact that they are linked does not mean that they are identical phenomena. Culture is deeper, more permanent, less easily influenced and involves values, attitudes and assumptions that tend to be taken for granted. Climate, on the other hand, is much more directly amenable to social influence. Events, success and other factors affect the climate much more clearly than the culture. The culture only changes in a restricted sense, indirectly and slowly, as a result of external social and economic factors. To some extent, the initial phase when the company is being built up is an exception. Here, the establishment of cultural patterns is reinforced if actions, statements and measures which express a culture in the making are regarded by the collective as performing a useful function in relation to desired objectives, and are hence considered to be "positive", "good" and "true" (Schein, 1985). In the next chapter, I will be returning to this process in the case of Enator and will examine the company's historic development from a cultural perspective. I will also attempt to analyze the importance of management and leadership.

Enator's rapid growth and success affect the climate. There are clear signs of a collective with the wind in its sails. In addition, the corporate culture influences the climate. Naturally, values, norms, rites and ceremonies and other cultural expressions affect the climate and the company spirit. This is true to some extent by definition, but, in principle, identical or at least similar climates can occur in different types of cultures and an identical culture can co-exist with different types of climate. This is because the climate is also affected by other circumstances. One such circumstance has already been mentioned: success and growth, which are of course largely determined by favourable external factors – primarily an expanding market for data consultancy services in the 1970s and the 1980s. The "image" which permeates Enator – a young, dynamic, attractive, successful and well-known company which has attracted attention in the media in Sweden – also affects the climate (and vice versa).

Another important factor is the composition of personnel. In 1986, 70% of the total staff were under 35. This means that the personnel were not only young but also a remarkably homogenous group in other respects, such as profession and education. A further factor is that Enator is in a good position to recruit new employees and that social criteria are regarded as an important factor in the recruitment process. Activities designed to create feelings of satisfaction in the workplace are more in focus at Enator than in many other organizations.

In certain respects, the management group is also homogenous. Of the 25 top managers in 1986, 19 were aged between 40 and 46. Most of the rest were a few years younger (Enator's annual report, 1986). All of them were men.

As I have previously mentioned, social homogeneity means a better chance of creating a corporate culture worthy of the name. However, the impact on work place satisfaction and climate aspects is greater and more direct. Agreeable working relationships and social cohesion affect the organizational climate rather directly, but it is considerably less certain that they will exert an influence at the cultural level, i.e. on deeper values, ideas and meanings.

What factors influence corporate culture? No doubt the organizational climate plays its part. A positive environment increases the probability of the occurrence of social learning, which means that people influence each other and that the ideas of key figures are likely to be accepted. There tends to be less involvement in a neutral or negative environment. However, the relationship between a positive climate and cultural influence is not at all clear. Social influence and cultural effects on approaches and attitudes occur even in anxiety-loaded contexts – one frequently quoted example in the corporate sphere is ITT under Geneen (Deal and Kennedy, 1982), another is the FBI under Hoover (Kets de Vries, 1980).

A rapid survey of the literature of organizational cultures indicates that it is commonly believed that leadership, particularly when exercised in the early social development of the organization, both in the establishment of the company and in the handling of major crises, is most significant for the development of corporate culture. Deal and Kennedy (1982), Peters and Waterman (1982) and Pfeffer (1981a) are all proponents of the management angle. The social learning approach has been highlighted by Schein (1985) who, however, also stresses the role of the founder/leader. Other ideas, mentioned above, about what may lead to cohesive cultural patterns have been presented by Wilkins and Ouchi (1983), who consider that the factors which determine whether a distinct, local culture emerges or not are largely determined by social interaction between the members of a collective (a society, a group, etc.), long-term membership of such a collective and the absence of strong social and cultural influences from sources outside the organization in question. Van Maanen and Barley (1984) consider that "occupational communities" within an organization determine the cultures or sub-cultures which exist in every organization. I have emphasized, in other contexts, the importance of typical conditions of work for cultural situations in the workplace and the influence of the macro-cultures which constitute the organizational context in society, at the regional level and in the industry concerned (Alvesson, 1993a).

Most people would agree that an organizational culture is formed and developed as a result of several complex interactions between factors at different levels – ranging from societal and historical forces to the influence of key actors and important events in early, critical stages in the organization's development. Practically all the above-mentioned possible determinative factors are relevant in understanding Enator's corporate culture. One obvious point at Enator is the influence exerted by the founders and their leadership as major determinative factors. It is not clear whether this is equally important in the longer term, but when my study was conducted this influence was tangible. I will return to this in the next chapter.

The professional activities involved – computer consultancy services – affected to some extent by management and business ideas about how such services should be undertaken – also sets its stamp on the culture of such activities (cf. Hofstede et al., 1990; Sackmann, 1992). In this case we have well-educated and competent personnel who are interested in what they are doing. The actual work is either individual and independent – investigations or other one man-assignments – or it may involve project groups which function autonomously in relation to other areas of operations. The assignment-based nature of all project activities should also be noted in this context. This contributes to the fact that bureaucratic tendencies in the organization – formal hierarchy, standardization and formalization of work assignments, separation of planning and implementation operations, directly supervisory management, etc. – are not particularly central features. Flexibility, informality and other anti-bureaucratic values are associated with this form of organization. The self-governance which is implicit in operations creates, *per se*, what amounts to a strong need for social-integrative actions, which are then reflected in the rites which have been described.

The professional nature of operations and the qualified nature of personnel means that an extensive social differentiation does not divide the organization into two or more class-determined cultures. A company with an even distribution of highly different personnel groups, ranging from directors and qualified professionals to clerks and unskilled workers, provides a considerably more heterogeneous social and cultural picture. Enator's high degree of personnel homogeneity facilitates the reflection of cohesiveness, affinity and equality in the symbolic operations and value structures, as compared with hierarchy and social differences. At Enator, for example, it is possible to let *all* new employees participate in the project management philosophy course, thus signalling equality. This is something which would probably be considerably more difficult to apply in an organization with a heterogeneous labour force.

7.12 Summary

In contrast with the rest of this book, where culture is employed as a metaphor rather than as a sub-system, this chapter has treated corporate culture as a specific part of the company, encompassing the values, norms, beliefs and symbolic forms which are particularly emphasized by management. Such values etc. characterize large areas of the company and contribute to binding the collective of organizational members together. This means that those values and symbols that management attempts to control are highlighted. This is a relatively limited cross-section of the "total" culture in the company, even if this cross-section is crucial for the functioning of the organization.

The functional, rational and intentional elements of the corporate culture have been stressed, and also the somewhat "superficial" character of this culture. One important conclusion is that the youthfulness of the company and its rapid expansion mean that it is doubtful if it is possible to speak of a culture in a deeper sense, as synonymous with shared orientations which are based and stabilized in the organizational collective at a deeper level. On the other hand, the company demonstrates considerable originality and many special features, particularly regarding cultural expressions (symbols). It is possible to illustrate cultures (tendencies to form distinct cultural patterns) in terms of historic, social, psychological and "artefactual" penetration (Louis, 1985; Saffold, 1988). These concepts indicate various aspects of the range and depth of a culture. As far as Enator is concerned, these dimensions point in somewhat different directions. Historic penetration – stability over time as regards common attitudes and values – is weak, as has already been pointed out. But social penetration – that is to say impact throughout the entire organization – may be considered to be strong. The other two concepts lie somewhere in between. Psychological penetration represents consistency and homogeneity as regards the manner in which common values and ideals are precisely perceived, while artefactual penetration denotes the extent to which the culture is embodied in specific forms and expressions. Since Enator staff have had varying periods of service with the company and relatively different experience as regards projects, which often take place at the customer's place of work, a question-mark can be applied as regards the depth of psychological penetration, even if recruitment and management influence contribute to the homogenization of attitudes within the company. Artefactual penetration is probably relatively strong in view of the investment in corporate architecture, interior decoration and rites. At the same time, it may be noted that some of these rites are of a somewhat artificial nature and that their impact may have been weakened over time. On the whole, these four criteria indicate that unambiguous conclusions as to the depth and the distinct character of the corporate culture should be avoided.

It would appear to be fruitful to distinguish between *corporate culture as an intention* (management strategy) and as an *outcome* (the existence of distinct, local cultures in a company). It is true that the outcome does not necessarily have to be preceded by a deliberate endeavour. On the whole, the formation of a corporate culture is the result of processes which emerge organically, rather than the result of attempts to create a culture. In the case of Enator, however, the intentions are clear and strong. Corporate culture is thus undeniably an appropriate description of management's powerful efforts to influence values, norms and social cohesion within the organization. The concept of corporate culture encompasses this endeavour well in the case of Enator. In terms of outcomes, it would appear to be more doubtful whether Enator "has" a distinct culture of any depth (is best described in such terms). However, from the management's point of view, the leadership strategy may be said to be broadly successful – the organization is apparently permeated to a relatively high degree by the values and ideas advocated by the management.

One way of summarizing this viewpoint is to regard the concept of corporate culture – as I have used it – as a synthesis of two metaphors: the cultural and instrumental metaphors. Thus, corporate culture denotes the fusion of an endeavour to use corporate culture as a tool to achieve something and the partial realization of this in the form of certain distinct cultural values. My aim here is to spotlight the central role of the instrumental metaphor to illustrate what Enator's corporate culture refers to.

Another, more general contribution in this chapter concerns discussion of indications of a "corporate culture" worthy of the name – that is to say which means something more, something deeper, more stable and more uniform than an organizational climate. Among other things, a number of important dimensions were noted which should be taken into account in attempting to understand the extent to which we may speak of the existence of a corporate culture in the sense of a set of values, norms and ideas distinct for the company and broadly shared among managers and other employees. As far as Enator is concerned – and this applies in principle to all companies – age, the professional situation, the total/inclusive character of the organization, the degree of closure/openness as regards boundaries with the environment, expansion, length of service with the company, intensity of the corporate spirit and congruity in recruitment are highly important factors.

The concept of organizational climate has also been discussed. In my opinion, this is less "pretentious" than the cultural concept and as a result has more general application. But the climate concept also explains less. The relationship between organizational climate and corporate culture has been discussed. Climate was regarded as a phenomenon which is rather close to the behavioural and experience levels and is easier to observe than culture. It is also more limited as regards time, space, durability and depth, reacts more strongly to external change and is partially determined by culture. To some extent, culture demonstrates the opposite characteristics, compared with climate. However, the two concepts also overlap.

Leadership/management is one important factor influencing corporate culture and organizational climate which has not been discussed. But leadership/management is probably important in new companies managed by their owners. The next chapter is devoted to these issues.

Notes

[1]   As pointed out in Alvesson (1993a), Schein's own empirical examples hardly correspond to his theoretical definition of basic assumptions. The examples concern relatively superficial aspects rather than deeper taken-for-granted assumptions.

[2]   According to Kunda (1992, p 90): "Internally, Tech's distinct principles of organization are captured in the notion of 'culture' as opposed to 'structure'. Traditional forms of control associated with bureaucracy are relegated to a supporting role. Instead, control is thought of as the internalization of disci-

pline reflected in the attitudes, orientations, and emotions of committed members. The company is presented as informal and flexible, and its management as demanding yet trusting. The community is characterized as 'bottom-up', loose, free, a 'people company'. Discipline is not based on explicit supervision and reward, but rather on peer pressure and, more crucially, internalized standards for performance. There is little mention of the economic structure, and the importance of economic rewards is underplayed, even frowned upon. It is a fact of life, but not one to be emphasized; instead, rewards are seen as arising from the experience of communion, of belonging, of participation in the community as organizationally defined."

[3]   See Hofstede (1980), for example. I would thus maintain that Enator has certain special characteristics in comparison with Swedish society while, at the same time, this society has clearly left its imprint on the company and its local culture. These special characteristics apply in particular at a somewhat superficial and more obvious level, in the form of special activities and customs.

[4]   I have not found any variation between male and female interviewees in tems of reported satisfaction with the workplace.

8 Leadership as Social Integrative Action

In this chapter, I shall be dealing with certain features of the management of Enator which formed the basis for the functioning of the organization and the cultural patterns described in the previous chapter. I treat how leadership was exercised by the founders when Enator was being built up. The primary focus in the chapter is, however, leadership at the point in time when my study was conducted – which may to some extent be regarded as an extension of the action patterns and norms developed and institutionalized by the founders. Emphasis is here on the way in which leadership is exercized by subsidiary managers. The managers concerned can then be seen as belonging to the upper middle level of management. The emphasis in the chapter is thus a bit different from what is common in leadership research, in which the interest is concentrated on a leader and the group he or she is heading (or just on a leader and his or her traits, attitudes, personality, behaviour, style, etc.). I see leadership partly as an expression of the organizational context in which managerial work is carried out.

Emphasis is placed on the cultural and symbolic aspects of leadership, especially on how it contributes to social integration within the organization. Leadership is here conceptualized as social integrative action. This type of leadership is viewed as a reflection of the nature of a (particular type of) loosely coupled organization, including many knowledge-intensive companies.

The manipulative aspects of leadership are also briefly addressed although it is difficult to define manipulation, and the term will be used here to signal potential ethical problems and consequences of managerial action which make it difficult for employees to attain a critical understanding of their work situation and to evaluate their exchange relationship with their employer.

8.1 A Note on Leadership Research and a Thesis

I will refrain from the reviewing leadership research as there are several satisfactory reviews available (e.g. Andriessen and Drenth, 1984; Bryman,

1995; Knights and Willmott, 1992; Yukl, 1989; etc.). However, I will pay attention to the tendency of leadership literature to neglect the organizational cultural context of leadership. Most studies of leadership focus on how a person identified as a leader is behaving or interacting with a group of subordinates. In some cases, this group of subordinates is so large that it comprises an entire organization and in this way a few studies have looked at the leader's influence on organizational culture. It is then normally the founder of the organization who is the target of attention (e.g. Pettigrew, 1979; Schein, 1985). A few studies have taken an interest in leadership in relationship to cultural change (Trice and Beyer, 1989). In most cases, the leader is viewed as somebody who exercises a more or less far- reaching influence on culture. It is usually the top level leaders that are focussed upon. It is revealing that in Yukl's (1989) extensive review article of leadership research, the word culture is only mentioned a few times in passing, and then as something that is changed as an outcome of transformational leadership. In the present chapter ("average") leadership is understood more as an outcome of the cultural context. (An exception is when the founders of Enator are treated.)

A note on the relationship between managers and leaders (management and leadership) might be called for here. During recent years many authors have proposed a distinction between managers who are relying on their formal position and working with bureaucratic processes such as planning, budgeting, organizing and controlling, and leaders, who rely on their personal abilities, vision, agendas and coalition building and who mainly affect people's feelings and thinking by non-coercive means (e.g. Kotter, 1985; Zaleznik, 1977; etc.). Zaleznik views the influence of leaders as "altering moods, evoking images and expectations, and in establishing specific desires and objectives ... . The net result of this influence is to change the way people think about what is desirable, possible and necessary" (p 71). In comparison, managers are much less omnipotent types. Without denying that leaders have the possibility to influence people in a far-reaching way as proposed by advocates of the big L-type of leader, my experience is that most managers have a personal and non-coercive influence beyond pure (bureaucratic) "management" which combines elements of management and leadership, and that the latter element is far from unconstrained. The following definition of the two concepts captures this.

Management can get things done through others by the traditional activities of planning, organizing, monotoring and controlling – without worrying too much what goes on inside people's heads. Leadership, by contrast, is vitally concerned with what people are thinking and feeling and how they are to be linked to the environment to the entity and to the job/task (Nicholls, 1987, p 21).

We can find a combination of the two elements in the activities of many managers, including my research subjects. Leadership is thus not seen as "standing above" or being able to change culture, but rather as trying to influence people's minds.

I assume that the majority of people who have jobs in which leadership is a relatively important aspect of what they are doing are much more strongly influenced by local (corporate, workplace) culture than they are active in producing it. Apart from structural conditions (job task, resources, position, formal rights, etc.) the cultural context of a leader (here equated with a manager not relying solely on formal authority) might be seen as an important determinant of the way in which leadership is carried out. This aspect is neglected, as is the organizational context of leadership in general, in the leadership literature. One exception is Biggart and Hamilton (1987) who stress the normative ties between leaders and followers and the institutional context of these relationships. (These authors, however, deal more with the societal level than with organizational culture.) Of course, some recent models of leadership have organizational culture as one of many variables in a box from which an arrow points at leader behaviour (and also vice versa) (e.g. Yukl, 1989). On the whole, however, leadership research hardly acknowledges the significance of the cultural context as something that is necessary to consider for the understanding of managerial work. Only a few exceptions exist (e.g. Smircich and Morgan, 1982; Willmott, 1987). (A couple of critically oriented studies considering the leadership dimension have to some extent taken the societal cultural context into consideration in understanding how influence is exercised, e.g. Knights and Willmott, 1992; Rosen, 1985. In these cases, the interest is focussed upon top leaders and not on the more typical manager, and the leader is once again seen as being in control over cultural issues, effectively drawing upon macro cultural themes, rather than the other way around.)

The absence of studies on the consequences of organizational culture for leadership has partly to do with the fact that the cultural dimension has traditionally been neglected in leadership research (Trice and Beyer, 1989), but perhaps even more so with the tendency in leadership research to stress the manager as a superior, unidirectionally interacting with subordinates, thus neglecting the fact that almost all managers are also subordinates to a higher hierarchy (Dervin, 1990; Laurent, 1978). Sometimes, external dependencies and structural restrictions for leadership are noticed but the phenomenon of "cultural subordinancy" has not been treated seriously in leadership research.

In this chapter I will argue that most leadership styles are severely constrained by, and draw upon, the cultural and ideological context of the organization. Normal leadership is thus, among other things, an expression and reproduction of key elements of this context, as will be developed in the interpretation of the case study.

8.2   Leadership during the Expansion of Enator

The three founders have had a profound impact on the company which they ran for the first 7-8 years of its 10 year history. A closer look at their influence, especially during the formative years of the Enator, is called for.

People who participated in the first five years of the history of the company have almost lyrical tales to tell about how the three founders functioned. A consultant who started at Enator in 1981 tells:

You had a management that knew what people could do, that took an interest in them and that made demands. There were very strict guidelines during that time. If you had a 'conference' that went on half the night, there were no excuses for not arriving in the right time the following morning. If you did not arrive on time, you got a public reprimand. You had to be there at 8 o'clock in the morning, in fresh shape. You were allowed to do what you wanted until then but ...

Despite the fact that the work pressure and the demands of the owners were high, and a large part of the activities were carried out at the client's workplaces, there was a strong feeling of closeness and involvement within the company.

Right from the beginning they talked about having a culture: about being close to each other, knowing what everybody was doing, who worked with what and being able to phone and get assistance from people. Even if one didn't do that so often, the feeling was there.

The last sentence is, I think, illuminating. The influence of the leaders affected the beliefs and feelings of the employees rather than specific social practices. An element of manipulation is detectable here. It is the beliefs about reality rather than reality in itself which was affected by the owners. This distinction is, of course, far from clear-cut. Social reality is made up of beliefs to a large extent. When it comes to the feeling of being able to receive support it is, however, possible to distinguish it from concrete supportive behaviour.

According to the subordinates, the management, i.e. the three founders, were energetic, enthusiastic, always available and had a committed and supporting attitude to their employees.

One had a management that was very committed. You had direct contact with the management. The management was always ready, was always available and always listened. You always got a reason.

Some obvious circumstances, mentioned in the previous chapter, facilitated the positive atmosphere and widespread commitment reflected in these interviews: the youth of the company and its owners and personnel (25-35 years old, during the first years of the company), its rapid growth, the success of the company. In addition to these, at least four elements appear to have contributed to the creation and maintenance of a strong, tight, positive spirit, a powerful feeling of community and a strong commitment and loyalty to the company and its owners.

One of these is indicated above – a cogently expressed interest in the employees. Good performances were noted, acknowledged and communicated within the organization. Spotlights were put on the person who had done the right thing. He or she encountered positive feedback from all directions. A bottle of champagne was often opened to celebrate the achievement.

A second important element in management was that the leaders (founders) tried to, and succeeded in, tying together the everyday life of the personnel with the company's activities. The personnel became involved in the company and its business side. The founders managed to make the personnel feel that they were a central part of the company, not only with respect to different consultancy projects, but also in contributing ideas and business developments, including contracts on new projects, joint ventures and company acquisitions. The management passed on a lot of information – some of it on sensitive issues – and often presented events and processes in a dramatized way. The employees felt that they were participants, rather than spectators, to what was going on.

When we had morning meetings one of the owners was always there. We got a lot of inside information, about present development, etc. We felt very much a part of what was happening.

The fact that the company was still rather small, 100-200 employees, made it easier to accomplish this effect, but the nature of the work, whereby consultants normally worked at the clients' workplaces, presented obstacles. The founders made great efforts to distribute interesting, sometimes even "hot" information, and to create among the employees a sense of being part of the dynamic centre of Enator. It seems as though the founders sometimes overstressed the confidentiality and significance of the information they passed on, in order to influence the employees' feelings as strongly as possible. The employees' sense of being in, or very close to, the centre did not seem to completely correspond with their participation in decision making. The position of the founders in this regard was very strong. They listened to employees' opinions, but as owners, managers and individuals their power base was very strong and seldom questioned, and the final word was always theirs.

A third important aspect concerns social activities outside working time. On this point too, the founders were energetic.

The management was always there, was always at the centre. If we went out and took a meal one evening, they were always with us. They often took the initiative, found out funny activities. They were a part of the gang as much as anybody else.

On a more theoretical level, it might be argued that the founders broadened the sphere of social influence that leadership in corporations is normally about. By broadening and "dramatizing" information it acquired another character than if it was more concerned with "facts" and was of a more neutral and administrative nature. Through frequent participation in social activity, also outside normal working time, leisure time became, to some extent, a part of corporate life, which benefited the community, strengthened social bonds and was perhaps also conducive to more productive work. When a group of fellow workers meet in a pub there is a good chance that useful ideas and information will be exchanged.

At the same time as this illustrates the management's ambition to exploit the leisure time of personnel, there were probably important spontaneous elements in the fun activities. It is hard to evaluate where the border between calculation (and perhaps even "manipulation") and "spontaneity" lies when it is about back-patting, visible interest in the well-being of the employees and social activities outside the (purely) instrumental sphere. One could perhaps say that the founders were very good at utilizing their spontaneity and social orientation. On the whole, the leadership style was characterized by careful reflection and consistency, at least as it appeared from the perspective of the employees:

I am impressed by the fact that they sat down, often, and thought this through: what affects people? makes them feel good? and had a strategy for this. They had a common view which was spread and affected other people who thereby developed the same view.

A fourth important aspect was the recruitment policy of Enator which strongly facilitated a good spirit within the organization. Many of the employees were a part of the contact network of the three founders – who knew a lot of people from earlier workplaces or in other ways. A large part of the personnel employed during the first years of Enator came from a computer service company in which two of the founders had worked.

There is a general tendency for new organizations to start by recruiting a homogeneous group of people, in order to create a good base for confidence and mutual understanding (Kanter, 1977). Homogeneity in background and opinions helps social relations to function better, and this is particularly valuable in situations where the level of uncertainty is high and standards and maps do not exist or are undeveloped.

For Enator, social criteria were important when recruiting new person-nel. The management looked as much at people's social leanings as at their technical competence. Individuals with similar personalities and attitudes were – and are, at the time of my study – recruited. The personnel had, and have, considerable influence on recruitment.

The leadership style and the personnel that were recruited in combina-tion with a heavily expanding market and the possibilities for growth led to the formation of an organizational climate which was characterized by a positive atmosphere which had a strong sense of community, strong loy-alty and commitment to work.

1978 you would go through fire and water for the founders.
You felt you were part of the company, and made an extra effort.

This of course does not mean that the situation was idyllic. A high stress level at work was not uncommon. Some of the employees felt, in retro-spect, that what they got from work did not really correspond to their efforts and contributions during that time.

This history of leadership at Enator provides the background for the common features of the exercise of leadership within the company at the time of this study. The patterns they developed have been reproduced in the company and are the cornerstones of the "corporate culture".

8.3   The Founders

Given the significance of the three founders, a few words about their style (how they were perceived by their subordinates) are justified. When Ena-tor was established, the three founders – Christer Jacobsson, Hasse Lars-son and John Wattin – were between 30 and 35 years of age. They had rather different backgrounds and characters. Jacobsson was a former man-agement consultant, Larsson was a data-processing manager and Wattin was a salesman and subsequently manager of another computer consul-tancy firm. Wattin gradually drifted away from Enator operations after a few years, worked within the Pronator Group but moved on again. His shareholding was bought out by the other two founders. When my study was conducted, the two remaining founders were still the main sharehold-ers in the corporate group (i.e. in Pronator, which included Enator).

Those who knew and had worked with the founders (and were still working in the company) had almost entirely positive things to say about them:

They are incredibly charming and pleasant people.
Everyone liked them.
Christer Jacobsson and Hasse Larsson are looked upon as gods. They are never criticized. People look up to them.

There is a high degree of consensus regarding opinions about the founders expressed by people who know them. I have only met one person with divergent views, who considered that there was hidden dislike among some people in the company of the owners. The above quotations probably express widely held feelings about the founders, even if perhaps the picture is somewhat idealized in comparison with the conclusions which might be drawn by an outside observer.

Wattin is described as the "great entrepreneur", a strong, tough and competent man whose efforts lead to "success or everything goes to pot", as one employee put it. Wattin was particularly important in Enator's first 3-5 years of development, and was very good at establishing contacts and selling Enator's services, according to interviewees.

Larsson is referred to as a "cultural wallah" and corporate philosopher. He was considered to have exercised considerable influence at the level of ideas and values. There is also considerable evidence of his social skills in contributing to a good working atmosphere.

He has such an exceptionally fine attitude to life and to how life should be lived … and he's damn good at turning a problem around and making you see matters in a totally new light.
He has a galactic vision. When you talk to him, you don't get any concrete answers, but he does take you along on a mental journey.

Jacobsson is described as "a very good managing director", equally competent as an entrepreneur and as an administrator. People regard him as a positive and enthusiatic person with a strong personality.

He radiates enthusiasm. He can turn some damnable setback into something positive. He has exceptional charisma. Everyone wants to talk to him.
You can feel it in the air if Christer is around. And he takes the trouble to go round and talk to people, although not as much as he used to, because he doesn't have time for that. He is still on the friendliest terms with everybody – just like a big hug.

However, Jacobsson was also considered to be capable of taking tough action when necessary …

The founders' mixture of personalities and competence seems to have resulted in an effective combination, both as regards internal management of the company and in external marketing terms. In the company's initial period, the three founders normally met customers jointly at sales meetings.

As regards the technology and matters of that nature, I was the only one who knew anything about it. But when it was a question of gaining a hearing for our ideas, then we were an incredibly strong combination. No one licked us on any question, no matter who he was. ... We also had an enormous amount of enthusiasm. We have different personalities. John was fantastic at establishing instant contact and Christer was a pretty formidable character. It made an excellent combination (Hasse Larsson).

An expanding market, a business concept which was successful in the market place and a group of owners with good sales impact who, in addition, had a rich network of contacts to fall back on all meant that most sales initiatives gave direct dividend in the form of small or large sales assignments. In particular, an extensive social network appears to be an important feature underlying (successful) entrepreneurship (Aldrich, 1986). The combination of the entrepreneur/salesman, the manager/economist and the philosopher/computer technologist (Wattin, Jacobsson and Larsson, respectively) also appears to have been a powerful combination from a development perspective.

The combination of key figures in the company should also include people responsible for transmitting the business concept and specialists who support the overall structure and the various functions which mean that the concept can be realized (Normann, 1975). The three founders appear to have been an effective core group in this sense, particularly in the early years of the company's existence.

While Wattin originally played a crucial role and was also initially managing director, he gradually disappeared from the scene, while Jacobsson assumed the central position. This shift to some extent reflected conflicts between these two people. Broadly speaking, the division of duties between Jacobsson and Larsson may be described as follows:

Christer generates the cash, while Hasse represents the corporate philosophy (Consultant).

The founders' management style and their personal manner of operation appears to have made a clear mark on the company and on subsequent managers. Over a period of several years, the company was headed by three individuals who shared a common basic approach for which they were able to achieve strong support. Enator was managed by three, and subsequently by two, principal owners for most of Enator's first ten years which provided a powerful basis for influence. The fact that the vast majority of the employees were relatively young also facilitated the influence of the founder/managers impact on the company.

Far-reaching influence can also be traced in the organizational climate which characterized the company, particularly in the first 6-8 years of its existence, but also quite clearly at the time when my study was conducted.

This influence can also be seen in the locally espoused values and norms (corporate culture). Direct management influence was present in a personal form because managers functioned as models and provided inspiration, highlighting certain values, norms and ideals and focusing on specific ways of perceiving and interpreting reality. They also exerted an indirect influence on climate and culture, for example on the way business was conducted or employees were recruited. In particular, the recruitment of a relatively homogeneous personnel group, many of whom were personally acquainted with managers, contributed to the establishment of a positive organizational climate. It also helped to create relatively distinct and clear cultural patterns within the organization.

8.4   Charisma as an Attributed Characteristic

Interviews with employees gave a picture of the founders as "charismatic people". Charisma is usually defined in management research as the ability to get people to feel strong loyalty and devotion to a person and to achieve a strong propensity to comply with this person's will, without elements of compulsion or utility-mindedness (House, 1977). Compare this with Weber (19**), who defined charisma in the following terms: "the bearer of charisma enjoys loyalty and authority in the form of a mission which is considered to be embodied in his person" (p 199). Charisma is normally regarded as a personal characteristic and intimately associated with the following attributes: extreme self-confidence, dominance and a strong conviction of the moral value of one's own beliefs (House, 1977). However, the question is how to determine whether someone is charismatic without considering the effects on the environment. As far as I can see, we are obliged to take effects on the environment into account. Charisma then becomes a question of the attitude of subordinates/followers to an authoritative personality. Charisma is thus a collective reaction vis-à-vis a certain person. Alternatively, charisma may be regarded as a quality in the relationship between a leader and a collective, rather than as an abstract personality characteristic (cf. Israel, 1979). This approach complies with Weber's (1987) classic definition.

   House (1977) considers that a tautology between charisma as a personal attribute and charismatic effects on a group should be avoided. Tautology occurs if charisma as an attribute is considered to cause certain effects, while at the same time these effects are regarded as a criterion for the attribute. If this is the case, charisma becomes both cause and effect. House considers that assessments of an individual's possible charisma must be made independently of an investigation of the effects of such charisma. This might be achieved by basing an assessment of personal charisma on the opinions of superiors or colleagues, rather than on the reactions of subordinates.

I consider that this is difficult to achieve in practice. The only reasonable criterion as to whether an individual can be considered to "possess" charisma is that people in the environment perceive him or her in that way. The key factor then becomes the opinion of the persons in the environment – irrespective of formal hierarchic status – rather than the characteristics of the person in question. It might be possible to imagine that someone who acted as a leader for various groups and in various situations, and who was consistently regarded as charismatic, might be considered to possess charisma as a constant characteristic (a trait).

However, an empirical basis for an assessment of this nature would probably be extremely rare. In the absence of such empirical evidence, I consider that one should avoid talking about charisma as an attribute, but instead see it as one aspect of a specific relationship, or even as something which can be incorporated into a collective's common ideas. This means that the spotlight is not primarily focussed on the personality of a charismatic individual, but is directed instead at the group of followers/disciples and their interaction with the leader.

As Pfeffer (1978) suggests, there is a tendency to attribute considerable importance to leaders in various contexts, even if the extent to which the leader, de facto, has a clear influence on matters is often uncertain. This is due to a widespread desire to regard individuals, and particularly individuals in positions of power, as responsible for various outcomes. This makes the world seem more secure and controllable. Pfeffer suggests that the emphasis on leadership derives partly from a desire to rely on the effectiveness and importance of individual action, which is more readily controlled than the contextual variables which can also influence results.

Thus, there are good reasons for not focusing exclusively on the founders of the company in trying to understand Enator's development; we must also study the employees in order to be able to chart the influence of the founders on them. This means that subordinates are an important key in understanding Enator's successes, particularly in the initial years. Interest then focusses on the conditions which made it possible for the founders to be assigned charismatic qualities and have a far reaching impact.

Some aspects of relevance for illuminating this issue have been touched upon above, and in the previous chapter. I do not wish to provide further description and analysis of issues related to the founders as persons at this point, but will instead attempt to look at the other side of the coin by emphasizing the importance of subordinates. A summary and one or two supplementary points are perhaps in order.

Being an entrepreneur in an industry which is growing extremely rapidly, as was the case in the Swedish computer consultancy business in the mid 1970s, naturally increases the likelihood of being regarded as charismatic. Recruitment policies can also have positive or negative effects on the social construction of charisma. People's general receptiveness to "charisma" probably varies, and the propensity to react in a highly positive way to a particular individual probably varies with the cultural context. (For example, Hitler and Ghandi were well-known personalities experienced as charismatic, but they were two completely different individuals who probably appealed to different groups in different cultures.) In the case of Enator, the employees were originally recruited from the founders' network of contacts. It is thus possible to imagine that a certain degree of selection occurred which meant that at any rate people who were inclined to develop a charisma attributing attitude to the founders were not likely to have been underrepresented amongst the recruitees. Most of them were young – under 30 – when they were recruited.

In addition, the importance of the founders' status as owners and managers of operations should not be forgotten. This helped to establish a basis for their power position and gave a freedom of action which meant that it was possible to regard them as possessing a powerful personal impact, as compared with a situation with more external restrictions and a weaker material power-base.

Naturally, this does not negate the possibility that the founders' personalities were also highly relevant factors per se. Not everybody is fortunate enough to be experienced by people in their environment as a powerful or strong personality, even under favourable social and material conditions. Thus, if we are to comprehend the strong impact that Enator's founders had in the company's initial years, at least three aspects must be taken into account: the founders themselves, their subordinates and the corporate situation which encompassed the interaction between the founders and their employees.

8.5   Management Principles and Corporate Culture

As I indicated in the introductory chapter, I am not greatly interested in the more traditional aspects of management, such as the regulation of behaviour or the planning and control of results. Such aspects obviously represent an important part of any company's operations, including Enator's, but I prefer to concentrate on features which are particularly characteristic of my case and, arguably, for many other knowledge-intensive companies.

As one of the founders put it in an interview, companies of Enator's type are "human companies" rather than "service companies". In the latter, other resources are important as well as people, for example aircraft for an airline, food and furniture in a restaurant, etc. In a consultancy company, people are the only asset and the only major factor for management to pay attention to. The need for capital is also small, so the financial side demands relatively little attention, at least for the sake of operations, compared with other types of corporations. This means that personnel and social relations become of decisive importance in the corporation, in a way that clearly differs not only from manufacturing companies, but also from most service companies. The ability to utilize (exploit) the personnel as much as possible is crucial.

It is common in knowledge-intensive organizations that the professional, technical competence is highly valued. In Enator, purely technical qualifications are downplayed, to some extent, in favour of interpersonal and social ability. In jobs as manager and project leader, the ability to manage a project might be seen as a professional skill, but this is more related to general project and personnel management skills than to strict computer technical knowledge.

Many people within the company emphasize that they are not more skilled, in a technical sense, with computers and programming than people in other companies. However, they think Enator is superior with respect to its social part, including its competence in running projects. The social aspects of the project work have to do with cooperation, planning, communication, leadership, relating the project to the client's organizational conditions, etc. An important internal principle in the company is to emphasize the interpersonal functioning within the company, and while the strictly technical qualifications are important, they are far from decisive when new people are recruited. It is assumed that the success of the project tasks are less contingent upon technical problem-solving as a critical factor, than on how social relations are managed, both within the project group and in relationship to the client's management and operative personnel. Organizational climate – the spirit and felt milieu of the organization, to a high degree influenced by the shared values, understandings and ideals of the members – and social relations are thus seen as a critical factor concerning both the functioning of the employees and the company's results. This is emphasized by management.[1]

Enator's top management argues that the significance of people for this kind of business, and the sensitivity of the performances of the personal and interpersonal functioning of the consultants makes it important that employees feel satisfied and that the managers know how they feel. People are not supposed to be absent from work other than in exceptional cases. When they are, they are sometimes expected to work overtime in order to compensate for the income lost by their absence. The structural arrangement of the company, whereby subsidiaries employ a maximum of 50 people each, is grounded in the idea that every subsidiary manager should know every employee. It is assumed that the two life spheres clearly affect each other and that good project planning also includes consideration of the private situation of the employees. Furthermore, Enator's managers believe that the well-being of the employees directly influences the quality of their work. As expressed by a senior consultant, "One of the strongest sides of the company is the ability to keep people satisfied":

The company succeeds in making people feel happy with the company and so that they also feel better in the work they are doing and the job is performed a bit better and then our customers also become happy.

Another important part of the management principles of Enator concerns the development of new ideas and innovations in the organization. One idea is that situations and connections apart from the on-going, goal directed work make it possible for new thoughts and impulses to be developed, perhaps when one has a coffee break or talks with the co-workers over a beer after the working day. To a large extent, it is in the activities around the work itself that important contributions to the organizations are generated. As mentioned in Chapter 7, these ideas on management are expressed in the design and interiors of the corporate building.

8.6   Integration, Differentiation and Fragmentation

One almost classic theme in management studies involves the relationship between the integration and differentiation of operations. It is claimed that companies that operate successfully must have organizational sub-systems that correspond to the external environments on which the company is dependent – for example market segments, the technological environment, etc. Integration is a question of establishing uniformity of action so that the organization's overall operations correspond to the overall demands which the external environment makes on the organization in question (Lawrence and Lorsch, 1967).

In the case of companies like Enator, differentiation is not a serious problem. Achieving an appropriate degree of internal variation in competence, orientations and other attributes is not too difficult in knowledge-intensive service companies which employ simple and flexible "technologies". This is especially true in comparison with industrial companies, for example, where production, purchasing, product development, sales, etc. are functions which require a broad range of ways of acting. On the other hand, the question of integration is critical for Enator, although not in the same way as for companies with operations which are based on a high degree of differentiation and division of labour. In the latter type of company, integration can be largely achieved by applying technical and formal instruments. But it is much more difficult – as well as less necessary – to achieve a high degree of integration in a company such as Enator.

This is partly because operations are decentralized in terms of a number of different projects which function relatively independently, with little supervision (apart from at the project level) and direct management control. As Mills et al. (1983) point out, the operative units function for the most part as "mini-companies". Enator considers that those who are responsible for projects should function as project "managing directors". In addition to the loose coupling of the work process itself and the relative independence of the rest of the company, most Enator consultancy projects are also characterized by decentralized physical location of operations, at the workplaces of the clients.

Since operations are loosely coupled and dependencies between different units are limited in a purely concrete, physical sense, specific demands are made on integration functions within the company. If integration fails the company is at risk in a number of respects, these range from poor quality of projects to excessive heterogeneity and divergence. This is because different units work in different directions in terms of assignments and principles for project work. Perhaps the greatest risk is that individuals or groups of employees leave the company, taking their customers with them. Customers are sometimes more interested in a specific employee (project manager) than they are in the company that employs them. A great deal of the customer/consultancy contact area goes via the consultant who is responsible for the project and is only partially subject to top management control (cf. Mills et al., 1983).

One of the worst setbacks in Enator's otherwise successful corporate history occurred when a majority of the employees in the Norwegian subsidiary – which had previously reported the best financial results achieved by any of Enator's foreign companies – resigned after a disagreement between the subsidiary manager and Enator management, and formed their own computer consultancy headed by the Norwegian subsidiary manager.

A company can counter the risk of losing key personnel in this way by applying traditional guidance and control mechanisms such as formal agreements, rates of pay, promotion policies, profit-sharing, etc. This means that the company provides incentives to retain personnel and to get them to act in the manner desired by top management. In addition, top management can try to influence personnel by establishing loyalty to the company and a sense of identity, by improving social cohesion between employees, building up common values, points of reference, etc. This is a question of attempting to create and reinforce social and affective ties. Concrete expressions of such attempts were described in Chapter 7. Formalized as well as normative control are also used to counter other forms of fragmentation, such as a considerable degree of heterogeneity regarding project management and project organization, or lack of interest in cooperation and the achievement of synergy effects between different projects and subsidiaries.

Other aspects associated with the theme of fragmentation and ambiguity involve a propensity for conflict in companies like Enator and a high degree of dependence on personnel which characterizes activities where personnel resources are the only production factor worth talking about. (It is true that employees work with computers, but they can hardly be regarded as an input factor in Enator's production. Enator only makes marginal use of its own computers to achieve its objectives, but utilizes the machines of the customers.) The literature in the field emphasizes the tendency for conflicts to develop between customers and consultants; the strong mutual dependency required for the execution of assignments tends to generate frequent conflicts (Mills et al., 1983). Conflicts also develop as a consequence of tendencies for the establishment of autonomous centres of power within the company resulting from the decentralization of operations and the existence of knowledge-based authority as a source of power in parallel with the formal hierarchy. As we saw in Chapter 6, Mintzberg (1983) and Robbins (1983) mention a propensity to become involved in conflicts, resulting from changes, uncertainty and ambiguities in the work and in the organization.

As already indicated, in Enator's case conflict-propensity is not particularly characteristic, but this does not mean that there are no risks of this kind, especially under less favourable market conditions than those characterizing Enator up to the time of my study. One important aspect of management is the prevention of serious conflicts and the channelling of such forces in a constructive direction. This ties up with the integrative theme.

Enator, like other knowledge-intensive companies, is extremely personnel sensitive in that successful operations depend on the competence of individuals, particularly senior consultants, and their willingness to make special efforts when required. The quality of consultant endeavours – as they are experienced by customers – has a direct effect on results. This is in sharp contrast to manufacturing industry, for example, where the final product depends on a multitude of factors, of which the efforts made by employees are only one element.

In advanced and demanding consultancy assignments, pure allocation of resources is less important than the willingness of employees to do their best. In other words, morale, motivation and involvement are crucial factors in achieving good results. More so in knowledge-intensive companies than in most other organizations.

8.7   The Company as an Institution

As mentioned, the activities of Enator are very different from the closed system logic that characterizes large parts of many manufacturing industries and other "machine bureaucracies". To borrow from Selznick (1957), it is vital for Enator to function as an "institution", i.e. what the organizational collective attributes to the company become values in themselves.

Instead of just functioning as a platform for work, wages, etc., Enator is considered to have a character, an identity, which embodies certain ideals and values with which the employees identify and to which they are prepared to commit themselves. For organizational members, a company that is functioning as an institution is a source of identification and emotional involvement, which generates an extra strong motivation. The members accept and support the ultimate purpose of the organization, its mission. You can say that an organization is "value-driven" rather than "control-driven" through formal means (Berg, 1986). Leadership is, to a considerable degree, carried out by means of ideas rather than instructions (Beckérus et al., 1988).

All this goes beyond the feeling of community and good social relations in the company. It concerns not so much people-in-the-company, but rather the company-in-itself. This distinction is important, and is not always recognized in the literature on organizational culture.

Selznick (1957) suggests that the integrity of an organization goes beyond efficiency, organizational forms and procedures, and even group cohesion. The integrity is determined by a certain orientation being anchored so strongly in a group's life that it affects and governs various attitudes, decisions and organizational forms. The creation of integrity is an important part of what Selznick refers to as "the institutional embodying of goals" and is an important management task in some organizations. In a strongly market and profit oriented company such as Enator, the importance of institutionalization is probably much less, for example, than in some voluntary organizations, but the structural conditions of the company make it important for management to avoid the development of a strong instrumental and "egoistic" attitude on behalf of the employees.

Strong and systematic efforts of management attempt to communicate the positive sides and aspects of the company, to draw attention to these and to conceptualize ambiguous phenomena in a positive way. These posi-

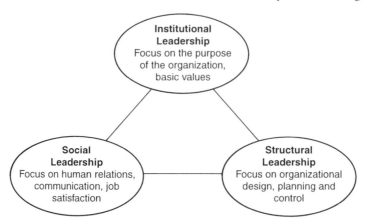

Figure 8.1

tively biased evaluations of what the company stands for are also, to some extent, an attribute of the corporate culture and a part of the organization's (the participants') self-understanding, fuelled and reproduced by management, but not primarily in a manipulative and conscious way. Managers are also socialized into these values, beliefs and affective reactions.

To some extent, managers can influence the corporate culture, but it must be noted that it is "above" individual managers, so that new managers are under strong pressure to adapt to it.

8.8   Leadership as Social Integrative Action

Selznick (1957) clearly distinguishes between the institutional manager and the human relations manager. The latter is interested in facilitating human communication and interaction, increase job satisfaction and reduce destructive anxiety.

Based on this we might imagine three sorts of orientations in management and leadership. (See Figure 8.1.) The three forms of leadership are not mutually exclusive, but every leader's temporal restrictions and personal attributes in combination with the nature of a particular management task and organizational situation probably prevent the scoring of 9/9/9 on all three dimensions. A certain emphasis is put somewhere in the triangle of Figure 8.1.

In Enator and, I assume, similar companies, management is characterized by a certain emphasis on the institutional and social elements. I call

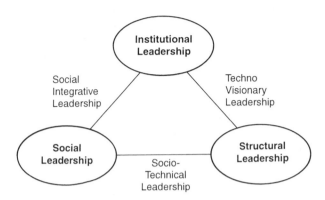

Figure 8.2

this *social integrative leadership*. (See Figure 8.2, in which I also put some concepts on two other "hybrids" in terms of leadership orientation.)

It is probably highly unusual for business organizations in the long run to emphasize institutional leadership as the dominating element in leadership. Sometimes the literature on organizational culture highlights values, assumptions, philosophies, etc., stressing qualitative virtues, which are instrumental in achieving corporate goals and forget the almost hegemonic status of profits and corporate growth as the ultimate values (Alvesson 1993a). It is probable that these values can seldom evoke the same feelings and commitments as, for example, social movement organizations or other organizations with "higher" goals than profits and growth.

Social integrative management differs from institutional leadership while the ultimate purpose of the organization, in principle, is taken for granted and does not function as a primary motivator. For Enator, the goals of the company are relatively clear. The company has, however, established certain elements of institution for large groups of the personnel and management aims to maintain it. Enator has been reasonably successful in this regard, even though the increasing corporate size and other changes has decreased the institutional character somewhat. The elements of institutional influence are closely connected with social matters. The management of Enator strongly emphasizes the social element of the workplace. Group cohesion, friendship, openness, fun, low conflict, openness with information to the employees, etc., are important sub-goals (means). This social level is combined in various ways with institutional elements. The value and meaning structure ("the corporate culture") point at the importance of these social virtues. The workplace and the company should be more than a source of jobs and wages. An important goal of the company is to make it function as a second "home" for the employees, a source of comradeship, where people have fun and so on. These ideals are linked to the economic performance of the company. "Fun and profit" is a slogan. Certain social rewards, such as "conferences" in nice surroundings for the entire subsidiary, are partly contingent upon the economic results.

Basic values such as openness, a positive attitude and a lack of emphasis on organizational hierarchies are attributes that are associated with Enator as an institution, as an organization containing certain values and ideals. At the same time, these values in a realized form facilitate the good social functioning of the company in true human relations style. What Enator is supposed to represent in terms of business concept and working style is also partly of an institutional character. The ability to manage projects and relate computer issues to the client's management perspective is a source of pride to large groups of the personnel (Chapter 10).

From the view of Enator's top management, an important task is to create a totality, to bring the various parts of the company together. Social integrative leadership is a matter of inducing a common orientation and direction to the operative units (the subsidiaries, the project groups and the individual consultants), to contribute to the identification with the company and to a feeling of loyalty; to achieve social cohesion both at the micro level, within work groups and subsidiaries, and at the macro level within Enator as an entity. Social integrative leadership is of relatively limited operative use. The purpose is not on this level. Instead, it is a matter of transferring ideas, representations and orientations that counteract the disintegrative tendencies inherent in this organizational form and facilitates convergence in thinking, feeling and acting, which increases the chances of people staying in the company, getting along, cooperating efficiently within and between units, and adopting a not too divergent or diffuse style in project work and in interactions with customers.

Social integrative leadership might also be formulated as a way of counteracting "negative" reactions from employees concerning the high degree of work pressure within the company. As mentioned above, the demands for effectiveness and, at least occasionally, for long working hours, are rather strong and this might be experienced by the work force as exploitation. The "hard core" of the exchange relationship between company and employee is "softened up" by social integrative strategies. The latter make people more prepared to accept hard work pressure.

In the next section, I will explore leadership on a more concrete level and provide some illustrations.

8.8.1   Aspects of Leadership as Social Integrative Action

In terms of the social integrative aspects of leadership, four functions appear to be crucial in Enator and companies of this type, especially for subsidiary managers. (This group, i.e. upper middle management, is crucial to the company and exercises the most significant leadership styles, in separate, largely autonomous units. The type of leadership exercised by the executive and project managers have many of the features described below, but their managerial situation is slightly different.) I will call these the boundary keeping function, the sparring partner function, the cohesiveness function and the pride-enhancing function. Other aspects and roles, well known in the literature, are not discussed here (Andriessen and Drenth, 1984; Yukl, 1989; etc.).

The first function has to do with *maintaining the boundaries* of the organization. In most organizations, it is completely clear to personnel where they are employed, to whom they are supposed to be loyal and to whose interest they should give priority. In consultancy companies, as in some other service companies, as well as in some industrial companies producing complex products that call for close cooperation between seller and buyer, the boundaries between company and customer are often unclear. The projects are carried out on behalf of the client, in cooperation with the client's personnel and often at the client's workplace. Some computer consultancy missions take a long time, sometimes several years. It is not uncommon for the consultant to work on his or her own. The recently employed consultant will often know the client better than Enator. Loyalty conflicts and identity problems may result. Whose interests are most important? Were does one belong? In which situations is one an "insider" and when is one an "outsider"? Even the more experienced consultant may run into similar problems:

You are out there with the customer and play the part, but you can easily get into problems with loyalty. To keep on the right side of the border you have to go home occasionally and discuss the situation ... (Consultant).

The subsidiary manager has the task of reminding consultants that they are employed by Enator and of making them feel that they are a part of, and important for, the company and the other employees as a whole. It is thus a matter of trying to create and maintain strong social bonds between the company and the consultants.

If you are working for a customer all on your own, you have a tremendous need to have contact with your manager, to feel that you are not only earning money, but that you also are a person and important as such (Consultant).

The subsidiary manager is important here as a representative of, and symbol for, the company as well as having a personal relation with the consultants. Both the formal representation of the company and the personal, friendly contact are important. These two tasks must be combined in the person of the subsidiary manager. It is important that he (all managers were, at the time of my study, men) is both respected and well liked.

A second important function is to be a *sparring partner* for the consultants and project managers. This concept is used frequently in Enator and in similar companies (Sveiby and Risling, 1986).

It is not that easy to sit out there as a consultant, alone, for half a year, perhaps with great responsibility. You have to have a sparring partner (Consultant).

The subsidiary manager and his deputy are then functioning as advisers. While the boundary-keeping function is primarily about identification, the sparring partnership means that the manager provides intellectual, social and moral support for carrying out the job. It thus goes beyond problem-solving or task-oriented leadership. The instrumental aspect is socially embedded. Project managers and others might check ideas, discuss problems, both technical, social and personal, and get assistance in evaluating whether the project is right in relationship to time and cost plans and with regard to the quality that is required.

The third crucial function concerns the internal social cohesiveness and atmosphere within the company. The subsidiary managers should be socially active and express a positive and engaged spirit. The expectations are high in this regard:

There is an opinion, a certain education that you get on how to be a manager in this company and that comes from the old leaders, the founders of the company. The leaders are seen as very important, as a sort of cultural carrier and an ideal for the personnel. As a leader you must participate in all social arrangements. You should preferably be the funniest of all, you should be visible all the time and give direction to the company and the personnel in the way you wish the company to function, hold nice parties, tell entertaining stories and things like that (Subsidiary manager).

A leadership style that contributes to satisfactory social relations and interaction, both within and outside normal working time, provides a base for good fellowship and, to some extent, also an identification with the company, as well as a social-emotional background resource for project groups, which facilitates their smooth functioning and counteracts conflicts between the members. An important aspect of the creation of social togetherness and strength is to manage the company as a collective and not only as a group of individuals (Berg, 1986). It is important for the leader to emphasize the collective at least as much as individual employees. This has to do with the possibility that only a minimal level of collective feeling will emerge in this type of loosely coupled organization, if specific means are not used to encourage it.

The *pride-enhancing* function means that managers point at (and perhaps exaggerate) the distinctive features of the company. Through various symbols (such as verbal expressions) the identity of the company is reinforced. While the boundary-keeping function is a matter of regulating the group belongingness problem inherent in this type of work, the pride-enhancing function connects the employee to the principles and virtues of the company and, in subtle ways, reminds him or her about the good side of what Enator stands for.

Apart from certain overall and common principles in the exercise of leadership, there are great variations in the ways these principles are expressed in specific situations. Of crucial importance for the functioning of managers are situation specific circumstances. A critical factor for consultancy firms is to get projects so that the employees have enough to do, and so that they can be debited to a high degree. The functioning of managers in terms of the classical, but somewhat abstract and sterile dimensions, personnel (consideration structure) and task orientation (initiating structure) are sometimes more a matter of how the subsidiaries score in relationship to market, customers and order books, than about leadership style as a static, situation-independent attribute. Variations in situation have a crucial impact on how leadership is carried out:

What it is all about is to have the capacity to be interested (in the personnel). To have the time and also the courage to do so, even if you have customers waiting in all directions. Sales efforts easily take all the time (Consultant).

The form of leadership is thus dependent on many factors. The corporate culture is an important one, in that it gives an overall direction to how leaders are expected to function. Especially important is the demand on subsidiary managers to be active in social arrangements, to downplay status and prestige and to emphasize close and informal social relationships; to put personnel orientation and team building, to some extent, into focus. These principles more or less radically break with traditional hierarchies and produce some broad parameters for the action space of subsidiary managers.

8.8.2   Illustrations of Leadership in Practice

I will now give a couple of brief illustrations of how leadership in Enator is exercised. One example came from an interview with a manager, which took place the same day as a recruitment advertisement was being published. The subsidiary manager got several calls. He asked the interested persons to write to the company and say something about themselves and their qualifications, what they wanted, and what they were like as a person. He asked them not to send academic grades, etc. He was not interested in formal documents.

Another example, also from the recruitment process, came from another manager. He also saw his management duty as comprising a social advisory role: "People came to me and talked about their problems." This manager starts by indicating his position at the time of the recruitment process. He asks personal questions such as "Are you religious?", "Jealous?", "Is it important for you to speak the truth?", etc. He also talks with the potential employee's spouse about the job, and what it might mean in terms of travelling, being away from home, etc. before agreement of employment is made.

Both examples illustrate the symbolic aspects of leadership (Peters, 1978; Pfeffer, 1981a; Smircich and Morgan, 1982). In the first case, it is signalled that the personal attributes are the crucial ones and that purely educational merits carry less weight. Informality and trust in people's honesty are also communicated. In the second case, something similar is signalled, but also a more holistic view of the personnel, their functioning and the appropriate behaviour in the workplace is included. The manager goes far outside what is traditionally conceived of as being part of the work role. Thereby, it is indicated that his and the company's interest in the personnel goes much further than their way of solving computer problems between 8 am and 5 pm. Openness and informality, as well as the importance of personal life and the connection between work and home life are stressed. (Less positively, the right of the company to interfere with the employees' private life is also expressed.) The new employee and his/her spouse are also forced to commit themselves to the demands of the company in terms of overtime, travelling, etc.

A third example is the meeting every second week, treated in Chapter 7, when all the employees of a subsidiary company come together in order to receive information from the manager and discuss things of importance.

These examples illustrate how the boundaries between Enator and the external world are maintained by stressing the characteristics of the company, and by using the (few) internal social gatherings to reinforce community feeling. The sparring partner function is facilitated by emphasizing informality and openness and – thereby – the rapid dissemination of information and informal communication. Opening up the personal dimension of people's functioning makes it somewhat easier for people to report about potential problems and difficulties. This is important as the possibilities for management to exercise control are relatively small in this kind of business. The social cohesiveness of the company is promoted by communicating to new employees the ideals of being personal, open and informal at the workplace. Leaders behaving in a way which corresponds reasonably well with these virtues, who downplay prestige and formal positions in many situations and who use social gatherings as vehicles for the promotion of a feeling of community in the companies fulfil this function.

Another example of symbolic leadership, which addresses the client side of work, concerns how leaders try to anchor certain principles for project management among their employees. The company takes a pride in putting information technology and its usage in a top management perspective. The projects, which normally concern the development of software, should involve efforts to communicate with the top management of the client as a crucial part of Enator's advanced business concept of relating information technology to the business and strategic situation of the client (see Chapter 10). Leaders try to stress this ideal and remind the consultants of the principles of Enator, and what the company stands for. One manager regularly asks his consultants when they last talked to the managing director of the customer company for which they work. Another says that the consultant, who is not familiar with the business concept of the client, does not run his or her job properly. These messages are not to be taken too literally. They are rather expressions of the ideal in which Enator believes and for which it is striving – although departures from the ideal are common – and mark the identity of the company. They remind the consultants of the company's ideals and its uniqueness, thereby playing upon the institutional qualities of the company.

8.9 Discussion and Conclusions

As emphasized in previous chapters, the structural situation of Enator and other knowledge-intensive service adhocracies differ substantially from bureaucracies. This means that other aspects of management and leadership than those traditionally being focused upon must be highlighted in order to understand how personal influence is exercised. I have summarized this leadership style as social integrative action. This includes efforts to tie employees closely to the company (the employer), to influence projects mainly by effective informal discussions and by anchoring general virtues and principles among the employees to strengthen community feelings and collective bonds within the subsidiary (and, indirectly, within the company as a whole).

The traditional metaphors of the manager as a plan and control bureaucrat, a task-oriented technocrat or a consideration oriented personnel specialist have recently been succeeded by the vision of the manager as a manipulator of symbols (Peters, 1978; Pfeffer, 1981a), a manager of meaning (Smircich and Morgan, 1982), an agenda setter and coalition builder (Kotter, 1982) and a player of ten roles, mostly related to communication (Mintzberg, 1975). The view proposed here is broadly in line with these conceptualizations. The specific metaphor suggested is the one of the leader as a social integrator, as a counterweight to the tendencies of decoupling which are inherent to many new organizational forms. As such, socially valuable and legitimate tasks, as well as manipulation, are exercised.

Enator is a relatively homogeneous organization, mostly because the majority of the employees belong to the same occupational group, are of a similar age and attitude, and partly because of efforts to influence and maintain a certain set of values, ideals and understandings. How does this fact affect the salience of leadership as social integrative action (the value of this metaphor in relationship to different empirical contexts)? Two themes of generalization may be invoked here, as the points made in this chapter may be of relevance across quite different types of organizational and leadership contexts. The first concerns what facilitates social integrative action. The other concerns when is it motivated for managers to bother about what may be accomplished through such action.

Social similiarity among employees facilitates social integrative action. The structural conditions of organizations such as Enator – especially geographically dispersed work – make it harder and call for the centrality of this kind of leadership. Many, probably the majority, of all organizations are much more differentiated than Enator in terms of shared values and other cultural manifestations. This does not, however, necessarily affect the work of a particular manager: the people in his or her area – for example a marketing or personnel department – might share certain personal and social features. Even a top executive might be less directly concerned by differentiation on lower levels in the company, than by the degree of homogeneity or consensus among his/her closest subordinates. But how are the social integrative aspects of leadership affected by an immediate context characterized by cultural differentiation, either in the form of distinct cultural groupings or ambiguity and uncertainty? Such a situation might make leadership more difficult, but may also make the manager as a social integrator more salient. In the absence of the integrative force of organically developed shared meanings, understandings and values, leadership processes, which tie employees to each other and clearly relate them to the organization, social integrative managerial action might be extra significant. (The importance of this aspect is partly dependent on organizational characteristics. If, for example, a physical production process integrates the work in a material way, the importance of social integration may be reduced.) In the case of organizations characterized by cultural differentiation, the outcome of social integrative leadership might be a moderate degree of commitment and moderate feelings of shared purpose and belongingness, in comparison with the rather high scores on these dimensions aspired to – and achieved – by the managers in Enator. This does not, of course, necessarily mean that leadership as social integrative action becomes less significant (of limited value for understanding of managerial work) in such contexts.

Another aspect of leadership highlighted in the case study is the role of the leader as an agent and reproducer of corporate culture. In contrast to many normative authors, who optimistically talk about managers' active engagement in "managing" or "controlling" culture, I am stressing the passive side of reproducing it. The ideals, espoused values, norms and verbal symbols developed by the founders and reproduced and refined by later managers in Enator prestructure the ways in which managers exercise influence. It is hard to say to what extent this occurs but it is vital to note that in the company the personal qualities of new managers are considered very important and a lot of energy is put into their socialization. It is sufficient here to suggest that elements of corporate culture simultaneously restrict the space for leadership behaviour, and functions as an important resource upon which managers can draw.[2] An important aspect is thus that corporate culture to some extent controls managers (as well as employees). A further illustration of this was the recently employed manager in Enator who was forced to resign following the initiative of his subordinates. As mentioned in Chapter 7, a major reason for his resignation was that subordinates accused him of not being "open enough" about passing on information to the personnel. The values and expectations of the personnel set restrictions on what was considered acceptable in managerial behaviour. As Biggart and Hamilton (1987, p 435) put it:

All actors, but perhaps especially leaders, must embody the norms of their positions and persuade others in ways consistent with their normative obligations.

This can also be formulated as corporate as well as other forms of culture framing and constraining leadership. It comprises a background, including expectations and preunderstandings from various sources – top management, subordinates, colleagues, the manager him- or herself – which facilitate as well as constrain the interaction and social relations within the company. Of course, in many organizations, there are no distinct, organization-specific cultural patterns, but in that case other cultural manifestations, for example those associated with occupational communities, affect and constrain leadership.

It is possible that top management might be less constrained by culture than lower level managers. Some of the talk about leaders with a capital L would indicate this (e.g. Zaleznik, 1977). Taking the issue seriously, would call for a discussion of the possibilities of cultural change – something which falls well beyond the purpose of this chapter. It is sufficient to say here that most reflective writers treating this topic downplay the chances of intended cultural change (Fitzgerald, 1988; Lundberg, 1985). Cultural manifestations shared by a larger collective (or perhaps, which is the common situation for a top executive, different kinds of manifestations corresponding to several collectives working within the boundaries of a formal organization) comprise a very heavy counterweight to the possibilities of a top figure exercising influence on people's thinking and feelings. Such a task is, of course, severely constrained by cultural manifestations, held not only by a large number of the employees, but also by many top executives themselves, especially those promoted from within. A more modest, but often difficult and important task not only for middle management, but also for top management is to maintain and or modify certain values, ideals and virtues in the organization (Nord, 1985). The point with the concept of culture is that it refers to a whole collective of organizational participants, including those at the top. My observations of Enator support the view that also top managers, after the formative years of a company's development, are constrained by those values and meanings that are shared by organizational members, at least when it comes to the possibilities of exercising influence on a cultural level. After the departure of the founders, the new top executives did not deviate from their predecessors and from the organization at large in terms of values, ideals and attitudes.

In the culture literature, there is a peculiar emphasis on the highly extraordinary situations of planned cultural change and top leaders who "stand above" corporate culture. The normal leadership situation is far less spectacular and grandiose. One of the purposes of this chapter is to draw attention to the transmission of culture by managers and to their "subordinate" rather than "superior" relationship to culture. Recognizing that there might be exceptions, leaders are normally better understood as "transmitters" or reproducers rather than "masters" of culture.

As a final point it must be emphasized that leaders as social integrators and transmittors of cultural patterns are not the same thing. In a sense, social integration always involve ideas, symbols and meanings, but may focus on belongingness to the company and a common social identity more than particular ideas, values and norms. A distinct cultural content may be drawn upon to a greater or lower extent in social integrative action. On the other hand, cultural transmission may not necessarily lead to strong feelings of community. Cultural ideas may, for example, concern individualism, rules for long-term rewards, etc. (See Alvesson and Lindkvist, 1993, for an exploration of this theme.) In a company like Enator, social integrative action and shared cultural ideas and values mutually support each other. The two metaphors, leadership as social integrative action and as cultural transmission, thus illuminate partly different theoretical points, but at least in the case of Enator, overlapping empirical phenomena.

Notes

[1]   In terms of the distinctive competence of Enator, the traditionally salient aspects of expertize – intellectual, technical and abstract knowledge – are downplayed in relationship to forms of knowing that are situated, social, distributed and processal (cf. Blackler, 1993, 1994).

[2]   Perhaps a warning against the reification is motivated here (and at other places in my text). For reasons of economics, sometimes reified expressions are called for. This does not mean that the author tries to express results of thinking, in which social phenomena or theoretical constructs are viewed as thing-like objects. As Johansson (1990) says, it is reification at the level of cognition that is the problem, not at the level of writing. When I am talking about, for example, corporate culture as something that has certain effects, hopefully the reader reads this as a matter of local patterns of values, ideas and meanings encouraging certain actions and discouraging others. Corporate culture is not a supra-human form or a causal factor, but an aspect of how people construct and make sense of their intersubjectively shared worlds.

9 Personnel and the Work Situation

This chapter will cover work and organizational factors at Enator, focussing primarily on the employee perspective. In other words, the psycho-social aspects of consultancy work will be studied. The corporate culture and the importance of management in relation to the employee's work situation will also be discussed.

This chapter will also discuss how control via values, norms, definitions of reality and influence, reinforced by special social-integrative activities such as quarterly conferences, impinges on the consciousness of employees. The question is whether this influence means that personnel are uncritically exposed to management's ambitious endeavours to get staff to think, feel and act in the way which owners and management want? Is it possible to speak of manipulation, indoctrination and other such terrible phenomena?

Social institutions always have an influence on people's ideas and values – culture always forms part of all action and thinking in one sense or another – but if "culture" is expressly and deliberately employed as an important aspect of the arsenal of instruments of influence available to management it is particularly important that this should be investigated.

Based on my interviews, I will provide a picture of certain important characteristics of the consultants' work situation. I will focus, to some extent, on factors which are potentially problematical for staff members. The same phenomena may sometimes also mean stimulation and development at work or denote other positive aspects of the job situation. Cultural control can seldom simply be evaluated in terms of good and bad.

9.1 Work Conditions, Strains at Work

Consultancy operations make relatively high demands on personnel. As far as customers are concerned, consultants are expensive labour. Consultancy companies are sensitive to the market and to customers' views, at any rate where keen competition prevails. While someone with a permanent position in an organization may make a mediocre contribution for a time without being dismissed, it is easier for a customer to get rid of a consultant. As a result, computer consultants must be more "on the ball" than employees in the customer company.

As a consultant, you are in an exposed position. You are expected to have a good grasp of the situation, know what has to be done next and be efficient and effective all the time (Enator manager).

Another general characteristic of work at Enator – as well as in consultancy work in general – is the considerable uncertainty often involved in the tasks to be carried out. The consultant's own background and competence does not always comply with job requirements. For a start, what has to be done is often extremely unclear. The first phase of many consultancy assignments means dealing with the confusion of the unsorted pieces of a jigsaw puzzle. It is difficult to know what the puzzle is supposed to represent – what the customer wants – and it is also difficult to know how the pieces fit together. The first month is often chaos, according to one interviewee. Perhaps the customer's requirements are regarded as strange, the consultant has no experience of the customer's computers and he or she does not know who makes the decisions in the customer company.

You can land up in a project where you know nothing about the hardware. The people you are sitting with don't really want to have you there, since the project has been sold at the wrong level in the customer company. Personally, you think that the timetable has been misjudged, that the equipment doesn't work and you realize that you have taken on too much responsibility. Everything can be up the creek.

Another problem experienced by consultants is lack of appreciation on the part of some customer personnel with whom they have to work.

As consultants, we are in an exposed position. Customers prefer to put the blame on us if there are failures. Some have negative views about consultants and think that consultants are expensive, etc.
Some customers regard consultants as something that the cat dragged in.

A further potential problem the relatively frequent changes of workplace. Personnel seldom get much advance information about future assignments. Many consultants do not know where or with whom they will be working in a few weeks' time. Where they wind up, and the quality of the new environment, can vary considerably.

Perhaps you get a dream job ... like two girls working on the top floor of the NK department store, with a view over the park in central Stockholm. They can go down into the park from March until September, eat lunch and dance in the open air. But you might just as easily wind up in an industrial area in the suburbs where you sit at the far end of a grey corridor and eat plastic food in the staff cafeteria.

Apart from the uncertainty associated with solving the actual job assignment, there is also the uncertainty of not knowing what lies in store and being forced to adapt to a new place of work and a changing situation. It is almost equivalent to changing jobs. Similar problems are described by Reeser (1969) in a study of personnel working in project organizations in the space industry in the United States.

Tight schedules and the obligation to work overtime in order to meet deadlines are other possible stress factors in consultancy work of the type carried out by Enator. This problem is also salient in the engineering division of a high tech company as studied by Kunda (1992). In a really bad case, the situation might be like this:

Initially, everyone thought that the project was fun, but it really turned sour. The project meant pretty tight time pressures. Finally, it was a question of having something completed by a deadline which approached steadily and then you can't really be structured. It was a question of banging away and hoping that something would work. Subsequently, you didn't really want to get involved in it again (Enator consultant).

This sounds rather off-putting, and it might be expected that there would be considerably higher personnel turnover than Enator's extremely low figure, which is generally well below 10%. Many of those who resign probably do so as a result of the factors mentioned above. Apparently, another common reason is that it is not possible to specialize much at Enator, to get proper experience of a particular hardware item or to become an expert on it. The nature of consultancy projects varies considerably and, on the whole, consultants have to adapt to this situation, even if they can sometimes refuse an assignment and occasionally have certain alternative choices. This depends a great deal on the market situation at any particular point in time. Many of the work factors mentioned also involve certain positive aspects. The job can be exciting, challenging, stimulating and dynamic. The problem-solving may also involve creative aspects.

The work assignments are often exciting and challenging – particularly because you usually don't know so much when you start a project. Then you can see things in a positive light, as I do. Look upon it as a challenge and think about how to solve this puzzle. Some people don't think it is so much fun. They want to feel that they master something fully and that they have real expertise.

While some of the research literature on project organization emphasizes the difficulties involved in frequent changes of project and the need to adapt to new people and constellations at frequent intervals (Reeser, 1969), in practice the opposite also seems to be a problem at Enator. Not everyone likes projects which last for a long time.

If projects go on too long and last for several years, then you pass the pain threshold. But that's not why you work as a consultant.

For the most part, consultants appear to be extrovert individuals who are prepared to take on new tasks. They look for flexibility in the job situation and variety in their project assignments.

Project work is characteristically a pulsing phenomenon, with phases of varying intensity and content. Sometimes, consultants have to work far more than normal in order to make things work. The way in which people react to such working conditions is partly a matter of their personality. Moxnes (1981) identifies two psychological approaches to work and organizational circumstances. One approach is characterized by a predilection for structure, order and discomfort and anxiety when faced by chaos and disorder. The other approach means that there is a high degree of tolerance for things which are unstructured, flexible and chaotic, while systems, rules, planning and other structural features are regarded as a social straitjacket leading to aversion and dissatisfaction. As far as Enator and similar types of activity are concerned, they probably primarily attract individuals with the latter psychological approach, who then stay with the organization in question.

9.2   The Importance of the Organization for the Work Situation

To what extent do corporate culture and other overall management and organizational circumstances characterize the work and work content in specific terms? Do these factors permeate project work, or do they function more as a kind of social superstructure based on the project assignments?

It is very difficult to answer these questions. On the one hand, it is hardly possible to determine what background and decisive factors are at work, and in exactly what degree they affect the design and implementation of consultancy projects. On the other hand, the character of consultancy assignments varies enormously – ranging from purely resource reinforcement assignments, in which a customer temporarily needs an additional programmer or various types of one-man assignment, to major projects which are completely run by Enator. Enator's business concept and strategy provide certain guidelines for deciding which projects the company wants to take on, but this does not mean that projects are homogeneous. Market requirements mean a great deal more than the preferences of Enator management and employees as regards what projects are desirable or not.

Inspired by Harris, Reed (1985) makes a distinction between primary and secondary social practices. The former are a question of activities which mean the concrete creation of values in the form of goods or services. The latter

are directed at achieving overall integration and regulation of the former through the design, implementation, monitoring and redesigning of various administrative, political, and judicial mechanisms which combine the multifarious primary practices in which human populations are necessarily engaged. They are imposed with the aim of coordinating the diverse and complex array of primary 'productive' practices in which communities of human populations are engaged into institutional structures which provide the required degree of normative coherence, social control, and stability necessary to sustained continued productive activity (Reed, 1985, p 121).

According to this view, organizations are a kind of secondary social practice, functioning as integrative and regulatory mechanisms which lead to the productive work taking the form of cohesive social patterns. Secondary social practices include organizational structures (regarded as repetitive patterns of action associated with social relations), routines, standards, corporate culture, management, etc. Social-integrative leadership and management, a concept which I introduced in the preceding chapter, is another example.

Thus, secondary social practices can be equated with various ways of achieving control and the integration of operations. In the case of Enator, primary social practices are programming, reports, investigations, etc. (In certain cases a secondary social practice is also sold, for example, when a consultant conducts a strategic study or functions as an acting development or computer manager in a customer company.) In the border area between the primary and the secondary, we find project management, an activity which may require considerable numbers of personnel. In an extremely large project, for example, which employed approximately 25 people at the time my study was conducted, the staff included a project manager, a project leader (head), three coordinators and four sub-project leaders, most working with programming and management and integration tasks. The primary task – programming – and the actual work content are only marginally influenced by Enator's management style, corporate culture, etc. Project management and implementation are strongly characterized by the nature of the task and the competence, experience and size of the project group and also the extent to which people involved in the project know each other. But secondary social practices, including practices which can be seen as part of the corporate culture, are also relevant. Thus, the concrete work situation is affected to some extent by the organization's overall manner of operation. A consultant described the project in which he was working as follows:

We don't worry about protecting our own personal domain, and we are not afraid to stumble into each other's territory. We don't work in hierarchies at all and we rarely give a single individual an assignment since we believe that you get results quicker if two people share a job and discuss their way through to a solution.

Here, the method of work is regarded as an expression of a particular subsidiary company's manner of functioning. Thus, organizational factors to some extent influence the concrete work situation faced by personnel at the point of intersection between primary and second social practices. Influence seems to be most powerful in the older parts of Enator, that is to say areas which are primarily encompassed by the corporate culture. At the same time, the actual core of operations – usually programming – is determined by factors which are not organization-specific. A consultant from another subsidiary than the previously quoted interviewee stated that:

The job is the same as elsewhere. If I'm working at programming, it doesn't matter whether it says 'Enator', 'Programmator' or 'Datalogic' on my back.

In a way, it might be said that "the culture" is stronger and clearer the further removed employees are from primary social practices as regards activities carried out within the company's area of business. Values such as social affinity and comradeship, and the metaphor of "the Enator corporate building is a home", etc. have their greatest impact several stages removed from the concrete production of services.

The name Enator is associated with champagne bubbles, the beautiful headquarters building, ambition, rocketing share prices, and the acquisition of new companies and so on. But it is easy for us who work for the company not to notice all that. We can see it at the 10th anniversary and at the Annual General Meeting. Sometimes it even irritates us. Because this company does not pay top bucks. The reason for staying on is that you have fun together. We have a good team in our subsidiary.

This interviewee added that it was activities around the actual job – parties, quarterly conferences, involvement in the art club and the choir, etc. – that meant that employees "got something special out of Enator".

The above statement indicates that the corporate culture – that is to say the values, rites, and style which are specific for the organization – are of considerable importance in several respects, but that they sometimes have limited impact on actual project operations. But, even if the culture is largely a superstructure phenomenon, and the actual job is primarily determined by something else, no strict line can be drawn between "cultural superstructure" and everyday activities. Instead, the corporate culture may be regarded as an overall frame of reference and a reservoir of (rules for) feelings, ideas, and social and emotional ties which have *some* effect on everyday project work. These ties influence the willingness of individuals to work, providing a slight tinting of their interpretative filters (chiefly in the social aspects of project work), and they help to create social bonds, both as regards ties between individual employees, and between employees and the company. Corporate culture is a "resource" which managers can utilize in the day-to-day influence they exert on individuals.

The corporate culture affects individuals not just at a general level – making employees relatively satisfied, fostering a positive feeling for the company, or ensuring that they tend to stay with the company longer and perhaps work a little harder. Management is very much a question of re-calling and linking up with values, norms, frames of reference and other cultural elements and tying them up with concrete projects. This may, for example, be a question of getting experienced consultants to feel that even boring, routine assignments are meaningful and worth carrying out in the best possible manner so as to build up customer confidence and to see the additional potential for consultancy tasks implicit in such assignments, etc.

Motivational psychologists sometimes refer to "task significance", that is to say the perceived social significance of a work assignment. This is considered to affect motivation in a positive direction (Hackman et al., 1975). The extent to which a routine task can be regarded as significant and to what extent this really affects job satisfaction can be assumed to depend on how strong identification and involvement in the employee's company is. Thus, culture can be assumed to increase the propensity to view tasks which may possibly benefit the company as more important and also to accept less agreeable assignments. This operates both directly (*per se* as a result of the acceptance of key values and ideas by individuals), and also via managers who recall and play on the "psychological contract" which the corporate culture helps to establish.

There is a heavy emphasis on loyalty. The culture is there to build up a we-feeling and loyalty to the company. If we didn't have it, people would be resigning all over the place. It's there for egoistic reasons on the part of the company. But it doesn't need to be negative. It's also fun. You don't say 'I don't give a damn about this', or 'I'm not going to do it', or 'I'm not going there'. People just don't do that. And naturally, you take your responsibility. Perhaps company debiting is in a poor state, a budget has to be complied with, maybe the project will lead to additional sales or we have worked there before and they need us now. There isn't anybody else ... . There are many arguments which can be used.

Another aspect of the influence of corporate culture on everyday work is that it improves the social prerequisites for the functioning of project groups. Since social ability is to some extent given priority in the company, in recruitment, the composition of groups and in day-to-day contacts, the probability of reaching agreement within project groups and achieving effective cooperation is increased.

Openness as a central lodestar at Enator may also have a certain impact on the implementation of projects. It is considered to be highly important that people "feel good". Since it is considered that the well-being of personnel can easily affect the quality of consultancy assignments, subsidiary and project managers must know something about the personal situation of their staff in order, for example, not to give people assignments which would mean staying away from home if this would lead to family problems.

This is an example of how the superstructure, which corporate culture must primarily be considered to constitute, affects primary social practices. However, corporate culture, in the sense of something which is primarily created and maintained by management, operates mainly at an overall social-integrative level, with partial parallel links with productive operations.

9.3   Cultural Influence and Awareness of Problems

As the previous chapter has indicated, considerable efforts are made at Enator to integrate employees into the company, and to create a sense of well-being and social cohesion. The classic conflict between the individual's psychological prerequisites and the organization's sophisticated division of labour and bureaucratic methods, leading to a frustration of the individuals' needs (see e.g. Argyris, 1964), cannot be found to any appreciable extent at Enator. The company has no detailed control of work or of the division of tasks into various routine assignments. This is primarily related, of course, with the nature of operations and is not particularly linked to specific management ideals and other attributes which are specific for Enator. Nonetheless, Enator's special style contribute to achieving integration between company requirements and the individual's demands and prerequisites.

Job satisfaction is reported to be high, the company spirit is excellent and personnel turnover low. There is no local trade union at Enator and staff are not members of a union, possibly because it is considered that management is extremely sensitive to the wishes of employees; there are no serious sources of frustration. Can we conclude from this that Enator offers its employees satisfaction in a broad sense?

Not necessarily. Several authors who discuss the consequences for staff of a management which is based on "soft" methods (i.e. with the help of values, norms, measures which encourage affinity, the anchoring of corporate identity with the staff, etc.) point to the risks of the seduction of personnel, of manipulation and of control of employees' perception of reality "from above", by an élite group with powerful resources which runs the company (Alvesson, 1987; Alvesson and Willmott, 1995; Kunda, 1992; Sandberg, 1987; Willmott, 1993). According to one author, "there is an obvious risk that employees will become mentally exhausted, financially exploited, socially indoctrinated and politically manipulated" (von Otter, 1983, p 93). It is also possible to speak of the exploitation of employees' emotions or the colonization of pleasure in the interests of profits and the owners of the company (Burrell, 1992).

Naturally, what is considered to be economic exploitation, indoctrination and manipulation is in many respects a question of taste. However, this is a genuine problem in all issues concerning management and in all types of social influence and in particular in cases where there is an attempt to employ symbols, culture and a group spirit as tools. In this context, I will look at certain potential problems for employees resulting from Enator's management methods. I will then take the risk of making an assessment of how cultural control relates to forms of consciousness in the company.

One potential problem for personnel is the powerful norm of emphasizing positive aspects, while applying a restrictive approach to the presentation of criticism. Some employees I spoke to were not fully satisfied with the situation. They felt it was somewhat inhibiting. The collective pressure to think and act in line with this positive company spirit can create problems at two levels. Firstly, it is more difficult to be aware of negative conditions. The propensity to indulge in criticial examination is reduced. Secondly, the tendency to bring up and emphasize any unsatisfactory circumstances which are perceived is reduced. As a result, there is little mutual exchange of information between employees regarding factors at the workplace which are (or could be) considered unsatisfactory. This affects the feeling of dissatisfaction experienced. Reduced awareness and focus on negative factors also reduces the perceived importance of such factors. A feeling of satisfaction, at least at a superficial attitudinal level, may in other words be affected positively by the fact that social information processes at the place of work inhibit exchanges of information concerning negative factors (cf. Salancik and Pfeffer, 1978).

To some extent, an emphasis on positive factors at the place of work may be in the employees' interest. The organizational climate is probably felt to be better if people are positive, compared with a situation in which complaints and criticism are often raised. But this feeling of satisfaction may be treacherous and illusory. At a deeper level, psychological reactions, which the individual employee would not wish to recognize, may be in the offing.

Conditions at work also affect the individual in many other ways, apart from feelings of satisfaction. The individual can be influenced psychologically, socially, cognitively, etc. in indirect, insidious ways which are not consciously registered. Suppressed conflicts and difficulties at the work place, of which the individual employee is perhaps only vaguely aware and which do not seriously affect his/her attitude to the work, may be expressed in a psychosomatic form or by compensatory release of irritation on the family. A feeling of satisfaction is far from being the only or most important aspect of how work affects people in psychological terms (Kohn, 1980).

Thus, certain aspects of the company's system of values and norms may contribute to a reduced propensity on the part of employees to define problems and to take measures to deal with them. A tendency of this kind may be reinforced by the management's skill in arranging social-integrative activities around the actual work, which generate pleasure. In other words, parties, quarterly conferences, choir sessions, etc., may lead to feelings of loyalty and a positive fundamental attitude towards the company which both contribute to establishing positivism as a value and as a behavioural norm, and also reduce the propensity to be conscious of or to stress problems.

These comments are primarily an indication of potential problems, rather than problems which I know exist for certain. However, I have encountered some information which suggests the existence of this type of "restraint" on the part of personnel when it comes to problem awareness and making demands. For example, many employees note the discrepancy between high rates of debiting and not particularly high salaries, even if they do not "take a stand" when involved in pay negotiations.

Since Enator takes such good care of its staff, the level of tolerance is relatively high. You cut back on your demands for personal development in your career because you get so much else out of the job.

A high degree of persuasion exerted by management at the value, norm and awareness levels may lead to a weakening of the employee's negotiation position. The employee's individual insights and overview regarding the fine print in the psychological contract are crucial in this context. (The concept of the psychological contract involves the informal mutual demands and expectations which the employee and the employer/boss have on each other and which regulate rights and obligations.) A reasonable balance means that the individual's work performance corresponds in terms of time, quality and involvement in proportion to what the company offers him or her in a broad sense. The company offers the employee rewards and other benefits, but also job assignments which involve difficulties and frustration. If the individual has good, broad insights into everything the employer does for him/her, (s)he will have a good basis for trying to provide a reasonable compensatory achievement (e.g. by working over-time to a certain extent and perhaps by spending his/her leisure in the pursuit of activities organized by the company, etc.), thus achieving a bal-ance between what is given and received at work. Influence exercised via a corporate culture such as Enator's may, however, mean that the individual finds it more difficult to understand what the psychological contract means. The positive sides of what the company has to offer the employee are emphasized, while the more debatable aspects are not allowed to emerge to the same extent. When, in various contexts, representatives of Enator's management exert cultural or social-integrative influence, this may be regarded as a public relations description of the company's share in the psychological contract: there is talk of what is expected of employ-ees and a description in flattering terms of what the company has to offer. In this situation, cultural influence may lead employees to make more ef-fort than is reasonably called for.

It has clearly been the case that some employees have operated on the basis of a psychological contract which they subsequently became doubtful about:

What do we get out of this? What's in it for us? This feeling didn't exist at the start, in the first few years. But then it started to appear. What the hell do you get out of working yourself to death, working so damn hard?
People don't talk so much about this today. There was a time when they did. But nowadays you don't work yourself to death even if there are actually quite a lot of people who do, and then they work like hell.

This quotation illustrates how employees at a certain point in time can feel that they are contributing more than is reasonable in relation to what the company gives them in exchange and what the owners gain from the com-pany's profits and success.[1]

I would hardly propose to lay down any moral rules or yardsticks for what is reasonable work performance in relation to a given reward struc-ture. But, on the other hand, I would like to indicate the desirability of employees having good opportunities to make a broad-ranging assessment of the pluses and minuses in the exchange relationship with their em-ployer. To the extent that cultural influence means difficulty in achieving a broad picture, for example as a result of a biased flow of information, this is a potential problem from the employee's point of view. This problem always exists, but it is particularly relevant in workplaces where corporate culture is successfully employed as a method of management and where there is a normative bias favouring positive attitudes and discouraging crit-icism.

It is interesting to compare the relative importance of cultural influence – including guidelines for interpreting reality – with the spontaneous, direct observations of their environment made by individuals. In other words, what is the role of corporate culture as regards how individuals perceive everyday phenomena which are dubious in relation to the content of this culture (according to an external observer who is not influenced by the local interpretative framework of the corporate culture)? It is obviously difficult to study this question. On the one hand, it is difficult to switch off the corporate culture as a factor of influence in relation to other factors while, on the other hand, it is also hard to find criteria to determine the clarity/doubtfulness of everyday phenomena in relation to the content of the culture.

In analytical terms, however, a scale of cultural influence might be imagined which ranges from, at one extreme, a situation in which management's systematic cultural influence totally determines consciousness to, at the opposite extreme, determination of consciousness by concrete, "objective" material reality ("existence determines consciousness"). These extremes would not appear to occur in modern companies since cultural indoctrination hardly involves brainwashing, nor does it permit measurement of the "objective circumstances". "The truth" is relativistic vis-à-vis the individual's cultural background and the way in which human beings work at a psychological level. A complicated reality is understood in an "intersubjective" and/or a "subjective" manner. Berger and Luckmann (1966) tell us that reality is a social construction. Also the researcher's point of view involves the construction or the interpretation of social reality, rather than the establishment of social facts.

What is the actual situation at Enator regarding the relationship between its celebration of ideals and values such as a flat, unhierarchical, open and non-bureaucratic organization on the one hand, and corporate practices on the other? Do the assertions and interpretative rules of the corporate culture permeate employee perceptions so strongly that deviations from what is prescribed by the culture are not registered or are explained away? In other words, is it the case that "reality" (e.g. everyday behaviour, corporate practices) does not directly correct and modify about the ideals and values which apply de facto? Or does "reality" get its revenge by ensuring that deviation from what is preached means that the preacher and his sermons are taken with a pinch of salt? The answer to the last question is that this is what happens, to a considerable extent. It is primarily a question of ambiguous phenomena, which are either interpreted in accordance with the espoused values and norms or where the lack of compliance does not have any major impact in the form of scepticism and disillusionment.

However, in a couple of cases I have observed that management's definition of situations tends to influence employee expressed views more
than their direct experience. In the course of an interview with someone
who had been employed at Enator for nine months, I asked the interviewee to compare Enator with his former place of work. It was interesting to
note that a great many of the points he mentioned appear to be derived
more from the company rhetoric presented in the project management
philosophy course and in other official contexts than from his own, direct
experience.

The interviewee said that one important difference was the relative lack
of hierarchy. At his previous place of employment he had a group manager as his immediate superior, while at Enator there was a flat structure.
"My only boss is X (subsidiary manager)", he said. A few minutes later in
the interview, we started to talk about the interviewee's possibilities of
having an influence on the type of assignments he received. It turned out
that the last time he received a new assignment, he had been given the job
by Y, without being asked whether he was interested or not. I then asked if
Y had managerial responsibilities and received the answer: "Yes, he works
directly under X." Thus, in practice Y functioned as a middle manager
with semi-formal status as second-in-command. As far as the interviewee
was concerned – a graduate engineer with several years of working experience – there was no doubt that Y was a superior. But, at the same time this
was less prominent in the interviewee's conceptual world when he thought
about his place of work than the official – but from his own concrete experience, half-true or even erroneous – version of a flat organization, where
his only boss is the managing director of the subsidiary.

The corporate culture emphasizing a flat organization may thus influence consciousness at the expense of the individual's own experience. The
interviewee's response was not explained, as a critical reader might perhaps suspect, by his desire to present the company in favourable public
relations terms. There is always the risk that people hesitate before they
say something unfavourable and that they allow loyalty to the company to
control their tongues. However, in this interview, the interviewee was not
afraid of expressing negative opinions in other contexts, and hence I consider that the interview extract cited above reflected his conscious views
on this point. But on the whole, this type of "false consciousness" is very
hard to prove.[2]

The conclusion that may be drawn is thus that systematic management
influence may give rise to ideas and forms of consciousness which to some
extent contrast with the concrete experienced reality which characterizes
the existence of individual employees.

While some people are sometimes all too easily prepared to accept officially marketed versions of how the organization functions, this is not the

general tendency in Enator, in my experience. As I hope this book has demonstrated throughout, I met many people with critical, balanced and sensible views regarding the company. I also have the impression that management has an open attitude as regards management style and methods of exerting influence. In a study of an American high technology company with in many ways the same style at corporate level as Enator, Kunda (1992) noted that many employees distanced themselves from the culture, and I also have the feeling that this applies to most employees at Enator. People are not easily brainwashed in companies.

For the most part, in my opinion corporate culture is *not* normally a question of any general far-reaching indoctrination of personnel resulting in the determination of ideas and consciousness by management. Influence exerted by the corporate culture involves a *slight* or moderate tendency for personnel to perceive organizational and work conditions on management terms. There are isolated examples of how statements and assumptions which emanate from the "culture" predominate and eliminate actual circumstances as a primary source of consciousness in a specific question.

9.4   Enator and Trade Unionism

There is no local trade union at Enator and employees do not belong to any national union either. This phenomenon, which does not comply with Swedish traditions, has recently become increasingly common in youthful and often technologically advanced companies (Geijerstam and Reitberger, 1986). I will not examine this question in detail, in the belief that a couple of comments will suffice.

As Ouchi (1981) points out, for example, a good relationship between employers and employees on both sides can escape overheads in the form of time and money and "bureaucracy" which formalized union-employer relationships involve, may benefit both sides. If employees receive good pay, security and stimulating working conditions, it is not felt that there is much need for a union. In a company like Enator, where the personnel are undeniably of decisive importance (and in fact the company's only resource worth talking about), it is in the employer's interest to treat staff well. And Enator employees would agree with this view, at least at the time when my study was conducted.

However, from the personnel point of view, the lack of the security which union membership provides involves two types of problem. The fact that an expansive and financially successful company has a satisfactory personnel policy does not, of course, mean that everything will work peacefully and smoothly in a period of financial stringency and hard times. If there is a serious deterioration in the demand for computer consultancy services of the type sold by Enator, there may be a rapid change in employees' perception of the need for union membership. However, setting up an effective union organization takes both time and energy. In addition, it would appear that cyclical changes are rapid in the consultancy business.

Another problem from the employee point of view relates to older staff members. So far, there are very few of these at Enator, but in a few years perhaps some employees will have passed the 50 mark. This may be a problem in a computer consultancy, partly because the job sometimes involves stress and partly because customers seem to expect the consultants to be young. At Enator, it is thought that perhaps employees will not have sufficient energy to be consultants throughout their working lives. Management, for example, has recently started to talk about "happy exits". This is an attempt to disseminate the idea that it is wise to look for another job when a career as a consultant begins to feel burdensome or when the consultant's customer-attractiveness starts to diminish.

Just as the company has a considerable interest in taking good care of its more profitable staff, it is not too difficult to imagine that there is less concern when employees are not considered to be quite so profitable. The problem with companies like Enator is that consultants are expected to meet high standards of efficiency and effectiveness, and that there is an extremely limited number of administrative and other positions which are somewhat less exposed to such demands. This means limited opportunities for the relocation of consultants who cannot really cope any longer. There is a greater interest in getting rid of unprofitable labour in knowledge-intensive firms such as Enator than in many other types of companies. Thus, the lack of a union or staff association at the place of work means potential problems in the long term. But these problems will not necessarily become acute. In the short term, there are no strong reasons for Enator personnel to unionize.

The question of what the establishment of a union branch would mean for the cultural patterns which currently characterize the company is interesting but purely hypothetical. Would the establishment of such a branch primarily comply with the tendencies established by Enator's style of management and values system, for example informal action and a positive rather than a critical approach to matters? This would involve partial subordination of the union to Enator's corporate culture. In a company like Enator, it is probably difficult to set up a union branch which develops a distinct union culture vis-à-vis the company. Obviously, poor prerequisites for a distinct union culture reduce the potential effectiveness and opportunities for union activities to exert an influence.

Some views on factors in the organization which facilitate or limit employee influence are presented in Alvesson (1993d).

9.5   Summary of Chapter 9

In this chapter, I have raised a number of points relating to working conditions at Enator and the functioning of the company in a personnel context. The nature of consultancy work has received special attention, and this also applies to the importance of management and organizational factors in the job situation faced by employees. The work situation involves a number of uncertainties and difficulties, but the problematic aspects of work at Enator seem to be less explicit than in many other organizations in which project operations are the essential feature. Several authors, for example, Kunda (1992), Mintzberg (1983), Robbins (1983) and Reeser (1969), emphasize that uncertainty and high demands in adhocracies and project organizations mean considerable strain on personnel. At Enator, however, there is a sense of well-being and low personnel turnover. This might be partly explained by selectivity in recruitment or because the corporate culture and the organizational climate function as a kind of "social shock absorber" which reduces some of the strain in the actual work operation. Also, the favourable business situation may facilitate a positive work situation.

In this chapter, some latent problems in the company from the personnel point of view have also been indicated. Of course, it is not certain that a youthful, successful company, which staff considers to be good at taking care of its employees and making them feel good, can demonstrate an equally harmonious personnel/company relationship in situations with a tougher climate and an ageing work-force. Many of the positive factors at Enator can be ascribed to the fact that the company, at the time of my study, is in a growth industry and that the favourable labour-market for computer staff means that there has been keen competition for labour.

9.6   Summary of Some of the Themes in Chapters 7-9: Management and the Job Situation for Personnel

Figure 9.1 provides an overall picture of relations between some of the central themes in the company's control of personnel and the work situation of employees, and also the feelings and experiences of employees at work and in the organization. The figure also summarizes aspects which have been treated in this chapter and in the two preceding chapters (Chapters 7 and 8).

The central idea is that the total work situation faced by employees is determined by three central dimensions: concrete, material working conditions; social relationships; and the corporate identity. The former are undoubtedly normally the most important dimensions, but they are outside the main focus of this book. They include work content (what you do and how you do it), the physical work environment, working hours, pay, etc. Social relationships express the quality, frequency and forms for interpersonal interactions within the company. Group spirit, a feeling of comradeship, cooperative structures, participation and hierarchy also come under this heading. Corporate identity denotes the feeling of being part of a totality, of belonging to the company as an institution and of contributing to its total results.

Although working conditions are the most important factor for an employee's feelings, experiences and satisfaction at his/her place of work, from the management point of view corporate identity and social relationships are of greater interest, at any rate in companies like Enator in which an impoverished job content and a poor physical environment normally do not constitute a significant problem. It is somewhat easier for management to influence corporate identity and social relationships in the work place, since the scope for action is somewhat greater. The actual working condi-

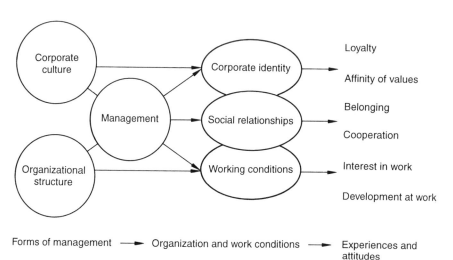

Figure 9.1:   Model describing management influence on the employee work situation and attitudes to work and the company

tions are determined to a large extent by the nature of the assignments which come in, which are in their turn decided by customer requirements and wishes, and market and competitive conditions. The "substantive" aspects of the company's operations are largely determined by external dependencies, which substantially reduce management possibilities of having an influence on what projects and working conditions which consultants have to cope with (cf. Pfeffer and Salancik, 1978). The company can, to some extent, make "strategic choices" with respect to market segments and the kind of project assignments preferred, but Enator's size and growth objectives mean that the company cannot be very selective about customers and jobs. However, the scope for influencing corporate spirit, attitudes, employee perceptions of the organization and other "non-concrete" aspects may be quite considerable. External resource dependencies and restrictions are less significant in this context (Pfeffer, 1981a). Managers may, for example, have considerable impact on the degree of openness which characterizes an organization (Hofstede et al., 1990).

The three central dimensions – concrete working conditions, social relationships and corporate identity – overlap to some extent. A strong corporate identity affects feelings of comradeship within the organization, while social relationships and concrete working conditions overlap in project group operations. On the whole, however, it may be wise to make a distinction between these three dimensions.

Three main forms of management influence may be distinguished: organizational structure, corporate culture and leadership. Organizational structure and corporate culture are more systematic, exert more overall effects and are linked to the total corporate entity, while leadership is to some extent a varying quality, tied to individual managers. However, leadership is also heavily affected by organizational structure and corporate culture. To some extent, leadership may be regarded as the transmission of certain structures and as the administration of the corporate culture. As the figure indicates, corporate culture primarily influences corporate identity and social relationships, while organizational structure affects social relationships and working conditions.

Corporate identity, social relationships and working conditions affect a number of central experiences and attitudes on the part of employees vis-à-vis the job and the company. These include loyalty, shared values, belonging, a propensity to cooperate, interest in the work and a feeling of personal development at work.

Of course, a number of factors which are not directly represented in the model also affect such feelings and attitudes – for example the backgrounds, personalities and competence of individual employees. And, of course, a number of external factors are also actively involved – for example market conditions and the state of maturity of the company and the industry. Nonetheless, the model points at several major internal decisive organizational factors which are at the root of the overall job situation faced by employees.

This chapter concludes the section of this book which focuses on personnel and organizational conditions and internal aspects of corporate management. These aspects will be dealt with more indirectly in future chapters but will come increasingly into focus once more in the two final chapters of this book.

Notes

[1]   Similar experiences appear to be relatively common when companies that originally were characterized by strong feelings of community and people-oriented values grow and become larger than companies (Martin, 1992; Wilkins and Dyer, 1987).

[2]   This interviewe episode also illuminates that consciousness can be seen as fluid and fragmented, rather than consistent and integrated. "Recognizing" the former qualities does not, however, indicates that contradictions as strong as those expressed by the interviewee, should be seen as the "normal" way of relating to workplace experiences.

10   The Business Concept as a Symbol

While Chapters 5-9 treated organization, leadership and personnel, the present and the following two chapters will deal with business and marketing themes in Enator and, by implication, knowledge-intensive service companies in general. This category is sometimes referred to as professional business service companies. (The service character of consultancy firms is significant in terms of exchange relations with the environment, which means that parts of that which is being treated in Chapters 10-12 is of less direct application for the understanding of manufacturing knowledge-intensive companies, i.e. high tech companies.) The focus mainly concerns the external dimension of corporate management, but this does not mean that organizational aspects are neglected. Even though the following chapters draw primarily upon literature on corporate strategy and marketing, organization theory is still significant as a source of inspiration and interpretation. As in previous chapters, the goal is to transcend a narrow empirical focus on the case study and to say something of a more general interest for the understanding of business concept (mission statement), strategic processes and the marketing of knowledge-intensive services. Empirical descriptions are treated in less detail in order to provide more space for literature reviews and more general discussions.

In this chapter the business concept is treated, the next will focus on strategy (strategic processes) whilst Chapter 12 addresses marketing.

10.1   The Notion of the Business Concept

Normann's (1975) notion of the business concept has had a considerable impact on management studies and possibly also on practice in Sweden. His concern was the complicated and "hard to pin down" know-how that is built into the organization and that can give the company superior capability in relation to its environment (the market). According to Normann, the term "business concept" is perhaps not really ideal partly because the interest is with concrete relationships as well as ideas and partly because it references a complex system and therefore cannot be reduced solely to a single concept or an idea. Normann defines the business concept as a "system for dominance" in a given market segment. One problem with this comprehensive notion of the business concept is that it includes too much. Many writers prefer to split up the product/market relationship and the company's competence (technology). Sjöstrand (1985), for example, speaks of the exchange idea to describe the basis of a company's relations with its environment. Understanding companies such as Enator requires seeing the notion of the business concept in relation to the company as a whole. I therefore associate myself with a broader notion of the business concept, similar to Normann's approach. The problems associated with this broader idea of the business concept will be discussed further in this paper.

The business concept combines a number of factors within and outside the company and weaves them together into a complicated pattern that consists of various compatible components. These components are the niche/market segment, the company's product system, and the company's organizational structure and competence. Thus, a functional business concept means that a company, operating in a given market, offers the customers products that are adapted to the market niche, with an organization that is structured so that technology, competence and management style are precisely balanced for the product and the market involved. Expressed in the very simplest terms, a business concept represents a harmony between the market, the product and the organization.

In this sense, the notion of the business concept is one variation of a large number of more or less closely associated conceptualizations of a company's fundamental relationships with its market. Levitt (1960), who was a central source of conceptualizations, argued that one should try to avoid thinking of a company's operations in terms of the technology or products with which it worked, and instead to extend the perspective to look at the company and the industry on the basis of the customer's needs or functions that are satisfied. He challenged his colleagues to adopt a less short-sighted, myopic approach to the market. As many authors have pointed out, this in itself, is insufficient and it only describes one aspect of how the "business concept" is basically evolved. Conceptualizing one's own operations, for example regarding oneself as a railway or tin can manufacturer or defining operations as a company in the transport or packing industry, possibly facilitates the understanding of one's own role in relation to the customer's situation and competitive conditions, but it does not say very much about what should be done in concrete terms or about what the company's distinct competence looks like.

Different authors have tried to arrive at definitions of operations in ways that are sufficiently viable to serve as a starting point for well thought-out strategies. Abell (1980) suggests, for example, that "defining the business" is a question of determining the combination of customer functions, customer groups and the company's own technologies. But Normann's (1975) conception is advantageous for my survey. His notion of the business concept does not have the same bias towards marketing as those applied by most authors in this field and he seriously examines the organizational dimension. He also typifies a considerable number of books in the area that also develop the system of "components" – the market, the product (service) and the organization (competence, resources) as a proper object for study (Ekvall, 1989).

According to Normann (1975), the notion of the business concept has a deeper meaning that encompasses various intraorganizational structures as well as the product/market considerations:

> We not only wish to include ideas about the market and the company's role – what is to be dominated – in the notion of the business concept, but also how this is to be achieved and the conversion of these ideas into concrete arrangements. It is not enough to say that you are in the transport business – if this is in any way a statement endowed with insight in a given situation. You do not have any kind of business concept unless you also have a formula for how "you can make money" in the transport business and unless you have been able to translate this formula into organizational and other types of arrangement (pp 48-49).

Normann refers to Selznick (1957), who emphasizes the importance of an institutionalization process through which understanding of the organization's external mission and special competence is embodied, permeates the organization and is anchored in the values of the members of the organization.

10.2   Enator's Business Concept

Enator's management indicates that the company's business concept is a matter of "combining management know-how with technical computer know-how, so that clients become more competitive and efficient" (Annual report, 1986). Almost identical formulations emphasize the goal of helping clients to integrate a strategic perspective into their data processing systems and to improve the clients' business:

> We sell opportunities to improve efficiency and competitiveness with the help of data processing (CEO in an interview).

Enator's market segment is comprised of medium-sized and large companies and, is thus primarily composed of top decision makers. Such clients are offered data processing services that can help customers to improve their business. The products are computer consultancy services in the broadest possible sense of the term, ranging from the implementation of major computer development projects to specific services such as "management for hire", training, investigations, project management, and so forth. The organization is characterized by a number of operational subsidiary companies with different market orientations, project organizations and areas of competence, with programming and project management as their primary features.

Enator pushes its business concept hard. As we saw in Chapter 5, the business concept has a crucial role in the training and socialization of new recruits. It is often mentioned in corporate publications and also often crops up spontaneously in my interviews.

Like Normann (1975), we could assume that a company's business concept is a decisive factor in its success and that the degree of agreement and harmony between the various parts of the company determines whether the business concept works – or fails to work. Perhaps we should conclude that the concept has been realized and has a powerful impact, in view of Enator's splendid successes in the form of high profits, rapid growth, good market reputation and a high degree of personnel satisfaction. But the question is whether matters are really as simple as this.

10.3   A Mystery

According to Asplund (1970), two important element of social science research are supposed to be 1) the formulation and 2) the solution of mysteries. So I am now going to depict a small mystery.

The ten or so people that I interviewed about Enator's business concept gave me what can only be described as highly divergent responses when questioned about the concept – despite the fact that all my interviewees should have had a good insight into the company. Most of them had several years of experience at Enator and they were project managers, subsidiary managers, etc. – not just junior consultants.

Some of my interviewees considered that the official business concept describes actual conditions rather well and that Enator's successes were largely a result of close adherence to the concept. Here are some typical responses:

Linking the development of a new system to the customer's business concept and area of operations is our basic philosophy.

I don't believe we are any better (than other companies) from a purely work point of view. We are better at some things. And that is precisely the fundamental business concept: management and computer development. But we are no better at computer development, perhaps worse in some cases. But on the management side – our way of handling customers – that's where we are better.

Our target group is corporate managements, not data processing departments.

But other interviewees give a different picture:

We are supposed to be computer consultants, combined with management consulting and this has been part of our business concept for several years. But Christer, Hasse and John (i.e. Enator's founders) represented the management side. They didn't recruit people at a lower level with that orientation, they wanted computer consultants – programmers and systems analysts.

Question: The connection between computers and management, that is to say the business concept, does that apply to the technical subsidiares?

Response: Yes, that's true on paper, but we have never worked with it ... My impression is that there is something slightly strange about computers and management, computers and business concepts, working with such things consistently, especially when you have a lot of technically based activities ... . As an ambition back in 1977, it was no doubt an exceptionally fine service. But then we couldn't really make it. Of course, if you send out Christer Jacobsson (the chairman of the company and one of the founders) as a consultant, he can probably fix up a good strategy and combine computers with management, and no doubt that's what he did in the early days. But it is all very bound up with a couple of key individuals.

When I was recruited, I asked my boss what the management assignments were like. He was very honest and replied 'What the hell, no way'. Well, he expressed it more elegantly than that, but that's what he was trying to say.

Another interviewee maintained, rather cynically, that the real business concept, when the company started up, was to recruit programmers, who were a scarce resource on the labour market at that time, and by the skilful use of social attractions, to retain them in the company and to make money by selling their labour in the form of consultancy services. (Strictly speaking, this does not contradict the official business concept).

Somewhat confused by the various statements made about Enator's business concept – which cannot be wholly explained by differences in the position of the interviewees or the fact that they worked for different subsidiary companies, etc. – I asked a subsidiary manager how things "really" were with the management aspects – and received the following answer:

Good question. It is excellent that it is included (in the formulation of the business concept). The fact is that, both traditionally and currently, Enator has had extremely good contacts at top level with customers, compared to other consulting companies. We have found this very useful, especially on the technical side. In most cases, our competitors only work at a lower operative level, dealing with development managers, for example. And we do that too. But in practice, we also have a contact network at a higher level. Damn useful! And that's the level you sell at.

There are also consultants who have this profile, on the technical side too. Not here with me, but with X. X and Y could take on a major consultancy assignment which involved starting up and operating a major development department in a company. But then on the technical side, we interpret these things differently. In our world, management means development managers. At Company EX, the development

manager has a budget of SEK 400 million. We don't just talk to him about programming, we also talk business. That's the kind of relationship we have.
Management is not just running the company, it's also project management. I don't
think we can say that we have smarter technical people than our customers. But
nonetheless we work much better in projects than they do. That's because we bring
in some project management. It permeates our whole approach. Push things forward until you achieve objectives. This has been expressed in the project philosophy course and this is an approach which characterizes Enator's whole method of
working.

Some other interviewees also provided information which was somewhere
in between these rather contradictory views of Enator's business concept.
In other words, I have obtained responses which are extremely varied
from a number of individuals who might have been expected to have a
good knowledge of the company's operations and who ought to have been
acquainted with the business concept as applied at Enator and the key
terms utilized in this concept – for example "management".

What is the "real" state of affairs? Is Enator's real business concept, the
actual way in which money is made, identical with what is expressed "officially", or is the company's business concept rather different? The business concept is clearly misleading, if management's formulation of the
business concept is considered to be a question of giving business and
strategy issues the same weight in Enator's operations as data processing
matters in quantitative terms in project work or in the competence profile
of Enator's consultants. But if the business concept is interpreted as meaning that data processing services, in a wider sense, are the primary feature
and that an attempt is also made to describe and handle such data processing aspects from a management and business perspective, then this formulation is valid.

It might be said that data processing is the core of Enator's operations.
The management perspective comes into its own in three ways 1) in the
form of minor management assignments, for example strategic information studies, 2) as a sales channel, where the contact network means that
consultancy services are anchored at a high level in the customer company,
and 3) because in many cases there is an attempt, in parallel with the main
consultancy project operations, to relate day-to-day activities with overall
business, strategy and management issues. To the extent that management
also includes project management, then obviously this is an important part
of Enator's operations. But, at the same time, management aspects in the
sense of strategic or top management questions are a limited aspect of
Enator's operations in volume terms. Only a very limited number of individuals have any extensive competence in the management consultancy
area. Several projects are to some extent linked to business and strategy
issues and involve an interaction between Enator employees and customer

management, while in other (most?) projects there are no such links and interactions.

It is important to note how the meaning of the business concept has partially shifted at Enator, even though the formulation of the concept has remained unchanged since the formation of the company. Originally, Enator was only concerned with administrative data processing and business and strategy aspects were more central parts of the projects. The three founders of the company also represented a considerable fund of corporate management competence. But as time passed, considerable technical competence was developed, together with expertise in other operational areas that do not have the same clear business orientation (regarding the contents of consultancy projects) as the dominant themes of earlier years. Concepts such as management, strategy and improvement of the customer's competitiveness are also rather broad and imprecise; they can cover almost anything and various types of couplings are possible. For example, skilful, competent project management can be regarded as a form of management, but it is hardly strategic management.

Primary in the business concept at Enator is that it represents an endeavour, their ideal ambition is to:

enhance the focus on computer questions so that it is no longer purely the computer departments which are concerned with data processing, but instead it becomes an aspect of the company's operations which is just as important as personnel questions and other product resources (Subsidiary manager).

In this light, the fact that ambition is not always realized is not that significant. The company comforts itself with the thought that there is a chance of achieving this objective, even if there may be projects which do not fully achieve Enator's business concept. Projects which deviate considerably from the business concept are legitimized because they permit Enator to mesh itself in with the customer company. Perhaps it is possible to see new opportunities, to ask questions and to point out interesting circumstances in the customer company which lie outside the actual consultancy project. It may also be possible to utilize a given assignment in other ways as a springboard to establish contact with corporate management and thus relate computer questions to the business and strategy level where Enator claims it belongs. This is how Enator bridges over the contradiction between ideals and (perceived) reality.

The business concept has a function which supplements the purely descriptive aspects. The possible purposes of this function will be taken up next. My response to the question of why various versions of the "true nature" of the business concept exist at Enator is that the business concept may have various functions, that can be persuaded or toned down, in various ways. The complexity of these functions constitutes an important

background dimension that contributes to informing Enator employees –
and probably applies in any other kind of operation – about the form that
matters "really" take.

10.4   Possible Functions of a Business Concept

I am going to examine six possible functions of a business concept such as
Enator's: analytical, integrative, controlling, ideological, marketing and
image-transmitting functions.

The *analytical* function is a question of capturing the core of the operations as precisely and "realistically" as possible (i.e. what characteristics of
the company and what aspects of the market have an effective exchange
relationship and what are the decisive features of this relationship). In
other words, this function calls for a creative picture of and insights into
what the corporate operation is about. The analytical functions is a question of providing as good a basis of knowledge as possible for management's intellectual functioning and corporate strategies. This is primarily
what Normann (1975) is referring to with his notion of the business concept. Much the same applies to other authors who speak of the "definition
of business" or intone similar expressions (e.g. Abell, 1980).

The second function is *integrative*. In other words, the business concept
constitutes a cohesive link in operations. This is not the same as Normann's reference to coherence and harmony in the business concept (the
system for achieving dominance). For Normann – and for most other authors who speak of the business concept – this is mainly a question of
control from above so that the various components match and support
each other. When I refer to the integrative function, I am thinking more of
the anchoring of the business concept with various sub-units within the
company, which makes it cohesive in what might be called a voluntary
manner. Thus the business concept is not, as in Normann's case, that which
guides (lies behind) various control and coordinative measures, but is in
itself the (symbolic) means of achieving integration. The business concept – if the personnel are familiar with and positive to it – transmits a
feeling of belonging to a totality. The business concept's integrative function is a question of indicating frameworks for operations, which then tend
to be retained in addition to the use of direct control via budgets, marketing plans and other formal control systems, thus the integrative function is
mainly a matter of the avoidance of disintegration. The business concept
has a power to unify.

The third function is *controlling* (steering). I imagine that, in purely concrete terms, the business concept provides guidance for company man-

agers, consultants, etc. in their operative action. Knowledge of the business concept means that it tends to indicate the direction to be taken in ambiguous situations. This controlling and guiding function differs from the analytical function in that, in this case, concrete action – not analysis and decision making at a strategic level – is in focus. In a similar manner, the controlling function differs from the integrative. While the integrative function primarily involves the maintenance of the "system" and linkages within the organization, the control (steering) function is linked directly with what is to be implemented.

Naturally the business concept exerts control in a variety of different ways. (All the functions discussed here are a matter of control.) What I am interested in here is direct control, that is to say, how the business concept, in itself, affects actions. I thus imagine that a business concept with which all employees are more or less acquainted and accept has a certain direct operative influence. This is something quite different from a business concept that exists in the minds of corporate management, and then materializes in the organizational structure, technology, the competence of personnel, etc. In this case, the business concept itself has no meaning for the actions of employees, but only the arrangements which result from the business concept. However, in a company such as Enator, the influence of the business concept is not limited to the influence of the actions of employees only via other means (systems and structures). It exerts an influence not only indirectly (through means for the implementation of the business concept) but also directly, because the personnel are acquainted with the business concept and are expected to act in accordance with certain, situation-dependent interpretations of this concept. Thus, management can exercise control by telling people what the business concept is and reckoning that, to some extent, it determines the orientation of productive behaviour. It must be emphasized, however, that the business concept far from always having a strong and direct impact on project work can sometimes have a modest or even insignificant impact on work behaviour, as projects do not match the ideals of the business concept.

Something along the same lines applies to the *ideological* function. In using this term, I wish to indicate that the business concept can mean that the company's operations are characterized in a way which legitimizes and evokes positive attitudes to them, both internally and/or externally. The ideological function means that the business concept is formulated in an attractive manner which appeals to the personnel. It must be associated with broadly shared values and contain key words which are positively loaded. However, the ideological function also requires that the business concept is regarded as more or less "correct" (or perhaps not too "incorrect"). If there is a discrepancy between a glamorous formulation of the corporate mission and the view held by internal and external interested parties of the "true nature" of operations, the business concept's ideological function does not work. However, the degree of "correctness" and precision of a business concept differs markedly between what follows from the analytical and ideological usages of the concept. The analytical function of the business concept is fulfilled best if the "company's way of making money" is formulated rather precisely and takes the inevitable degree of complexity into account. From an ideological perspective, however, the "positive" elements are emphasized. A rather simple message is also normally required.

The fifth function which I wish to examine concerns *marketing*. I am referring here to marketing in a rather narrow sense, primarily sales and other marketing areas which are directly linked to the establishment of exchange relationships between companies and customers. Since the product offered by Enator and similar companies is not of a material nature and is difficult to describe, other methods of trying to explain the product (service) become more important. Communicating what you are doing at a comprehensive level is one way of trying to indicate what is being offered. Thus, the business concept constitutes a message which can be directly utilized in a marketing context, especially in companies such as Enator. A potential customer probably benefits directly if he (more seldom a she) knows that Enator is involved in combining computer and management know-how in order to improve the customer's business and general efficiency. This is a sales message which, although perhaps somewhat vague and debatable, says something about what the customer can get out of the company. In other areas of operations, where the product (concrete, visible and measurable) can be studied by the potential buyer directly, the seller's business concept is of minimal interest from the marketing point of view. If I am a potential passenger, I am not necessarily interested in the contours of the airline company's business concept. Flights, prices, comfort and other elements in the product are the decisive factors. The same applies to the purchaser of a Ford or a Volvo. Interest centers on the specific characteristics of the car. It does not matter much whether Volvo's managers regard the company as a car manufacturer or if they think they are in the transportation business. The potential Volvo buyer is probably not considering the purchase of a jet engine.[1]

Thus the marketing aspects of a business concept means that the concept is formulated so as to provide information which facilitates sales and interactions between Enator and customers when working on projects.

The *image* aspect represents a further function. A company's image is a comprehensive summarized picture of the company held by a certain section of the environment. The image thus refers to an overall view of an object. Sometimes it is maintained that it is possible to have an image about anything. As a psychological concept, an image is a dimension of how people conceptualize and perceive an object. But I consider that, in contexts such as the one discussed here, the concept is only meaningful if there is a certain distance between the observer (the observing group) and the object in question. If the observer is very close, or is even part of the object (e.g. a particular company), the object becomes too complex to permit discernment of any special "image" (Alvesson, 1990).

While the marketing aspect of a business concept is linked with sales and specific exchanges on a market, the business concept as a component in a company's image has a broader meaning. The target groups are larger – not merely potential customer companies but also people who may be of interest as recruits and employees, the general public, etc. Thus, from the image perspective the corporate business concept should be formulated in a manner which facilitates the desired image. In relation to the functions listed above, this means that the business concept should be simple, easy to grasp and – thus – easy to communicate. The great general public are less well equipped to understand what Enator does – and are of course less interested – than the company's customers and personnel.

I have indicated six functions. They are summarized in Figure 10.1 and Table 10.1.

The order in which I have arranged these six functions also suggests the space for complexity and precision in the formulation of the business concept. The analytical function needs these characteristics to a high degree, while the contrary applies for the image-oriented function. An ideologically formulated business concept is not a successful instrument for corporate management's precise analysis of "the company's way of making money", nor is it really appropriate as the lode-star for concrete action. Action requires a feeling for when deviations from a theoretically correct course of action are justified and a subtle understanding of what the business concept means at a down-to-earth level. Concrete action also deviates from the understanding of the business concept that is appropriate from an analytical point of view; a fairly high degree of abstraction and an overall systems perspective are more justified from an analytical perspective.

But naturally there are also common features. Despite everything, there is a common core – that the business concept should capture what the company really does in order to earn money.

Enator's explicit business concept – the concept which is formulated and embellished – probably provides a form of compromise between what would be optimal on the basis of the various functions, with a certain bias towards the ideological, integrative and image functions. The analytical and controlling functions require more complex descriptions and interpretations than the business concept formulations which are most commonly presented in official and half-official contexts. The meaning and interpretation of the business concept varies between different groups of inter-

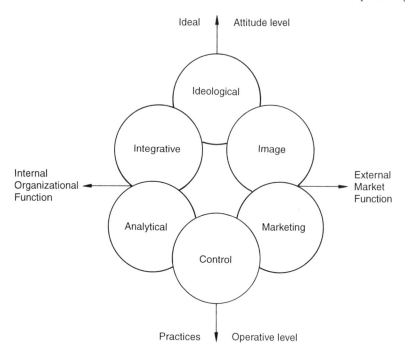

Figure 10.1:   Various aspects of (the functions of) a business concept

ested parties and also from one situation to another. This partly accounts for variations in my interviewee responses about Enator's business concept. Different functions surface to a greater or lesser degree for different individuals, faced with differing situations and cognitive problems. A number of functions, with their accompanying specific interpretations, gives rise to multiple ideas about the core of the business concept.

At the same time, it is difficult to imagine excessive variations in the interpretation of the business concept as a result of the "official" business concept being accompanied by a number of different definitions held by different groups of employees. Excessive variations would lead to too much confusion, and other experienced difficulties. I believe that it is not possible to make any clear distinction between "official" and "real" business concepts or espoused business concept and business concept(s) in use. The official version is "real" enough, and widely subscribed too. Even if it might be advantageous to have different business concepts for different situations and for different groups, this is hardly fully possible in practice. The business concept is needed as a summarizing, comprehensive description of the nature of the company's operations. Belief in one business concept at corporate management level, communicating it in a markedly dif-

Table 10.1: Possible functions of the company's business concept in relation to different target groups and possible (from top management's perspective desirable) consequences

Function	Target Group	Purpose, Possible Effect
Analytical	Corporate management	Cognitively acute conceptualization of company operations
Integrative	All personnel in the company, chiefly managers at lower and medium levels	Mutual understanding, feelings of cohesion, common frame of reference which facilitates collective action
Controlling	Ditto	Action and priorities in day-to-day operations which are in line with the company's basic manner of operating, without being controlled formally or directly
Ideological	All personnel in the company, not least at lower levels, to some extent external interested parties	Attractive opinion of operations, corporate pride, involvement in the work
Marketing	Actual and potential customers	The picture transmitted of products which the company can offer
Image	Potential customers and other relevant sections of the general public	A relatively simple total picture of the character of the company in line with the way the company wants its environment to regard it

ferent form to employees and then formulating it for the general public in terms which differ once again would be counterproductive and would not result in a common understanding of the essence of operation. It would also hinder the communication of the business concept and would cast doubts on the integrity of the company. In Enator, such doubts clearly exist among employees.

Variations on the business concept are thus not a question of whether there are distinctly different formulated concepts. But there are differences in the interpretation of the business concept, especially when it is a question of how strictly or how liberally the concept may be interpreted. Since the business concept constitutes a synthesis of various goals and considerations, it is not merely a direct reflection of the "company's way of making money", in the manner which complies most closely with the analytical function; all the other functions also enter into the picture. The business concept when relating to operations as a whole is not devoid of tension. Contradictions can be seen in the divergent information supplied by the interviewees when asked about Enator's business concept. The ambiguity of the concept (and the company's practices for that matter) is considerable, but not so great that it can prevent some organizational members from perceiving it as misleading or irrelevant in relationship to the consulting projects actually carried out and to some extent it triggers cynicism.

The space for different interpretations of the business concept can also be seen in certain concrete problems. According to one subsidiary manager, the problems of another recently started subsidiary were partly due to incorrect interpretation of the business concept. The corporate management aspects of operations were over-emphasized and many of the consultants recruited were highly qualified and expensive, and not particularly suitable for "normal" programming assignments. Perhaps one might say that in some cases the business concept was interpreted on the basis of an ideological version, where exquisite formulations are taken literally rather than based on a controlling (steering) function, which is more pragmatic and operational – and more appropriate in the context. However, this unfortunate interpretation of the business concept did not seem to be common amongst subsidiary managers. Generally speaking, the concept was interpreted pragmatically, that is to say in line with the function which matched the context. Managers, on the whole, did not appear to be religious about the business concept in relationship to project work.

A certain degree of uncertainty in contacts between Enator and a particular client from the public sector may also be interpreted in terms of the client focusing on Enator's business concept image rather than applying a more appropriate marketing interpretation. This particular client was surprised that Enator was interested in doing business in the public sector, since Enator was considered to have a typically "private industry" orientation. In particular, the business concept employs key words such as "corporate management", "business", "competition", "strategies", etc. which may be interpreted as implying that Enator is not interested in the public sector. Thus, in this case it can be seen that the corporate image hindered marketing and the establishment of an exchange relationship with the client. The correct (pragmatic) interpretation of the business concept, in terms of client types should be that Enator is interested in offering computer consultancy services to an extremely broad spectrum of customers and that, prior to the assignment and while the assignment is going on, Enator wants to establish contact with the customer's management and to get the customer to see data processing in a comprehensive corporate perspective.

I thus consider that it is valuable to perceive the business concept as a phenomenon with many facets which, in itself, can contain various kinds of tensions in terms of interpretations and perspectives.

10.5   Proposals for Extending the Notion of the Business Concept

Now it is time to return to the current view of the business concept, as propounded by Normann (1975), and to compare this view with the conclusions I have reached (above). Normann primarily employs the business concept as an analytical notion, regarding it chiefly as an instrument for corporate management to use in clarifying the company's orientation and the degree of cohesion between the three components contained in the notion: the market niche, the product and the organization. Similar standpoints are adopted by other authors who speak of "the company's mission", "defining the business", etc. Clarifying the business concept means determining the starting point for the corporate strategy (Abell, 1980). However, my discussion (above) has also stressed the possible meaning of the business concept in direct relationship to other groups of interested parties. The social and cultural functions of the business concept have been spotlighted and are not just strategic aspects, but wider organizational and marketing perspectives have also been related to the business concept.

Two types of views appear to be relevant in understanding how the notion of the business concept which I have proposed differs, for example, from Normann's. One type of view involves theoretical assumptions and focuses. Normann assumes the corporate management perspective – and sticks to it almost exclusively. He uses – and to some extent mixes – many metaphors, including ecology, organisms and systems and also social concepts such as values, learning and actors. Relatively heavy emphasis is placed on biological metaphors, however. There is talk of niches, systems for dominance, revirs, the "embodiment" of systems etc. The business concept is also likened to a "well-oiled machine" (Normann, 1975, p 53). My own approach is characterized partly by a greater stress on social and cultural aspects and by limited reliance on biological and mechanical metaphors.

The other type of perspective is connected with the fact that Normann's assumptions primarily involve industrial companies, which often differ markedly from knowledge-intensive service companies – for example in the respects which are discussed here. Business, strategy and marketing questions cannot be centralized and concentrated in companies like Enator in the same way that they can in most companies that produce physical goods. It is tempting to view the business concept as anchored on a broad front within the company as a result of the service company's marketing situation and also to see it as linked to the company's measures to influence images.

Using the business market concept, in addition, as a feature in corporate communications seems to be a characteristic of the computer consultancy business – and probably of many other service companies too.

The importance of the business concept as a cohesive force seems to be much greater in knowledge-intensive service companies than in several other types of operations. At any rate, this is what Enator's corporate management feels:

> ... something which I think is characteristic of knowledge companies is that there has to be a fantastically powerful business concept which holds things together, irrespective of objectives and strategies. I think a business concept is even more important in a knowledge company than in any other type of company. It is a major parameter to hang things on. There is no product which can rely on if you land up in a tricky situation, when you have to explain what you're doing. There's just a business concept (Executive).

In a case study of an American computer consulting organization Deetz (1994) also illustrates the significance of the business concept along the lines I have indicated above.[2]

On the basis of the case study and the above discussion of the functions of the business concept in companies like Enator, I would like to suggest a further development of the current notion of the business concept. Normann (1975) lists six characteristics of the business concept. I concur with many of his points, but I would like to propose modifications of some of them so as to capture the phenomenon represented by companies of the Enator type.

1. Normann maintains that the business concept has a systems character, that is to say it consists of many different components which form a complex pattern. The business concept expresses the "totality" of this system. An alternative formulation would be that the systems character is considerably weaker than is implied by the systems concept. Different activities diverge and fail to form a well-integrated totality. Instead, various projects and activities are loosely coupled. Consultancy assignments do not function as "components" in relation to each other. The degree of freedom and independence between different projects is normally greater than this. To the extent that the business concept at Enator is to be described in systems terms – which is perhaps not such a good idea – it becomes a highly "loosely coupled" concept (cf Weick, 1976).

2. To counter the idea that: "the business concept is an expression of concrete circumstances which exist in a company, it describes the actual way in which the company functions or ... its 'way of making money' (Normann, 1975, p 53), it might be said that the business concept is not just an expression of what is "purely actual" in social practices. The use of the business concept is determined by many factors: including ideological, cul-

tural, and social. The espoused business concept is an ambiguous representation of the "the company's actual way of working". Several different descriptions can be imagined which makes more or less sense in relationship to observable behaviour patterns. It is common practice to select a variant which describes operations in an attractive manner which arouses enthusiasm. An idealistic gloss thus tends to characterize the formulation of the business concept.

One important aspect of the business concept is that it tends to encompass itself. To the extent that there is a business concept and that it is familiar to, and taken seriously by, management and employees, the business concept constitutes an important part of the company's way of functioning. The business concept is an image of the company, but it is also an important part of what is depicted. This image is a "part" of the company. However, I do not believe that the slightly tautological character of the business concept constitutes a serious theoretical problem. But it is important to note that the formulation of the business concept is to some extent self-fulfilling. The way in which you describe how you make money has consequences for how you really do make money. For this reason too, it is reasonable to imagine that the business concept is described to some extent in a manner which contains an ideal state of affairs which is strived for.

As a result, I would like to suggest that the business concept does not express concrete circumstances and the company's way of working in purely "neutral" terms, but is instead a kind of synthesis between what is purely factual and the ideal of affairs. Thus, the business concept expresses not just what you do, but also what you are striving for and how you want to be perceived. It is a normatively loaded representation of corporate practices.

3. According to Normann, the nature of the business concept is characterized by harmony and agreement/compliance.

A business concept can be likened to a complicated and well-oiled machine, where all the parts fit in with each other and contribute to the whole (Normann, 1975, p 53).

My case study is not easily captured by the machine metaphor. As already pointed out, the parts do not necessarily fit together, and they may operate relatively independently without affecting other components. The umbrella is a better metaphor than the machine for Enator's business concept. Operations are rather broad and dispersed; assignments cannot always be fully described on the basis of the business concept and sometimes they do not live up to the concept particularly well. Rather than organizational operations being characterized by cohesion, consistency, system design and the reflection of this in the business concept, in practice it is more likely that there is room for divergency, including variations in how closely activities are related to the business concept. Generous, broad interpretations of the concept are also possible.

All this can also be illustrated in terms of base and superstructure. Normann sees the business concept as reflecting the base, that is to say the material practice which permits the company to make money. But I am also trying to take the superstructure aspects into account. This means that what is concrete and actual, that is to say the material, "objective" aspect, is not the only factor to be taken into account in understanding the business concept. The cultural dimension is crucial if we are to understand the business concept. Interpretations, ideologies and variations on individual considerations and actions enter into the picture. Taking both the foundation and the superstructure dimensions into account also means that the discrepancies and contradictions surrounding the business concept, in the sense of reflecting "actual circumstances", come more into focus.[3]

10.6   The Symbolic Value of the Business Concept

As implied above, the business concept – at least in the case of Enator and, in many other companies too, also outside the category of knowledge-intensive companies – has considerable symbolic value. First, I am going to comment on the business concept as a symbol and I will then link the contents of the business concept to the value system of the environment and the market.

As said in Chapter 3, I adhere to Cohen's (1974) definition of a symbol: "Symbols are objects, acts, concepts, of linguistic formations that stand ambiguously for a multiplicity of disparate meanings, evoke sentiments and emotions, and impel men to action" (p ix).

As should now be apparent, the business concept as a symbol has quite varied meanings for the entire collective working at Enator. Variation occurs not only between different people, but even more so between different contexts. For those in the company who consider that the business concept does not cover core operations, the formulation of the business concept tends to be a historical by-product or some kind of notation of a ceremony, something to know about and perhaps to feel some respect for, but of no great concern in daily and concrete actions. For a few people, the business concept is hardly more than a publicity stunt:

You use the business concept to get yourself an image in the market. If you tell people that you are a humdinger at bending pipes and people then come to you, get their pipes bent and are satisfied – well then you are a humdinger at bending pipes. That's the image you have on the market. And if you have never bent a single pipe before and you have just done it for the first time for a customer, it doesn't make any difference to the customer. The whole business concept, then, is a question of fooling people, and making money. But that's another story (Consultant).

For other people – and this seems to include corporate management and other leading actors – the business concept has another meaning. In essence, this is a question of the business concept's depiction of the company's way of working, at any rate its ambitions for its work. This interpretation is probably the most widely held within the company and it is the most important, at any rate in integrative and ideological terms. The dynamics and flexibility of the business concept must, however, be emphasized. The meaning is contingent upon if the concept is invoked in strategic analysis, in sales talk, in project management or in PR work.

The business concept is a complicated symbol, with different meanings. One significant aspect of the business concept involves history. Within the company, it is thought that Enator based itself on the business concept and its idea of combining corporate management and computers right from the start, and that the business concept has stood the test of time ever since, for the most part at least. If one compares competitors' descriptions of themselves with Enator's, there is hardly any noticeable difference: everyone in the business places computers in a wider perspective and emphasizes that:

information processing can be a highly important competitive tool from a strategic point of view and may open up opportunities to offer new services (Programator, Annual Report, 1986).

I have no basis for assessing real differences and similarities between different companies in the computer consultancy business in Sweden. Sveiby and Risling (1986), however, consider that they have this kind of insight and they maintain that Enator and Programator possess integrated information processing and management know-how to a greater extent than other computer consultancy companies in the country. They claim that Programator has made the greatest progress in this context (p 43). However, it is interesting to note here that for (most) Enator employees the business concept expresses the idea that the company was one of the initiators of this perspective on computer questions and that management and strategy know-how are deeply imbedded in Enator's methods. In other words, the business concept expresses the far-sightedness and a go-ahead spirit which are considered to characterize Enator. The continuity in the Enator business concept means that the personnel believe that concept denotes consistency and purposefulness and that the market has confirmed the company's good qualities. (Market research, at the time of my study, gives Enator a very good rating.)

Thus, the business concept may be regarded as a symbol for the organization, expressing the company and its qualities. A great deal of the corporate pride which I encountered in the course of interviews with employees centers on the business concept. One person said: "This is what we are good at. This is Enator's strength." The business concept spotlights the areas where Enator is better than other companies and is not merely a neutral description of the "company's way of making money". For certain personnel groups, this has an expressive-affective loading and thus has "institutional" qualities (i.e. for many people it transmits signals of Enator as an institution) (Selznick, 1957).

Enator's business concept, as formulated, also contains several key words with a positive loading in Swedish society, working life and industry in the 1980s, in particular: "management", "strategy", "business", etc. Data processing also has some positive connotations, but it is perhaps not felt to be so new and exciting any longer, at least not where rationalization and cost-savings are concerned. However, it is precisely the combination of computers and management which probably achieves a positive impact. Data processing is given a different, broader meaning: it becomes a matter of concern to corporate management, a question of strategic and business significance, a method of improving competitiveness and opening up opportunities for new facets of enterprise. Quite apart from the realities in this area, ideas about such factors – expressed in a concentrated form in the business concept – have a special meaning for people involved in such activities

The positive associations surrounding concepts such a management, business and strategy can also be seen in the market, of course. Rhenman (1974) regards the success of an organization as a question of whether the organization's system of values both agrees with other sub-systems in the organization and whether it also complies with values in the environment. Rhenman is no doubt primarily concerned with relatively concrete factors, such as prices and products. But the idea should also apply to the language forms employed and what the language used particularly denotes.

In the 1980s and 1990s, it appears that words like strategy and management have acquired greater impact in Sweden, in private industry and in society at large. The term "corporate management" creates more positive reverberations than it did 15 years ago. It would take far too long to speculate about why this is so. It suffices to note that this is in fact the case and that Enator probably has a good response as a result – not simply for strictly business and economic reasons, but also for symbolic reasons. An exchange relationship which includes, for example, the "corporate management" symbol and signals a valuation involving a combination of computers and management has a more positive connotation in the current societal system of values than an exchange relationship which does not contain these elements. Expressed in another way: the exchange relation-ship cannot be simply reduced to a question of technology, economic util-ity, visible work inputs and results. There is also a symbolic dimension, which is in reality interwoven with instrumental aspects and can perhaps only analytically be separated from what is instrumental, but which is nonetheless important to consider.

   To sum up: one important aspect – the value of and respect for Enator's business concept – is that the business concept encompasses words which have considerable symbolic value. Obviously, if the words are to have any effect they must based on competence and practical achievements. The symbolic value of the business concept lies in denoting such competence and achievement.

Notes

[1]   Of course sometimes broader business offers, involving a combination of products/services may lead the customer to some interest in what the seller's overall idea regarding the company/market exchange. But also in such cases, the specific core product/service combination is normally of greater interest than more abstract formulations of how the company defines its mission.

[2]   Deetz (1994) uses the aspects of the business concept that I have developed here and shows that the points made here clearly go beyond that which is relevant only for my case.

[3]   As stressed before, the material, behavioural aspects must also be understood in terms of shared meanings. Without cultural meaning, "objective" reality does not make sense. Emphasizing the cultural dimensions of the business concept means that not only actions and practices but also wider ideational aspects are taken into account.

11 Strategy

11.1 The Strategy Concept in General Terms

Strategy is one of the most popular terms used by executives and business researchers and to an increasing extent by people in general. One factor which contributes to the frequent use of the strategy concept is the considerable possibility of variations on a theme. An increasing number of definitions and approaches to strategy have been offered to readers of articles and books on management and corporate strategy (Schoemaker, 1993; Whittington, 1993; Zan, 1990). Some writers have been concerned with internal situations in companies – thus, for example, corporate culture may be regarded as a management strategy. However, this chapter confines itself to consideration of strategy issues which involve external circumstances, i.e. the environment or the context of an organization. Congruity within the literature describing strategy with an external orientation is limited to certain general premises, for example that strategy is a question of the relationship of organizations with their environment, and that this involves overall, non-routine questions and circumstances which affect the functioning and possible "survival" of organizations (Chaffee, 1985). Otherwise, there is little conformity of views.

Some time ago, matters were simpler. Strategy used to be defined in approximate terms as a plan which expresses corporate goals and methods for realizing such goals in concrete terms. Strategy represented the overall, long-term orientation of corporate activities which guided operations. Formal planning was the basis of such operations. Analysis and planning were crucial aspects in the formulation and development of strategy, as was the optimization of decision rationality before implementing a plan. The good of the company depended on a well-thought-out strategy. This approach to strategy tends to require research endeavours which emphasize the content of strategies rather than strategic processes, and purely analytical decision making rather than the social action which supports or fails to support (formulated) strategies.

This view of strategy and its formulation has been described in varying ways by different commentators. Whittington (1993) refers to it as the classical approach, Mintzberg (1973; Mintzberg and Waters, 1985) has called it the planning approach, while Ansoff (1987) speaks of a systematic management model, Schoemaker (1993) uses the term the unitary actor model, Chaffee (1985) refers to the linear model for strategic management and others, for example Peters and Waterman (1982) and Pettigrew (1985), speak of the rational model. Apart from Ansoff, these authors are more or less critical of this model, at least as regards the manner in which it is employed by its many proponents. Pettigrew (1985), for example, offers the following combined characteristics and criticism of the rational model, which has dominated in a traditional perspective:

As applied to the formulation of strategy, the rational approach describes and prescribes techniques for identifying current strategy, analyzing environments, resources, and gaps, revealing and assessing strategic alternatives, and choosing and implementing carefully analyzed and well-thought-through outcomes. Depending upon the author, explicitly or implicitly, the firm speaks with a unitary voice or can be composed of omnipotent, even heroic general managers or chief executives, looking at known and consistent preferences and assessing them with voluminous and presumably apposite information, which can be organized into clear input-output relationships (p 276).

This criticism is also considered to apply to models based on the idea of "bounded rationality", in which analysis and decision making are far from perfect but where there is still an emphasis on analysis and decision making which are seen as the crucial aspects in drawing up strategy, while implementation is reduced to being a result of the plan.

This criticism is closely associated with criticism of most research dealing with the content of strategy. Research on the content of strategy is widespread but it is considered that proponents of a process-approach to strategy and strategic change miss the most important points in this context: how strategic change takes place and how strategic decisions are made in an organizational context (e.g. Johnson, 1987; Melin, 1987). This context, involving complexity and a multitude of actors with different priorities and perspectives, as well as the often unstable nature of the environment, means that identifiable, big decisions are not very significant and may be an unproductive focus for research (Mintzberg, 1990; Mintzberg and Waters, 1990).

Newer approaches to understanding corporate strategy focussing on the processual, dynamic character of strategic management must be understood in the context of changes in the economy over the last two decades. Turbulence is considered to have increased dramatically as a result of increased international competition and rapid technological change, for example. Rapid environmental changes lead to shorter reaction times and a heavier emphasis on rapid adaptation at company level, thus destroying the value of long-term planning and of the traditional strategy approach.

Authors within the strategy area like to paint dramatic pictures of the rate of change and turbulence (see e.g. Ansoff, 1978). Theoretical developments within the organizational discipline, which to a greater or lesser degree influence and permeate strategy research, also play their part. In particular, criticism of bureaucracy models and the rejection of rationalistic approaches to decision making and operations in organizations have paved the way for an approach in which strategy is not merely described in terms of planning/decision/implementation, but in which the formulation and implementation of strategy are also regarded as considerably more complex social processes, in which politics, sluggishness, random factors, values, the actors' interpretation of the environment, and socially constructed representations of the world, etc. are concepts denoting major factors which need to be taken into account. Naturally, the sheer volume of studies of corporate strategy over the past decade has also paved the way for a variety of approaches and definitions (Ansoff, 1987; Chaffee, 1985; Whittington, 1993). The reader is referred to Knights and Morgan (1991) for an interesting, broader and more historical examination of the extensive background to strategy studies in the post-war period.

As an example, definitions of strategy as "a pattern in a stream of decisions", or even as behavioural flows in which patterns or consistencies may be identified (Mintzberg and Waters, 1985), are worth special note. Greiner (1983) goes even further in rejecting the analytical, rational concept of strategy as a plan, followed by action steered by objectives:

Strategy is a deeply ingrained and continuing pattern of management behaviour that gives direction to the organization – not a manipulable and controllable mechanism that can be easily changed from one year to the next.

Strategy is a non-rational concept stemming from the informal values, traditions, and norms of behaviour held by the firm's managers and employees – not a rational, formal, logical, conscious, and predetermined thought process engaged in by top executives.

As Weick (1985) notes, this definition could equally well apply to culture, as this concept is defined by a great many writers. This illustrates variations in how the concept of strategy may be employed and may also raise the question of its usefulness. The considerable problems involved in giving the concept of strategy a clear and delimited theoretical content mean that the concept is in danger of being reduced to a slogan which covers everything and nothing (cf. Zan, 1990).

Another question closely associated with the development of a view of how to conceptualize strategy involves, on the one hand, the determination of various types of strategies, and, on the other, the formulation of various theoretical perspectives.

Mintzberg has been particularly prominent in establishing a typology for strategies. In an early article he identified three variations of strategy formation: *entrepreneur-dominated, adaptive* and *planned strategies* (Mintzberg, 1973). The first of these types is characterized by the fact that the strategy primarily reflects a dominant actor, whose intentions and actions are characterized by risk-taking and a search for opportunities. The entrepreneur's strong position means that intentions have considerable impact on the functioning of the organization. The adaptive strategy is characterized by adaptation to external conditions and may also involve internal compromises. "Reactive" solutions to problems which occur (perceived constraints) are more common than a planned exploitation of opportunities. Decision making and implementation take place in steps in the adaptive strategy. Planned strategies mean extensive planning and analysis, the formulation of objectives in detail, and the development of formal, cohesive plans which are accompanied by predictable, integrated action within the organization.

Later, Mintzberg and Waters (1985) developed this typology and identified a total of eight types of strategies, two of which have been mentioned above, namely planned and entrepreneur-directed strategies. As already stated, these two kinds of strategy exhibit considerable differences, but their common factor is that both regard strategy as controlled by management, and as a well-integrated and controlling factor for the entire company. Examples of the converse might be the *umbrella strategy* and the *unconnected strategy*. The former is characterized by an indication of frameworks and/or overall goals for management activities, which then gives various actors at lower levels a greater degree of freedom within which they can operate. The umbrella strategy is often the result of complex and turbulent conditions in the environment which can hardly be predicted and which require responses from comparatively autonomous sections of the company. The unconnected strategy is characterized by actors who are loosely linked with the organization in other respects and who develop patterns of action in the absence of centrally and broadly formulated guidelines. In such cases, most authors would probably refrain from speaking of a strategy.

The distinction between *deliberate* and *emergent* strategies (or elements of strategies) provides an important basis for Mintzberg's approach. The deliberate strategy is characterized by the fact that it is implemented as intended. It is thus a question of intention followed by action. The emergent strategy is characterized by patterns and consistency in action which have occurred in contradiction of intentions, or in the absence of clear intentions characterizing a development phase, before the establishment of patterns of action (Mintzberg and Waters, 1985). The emergent type of strategy differs markedly from other approaches, in which intentions and

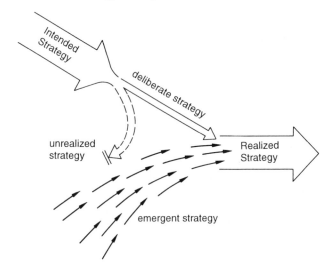

Figure 11.1:   Fundamental forms of strategy (based on Mintzberg and Waters, 1985)

plans are regarded as important aspects of strategy. The idea, however, is that purely predicted strategies are extremely uncommon. The prerequisites – precise and detailed intentions, uniform and well-integrated action on the part of the entire organization and an environment (market, competitors) which has been perfectly predicted – occur infrequently. A purely emergent strategy is also relatively uncommon; a total lack of intention behind a strategy which is implemented is probably unusual. In such a case, it is misleading to talk about a strategy. Mintzberg's thesis is that many strategies contain a combination of deliberate and emergent elements. In some cases, the deliberate strategy dominates, while in others the strategy is primarily of an emergent nature.

Figure 11.1 illustrates Mintzberg's and Waters' strategy typology and the relationships between them.

The figure indicates that intended strategies may lead to either implemented or unimplemented strategies. Implemented strategies may be either deliberate or emergent. Mintzberg thus considers that there are three fundamental possibilities as regards strategies: unimplemented, deliberate and emergent strategies. In a "normal" strategy, all three types of strategy are at work to some extent: some of the intended strategy is implemented, certain aspects are not achieved and there are features which were neither planned nor initially intended in the consistencies and patterns which characterize the behaviour and decisions which are implemented. Distinctions between intended and emergent strategies and between imple-

mented and unimplemented elements of the strategy are important. However, in reality, what is classified as one type or the other is strongly dependent on the time perspective applied. The shorter the time horizon, the
greater the agreement between intended and implemented elements. In
the long term the scope for emergent elements is greater, and this also
applies to unimplemented elements. It is often not clear what is the most
appropriate time perspective in answering this question. In addition, the
level of analysis also influences the picture that is produced. As Schoemaker (1993, p 121) says, "the more paramorphic or distant the observer
is, the more the rational model will appeal".

Other authors have also discussed and confronted traditional views by
introducing new theoretical perspectives on how strategies and strategic
change should be described. Quinn (1978, 1984) considers that a strategic
change does *not* normally occur in the form of the drawing-up and documentation of a major, overall plan which management at some point
presents to subordinates for execution, but instead takes the form of what
he terms "logical incrementalism". This means that the processes which
lead up to the total strategy are normally fragmentary, evolutionary and
largely based on the intuition of the top management. However, managers
have relatively clear ideas about the main lines for strategy. The process
takes place slowly and is characterized by combinations of internal decisions and external events and by dealing with various strategic sub-prob-
lems step by step. Both cognitive and process factors make it impossible to
apply a total overall approach which is determined in advance. The overall
strategy occurs over time as a result of control over the total process by a
management which step by step tries to link together various aspects and
to create a consensus for the strategic plan whose exact contents are determined as late as possible, partly because the constraints make this essential
and partly to avoid opposition, locked-in positions and blocking.

This approach deviates considerably from the traditional, planning-ori-
ented concept, but several commentators emphasize the similarities between the planning approach and the "logical incrementalism", which is
sometimes regarded as an example of an adaptive view of strategy (Chaffee, 1985). Both variations emphasize a strong degree of rationality and
control of the formation of strategy by top management.

(The view) ... is that strategy formulation can be accounted for by logical, rational
processes either through the planning mode or through the adaptive, logical incre-
mental mode. In either event the manager is a pro-active strategy formulator consciously seeking to understand a complex environment, so as to establish causal
patterns and formulate strategy by configuring organizational resources to meet
environmental needs (Johnson, 1987, p 8).

An alternative viewpoint which has gained ground in recent years involves examining strategy on the basis of an interpretative model (Chaffee, 1985; Johnson, 1987; Smircich and Stubbart, 1985). The interpretative view of strategy rejects objectivistic ideas about the company's external "environment" and instead emphasizes reality as a social construction. The consequences of the environment for the organization and its action are revealed in the interpretations, frames of reference, perceptions and forms of understanding which characterize the strategic actors. Ideas about the market and the environment in general determine organizational operations, not external circumstances *per se*. The environment is seen as a social construction.

Another characteristic of the interpretative view is that organizations are understood in terms of shared or differentiated meanings, ideas, values and assumptions and the way in which corporate processes are informed by as well as give rise to patterns of interpretation and understanding. Organizations are not regarded as the sum of objective, stable structures which can be measured and described in statistical terms. Instead, organizations are a question of ongoing patterns of interaction, whose establishment, reproduction and change are characterized by dynamism and process (Smircich and Stubbart, 1985). (Cf. the view of organizational structure presented in Chapter 6.) This means that the realization of a strategy requires carefully taking into account the manner in which the collective involved gives meaning and content to different aspects of the environment. Shared meanings are the basis of collective action. One definition of strategy based on this approach might read as follows:

Strategy in the interpretative model might be defined as orienting metaphors or frames of reference that allow the organization and its environment to be understood by organizational stakeholders. On this basis, stakeholders are motivated to believe and to act in ways that are expected to produce favourable results for the organization. 'Metaphors' is plural in this definition because the maintenance of social ties in the organization precludes enforcing agreement on a single interpretation (Chaffee, 1985, p 93).

This approach will indicate that managers and other strategic actors should study how people think about environments and product/market combinations, rather than try to investigate such phenomena *per se*. Rather than concentrating on decisions and methods of structuring decision situations, managers should study the values, language, dramas, symbols, etc. which constitute the background for decisions. Rather than relying on a technical analysis of organizational structure, the emphasis should be on learning to understand and utilize the social and emotional basis for the functioning of the organization (Smircich and Stubbart, 1985).

This means that the approach to strategists changes. Traditionally, the strategist has been regarded as an analyst, decision maker and drawer-up of plans. But representatives of an interpretative approach tend to emphasize the strategist as a creator, and even as an artist. Creativity and imagination in effectively interpreting the environment and in mobilizing involved action in the organization, are regarded as important characteristics of the strategic manager.

Like Smircich and Stubbart, Berg (1985a) assumes a cultural-symbolic perspective on strategy and organizational change. Berg considers that strategy should be regarded as a more or less synthesized abstraction of the aspects of the company's identity which are to be developed. He considers that organizational and strategic change is primarily a question of transforming the underlying organizational symbolism holding the organization together and providing points of reference for social action (p 289). Seen in a symbolic perspective, the explicit strategy is reduced to a conscious formulation of aspects of "the corporate myth", that is to say emotionally-loaded ideas with a historical basis about the fundamental character of operations (cf. Hedberg and Jönsson, 1977; Jönsson and Lundin, 1977). In common with these authors, Berg (1985a) rejects the planning approach, maintaining that "A strategy is not regarded as a plan, but as a collective image that can be acted upon" (p 295). This approach means that strategic planning is regarded as a renewal rite, in which the collective process, links with fundamental values and ideas and the plan/rite as a manifestation of the corporate mission and vision are emphasized. Similar views have been expressed, for example, by Broms and Gahmberg (1983, 1987).

New metaphors to illustrate the position of the manager/strategist are also proposed by Bourgeois and Brodwin (1984) in a survey of models for the implementation of strategy. Like many other authors in recent years, Bourgeois and Brodwin heavily criticize traditional strategic management which they term "The Commander Model", due to its strongly normative orientation towards central control. This model sees the manager as "the rational actor". Other models and metaphors place greater emphasis on organizational circumstances and the uncertainty associated with such circumstances. Regarding the managing director as an architect is close to the "Commander Model", while metaphors such as "coordinator" or, even more, "coach" are more remote from the commander concept. The greatest contrast can be found in the view of the strategist as a developer of premises and an assessor of strategies. Particularly in the latter case, strategies are regarded as emanating from the bottom of the organization, that is to say "at the front", rather than moving in a top-down direction. In this case, the manager's function is to define the purposes and prerequisites of the organization in a manner which creates innovation and possible lines of development and to assess and select projects or strategic alternatives which then emerge. This way of characterizing the manager's task complies with some of the strategies described by Mintzberg and Waters (1985), for example the umbrella strategy.

This review of some of the current theoretical approaches to strategy and strategic processes – in which, as I have indicated, research about the content of strategy has been excluded – may be briefly summarized in the form of some important dimensions which must be taken into account if concrete strategic processes are to be described:

- *strength of intention*: the extent to which there are detailed intentions, clearly stated in advance, underpinning the strategy; the relative dominance of intended or emergent elements in the strategy;
- *rationality*: Strategy as a "rational" project, in relation to strategy as an expression of values, traditions and other "non-rational" factors;
- *degree of centralization*: Centralization/decentralization as regards strategic behaviour: is the managing director/management responsible for leadership or is strategy a question of collective action, to which major areas of the organization contribute, not only in an implementive role but also as designers of the patterns of action which are implemented?
- *degree of integration*: Strategic action as an integrated, comprehensive pattern of action or a strategy which emanates from (or guides) actors who are only loosely linked with each other: convergence within the organization/divergence in strategic action;
- *planning*: The relative dominance of strategic planning and logical incrementalism as compared with non-planned, "spontaneous" processes in implementation of a strategy;
- *adaptation/creativity*: Strategy as a reflection of attempts to achieve adaptation to and compliance with the external environment versus strategy as an expression of individually or collectively based creative/non-creative interpretations of the organizational context.

Some of these dimension tend to go together but they do not fully overlap. Strong intentions and planning, for example, often co-exists, but it is perfectly possible that strong intentions about objectives may be followed by a rather loose and flexible approach. As we will see, the internationalization of Enator is characterized by this combination.

In the following, I will describe Enator's strategic development, employing Mintzberg's definition: strategy as a pattern or as a consistency in decision making and action. I will then return to the dimensions described above. First, however, a brief critical comment on the applicability of the strategy concept.

11.2   Critical Comments on the Strategy Concept

The rich variation which characterizes the employment of the strategy concept in a corporate context means that its usefulness is open to discussion. This certainly applies to opportunities to elucidate specific circumstances. Knights and Morgan (1991) point to other reasons for managers to link up their understanding of themselves and their activities with the strategy concept and they also explain why practitioners and researchers try to give meaning to all possible phenomena in terms of strategy. Knights and Morgan consider that strategy as a discourse – in the sense of a systematic thought process which is both based on and produces a certain social practice – is not "natural" or self-evident. Instead, this discourse occurs in a particular context when managers feel the need to clarify for their own benefit what they do and explain it in persuasive terms to others (subordinates, shareholders, the public). Knights and Morgan claim that the strategy discourse fulfils the following functions:

- It provides managers with a language for rationalizing successes and failures.
- It maintains and reinforces managerial status and provides a defence against other organizational perspectives by depicting strategy as the hub around which everything else revolves.
- It contributes to providing managers with a sense of personal and organizational certainty.
- It reflects and maintains a strong feeling of masculine identity for male managers because it offers an understanding of the situation faced by the company and its executives in masculine terms.
- It demonstrates (the possibility of) managerial rationality to significant and relevant areas of the environment.
- It contributes to the creation of a certain managerial identity and self-image, and it also ensures a certain view of reality amongst people who are involved in strategic discourses and practice. Thus, managers develop an understanding of themselves as "strategists".

It is not clear whether these functions can be considered to have been satisfactorily fulfilled. But, broadly speaking, the strategy concept tends to express a form of understanding which rejects or downplays ambiguity, complexity, passiveness, dependence on external resources and the importance of most of the company's employees, while it emphasizes opportunities for (top) managerial rationality, dominance, purposive activity, a clarified corporate context and, especially, the central importance of top management. The fact that certain theories – for example those which have been referred to above which emphasize process and emergent strategies – to some extent negate this picture does not seriously affect what the strategy concept, as normally understood, is signalling. Perhaps it would be preferable to completely abandon the strategy concept when dealing with, for example, phenomena which Mintzberg terms emergent strategy, umbrella strategy and unconnected strategy or, alternatively, to employ the symbolic-cultural perspective on corporate change. Possibly, the reason why the strategy concept is used to explain the most varied phenomena and forms of understanding lies in its ideological advantages for managerial elites and academics interested in associating themselves with this group rather than in its intellectual attributes.

Thus, personally I am doubtful about referring to strategy (Willmott and Alvesson, 1995). But this is not the place to introduce any extensive conceptual reorientation, however, and I will content myself with utilizing the concepts referred to in the literature, under slight protest. I will refer to theories and ideas which do not particularly favour "a command model", but which tend instead to indicate the "non-strategic" nature of strategies and managers. My empirical interpretations also point in this direction, and I hope that this means that this chapter does not contribute to the predominant functions of the strategy discourse as described by Knights and Morgan (1991).

It is now high time to return to my case study.

11.3   Enator's Development from a Business and Strategy Perspective

When Enator was set up, the first employees and the first customers were friends or acquaintances of the three founders. Those employed after that were often friends or acquaintances of the initial employees. Veterans from Enator's first few years speak of a strong feeling of belonging to a family.

In the first two years it was very much a question of confidence in and loyalty to friends, both as customers and as consultants employed by the company.

This company's initial orientation was confined to administrative data processing. The idea was to offer a management approach to computer questions, to propose the correct solutions on the basis of this approach and then to take full responsibility for the management and implementation of projects. The market was confined to the Stockholm region.

This area of activity has expanded by 20-25% on average, in terms of Enator's invoicing over a ten-year period, with some tailing-off in later years. Two companies have been formed since the splitting of the original unit. Approximately 120 employees were involved in this sphere of activity in 1987.

Another type of activity started up a couple of years after the company was founded – technical data processing – with customers who manufactured computer systems or whose products employed computer technology, for example in process control equipment. The difference was that the market was manufacturing industry, rather than administrative companies in commerce, transport, banking, etc. Enator's technical subsidiaries had a different area of competence, with more than their fair share of graduate engineers. As a result, the business concept for this side of Enator operations was, and is, somewhat different than in the original company and its offshoots in the administrative services market. On the technical side, the market segment consisted of product development departments and Enator's function involved assistance in the technological development of software and computers and computer-based products.

The first technical subsidiary was established in 1979 and took the form of an intermediate stage between new recruitment and branching out.

New recruitment was involved to the extent that our manager and a few other people came from the former Datasaab company. But, as I recall it, originally they were part of the Enator group (the initial company) and then when they had enough experience, and developed their own muscle in the form of assignments, personnel, and the ability to stand on their own two feet, they were allowed to branch out (Employee since 1978).

This approach typified Enator practice when forming a new subsidiary. In some cases, subsidiaries were established in the form of a splitting-off process, in which the manager and the first employees in the new subsidiary were ex-employees of the parent subsidiary.

In the period 1979-83, Enator's technology sector developed at about the same rate as the administrative sector. Subsequently, the technology side moved ahead increasingly rapidly, and between 1984 and 1986 invoicing from the four technology subsidiaries doubled. The original technology subsidiary, Mikrotell, gave birth to other technology subsidiaries in 1983, 1984 and 1986.

The development of the technology sector increased Enator's product range. However, the strategy still involved a concentration of activity to the Stockholm region, even if individual projects might take place in other locations, of course. In 1981, in practice two additional strategies were introduced, in parallel with administrative data processing and technological data processing in the Stockholm region. These new strategies involved regionalization and internationalization.

Regional expansion took the form of setting up Enator Syd (Enator South) which was located in Malmö in southern Sweden. The original reason for this move was that one of the founders of Enator had a friend who was working in Stockholm but who came from southern Sweden and wanted to return to his home district. The founder proposed that he should open an Enator branch in Malmö and his friend took his advice. By 1987 there were 30 employees in Malmö. For some time, Enator Syd was the only example of regional operations under the Enator banner in Sweden, outside the Stockholm region. When I conducted my study there were signs of increasing efforts to pursue this strategy. A subsidiary had been formed in Gothenburg in 1986 and another company had been acquired in Västerås in the same year. Nonetheless, in 1987 regionalization in Sweden was a relatively peripheral strategy which represented less than 10% of Enator's total operations, in terms of personnel.

Enator's international expansion started with the establishment of a subsidiary in Great Britain. Further foreign subsidiaries were set up in 1983-86 in the following order: Norway, West Germany, Denmark, Switzerland, and Finland. By 1986, foreign subsidiaries represented roughly one third of all invoicing by Enator's operational companies. And about half of Enator's total turnover came from assignments outside Sweden (the Swedish operational subsidiaries had a number of assignments for foreign customers). I will return to the question of the internationalization strategy shortly.

Another business area for Enator involved sales of computer systems and systems installation competence, based on previous development projects. Enator established sales companies to market such systems in cooperation with former customers for whom Enator had previously developed administrative systems. Enator had stakes in two such joint-venture companies, together with a bank and an airline company. Enator's partners were primarily concerned in making money from the systems produced, thus reducing costs for their own investments, while Enator was primarily interested in receiving assignments in connection with the installation of such systems.

Prior to 1986, Enator's growth was exclusively the result of its own efforts, that is to say as a result of the increasing volume of assignments in existing subsidiaries. But in 1986 Enator began to acquire existing companies – for example in Britain and in Västerås. The transition to a growth strategy which included the possibility of acquisitions was partly the result of tougher market conditions and greater difficulty in continuing to expand at the same rate as before as a result of the company's own endeavours. (Most of the major companies in the industry in Sweden increased their turnover in 1985-86 by 20-30%, which was 10-15% below the average rate of increase in 1981-84.)

As regards the type of assignment undertaken by Enator, for example the extent and the nature of the project, the customers involved, etc., it is difficult to get a clear picture. Statistics covering the nature of previous assignments are not available, so I will refrain from comparison between phases in the company's development.

Enator has considerable competence and has received many assignments within the transport/travel/tourism sector and also in the computer/-electronics industry. The position in other types of manufacturing industry and in the public sector was less favourable, even if some assignments were carried out in practically all types of public and private sector operations.

However, in 1986-87 the picture changed somewhat in the public sector, as indicated by the formation of a joint venture with the city of Malmö to sell computer systems for health-care services and the setting up of major projects for the Post Office Administration, the Telecommunications Administration and the National Labour Market Board, for example.

11.4   The Internationalization Strategy

The Enator strategies described above differ from the more "spontaneous" emergent activities that subsequently result in patterns of action in regard to the relative extent of planning and in clarity of stated and implemented intentions. The clearest example of strategy with a relatively high content of intention and management control is international expansion. I will describe this in greater detail.

Originally, the background for investment outside Sweden was that Enator found that it possessed considerable know-how which was difficult to utilize in Sweden but where foreign customers constituted an appropriate market:

... in 1979 when we had completed the NK (department store) system and had acquired a great deal of know-how about retail operations, purchasing, order-handling routines, and other aspects of distribution, we had extremely good insights into how this industry, or this retail sector, functioned. The problem was that we couldn't simply go to Åhléns or Epa (two other retail chains) or to any other department store and tell them, 'we've been working for NK for two years and we know exactly how things work. So why don't we do the same for you, too?' The NK Managing Director wouldn't have approved. So we had all this know-how, but how were we going to exploit it without going abroad and selling it? That's how it started. We began with department stores – in Britain and Germany, at Stockmann in Helsinki, at Magasin du Nord in Denmark and at Gallerie la Fayette in Paris. We worked in all these places and then we started to develop our foreign market (Consultant).

Additionally, I have been told that the reason Enator initially established itself in Britain was that the exchange rates at that time meant that British programmers were cheap labour which, in its turn, meant that they could be flown over to Sweden for assignments on a highly profitable basis.

As time passed, other ambitions and motives underlying international expansion became clearer. The concepts on which the internationalization strategy was based at Enator were:

- Restricted market in Sweden due, on the one hand, to the limited size of the market and, on the other, to the fact that it was not possible to work for customers on certain types of assignments if they were competing with each other. Internationalization means that multiplier effects of Enator's know-how can be achieved.
- Internationalization as a method of building up know-how via foreign subsidiaries which act as sensors. One example is telecommunications and computers. In 1987, Enator bought up a British company with this speciality. Apparently there was relatively little competence in Sweden in these areas. The idea was that London would be Enator's centre for telecommunications know-how and that this would then spread to Enator subsidiaries in Sweden and other countries.
- Customers are becoming increasingly internationalized and it is an advantage for a consultancy firm to be able to offer local services in countries where customers have their subsidiaries.
- The spreading of risks. Fluctuations in the business cycle can be evened out if Enator has a presence in several markets.
- Recruitment and personnel policy advantages. Recruitment is facilitated and personnel will stay with Enator longer if they have the opportunity to work for a subsidiary abroad for a given period of time.

Apart from these business motives for expansion outside Sweden, there were also more "romantic" and light-hearted elements:

Last, but not least it is extremely stimulating to work in an international environment. You learn a great deal. The whole thing is fun (Enator manager).

Although Enator's management and owners emphasize that "the reasons for going international today are damn rational", they do not hide the fact that the founders' boyish dreams have also played a part in this process. Despite an open-minded attitude to the role of feelings and personal orientations, the management appears to overstress rational reasons or at least understress the difficulties in establishing consultancy services on an international market. Being "international" is an important success symbol, and the role of this symbolism seems to have been significant for key actors in the company.

Apart from Sweden, the six countries in which Enator has established itself have been selected on the basis of criteria that there should be strong similarities as regards ways of thinking, the business climate, etc. The idea was thus to work in markets where the "psychological distance" between Enator (Sweden) and the subsidiary companies and foreign customers was relatively limited. "Psychological distance" involves average differences as regards the perception of various circumstances which are relevant for exchanges between the companies involved (Hallén and Wiedersheim-Paul, 1979). Apart from the size of the market, physical distance between the home country and the country where exports/establishment take place is normally an important determining factor in selecting the sequence for setting up business abroad (Johansson and Vahlne, 1977). Enator was no exception. Norway, Denmark and Finland were obvious objectives. In other cases, the choice of country and the timing for setting up business operations was partly a question of "who you meet", as one of Enator's top managers put it.

Foreign companies were established at a rapid pace, with an average of one new subsidiary per year in the period 1981-86. The original strategy was to find an entrepreneurially oriented person in the country in question, to support him or her and to build up operations from nothing. The original intention was also to work solely with wholly-owned subsidiaries and to find an increasing number of markets in which to establish operations.

While the actual establishment of operations seems to have been successful, it has proved difficult to achieve satisfactory growth and profitability, and it appears to have been much more difficult than anticipated to achieve unproblematic relationships between subsidiaries and Enator management. The worst example was in Norway, where the subsidiary manager and most of the personnel left Enator in 1986 following a schism, and then formed their own company. In two other countries, the initial subsidiary manager has also resigned or been replaced. Profitability has varied, but failed to meet expectations.

In 1987, the intended strategy for Enator's foreign operations changed. Instead of continued establishment in an increasing number of markets, Enator planned to concentrate on the six existing markets and to establish its roots deeper in these countries.

The original intention of only starting up wholly-owned companies also changed. Acquisitions began to be regarded as a possibility, and a company was purchased in Britain. At the same time, it appears that acquisitions were expected to be responsible for a major proportion of Enator's future growth. Enator's management expected, for example, that Enator would be employing a couple of hundred staff in West Germany within three to five years, and this was expected to take place along the following lines:

In Germany we have two subsidiaries with a total of 50 employees. Perhaps we'll start up another in Munich. These companies will expand. If we add in a couple of acquisitions comprising 40-50 employees over a three-year period, and succeed in assimilating these new staff in cultural terms ... (Top manager).

The previous policy of only having wholly-owned subsidiaries abroad was abandoned in 1986. Two companies were set up on a joint basis with Swiss and Finnish partners.

Thus, Enator's strategy for foreign operations was characterized by the fact that the original intentions – newly established, wholly-owned subsidiaries – had only been partially realized and that a new strategy had emerged after some years: concentration on six foreign markets, corporate acquisition as an important aspect of growth and joint ownership with local companies. This strategy had, however, only been achieved to a limited extent so far, but it had only been in operation for a few years at the time of writing. (Considering the rapid changes in the elements in the internationalization "strategy", this term may be seen as somewhat misleading, even in the light of the broad and imprecise ways the word strategy conventionally is used.)

The objective for the foreign side of operations was that it would amount to 50% of total operations. In terms of turnover, this figure was achieved in 1986, even if only one third of the total number of employees in 1986-87 worked in foreign subsidiaries. In the long run, the objectives for international operations were extremely ambitious:

If we have 400 employees in Sweden, we should have at least as many in Germany. That is quite clear. We can't just grow on the basis of our own efforts there, and this means that we must find strategic acquisition opportunities in order to achieve this goal. We have to have consultancy groups of 400-500 employees if we are to be taken seriously. Major players don't compete in the fourth division (Top manager).

Thus, Enator's strategy was extremely bold. The difficulties encountered did not result in a reduction in the level of ambition. Optimism was retained and the company was apparently prepared to abandon previous principles and plans regarding the way in which growth should be achieved. Dramatic international growth was the aim, even if there were signs that the market was tending to become mature. Enator's new strategy meant that the growth objective was retained, while there was less emphasis on previous sub-objectives of cultural assimilation and social integration of the new companies into the group. In any case, it is difficult to imagine that the companies which were acquired, and to some extent also companies where Enator was a joint owner, could provide the same opportunities for top management control as regards values, style, etc. as when starting up new operations.

A number of circumstances may be assumed to have facilitated the avoidance/abandonment of blocks/consistent action in relation to previous corporate policy: a young, dynamic company in which the central role played by growth represented a major feature of the world of ideas and relatively loose links between the new foreign operations and Enator's Swedish activities, which meant that most of the "older" personnel at Enator were not directly involved in the internationalization process. The basic nature of operations also meant that it was not possible to formulate long-term plans. Minimal capital requirements reduce the need for long-term planning. The mode of production, e.g. the formation of project groups which have to be rapidly assembled in accordance with the assignments which come in, and simultaneous production and consumption of consultancy services, requires rapid responses and flexibility on the part of management, resulting in a certain emphasis on a short-term time perspective. This then affects strategic decision making in a way that is hardly characterized by rationalism or fear of taking decisions. And the strategic patterns are characterized by short duration and rapid decisions, sometimes made because they feel right rather than on a factual basis.

11.5   An Emergent Strategy

At any rate in retrospective terms, the internationalization strategy appears, overall, to have been a deliberate and cohesive endeavour, designed to achieve continued dramatic growth and corporate establishment in a number of major north-European markets, even if, as has become apparent, this strategy differs to some extent from planning ideas and is partly characterized by emergent features. On the whole, Enator's strategy complies with the concept of "logical incrementalism" (Quinn, 1978).

Many of the other strategies developed by Enator have been of a more emergent character. An excellent example is Enator's establishment of operations in important areas in the public sector.

When I conducted my study (1987-88), a strategy of this type – to the extent that the term strategy can and should be employed – was in the process of crystallizing. Major assignments for some large public companies had commenced or were in the process of starting up. In 1987, Enator also launched a subsidiary, Malmator, in partnership with the city of Malmö, with the aim of selling computer systems in the health-care sector. The public sector, which ranges from profit-making agencies to municipalities and counties, is not at all uniform or easy to define in marketing terms, but from Enator's point of view this was mainly a question of new types of customers, compared with the medium-sized and large companies which Enator had previously worked with. Although some small assignments had been completed for public-sector organizations previously, it could be said that assignments for the Post Office Administration, the Telecommunications Administration and the National Labour Market Board, and cooperation with the city of Malmö, all signalled a new orientation for Enator.

How did public-sector business develop? Traditionally, Enator has worked with areas of operations where the founders and the initial employees had personal experience and contact networks. This meant, for example, transport, travel, tourism and the retail sector.

We gave priority to areas where we already had contacts or where we felt that we had the know-how. On the other hand, we were bad at anything to do with the manufacturing industry and suchlike. There we had hardly any experience at all and we didn't know anything about local authorities and government administration either. We thought this was a difficult area which didn't suit us (Top manager).

Enator's industrial assignments and operations in the technical area were established by recruiting some engineers to manage this side of the business. For many years, the public sector was regarded as not particularly interesting as far as Enator was concerned and no real effort was made to recruit customers in the public domain.

The specific background to Enator's attempts to establish itself on the market for state corporations and other areas of the public sector is as follows:

Eighteen months ago I came into contact with a number of people – at the personal level, that is – who were working in local authority administration. We began to talk a little and there were signals that 'we should be more businesslike' and 'why can't this be privatized?', etc. And then I started to get interested. Why not have a go? They were talking more or less the same language as me. Perhaps they weren't as complicated as I had thought. Actually, our initial discussions indicated that the decision process is much, much harder work than in an ordinary company in the private sector. Politicians have to decide, etc. But it started by Enator getting a few short assignments simply because we knew someone, but also because Enator Syd (Enator South) recruited someone who was an extremely competent consultant. He happened to come from the Malmö city administration. Then he got some work to do for Malmö city. And we had a few jobs here in Stockholm working for the city, due to my acquaintances and other contacts. Suddenly we began to … . Well, quite simply there was an enormous market there, with plenty of people working in it. We felt that we could function perfectly well here, with our method of working (Top manager).

It is interesting to note how factors and processes outside the narrow company context can affect strategy. Contacts at the personal level gave an important input to the manager I interviewed. A consultant who was employed at a lower level in the corporate hierarchy also had an impact on strategy due to his ability to establish relations between Enator and his previous employer and to pave the way for a joint project. The importance of actors at the "grass roots level" in the development of strategy is also illustrated by the manner in which Enator's assignment for the Telecommunications Administration started.

Early this spring, Enator recruited a fellow who has been working with the Telecommunications Administration previously, and who has good contacts. I must admit that when he began to talk about this, saying things like 'We should go for this' and 'within six months we should have the Telecommunications Administration as a customer', I felt that I didn't really believe in this. Why should the Telecommunications Administration contract out such a major part of their operations at Enator when they had no experience of us? Perhaps there were other people who they had already worked with. It felt strange in some way. But you have to admire a fellow like that. That's a characteristic which applies in all types of consultancy and to all consultants – being devoted to the job. The fact that although he didn't get much response from me or from other people at Enator either, he went on working quietly and made sure that something developed out of it. That's what makes a good job. It also provides some food for thought – that you shouldn't knock people who have ideas on the head, people who are working for something – you have to listen and encourage them in various ways.

Thus, this description of Enator's entry into the public-sector organization market clearly indicates how initiatives from personnel with a relatively modest position in the company can affect Enator's overall orientation and thus also its strategy – when this has to be explained. It is now time to try to say something in general about strategy and strategic development in the type of company exemplified by Enator.

11.6   The Formation of Strategy in Adhocracies

Mintzberg and McHugh (1985) attempt to identify the manner in which strategies are formed in an adhocracy, based on a study of the National Film Board of Canada (NFB). The organization which they studied is in the public sector and its function is to produce films. NFB also demonstrates certain of the adhocracy characteristics which can be seen at Enator. We should therefore look at what Mintzberg and McHugh have to say.

Mintzberg and McHugh ask themselves: how is it possible for consistency and patterns to occur in an organization like NFB?, after noting that both convergence and divergence of action can be identified. Mintzberg and McHugh maintain that the powerful force favouring convergence is the inner need to utilize the knowledge and skills which are developed. It is natural to exploit the opportunities implicit in existing competence. Other factors are fashion – things that are in the air and which give rise to similar action – and administrative needs for consistency due to efficiency criteria or economic and financial restrictions. Another route to convergent action, coming from the other direction, is when an individual project unintentionally becomes a model, and is then followed by other projects.

Additional factors which forced NFB in the direction of convergence included the simple need for a feeling that the organization represented something, that operations could be defined in common terms, irrespective of what part of the organization the employee belonged to, and strong external pressures from the environment.

Otherwise, at any rate in organizations of the NFB type, adhocracy is fundamentally characterized by a high degree of tolerance for divergence as regards activities in the organization. This contrasts, for example, with entrepreneurially led and bureaucratic organizations where the scope for divergent action in relation to a focussed strategy is extremely limited.

Machine bureaucracies, top-down and obsessed with rationalization ... focus on their target markets and chosen products, integrate production around them, and work to rid the organization of the vestiges of any leftover strategies. Adhocracies, in contrast, cater to impulse, to peripheral patterns tolerated or simply lost within the system. That provides their great strength – their ability to innovate – but it also gives rise to the problem of achieving focused direction (Mintzberg and McHugh, 1985, p 191).

Mintzberg and McHugh have constructed a model for the development of strategies in adhocracies, which they term "the grass roots model". This involves, for example, the following points:

- Strategies originally emerge like weeds in a garden. They are not cultivated in the same way as tomatoes in a greenhouse. At any rate, initially it is important to allow the pattern to develop, rather than to force an artificial consistency unto operations at an early stage.
- These strategies can take root in all possible kinds of situations, practically everywhere where human beings have a capacity to learn and where there are resources which support this capacity. An individual actor may come into contact with a certain market niche and develop his or her own pattern of action there. Alternatively, an individual or a group may take an initiative which subsequently inspires, and is followed by, a major endeavour which is undertaken centrally or which stimulates others to "spontaneously" follow the same route.

• These strategies become organizational when they become fully collective, that is to say when the pattern of action expands and sets its stamp on major sectors of the organization as a whole.
• Managing this process is less a question of foreseeing strategies than of recognizing their emergence and intervening when appropriate.

Mintzberg and McHugh draw the conclusion that strategic management in adhocracies is a question of creating a climate which permits considerable variation in strategies which can emerge within the organization. This requires flexible structures, supportive ideologies, and the formulation of guideline umbrella strategies. It is then a question of seeing what grows and takes root and also being prepared for the unexpected. It is important that the manager develops a feeling for when it is appropriate to exploit an emergent strategy and when encouragement of the development of new tendencies which can replace old patterns is justified.

This model complies well with several lessons which can be drawn from the Enator case study, particularly the background to the emergency of the ("umbrella") strategy for entering the public sector. At the same time, the "grass roots model" only indicates one aspect of strategic development for a company like Enator, since Enator differs in several respects from the empirical material on which Mintzberg and McHugh's model was founded. In contrast to the National Film Board of Canada, Enator is a private company, market-dependent, profit-oriented and with relatively strong management. The logic on which film production and computer consultancy services is based is also different, even if the similarities are probably greater than, for example, in the case of computer consultancy companies and manufacturing industry.

However, in manufacturing industry certain producer goods (business-to-business) companies differ from other industrial companies, since strategically important decisions are often taken at lower levels within the hierarchy (Turnball and Valla, 1986). Producer goods companies have close contacts between suppliers and customers. Customers are crucial and are handled in an individual manner. This may involve the selection of key customers, their special treatment, the allocation of resources to meet their wishes, etc., and this may have strategic consequences. From a network perspective on strategy, the relation to a set of distinct, related entities forming the context of the focal organization becomes crucial (Håkansson and Snehota, 1989). This process of relating and interacting may be influenced by actors who are relatively junior in the organizational hierarchy and who apply a perspective which diverges from top management's overall strategic plan.

This divorce of the corporate business perspective and the local, more operationally based, perspective is particularly relevant in industrial marketing, where strategic decisions are often actually taken at relatively low levels in the hierarchy (Turnball and Valla, 1986, p 7).

As in an adhocracy, it may thus be possible to imagine certain characteristics of the grass roots strategy in companies which produce goods for other industrial companies, even if the centralization and integration of the overall strategy is stronger in these companies than at NFB or at Enator.

11.7 Strategy Development at Enator

One way of describing the development of strategy at Enator is to regard it as a combination of the "grass roots model" and of initiatives and planned endeavours on the part of top management. As has already been indicated, internationalization of operations contained major elements of traditional top-down formulation and strategy implementation.

The central role played by personnel resources must be taken into account if we are to understand the development of strategy at Enator. These resources not only consist of competence and skill – they also mean contacts and networks. Almost all personnel have direct contact with the market. As far as junior consultants are concerned, this is not particularly significant – at least not from a strategic point of view – but a considerable number of senior consultants, project managers, subsidiary managers, etc. have an important contact network. The combinations of competence/contact networks which the company has at its disposal in terms of existing personnel indicates important opportunities, but also constraints in terms of corporate development. It is difficult to get major assignments in new markets, or of a type where the company has no previous experience, where there is no well-developed network. One of the most important factors for customers in selecting consultants in the computer area – and probably in other knowledge-intensive areas, too – is the competence of the project manager (according to market studies). The customer needs to have personal experience of the project manager in order to have confidence in his assessment of the individual concerned. (Marketing and sales of consultancy services will be covered in more detail in the next chapter.)

The significance of the contact network of senior consultants and other executives means that when the company recruits new personnel, it is also recruiting new, potentially useful networks to some extent.

Traditionally, Enator has relied heavily upon the networks possessed by the founders and the initial employees. The founders were able to build on a number of relationships with managers within Enator's major customer industries when the company started up, and these relationships have been maintained. The importance of contacts at other levels in the company was also clearly illustrated when Enator entered the public sector – in this case the experience of relatively newly employed personnel in their previous assignments and workplaces paved the way for new development. Thus, operative experience and actions of low-level employees feeds back into the strategic level. As often is the case in organizations dependent on a great deal of sophisticated expertise, people who are to "implement" strategies also become formulators of them. The dichotomy implementation-formulation collapses (Mintzberg, 1990).

The personal networks of other senior executives are also important, of course. Naturally, such networks are not confined to "purely" business contacts, but also include private relationships. It may be noted that one typical feature of this type of industry seems to be that the dividing-line between private and business relationships is often weak and diffuse. Since almost all types of organizations over a certain minimum size are potential customers in the computer consultancy world, this means that a relatively high proportion of a random collection of individuals in the higher echelons of society are potentially interesting from a business point of view – people on the golf course, in the business-class seats on the plane or acquaintancies in the personal sphere. It may be observed that the top managers work hard on sales. Customer contacts are a major management function and this means that top managers are not only the architects behind strategies but are also equally active in implementing them. To some extent, the actions of top management are in line with the "grass roots model".

There are a number of other reasons why the grass roots aspects and the emergent element in the formation of strategy are central features. The most important reasons are connected with the nature of operations. They involve flexible activities, designed to solve more or less unique assignments. There are no material constraints in the form of a sophisticated production apparatus, nor are the capital requirements significant. Various sections of the company also function autonomously. A cohesive, integrated plan which controls all areas of the company and closely regulates dependency relationships between them is hardly required. It may be said that the strategic and operative aspects of Enator's operations are very close. This contrasts with many other companies where the strategic and operative levels can be treated separately. According to Ansoff (1987), in the future strategy questions must be more closely related to the operative level. To the extent that companies of the Enator type become more common, the present study confirms Ansoff's views.

As previously indicated, tolerance for divergence in action is considerable. Enator, like other companies in the industry, has an extremely broad orientation, both in terms of products and marketing. Practically all types of customers are welcome. Enator offers a broad range of services and people at Enator stress the fact that the company has sometimes refused assignments when the customer's management were not involved, but in practice the company adopts a pragmatic approach. The overall goals are high growth and high profits. Amongst other things, this means that the consultants must have a full load and that an excessively restrictive approach cannot be applied when selecting assignments.[1] This is reflected in the fact that projects are of a relatively divergent nature. It is difficult to identify a distinct business concept from the company's operations.

At the same time, top management have a major strategic function in establishing boundary lines for activities which are not acceptable or in indicating the volume of "deviant" activity which is acceptable, and also in reminding employees of the central strategy, and working for it. The main strategy does not need to be maintained rigidly or consistently in this type of operation, but a certain minimum of integration of projects in relation to the business concept and the principal strategy (strategies) is probably necessary, both for external and internal reasons. The internal reasons involve cohesion, a feeling of corporate identity, prerequisites for synergy, etc. The external reasons are a matter of position in the market, image in relation to customers, and so on. If operations are excessively diverse, corporate identity will suffer and the market profile will become diffuse.

However, in certain situations, top management's importance from a strategic point of view is particularly great and – connected with this – some form of planning/implementation model, in which intentions precede implementation, has considerable relevance. This applies, for example, in situations where concentrated efforts are required, involving new resources, e.g. new products or establishment in new markets. The initiation and control of strategies for setting up businesses and investing in regional and international markets, the acquisition of companies and joint ventures are characterized by the influence of top management as a central strategic actor. It is interesting to note that Enator has not been particularly successful in these respects.

Some dimensions which are of central importance in understanding strategic processes have been formulated on the basis of the review of current strategic research with which this chapter commenced (pp 243). The experience of the Enator case can be described as follows, in these terms:

Broadly speaking, strategy formation in companies like Enator follows the emergent pattern. Long-term, detailed planning, which subsequently controls actions which fully comply with plans, hardly exists. Instead it is a question of a dynamic activity where many unforeseen events can take place. The important factors are flexibility and an open attitude towards any opportunities offered.

In terms of strategy as a "rational" project – in which clear, predetermined objectives are achieved with the assistance of a set of predetermined means – versus the concept of strategy as an expression of values, traditions, beliefs etc., I consider that Enator's strategy is not particularly well covered by either approach. It is true that Enator's strategy is characterized by rationality to the extent that the company has certain profit and growth objectives and strategies for achieving them. Values about what is considered good, desirable, etc. also play their part. However, for the most part Enator's strategy is characterized by pragmatism; a narrow concentration on the business concept, clearly thought-through formulae for objectives/means, and sacred values have to give way to tolerance for a broad range of projects and changes in orientation if new opportunities occur. Of course, this may be because the company is young and is largely working in new markets. Strategic action cannot be regarded as centralized, in the sense that management has a monopoly of initiatives which affect strategy. Naturally, management has important functions to fulfil in terms of the formulation of intentions and as a strategic architect. But it is a fair question to ask whether other roles are not more important in a company like Enator. Of the five roles which Bourgeois and Brodwin (1984) allocate to the managing director in the implementation of strategy – rational actor, architect, coordinator, coach and establisher of premises/umpire – the two latter roles probably count for more than the others. Important questions for the managing director will thus be:

How can I involve the whole organization in the implementation of a strategy? How can I encourage personnel to try to develop new, sensible strategies? (Bourgeois and Brodwin, 1984).

In other words, strategic action may be also exercised from positions outside top management.

The main feature of Enator's strategy is its broad scope. In Mintzberg and Waters' (1985) terms, this implies process strategy or umbrella strategy. Management establishes frameworks and objectives, and tries to influence the prerequisites for the process by deciding who is employed in key positions, what the structure is to look like, etc., without exercising control in detail or forcing consistency on operations. This means that the strategy is not focused and that patterns of behaviour do not converge. In the wide frameworks permitted by this strategy, there are considerable variations in terms of type of assignment and customers, for example.

11.8   Cultural Aspects of Strategy

Most researchers who are interested in organizational culture and corporate strategy place these two concepts externally, in relationship to each other, that is to say they see culture and strategy as two variables. In a company which functions satisfactorily, culture, the organizational structure and strategy need to be thoroughly correlated and should support one another. For example, the title of Schwartz and Davis' (1981) article is "Matching Corporate Culture and Business Strategy". Another view which harmonizes more closely with my own position would be that strategy expresses cultural patterns and thus encompasses values, ideals, beliefs, etc. Strategy is seen as a cultural manifestation. The features of an organization's strategy may thus have a symbolic meaning: internationalization, growth, establishment in new markets, the launching of new products – all have a deeper meaning in a collective sense. At any rate, this applies to a number of actors in most companies. It is true that large groups may have a more distanced, instrumental and perhaps even indifferent or alien approach to the content of strategy and the way in which it is specifically expressed. Actors who shape the direction of the company do not, however, share this attitude.

As previously mentioned, certain authors regard an organization as a cohesive collective, which provides a socio-emotional basis for the functioning of the organization and the implementation of strategy (Smircich and Stubbart, 1985), or which emphasizes the importance of a strong corporate identity and shared points of reference and understanding as to how the organization should function (Berg, 1985a).

The stronger the socio-emotional base and the corporate identity, the greater number of degrees of freedom which may be permitted as regards the development of strategy at a grass-roots level. Formal, material and administrative ties may be weak, but this is compensated by common ideas and meanings. The culture may function as a social glue. In a professional organization, each employee with a certain degree of competence may function as an entrepreneur in some ways (Mills et al., 1983). One prerequisite if this is to work in practice is, however, that there is a certain similarity in fundamental views. In the classic, traditional professions (for example, doctor, lawyer, priest) a shared professional socialization paves the way. In knowledge-intensive companies such as Enator, one important management task is to achieve shared values and views within the company.

However, the relationship between strategies which are realized and the organizational collective as a whole is often much weaker in a company like Enator. This is because the various sections of the company function rather autonomously. Enator's investment outside Sweden was soundly based in the values and ideals of top management and the owners, but was less clearly supported in the organizational collective as a whole. Most employees probably accepted the strategy, but the points of contact with traditional Swedish operations were relatively limited, although cooperation and synergy effects were discussed.

Growth is particularly interesting in this context. At Enator, turnover increased between 1982 and 1986 by between 30% and 56% per year. Economic growth has a particularly strong symbolic value in Western culture. Growth is associated with competence, rational thinking and acting, and is a sign of success and value. Ultimately, economic growth denotes the possibility for most people to live rich and good lives due to the employment opportunities, public-sector services and increased consumption which result from growth. In industry, growth tends to be equated with efficiency, adaptation to, or creative restructuring of, the market and other features which are considered to characterize good management practice. In purely concrete terms, it can be maintained that companies which grow find it easier to survive and to develop in the long term. Size is a competitive advantage. Growth and high profits are often considered to go hand in hand. Perhaps the relationship between the volume of operations and profits is often weak in the case of companies of the Enator type, since purely technical large-scale advantages are not particularly prominent.

The interesting feature in this context is, however, not the purely economic aspects of a growth strategy but its symbolic and cultural fruits. According to Berg and Gagliardi (1985), the primary objective of any organization is the maintenance and protection of its cultural identity. This identity is handled by means of "expressive strategies":

> Expressive strategies operate on the symbolic field and seek to protect the stability and the coherence of shared meanings. They may be internally or externally oriented: in the former case they enable group members to maintain a lively awareness of their collective identity, in the latter case they enable the organization to offer a recognizable identity to the outside world (p 11).

Enator's corporate identity – the collective's view of itself and of the company as a whole – is largely a question of youth, enthusiasm and dynamism, a strong corporate spirit and excellent social relationships. Dynamic investments in growth and international expansion are partly in line with these aspects. The company's history of success and the intensive spirit which have been partly created and maintained as a result of growth and the strong degree of positive interest – both internal and external – which has been associated with growth, pave the way for an understanding in which growth is regarded as something natural, and an expression of vitality and dynamism.

At this point, perhaps somewhat speculatively, one might link up to the idea of life symbols. Growth, the burgeoning of new companies, and the starting up of new subsidiaries all denote the early stages of the life-cycle, and youth, vitality and development towards something greater and better. Lack of growth denotes stagnation and may ultimately, unconsciously, be associated with ideas and fantasies to the effect that there are no guarantees for invulnerability and immortality. This antithesis of growth may gain greater currency in a stagnant market, with reduced or non-existent growth or even decline, in a company whose development has been characterized for some time by increased turnover, an expanding labour force and new exciting deals, etc. This may lead to an inability to accept a deterioration in external conditions and a propensity to hold on to quantitative development which symbolizes certain ideals which are hard to realize in the long run.

However, certain of Enator's corporate strategies also involve elements which do not harmonize particularly well with its "cultural core" or its corporate identity. The purchase of existing companies, within and outside Sweden, joint ventures with partners who were new and unknown to Enator and the goal of making Enator into a major international corporate group can all be placed in this category. This is virtually "anti-expressive" in relation to some significant corporate values: strong social ties, comradeship, an intensive corporate spirit, small-scale operations and a feeling of belonging. The corporate strategies which have come to characterize Enator's development in recent years have meant a greater distance between various parts of the group, not only geographically but probably also in social and cultural terms. It may perhaps be noted that the values associated with growth, expansion and internationalization carry more weight, at least in management and owner circles, than the importance of strong social ties within the company. When compared to an architect firm studied by Mintzberg et al. (1988), where broad values and normative beliefs about what the firm should work with set constraints for the company's development, to some extent, at the expense of financial success, Enator is driven more by profit and growth motives than by cultural values, when these values are not clearly instrumental in relationship to capitalistic goals.

At the same time, internal management strategies have emerged to combat the consequences of this development within the organization. The use of corporate culture as a general management tool is crucial here. The "Victoria" tenth anniversary may, for example, be regarded as a powerful manifestation of an endeavour to maintain cohesion and a feeling of community throughout the Enator group, in the context of heavy stress of expansion.

Note

[1]   Of course, these imperatives are a result of Enators strong orientation to
      profits and growth. Other companies may be more committed to other val-
      ues, such as focusing on a certain kind of work that one is highly interested in
      and/or competent at. This is characterizing some knowledge-intensive com-
      panies (Mintzberg et al., 1988; Starbuck, 1993). These companies, i.e. their
      dominating actors (owners) see corporate size as less important than attain-
      ing interesting work and achieving a high quality within a core area. By impli-
      cation, these companies tend to be smaller than Enator.

12　Marketing – External and Internal

Enator will be examined from a marketing perspective in this chapter. Some general themes of significance for the marketing of knowledge-intensive service companies will, by implication, be treated. Internal marketing will also be discussed and the concept scrutinized at a general level. Both external and internal marketing will be related to organizational dimensions. A few general perspectives are introduced before dealing with the situation which applies at Enator and in similar companies.

12.1　Marketing of Services

In recent years, researchers in the marketing field have persistently maintained that "service marketing" and "service management" are quite different from traditional marketing (e.g. Grönroos, 1984, 1990; Lovelock, 1981; Normann, 1983). This concept, in combination with the fact that the service sector has rapidly expanded and continues to do so, explains dramatic developments in the specialized literature in this area. (See e.g. Gummesson, 1994; Zeithaml et al., 1985, for overview.)

This literature is based on three fundamental assumptions. The first is that services have certain unique characteristics which distinguish them from physical products. The second assumption is that these unique characteristics result in certain specific problems for service companies which manufacturing enterprises avoid. The third assumption is that the marketing of services requires a special type of activity and a theoretical basis which take the special features of service activities fully into account (Zeithaml et al., 1985).

Despite the fact that the service sector – to the extent that reference can be made to such a sector – covers an extremely varied range of activities – from hairdressing to insurance and from air-travel to consultancy services – some authors claim that it is possible to observe certain common characteristics (Normann, 1983). One such common feature is that services are non-tangible. They are not goods. Amongst other things, this means that they cannot be stored, that they are hard to demonstrate and that customers are forced to buy "a pig in a poke" to a greater extent than in the case of physical goods. Another special feature is that most services consist of actions and interactions between the seller and the buyer. Social processes are thus significant. Keeping a tap on and controlling the interplay between company personnel and customers demands special management and organizational features. In addition, the production and consumption of a service are not clearly separated, since both take place simultaneously and at the same location. In other words, the manufacturing process takes place "in the field". This means, for example, that differentiation between various functions – e.g. production and sales – becomes blurred at the company level. A fourth characteristic is that the customer also participates in the production of the service. In the case of haircutting, visiting a restaurant, education and holiday travel, etc., the customer participates actively in establishing the quality of the service in question. This is important, particularly in a consultancy context. Cooperation with the customer is often intimate and the quality of the project partially depends on the customer's knowledge of what he (she) wants and his (her) ability to complete his (her) part of the work. Another important point is the degree of heterogeneity which is particularly characteristic of many services. The quality level is less standardized than in manufacturing industry. The essence and quality of a service can vary between different sections of a company and different employees, and between different customers and on different days (Zeithaml et al., 1985).

Sceptics or "traditionalists" counter the idea of proposing that service activities constitute the basis for a special "service management and marketing concept" by arguing, on the one hand, that all companies are in the service sector in a certain sense and, on the other hand, that it has proved difficult to demarcate and define services in an appropriate manner. The sceptics also maintain that what is sold always contains tangible and nontangible elements in varying degrees, irrespective of whether the good in question is presented primarily as a "service" or as a "physical product" (Enis and Roering, 1981; Levitt, 1981).

Authors who do not accept the idea that the marketing of services is sufficiently special to constitute a separate orientation which is quite distinct from "traditional" marketing do not deny that services and physical objects are of a different nature. But they oppose the idea that a clear division can be made and that this has special implications from a marketing viewpoint. Enis and Roering (1981) consider, for example, that the starting-point for the marketer should be the total benefits which the customer receives as a result of his purchase. It is not particularly important whether these benefits are achieved by something which is primarily a physical good or by something in which the non-tangible component dominates (i.e. a service). Thus for example, the same needs may be satisfied by McDonald's or by a semi-manufactured or fully manufactured food product, by a school or a publisher or a library, by a bank or a seller of security systems (safe storage of assets) or by a bank or a dealer in gold (investment), etc. From a marketing point of view, the fact that corporate activities consist of services or products or a combination of both is less important than the customer's needs and what the company can offer the customer in relation to competitors. As the examples above illustrate, it is not of primary interest whether competitors are producing services or physical products. McDonald's competitors can be found amongst companies manufacturing fast foods in deep-frozen packaged form, for example. Thus, Enis and Roering (1981) regard the manner in which a company operates – production of services or of physical goods – as not particularly important from a marketing perspective. They consider that what the company offers is neither a physical good nor a service, but rather a set of benefits, which normally include both tangible and non-tangible aspects.

The difference between these authors and representatives of a specialized service marketing concept is that the former take customers' "needs" as their starting-point, while the latter group are primarily concerned with the special circumstances and difficulties which characterize the production of services. Perhaps Levitt's (1960) famous "marketing myopia" thesis is relevant in this context – that companies sometimes concentrate heavily on current products or technology, ignoring the fact that customers' needs may be satisfied in various ways. Levitt's article may be seen as an important antidote to the literature which heavily emphasizes the specific production character of services. In addition, it may be claimed that service activities are particularly heterogeneous, especially in view of the claim that more than half the labour force in the most affluent countries are often working in the service sector, in what is sometimes known as post-industrial society.

Grönroos (1984) considers that the problem of demarcating services from other activities can be solved by applying the following highly atheoretical definition:

Services are transaction objects which are offered by companies and institutions which normally sell services or which regard themselves as service organizations (p 19).

Normann (1983) prefers not to get entangled in "speculations about words and definitions", perhaps wisely, but notes that "the difference between manufacturing companies and service companies is in the best case diffuse" (p 12). However, he implies that an increasing number of companies are becoming accustomed to regarding themselves as working in the service sector.

Despite the problem of defining any uniform category of phenomena to which the "service" label can be applied, there is nowadays "the almost universal idea held by academics working in this area that the marketing of services is different from marketing of goods in certain fundamental respects" (Zeithaml et al., 1985, p 44). A somewhat ironic way of summarizing the position of authors who believe in the specialized marketing of services would be to say that they do not really know what distinguishes services from goods, but at any rate they do know that there are differences in the marketing. Particularly in the type of company which I am dealing with in this book, there are good reasons for accepting the assumption that "traditional" marketing (i.e. "management of the marketing mix") do not provide a satisfactory picture or an appropriate indication of orientations for marketing activity. The characteristics noted above for services fit well: consulting is non-tangible, it is a question of complex interaction between consultancy and customer companies, and production and consumption take place simultaneously, at least in some respects.[1] The customer participates actively and the quality levels probably vary heavily compared to manufactured physical products.

In a great many other cases, questions may be raised as to whether the service characteristics referred to above really are valid for all or even most companies operating in the service sector, despite the fact that they are dealt with in all of the literature which tries to give service marketing uniform characteristics and an independent status and profile (Zeithaml et al., 1985). Let us take air-travel as an example. In contrast with the special characteristics listed above, it can be maintained that air-travel is a tangible activity. Passengers often know precisely what to expect: the aircraft, the on-board environment, and the airports. A considerable proportion of the service – the actual flight – takes place without the direct involvement of passengers. (Perhaps the quality would reach its ultimate heights if the passengers slept all the time.) Most of the functions involved can be distinguished quite clearly from each other: selling the flight, check-in, service on-board, and the actual transportation function. The standards of performance offered are almost as homogeneous as a stream of cars or milk packets coming off the production line. And air disasters, high-jacking, unfriendly stewardesses or serious delays are the exception rather than the norm. In my own case, at any rate, all the flights that I have made seem to be remarkably similar.

From a marketing point of view – and from a number of other perspectives – there are considerable differences between consultancy companies such as Enator and most other service companies. In this context, it is fruitful to distinguish between companies which are concerned with advanced problem-solving and organizations which offer more or less standardized services (Sveiby and Risling, 1986). Most companies in the service sector are in fact concerned with standardized products (services). In some cases, standardized products are most significant, but problem-solving operations are also offered. Banks, for example, are largely concerned with standardized production – routine incoming and outgoing payments, simple accounts procedures, etc. – but they also have smaller units working with specialized problems, for example major credit commitments. The special characteristic of knowledge-intensive companies, in contrast to other service companies, is that the former primarily offer non-standardized services which involve complex problem-solving (Sveiby and Risling, 1986).

I will shortly be examining this dimension and one or two others in more detail since they are important if we are to get a fuller picture of the marketing situation in companies such as Enator. However, the first step is to present some of the fundamental ideas involved in the marketing of services.

12.2   The Service Marketing Concept

As a practical activity, in contrast to academic disciplines or philosophies/ideologies, marketing has customarily been defined as follows:

Marketing management is the analysis, planning, implementation and control of programs designed to achieve the desired exchanges with target markets with the object of achieving organizational objectives (Kotler, 1976, p 7).

The core of marketing involves strategic and tactical management and administration of what is known as the marketing mix, that is to say the formulation and realization of measures with regard to the product, distribution, promotion (communications) and pricing.

Proponents of a special marketing theory for services regard this approach as appropriate for the marketing of physical goods, but far too narrow to be fruitful for the production of services. Major areas of the sales organization are directly involved in customer contacts in a service context, and this is not covered by traditional marketing concepts. Grönroos (1984) proposes the following definition as a basis for marketing theory for services:

marketing management is planning, infusing and managing all resources and activities within the company's area of control which influence the company's customer relationships ... (p 26).

One important aspect of customer relationships involves views about the company held by customers and the general public, the corporate image in the market-place.

The above definition of marketing reflects the fact that there is a broad area of contact between the company and its customers in a service company. A considerable proportion of the activities conducted involve contacts and interaction between personnel/customers. The marketing function is not restricted to a special marketing and sales department, but also permeates the area of the company which produces the services. Normann (1983) expresses this by saying that the company is "personality-intensive" in the daily production of quality. In this context the management of "human resources" become particularly important (Schneider and Bowen, 1993).

Another important aspect is that the quality of services is intimately associated with the customer's subjective experiences. Physical goods often have more objective characteristics, such as physical performance and durability. In the service sector, people refer more often to how the customer perceives the quality of the services offered. At Enator, for example, "customer-perceived quality" tends to be a keyword. The customer's perception of quality depends not only on the services which the customer receives and their technical characteristics (a clean house or a flight free from mishaps), but also *how* the customer perceives the service in question and the customer's expectations and ideas about the whole process. In this context, the corporate image is a vital asset – that is to say the picture of the company held by a specific relevant audience (e.g. current and potential customers).

This is illustrated in Figure 12.1, which distinguishes three dimensions of quality: technical, functional and interactive quality. The customer's perception of quality is permeated to some extent by the (consultancy) company's image, which filters perception and interpretation of actual achievements. To some extent, the diagram distinguishes perception of consultancy services in a strict sense from perception of the consultancy company. This may be a good idea, since the picture of the consultancy company itself is determined by many more factors than apply to the technical and functional characteristics of the consultancy service. The figure demonstrates that the propensity to place repeat orders is determined both by experience of services previously received and also by general ideas about the consultancy company.

One result of the close contacts between a considerable proportion of the personnel in a service company and customers, and customers' sensitivity to the behaviour of personnel in a broad sense, is that it is difficult to distinguish between internal and external effectiveness. Nor is it possible to regard revenue and costs as separate items. Attempts to cut costs will normally have direct and indirect consequences on customer relationships and hence on revenues (Grönroos, 1984; and Normann, 1983), either because the customer directly perceives the deterioration in what is offered or because cost reductions affect the motivation and interest of personnel in their work. The link between what employees experience at work and consumers/clients perception of service qualities is strong (Schneider and Bowen, 1993).

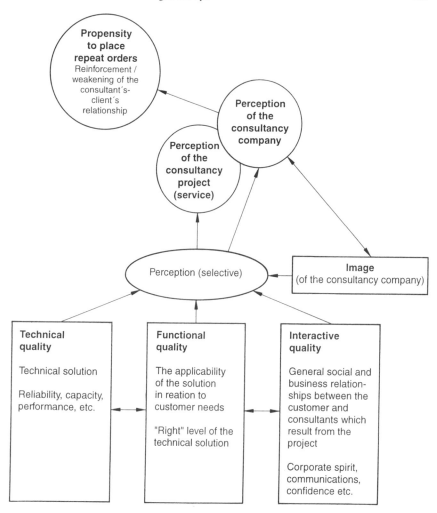

Figure 12.1:   The client's perception of the quality of consultancy services (cf. Grönroos, 1984)

Grönroos considers that strategic management in service companies should be based on interactive marketing between sellers and buyers. This means that the consequences for the relationship between customers and personnel who have the power to influence customers in a broad sense must be taken into account in decision making and resource allocation and that these are crucial aspects of the company's activities.

12.3 Industrial Marketing

An approach to marketing such as that presented by proponents of service management would appear to be adequate for the type of company dealt with in this book. The marketing situation for industrial companies is quite different. However, as previously indicated, the service market management approach is relatively general and therefore it provides an approximate and imprecise picture of the characteristics involved in the type of activity which is in focus. It would therefore appear that greater precision and a more sophisticated approach would be in order.

The distinction between the marketing of consumer goods and producer goods is important and is well-established in the marketing discipline, even if there are differences of opinion as to how great this distinction is. Some people, for example Kotler (1976), apparently regard the various markets as a question of differences in emphasis in the marketing mix and of the more complex sales process which occurs because the customer is an organization. Specialists in industrial marketing, such as the IM Group in Uppsala (e.g. Håkansson and Johansson, 1982; Håkansson et al., 1981; Håkansson and Östberg, 1975) do not agree, emphasizing that in many cases the marketing of producer goods is intrinsically different from the marketing of consumer products.

The primary difference is that the seller has often a limited number of customers or that a high proportion of production goes to a limited number of major customer companies. This means that customers must be treated individually. The situation is even more complicated if the manufacturing operation involves sophisticated goods. In such cases, relations with customers are often complicated and multi-faceted and a considerable number of departments and decision makers in both the supplier and customer company are involved in interactions to solve financial, technical, delivery and operational problems. In situations of this kind, it is not fruitful to employ a marketing theory which assumes that the company has a large number of customers who may be treated in a standardized or moderately individualized manner and that customer reactions can be dealt with as average reactions to a certain, given combination of competitive instruments (Håkansson et al., 1981).

Proponents of a service marketing approach sometimes point to experience in industrial marketing and employ it to counter the idea that one and the same fundamental marketing model can be employed in all possible contexts. Grönroos (1984) does this, even if he himself does not distinguish between consumer and producer-oriented service operations. The argument regarding the differences between the marketing of consumer and producer goods should also be highly applicable to the marketing of

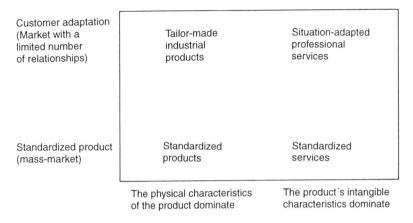

Customer adaptation (Market with a limited number of relationships)	Tailor-made industrial products	Situation-adapted professional services
Standardized product (mass-market)	Standardized products	Standardized services
	The physical characteristics of the product dominate	The product's intangible characteristics dominate

Figure 12.2:   illustrates the importance of distinguishing between two crucial dimensions: the proportion of physical goods/services in the product and the question of standardized/customer-adapted products (which broadly corresponds to the distinction between mass-market/limited market)

services. The differences between consumer and industrial/institutional markets may be considerable. In the case of Enator, for example, the company has a limited number of large and important customers whom it is both possible and essential to treat in an individualized manner.

12.4   The Marketing of Professional Services

A more precise definition of the marketing situation faced by operations such as Enator's also calls for a greater focus on the professional (know-ledge-intensive) character of such activities.[2] Professional activities can be loosely defined as offering advanced, complex products/services via well-trained personnel (often with a university degree and some years of experience) for relatively high prices. Advanced knowledge and know-how is the core of what is sold. The knowledge in question is primarily or at least partly of an intellectual, textbook-based nature, which can be formalized, in combination with experience based on such knowledge and, perhaps we should add, other acquired skills. Advanced knowledge may be of different types, for example in terms of craftsmanship or artistic skills – and perhaps there is good reason to beware of an approach to knowledge which only looks at the existing status hierarchy in the labour market as a measure of what is considered to be qualified or unqualified work (Knights et al., 1993).

Knowledge-intensive service work is normally placed in the same category as service work by authors on service management. This is feasible, but there are considerable differences between knowledge-intensive companies and the great majority of service companies. Advertising agencies, consultancy companies, law and accounting firms mainly consist of highly qualified professionals (knowledge workers) and services, while for example transportation companies, security and cleaning contractors sell services of a rather different nature. In Normann's (1983) book on service management, which chiefly attempts to cover all types of service activity without drawing clear distinctions between service organizations which are oriented towards the solution of advanced problems and more routine and standardized services, many of the arguments discussed are *either* applicable to problem-solving services *or* they are appropriate for standardized types of activity. Thus, there is good reason to distinguish the marketing of professional services from the marketing of other types of services. The idea of distinguishing services from physical goods is probably less debatable and more clearly fruitful in the case of professional services. On the one hand, many of the special characteristics which service management authors claim distinguish services from the manufacturing of goods, are considerably more marked in the case of professional services. We may take the degree of tangible/non-tangible features as an example. Even if services generally have fewer tangible aspects than physical goods, and are therefore more difficult to demonstrate, there are substantial differences regarding the relative input of tangible/non-tangible elements. McDonald's restaurants, taxi services, air-travel, libraries and the rental of bank safe-boxes contain a considerable proportion of physical objects. But in the case of most types of knowledge-intensive activities, such physical aspects are quite subordinate. The basis for the service in question is primarily in the minds of personnel in the knowledge-intensive company, and this is something which is more difficult to demonstrate in physical terms.

Criticism of the idea that the marketing of services is different from other types of marketing have a weaker case regarding professional services. These are arguable and distinctly different from "traditional" and "average" marketing. It makes sense to take the actual functioning of operations as the starting-point rather than the possibility that customer requirements may often be met either by purchase of goods or by the provision of services. As mentioned above, Enis and Roering (1981), for example, consider that the customer purchases benefits which may often involve either a service or a product, for example renting or purchasing something. From the buyer and competition perspective, the division into services/products is then not particularly interesting. In the case of professional services, there is relatively little competition with businesses outside the service sector. Possibly a doctor may compete with the manufacturer of gymnastic equipment in certain situations, a dentist with the manufacturer of toothbrushes and a management consultant with a publisher such as Harper and Row, who have published "In Search of Excellence". But, on the whole, these aspects of purchasing and competition aspects cannot be said to counter the idea that professional services should be regarded as a special and separate area with partially unique characteristics. The definition of a professional market for services does not generally mean automatically obtaining an incorrect picture of the alternatives open to customers or of the structure of the competitive situation. However, it should be noted that professional services may also be offered within the customer company. (Thus, consultants sometimes compete with the customer company personnel.) And of course it should also be noted that the technological development in the computer field has an effect on the computer consultancy market.

To sum up this section, it may be said that companies like Enator may be described in broad terms on the basis of models and reasoning derived from the discipline of service marketing. Knowledge-intensive companies do however, differ markedly in major respects from most companies, particularly those working in consumer markets. The differences mean that special attention must be paid to certain aspects of the marketing of professional services.

12.5   Standardized and Situationally-adapted Production of Services

At the risk of being accused of going into excessive detail, I would like to focus on a fourth distinction: the difference between standardized and individualized products/services. By standardized services, I mean services which are of a uniform nature and which are offered in a form which is specified in advance. Situationally-adapted services, on the other hand, are designed to meet specific problems and requirements. Naturally, many types of services lie somewhere between the unambiguously standardized and the totally unique extremes. It may be claimed that this fourth dimension has already been covered above, when discussing professional/non-professional activities. This is certainly the view of Sveiby and Risling (1986), who define the products of a professional or knowledge-intensive company as non-standardized, creative, heavily dependent on individuals and involving complex problem-solving. It is true that the non-standardized and professionalized dimensions often overlap, but they are not identical. There are two reasons for this.

The first reason is that non-professional activity may also exhibit characteristics which comply with Sveiby and Risling's definition of a knowledge-intensive company. Examples might include craftsmanship and many types of operation in the health-care and social sectors. (One example of an organization which is non-standardized, creative and dependent on individuals, etc. to a greater extent than most types of professional activities might be a programme for the care of drug-abusers. Such collective programmes sometimes directly reject the training and approaches which characterize professional operations in the health-care sector.) Secondly, and this is more important, a high proportion of all types of professional activities are of a standardized nature. As Mintzberg (1983) points out, most professionals may be found in what Mintzberg calls professional bureaucracies; activities provide a standardized product or service based on the knowledge and skills of professionals. This applies to most activities in health-care, chartered accountancy, social care, the educational system and universities. It is true that the service is normally to some extent situationally adapted to the customer's needs, but it is typically a question of choosing between standardized solutions to assist the customer. A broken leg, an appendix operation or a bad cold are normally treated by doctors on a standardized basis, without introducing a creative, complex problem-solving element. There is thus good reason not to equate professional/-knowledge-intensive services with non-standardization.

12.6   A Classification of Marketing Situations

Classifying products/services is clearly a popular activity for marketing authors. This applies particularly in the service area. See Lovelock (1983) for an overview of a number of proposed classification schedules.

My idea in this context is, instead, to provide a comprehensive picture of the main areas in marketing which should be highlighted and distinguished so as to arrive at a picture of the situation faced by knowledge-intensive companies such as Enator. This can be achieved by combining the four distinctions which have been described above. These distinctions involve physical products versus services (as most salient element in the product offer), the institutional versus the consumer market, professional versus non-professional activities and standardized versus situationally-adapted products (services). If these four different dimensions are combined, we arrive, in principle, at 16 different permutations as illustrated in Figure 12.3.

	Production of goods		Production of services	
	Professional activity	Non-professional activity	Professional activity	Non-professional activity
Consumer market — Standardized product				
Consumer market — Situationally-adapted product				
Industrial and institutional market — Standardized product				
Industrial and institutional market — Situationally-adapted product				

Figure 12.3:   Forms of activity on basis of dimensions which are important for the marketing of different types of products/services
The area market with diagonal lines indicates Enator's product range

I will not strain the reader's patience excessively by covering all these 16 possibilities. Perhaps a couple of them hardly occur at all in practice. Let us instead focus on Enator's position in the diagram. Enator is clearly a company which operates in an institutional market, offers services which are primarily of a professional (knowledge-intensive) nature. The degree of (formal) professionalization demonstrated by systems analysts and programmers is not, however, as marked as in the case of lawyers, doctors and chartered accountants. It is somewhat more difficult to deal with the question of the degree of standardization (situational adaptation) in the services offered by Enator. Activities are primarily concerned with more or less unique problem-solving, but there are also significant elements of a more standardized nature, at least from a marketing perspective. The standardized features include, for example, certain maintenance commitments and the renting out of purely programming competence. A consultant who is rented out and the manner in which such an individual is subsequently employed may vary – this is something decided by the customer. But in principle such transactions involve a specific resource, a consultant who temporarily assists the customer with sophisticated, but relatively routine work. Thus, Enator's services are primarily of a non-standardized, situationally-adapted character, but more standardized services are also offered.

It is now high time to describe marketing at Enator.

12.7   Marketing at Enator

Selling a major consultancy project worth perhaps several million kronor is obviously quite different from the act of selling a travel package, a visit to a restaurant, a particular banking service or any other type of service product at the consumer level. There are also strong differences from the selling/buying of a major industrial product, since the latter is more easily specified in physical terms, etc. Customers normally want clear indications of the competence of a consultancy company in general and, specifically, they want to know which individuals will be directly responsible for the project. There is a very high degree of uncertainty in the production of professional services. Since problem-solving is normally involved, uncertainty may arise from the nature of the problem and from the assessment of the consultant's/the consultancy company's competence (Wilson, 1975).

Building up, maintaining, and developing good relations with regular customers is of decisive importance in this situation. Detailed knowledge and good relationships between the consultant and the client may reduce this uncertainty. A good social network is of considerable value in this context. The qualities exhibited by the three founders in this respect appear to have been a highly significant factor in Enator's expansion and success. Many business contacts are difficult to categorize in terms of business or private relationships. Personal relationships and friendship proceed and result from business assignments. One of the bench-marks both for external contacts and relationships within the company at Enator is that employees try to make friends with people they meet at work. This means that customers, suppliers and other interested parties are treated as "friends". Of course, Enator is not alone in this endeavour. There seems to be a tendency to claim that "it is no longer enough for a company to have a large number of customers – we also need a lot of friends" (manager, quoted in Berg, 1986, p 558). This statement illustrates the importance of establishing close relationships which go beyond what is required in traditional marketing terms (where the customer/supplier is easily replaced).

Good social relations with customers are partly a matter of personal ability and a personal approach to business contacts, and partly a question of trying to deal with purely business aspects in order to maximize the congruence of objectives between the seller and the customer.

Of course, an inborn talent for achieving friendly relationships and the situationally-specific prerequisites for such relationships varies and cannot readily be managed or administered. But I feel that Enator has been relatively successful in achieving such a situation. Enator's managers and employees have endeavoured to avoid recruiting "awkward types". Thus, the ambition of recruiting extroverted and agreeable personnel – sometimes at the expense of technical competence – facilitates both internal and external cooperation.

At a more comprehensive level, it is important to attempt to achieve high economic congruence of objectives between the company and its customers, and this means avoiding short-term thinking and a narrow maximization of utility. Instead, efforts are made to build up long-term relationships based on trust.

Rational bonds are desirable where congruence of objectives means that the parties to a transaction can gain more from exchanges in which long-term ties of acquaintanceship and confidence replace anonymous forms of exchanges for a limited period which characterize the impersonal market (Bowen and Jones, 1986, p 435).

Building up and maintaining such relationships is expensive, in terms of time, resources and refraining from optimized debiting in the short term. It may pay, however, since durable and trusting relationships reduce transaction costs, i.e. the costs of investments which make the exchange possible and the costs of the monitoring of the exchange process. With regard to often complicated and ambiguous services which apply in the current case, considerable investments are usually required, on the part of both the seller and the buyer, to achieve the actual sale/purchase itself and also to control and the production of the service in question and the outcome, as well as to correct possible dissension regarding the outcome. However, the total cost is considerably less if both the buyer and the seller have established satisfactory, long-term relations. Thus, relationships of this type are important for the kind of operations in which Enator is involved and for many other types of activity in which there is considerable uncertainty about the exchanges involved (Bowen and Jones, 1986; Håkansson and Johansson, 1982, etc.).

With regard to marketing to institutions (companies and other organizations), personal selling is clearly the most important element in the promotion mix. Advertising is of relatively minor importance compared to the marketing of consumer goods, while publicity and sales promotion have roughly similar importance (Kotler, 1976).

In Enator's case, a distinction may be made between specialized sales activities and "assignment-based" sales. The former term refers to measures which can be defined as clearly sales and marketing oriented. They are defined in these terms by both the consultancy company and the customer and can be clearly demarcated as distinct from other activities. Assignment-based marketing is an integrated aspect of day-to-day production occurring in the course of a consultancy project. Thus, marketing is an integral part of the production of services. Enator attempts to look for and obtain project assignments that parallel its execution of projects which have already been agreed. Both formal and assignment-based marketing exist at Enator and the latter is the significant. As one employee put it: "At Enator we debit the customer for the time which we spend selling our services."

As authors interested in the marketing of services have pointed out, in a certain sense marketing always takes place when services are produced. The customer comes into contact with different sections of the service company and the net result means that a basis is established with regard to the customer's picture of the company, the quality on offer and the prerequisites for purchases. This also applies at Enator, of course. A well-executed assignment – in the widest possible sense – is the basis for new assignments with the same customer. But, apart from this, Enator, like other knowledge-intensive service companies, uses the project as a basis to track down and secure new assignments.

The company frequently takes on small assignments with the aim of using them to secure major projects in the future. Pilot studies and reports fit into this category, for example, and minor projects of a simple and uncomplex nature which are not linked to major projects may be used as a "foot-in-the-door", offering opportunities for a shot at major assignments. This is why overqualified consultants are sometimes used for simple assignments. This establishes customer confidence, and an experienced consultant can also see further needs and assignment opportunities. Behind the weaknesses and problems the customer is immediately interested in dealing with, there are more often complicated problems or opportunities for comprehensive improvements (more work for the consultants). An inexperienced consultant only concentrates on the needs the customer has specified, while a fully competent individual not only does the job he is paid for, but sees complex factors behind the symptoms and uses these insights to sell the customer additional major assignments. At least that is the reasoning employed at Enator.[3]

Thus, part of Enator's activities have a "spear-head function"; they serve as a spring-board to other assignments. The most important function of Informationsstrategerna (Information Strategists), a small Enator subsidiary which emphasizes the combination of management and computer know-how and which focuses on management problems, is to operate as a spear-head unit, getting further tasks for other Enator subsidiaries as a result of its own assignments.

This type of activity, which is characterized by a gradual establishment of closer relationships in the course of major consultancy assignments with customers – where small projects constitute an intermediate stage – is natural in view of the uncertainty involved in this type of operation. It is difficult for customers to fully understand, in advance, what they are buying. Services cannot be demonstrated before they are performed. As a result, the consultancy company must work hard to facilitate the customer's purchasing process so that the customer can evaluate the potential advantages and reduce his/her uncertainty. A small, well-implemented project may provide an excellent indication of the consultancy company's qualifications, making it likely that major, crucial assignments will also be carried out satisfactorily. This corresponds to what Normann (1983) terms "immediate mini-delivery":

A complex service cannot be experienced or demonstrated in its entirety, but a well-trained and experienced contact person creates opportunities – or takes opportunities – to show what he can do for the customer and that he and his company have something valuable to offer (p 82).

Wilson (1975) calls this "the intrinsic approach" in the marketing of professional services. The intrinsic approach demonstrates an ability to get to the heart of the clients problem which one can help to solve in the contact phase. This is much more difficult than an "extrinsic" marketing approach, where there is *no* focus on the client's problem, and where marketing consists of a general description of what the consultancy firm represents, with references to successful projects ("success stories").

Sales and marketing elements are also found in major projects, not just in small assignments. Enator's ambition is to systematically watch out for the customer's needs in all projects, needs which can be satisfied as a result of Enator contributions in addition to those specified in the assignment contract. The aim is to apply a "helicopter view" of the customer company in parallel with the implementation of the consultancy project, and to consistently attempt to establish and maintain a dialogue with top level decision makers in the customer's organization. Thus, sales take place within the framework for a specific project. The tools employed by Enator in its attempts to live up to this ideal include the course in project management philosophy in which all employees participate (covered in Chapter 5) and the quality control groups which provide project follow-up and support on a regular basis. However, it appears that enthusiasm and the ability to conduct sales operations while undertaking assignments varies amongst the consultants. Many employees are not particularly interested in this aspect of operations.

However, an appreciable proportion of the selling of consultancy services also takes place in the conventional manner, that is to say outside the framework of a specific, ongoing project. The marketing of professional activities is somewhat problematic since the marketing has to be carried out by primarily professionally qualified individuals. Skilled salesmen who have no training in the profession in question sometimes find it hard to market a complex product whose charactistics can neither be specified physically nor demonstrated and which depends on professional problem-solving competence. The marketing must be mainly taken care of by the professionals themselves, since only professionals are able to exploit every opportunity in the sales phase to focus on the customer's specific problems and to give some idea as to how they can be solved ("intrinsic marketing"). The problem is that it is difficult to perform marketing while fully maintaining individual professional competence (Gummesson, 1979). The most important element in this type of company is the establishment of personal contact and sales, and this is extremely time-consuming. At the same time, professional competence may fade if non-operative tasks become too dominant. According to Gummesson (1979) when professionals confine themselves strictly to marketing, development work or administrative tasks, the results are not good. Many professionals are not particularly interested in sales or marketing operations (Whittington and Whipp, 1992).

However, the distinction between different types of professional services is relevant in this context. Not everything done by a professional consultancy company is complicated, situationally-adapted and problem-solving. Some services can be handled in a more uniform and standardized manner, for example selling programmers as a resource or the maintenance of a data processing system. Some Enator subsidiaries employ full-time sales personnel who are skilled salesmen rather than trained computer professionals. Salesmen of this type are responsible for a high proportion of some subsidiaries' output.

Other companies consider, however, that it is too expensive and too inefficient to have specialist salesmen on the payroll. One subsidiary manager remarks that "We can't afford those pin-striped guys out there 'scanning'." Particularly in subsidiaries which do not have specialist salesmen, but also in Enator companies which have decided to employ specialists, sales of services are a matter of concern at the highest levels in the organization. This also applies in other professional companies (Gummesson, 1979). Most of the subsidiary managers whom I interviewed considered that their most important function was selling, although some of them felt that personnel management and development were equally important. In this respect, professional companies differ markedly from mass service companies where management is not normally directly involved in personal sales. The situation at Enator and similar companies is the converse of the normal state of affairs: at Enator sales operations are a task for management and other competent and experienced staff, whereas in consumer company services, selling operations are a job for parts of the lower hierarchical levels. Of course, this is due to the preoccupation of consumer-goods companies with mass-markets where the individual customer is an insignificant factor. At Enator, on the other hand, the number of customers is limited and this means that many of them are important.

The generous way in which managing director titles are handed out at Enator seems to facilitate sales operations. The magic words "Managing Director" on a business card pave the way for successful deals. As one subsidiary manager put it : "I can sell because I've been blessed with the title of Managing Director." In other words, Enator's organizational structure, which is characterized by a large number of subsidiaries, facilitates sales efforts. Another important aspect of Enator's marketing is to present various substitutes to compensate for the disadvantage of not having a clear and well-defined product which can be demonstrated. The general image of the company held by a certain target group is important in this context. Corporate image is determined partly by what the company produces, for whom, and who works for it, and partly by special measures which aim to influence the image. The former group of factors are the most important but sometimes, at least on a short-term basis, drastic effects can be achieved by manipulating the corporate image according to Normann (1983).

The image which Enator is striving for is that of a youthful, dynamic, rapidly-growing, creative, technologically relatively advanced and unhierarchical company with a strong and distinct corporate culture, skilled in social interaction and project management, working on strategically important computer consultancy projects, primarily for large companies. Enator's international character is also emphasized; Enator's corporate culture functions as a kind of instrument for communicating what the company represents, in ideal terms. By establishing certain ideas, values and principles amongst employees, the transmission of an appropriate external picture of the company is also facilitated. The corporate culture can thus be regarded simultaneously as part of the image and as a communications tool for imparting this image.

More specific attempts to transmit the image are also made. In 1987, for example, Enator conducted a profile advertising campaign, using the slogan "We are looking for a hundred new consultants". On the one hand, the aim was to recruit new personnel, but another objective was to give the company a market profile since Enator's rapid growth was part of the message. Enator annual reports – which prior to Pronator's take-over of Enator shares were thick and glossy, with considerable advertising/information about the company – took pains to emphasize the Enator corporate spirit and the principle of small-scale operations, rapid growth and sophisticated consultancy projects which were of major business and strategic importance to the customer company. Considerable space was devoted to Enator's managing director and a select group of consultants in many annual reports, which included photographs and their comments on professional matters and some relatively personalized comments. This is something which typifies companies in this industry (Normann, 1983) and to some extent it characterizes the present time (Berg, 1986).

One motive for giving Enator a stock exchange listing was to attract attention and goodwill. In the event, the company in a certain sense attracted too much attention – with too much emphasis on the stock exchange perspective. In combination with Pronator's many deals and "coups", this damaged Enator's reputation to some extent. Some customers were worried and confused, as one of the subsidiary managers relates. According to this manager the customer claimed that his reason for not signing an "interesting" (important) contract was:

I have worked with you and know that you do a good job. But what the hell are you doing now? Are you technicians or stock-jobbers? The only thing we hear about you now is your beautiful building and all your deals.

I will return to the question of the beautiful building shortly. At any rate, it is obvious that Enator's considerable success on the stock exchange and interest in the company from a shareholding point of view did not fully harmonize with the image which Enator wished to achieve. Possibly the fact that many customers and also some of Enator's own personnel reacted negatively to "smart stock exchange deals" and other share transactions is probably linked with the idea that professional activities require a clear identity, and also integrity. In addition, it may be concluded that this type of activity is image-sensitive and Enator's image does not appear to have been particularly stable. However, it should be mentioned in this context that the considerable attention which Enator attracted as a result of its success on the stock-market also had considerable positive effects. Enator became well-known and was regarded as a competently managed and successful firm.

Apart from the general corporate image, there are slightly more tangible and specific substitutes for services which are invisible and hard to assess. One such substitute is the ability to point to work carried out previously and to satisfied customers. If you can clearly demonstrate to customers that you have completed complicated projects which are similar to assignments for which the customer requires assistance, the customer's uncertainty is reduced. The ideal is large, well-known, successful customer companies where Enator has carried out major projects which implied clear advantages for the customer. In Enator's case, people are happy to point out that their customers include SAS, Ericsson, Philips, Lufthansa, etc. No doubt there is considerable marketing advantage in having joint subsidiaries with SAS, for example. A similar situation prevails in the case of some of Enator's competitors.

Normann (1983) speaks of the "club-feeling" which can occur among the customers of a particular company. A potential or existing customer asks what other customers have employed the company and a sense of forming part of a particular context may occur if they resemble the customer or the other companies have a good reputation. No doubt, the possible emergence of a "club-feeling" of this kind varies between different companies. Enator's (and particularly the founders') excellent social networks, some of the well-known names on the Board, and Enator's skilful utilization of social activities may contribute to the relatively good prerequisites necessary for the emergence of a "club-feeling" of this kind.

A further substitute for – or sign of – the quality of services may be visible phenomena which can transmit or symbolize the activity in question. Basically, non-tangible services are often linked to material circumstances in some way. Intellectual knowledge can be expressed by means of well-filled bookcases containing appropriate works, and the design of buildings, interior decoration and office furnishings may also communicate something. I have already discussed the architecture and interior design employed by the company. As indicated in Chapter 7, Enator's headquarters are rather special. From a marketing point of view, this is significant in three different ways. Firstly, it gives rise to publicity – Enator has even been on television, with the building in focus. Secondly, a well-known head office facilitates the building-up of contacts. If a potential customer is curious about the building, (s)he is perhaps somewhat more inclined to meet an Enator representative and perhaps visit the Enator headquarters. Customer contact meetings in the headquarters building presumably facilitate sales operations. Enator contact personnel do not need to travel and this means they can save time, they are on home base, they have the customer's undivided attention and they have ready access to other Enator personnel whom they can call in to the meeting if this is justified by the course of discussions with the customer. Thirdly, the building per se represents a powerful form of communication, or at least a natural introduction to and illustration of Enator's fundamental philosophy and method. It is much easier to describe the company in an interesting manner, taking the inner structure of the building as a starting-point, than it is to describe Enator in abstract terms. The building functions as a rhetorical device.

Despite these advantages, the building does not always function as an efficient and effective marketing tool. Some customers do not particularly like it. One subsidiary manager describes a visit from representatives of an insurance company – they felt somewhat uncomfortable in a room with glass-walls with no optical screening off. Excessive focus on the building may also draw attention away from the company's core product.

Naturally, a great deal more might be said about Enator from a marketing perspective, but perhaps the above points suffice as regarding the external aspects. The next stage is to examine internal marketing – a highly important dimension in operations such as Enator's.

12.8   Internal Marketing

Internal marketing has become fashionable again in the last few years, particularly in service companies (Berg, 1986; Grönroos, 1984). Grönroos identifies three marketing functions in service companies. One of these functions is *traditional marketing*, aiming to survey the market, to inform it and to make the initial sale as a result of an appropriate marketing mix. Another is *interactive marketing*, which is concerned with buyer-seller interactions and which constitutes the link between the company's production of services and the customers' purchases and consumption. These aspects have already been dealt with. The third major function is *internal marketing*. Internal marketing may be seen as a method of ensuring that interactive marketing actually works – that is to say that the customer is satisfied, that additional sales are achieved and that a lasting and satisfactory relationship with the customer is established. It is thought that satisfactory internal marketing is a prerequisite for external marketing (Flipo, 1986; Grönroos, 1983).

Grönroos (1983) defines internal marketing as follows:

The internal marketing concept involves influencing the organization's internal market of employees in the best possible manner, thus providing motivation for furthering customer interests and marketing-oriented operations as a result of an active marketing approach at the internal level, with the application of marketing measures. This is the best way of satisfying the staff's need for attractive and stimulating places of work (p 14).

The idea is to sell the company's activities and products to employees and to establish an awareness of quality aspects in relation to the interaction with customers, with a particular emphasis on functional quality. Internal marketing may also be described as "increasing business and market awareness, motivation and loyalty at all levels within the organization"

(Berg, 1986, p 562). Thus, internal marketing is a question of attitudes, corporate spirit and motivation. In more precise terms, the purpose of internal marketing is said to be

- to meet quality norms in the supply of services;
- to control and motivate employees to make them customer and sales-oriented;
- to recruit and retain personnel who correspond to the corporate image.

In addition, many authors (Grönroos, 1983, 1984; and Normann, 1983) also include a number of general objectives and aims concerning recruitment, the retention of good staff members, the promotion of suitable personnel and general motivation and quality awareness.

Grönroos (1983) turns almost all personnel and management issues into marketing questions. Motivation and involvement at the place of work are primarily regarded as a matter of attitudes and values. Companies try to control such factors in external markets, and they also try to achieve this internally, by means of internal marketing rather than through traditional concepts such as personnel administration or self-governing groups. The marketing concept is employed loosely to colonize an understanding of organizational and work phenomena. For example, the organization is regarded as an internal market of employees, while recruitment, selection and promotion are described as market segmentation, designed to achieve the best possible labour force. On the internal market, the company offers internal products in the form of job assignments and working environment.

Under the heading of "strategic internal marketing" Grönroos lists all the current methods and sub-areas in a company which influence personnel – motivational management methods, personnel policy, training policy and planning, implementation and follow-up systems. But in this context the marketing approach does not seem to contribute much new. The situation is somewhat different in regard to "internal tactical marketing". Here, the marketing concept is embodied as a replacement or supplement for traditional concepts. For example, pay and fringe benefits are regarded as a price for internal products and personnel attitude studies are described as market surveys.

The reason for this somewhat unusual terminology appears to be the idea that marketing represents an intellectual tradition which is purposeful and dynamic:

In tactical, internal marketing, it is important to retain an active, purposeful grasp on a continuous basis, where all measures are designed to reinforce the employees' motivation for customer-orientation and their interest in sales ... An active grasp of this kind can be maintained if the thinking is in marketing terms (Grönroos, 1983, p 23).

As already mentioned, the broad areas of contact between major sections of the organization and customers may possibly justify the central role of the marketing approach in internal organizational questions. It is interesting to note that this factor might just as well justify the opposite approach – that the organizational concept and organizational theory should replace marketing and reduce marketing to advertising and special sales promotion activities. Instead of locating the market within the boundaries of the organization, the converse tactic is applied, that is to say that the external market is subordinated to the organization. This might be justified by consumer participation in the production of services and the close relationships between producer goods companies and their customers, etc. In this case, customers are regarded as external participatory personnel. Market segmentation and sales are referred to as recruitment, selection and the employment of customers. The performance gained from the customer is money and the customer is paid in terms of the product or the service which the company works with (thus, air-travel or a consultancy service becomes a form of payment). The better managers are at managing, motivating, influencing and manipulating the person who is "employed" as a customer, the better achievement she or he makes – that is to say the more money she or he contributes. But this requires recognition in the form of even more flights or consultancy services.

This is not the right occasion to try to let organizational theory replace the marketing discipline. However, it is interesting to note that the boundary line between the organization and marketing can be eliminated from two different directions. In many studies of service companies, it is maintained that marketing is of crucial importance for the internal functioning of the organization, while, primarily in books about producer goods companies with complex products, the customer-seller relationship is often considered to be better illustrated on the basis of the organizational concept, rather than by employing purely marketing theory. (See e.g. Håkansson and Östberg, 1975.)

Turning established concepts of what fundamentally characterizes a certain object or the area of application of a theory upside-down may be useful. Nonetheless, I imagine that a concept such as internal marketing has its greatest applicability if it is given a limited interpretation which indicates certain new aspects of the functioning of a company. Its value is more dubious if internal marketing is interpreted as "an all-embracing sweep", covering almost everything from personnel policy, management and the working environment to advertising campaigns addressed directly to employees.

In my opinion, a more fruitful approach to internal marketing treats it as management ideas and specific measures which are directly aimed at selling the image of the company desired by management to personnel and providing a positive view of the services offered, and stimulating employees to voluntarily (i.e. without external pressures or incentives) transmit to customers the appropriate corporate image. In accordance with this definition, internal marketing is only one of many instruments for achieving the desired buyer-seller interaction and quality of services. Leadership, the organization of work, the rewards system, and training of a "technical" nature are examples of other instruments.

In certain cases, the use of an extremely broad marketing concept as a "frame of reference" for organizational management in service activities may have negative effects on attitudes and the organizational climate. Regarding and treating personnel as a market, perceiving work and the working environment as products and regarding surveys of personnel attitudes as market studies may mean focusing on and reinforcing more alienated and instrumental concepts of work and the organization among employees. The characteristic of a market is that it is an arena for potential exchanges in which actors are presumed to maximize their own utility. Relationships in a market are of a calculating, instrumental nature (Sjöstrand, 1985). Loyalty and involvement are not particularly prominent characteristics. Orientations of this nature virtually eliminate a pure market.

As Salancik and Pfeffer (1978) maintain, attitudes and evaluations are partially determined by the aspects of work and the organization which are stressed in the social environment. The social environment influences the factors which the individual focuses on or to which he or she only allots peripheral importance consciously. The individual's processing of information is also dependent on socially transmitted clues – particularly where complex circumstances are concerned – and these clues are crucial for the manner in which the phenomena are interpreted. (Salancik and Pfeffer were treated in somewhat more detail in Chapter 5.)

A broad and widely employed internal marketing concept, which affects and controls organizational and relations may mean that polarization and dissociation between employees ("the market") and management ("the marketers") emerges more clearly, rather than the view that everybody is participating in the same social unit ("in the same boat" or "family", which is not the case in a purely market relationship). In addition, this marketing concept emphasizes a utility-maximizing, instrumental approach to the company and work, rather than strong social ties and "commitment".

Obviously, it may be claimed that a calculating, distanced relationship between owners/management and employees provides a correct picture of what is involved – this is probably how most economists and Marxists would argue – but it is obvious that in most companies, relationships other than those which are centered on purely economic, instrumental factors are highly important (Sjöstrand, 1985). This particularly applies to companies which can offer personnel social working conditions and a good organizational climate (Alvesson and Lindkvist, 1993). This applies to a considerable extent at Enator. As Perrow (1986) maintains, the relative impact of utility-maximization and altruism in the way human beings function is partly dependent on social conditions (ideologies, incentives, etc.) and varies in line with these factors. To the extent that the market metaphor informs thought and action in a company, it reinforces the maximization of utility and egoism in the individual.

12.9   Internal Marketing at Enator

As indicated in previous chapters, Enator strongly emphasizes social ties. High priority is given to a spirit of comradeship within the company as well as loyalty to and involvement in the company. There is heavy stress on feelings of belonging and a "we-spirit". Enator is sometimes depicted as a family or a home. This is quite different from a market. It would thus be quite inappropriate to introduce the marketing concept or to work for such an objective at Enator.

However, this does not mean, of course, that practices that may be understood in terms of internal marketing in the more limited sense do not exist. One example is the project management philosophy course described in detail in Chapter 5. Roughly half the course may be regarded as an internal marketing campaign. In this course, Enator sells the business concept and the corporate approach to new employees. They learn, in appropriate contexts, to present what Enator has to offer customers in a positive and persuasive manner. The basis of a public relations approach to the company is established. Two stages are involved: First an "ideological" phase rather than a more advanced understanding of, acceptance of, and enthusiasm for the company and its business concept, and then the establishment of the prerequisites for the transmission of appropriate messages and signs of the company's competence and advantages to an external audience.

Many of the items covered in the project management philosophy course are powerful sales arguments, both for new employees and for external parties with a potential interest, and they are appropriate for effective further transmission. Enator's status as an "In Search of Excellence" company, its fine business concept, its projects with major, well-known customers and the intimate links with SAS and Jan Carlzon form part of this approach. Enator's business concept is particularly helpful in this respect since it both encompasses the company's operations (target groups, competence) and also contains a direct sales message. Thus, the business concept can be directly utilized in marketing, both internal and external marketing. A presentation of Enator's business concept simultaneously provides some information about Enator as a whole and also about what a customer may expect to receive in terms of services.

Another advantage of the business concept and the manner in which it is formulated is that it contains or reminds target groups of several concepts with significant contemporary symbolic value: management, business, strategies, computers in a strategic perspective, etc. As already mentioned, it is debatable whether the business concept covers Enator's operations, but it does say something about what goes on. The marketing advantages – at both the internal and external levels – of the manner in which the business concept is formulated should be considerable. In a certain sense, it may be said that the business concept is more useful as a marketing tool than as tangible guidelines for the control and implementation of operations.

Otherwise, there are certain specific features which can be classified as internal marketing in day-to-day management and control of consultancy projects. This is primarily a question of influencing employees so that they will be more inclined to seek opportunities for establishing customer contacts and for achieving additional sales over and above the contracted stipulations of a particular assignment. For example, when a subsidiary manager is accustomed to ask his staff from time to time, "When did you last talk to the Managing Director (in the customer company)?", his intention is to remind his personnel that Enator's ambition is to establish contacts with decision makers in the customer company and to use such contacts to obtain assignments of business and strategic relevance. Another example is the subsidiary manager who is accustomed to state that "anyone in this company who is not familiar with the customer's business concept is on the wrong track". Examples of this kind, like the encouragement/persuasion of consultants to carry out assignments for which they are actually overqualified, can however only be characterized in analytical terms as internal marketing if they are regarded as specific instruments for management of operations.

At Enator, the need for thinking systematically in terms of internal marketing is probably somewhat less prominent than in many other types of activity. The nature of operations, that is to say primarily professional work rather than pure routine operations, facilitate intrinsic work motivation. In a young, rapidly-growing company with a positive general climate there is hardly any need to launch a campaign for renewed, revitalized endeavours. For the most part, "internal marketing" takes care of itself as an element of everyday normative control (exercised by managers and other senior consultants). The fact that Enator is relatively small, particularly if subsidiaries are treated as independent units, reduces the need to undertake special campaigns with personnel as the target group. Enator hardly needs managing directors who write little red books or who make video recordings to reach the broad majority of their employees, at least not yet.

But perhaps this is something which will happen in the future. In parallel with the emphasis on small-scale operations at the subsidiary level, the number of employees is increasing, and also the distance between different groups of employees. The establishment of operations in foreign countries and corporate acquisitions may mean that the "correct" consciousness of the business and marketing aspects of the group as a whole will not be achieved "automatically" as a result of the ongoing action and statements of key personnel and other senior employees, permeating the workplace environment and spreading like circles in a pond. "Spontaneous" direct and indirect communication from the centre of the company to the periphery does not work for new employees who do not have a clear picture of how the company operates, based on their own experience, or who do not know who top management and other key personnel are. The interest of subsidiary managers in information seems to vary, as does their ability to supply it. Thus in time, formalised direct communication in written form between management and employees is a natural step. In this situation, special internal marketing campaigns may appear as an option for management.

12.10 Summary

In this chapter, I have described marketing in knowledge-intensive (broadly speaking professional) service companies in general, with particular reference to Enator. Both external and internal marketing have been discussed. In the case of external marketing two distinctions in addition to those which have been traditionally applied (i.e. between the marketing of services and products and between consumer marketing and industrial goods marketing) are introduced: professional versus non-professional services and standardized versus situationally-adapted activities.

It may be concluded that although Enator is undeniably a service company and is faced with problems that result from this in the form of a non-tangible product, it differs markedly from companies which provide consumer services on a mass market. The common factor is primarily the importance of an image in a marketing perspective and of social processes in the interaction between service worker and customer. Enator has considerable similarities with companies working on industrial markets and selling sophisticated products which need to be adapted to the needs of various customers. Well-developed customer relationships are highly important from a marketing point of view. The cost of relationships is an important item in the marketing budget, involving investments in building up, maintaining and developing good and close relationships with customers (Håkansson and Johansson, 1982). This cost may exceed the actual cost of selling operations.

It should also be noted that Enator's operations lie somewhere between professional and non-professional activities. (I am now talking about professions in the traditional, narrow sense of the word, i.e. an occupation with a specific education, authorization, a professional association, a monopoly of a certain kind of work, etc.) As far as many people in the computer world are concerned, Enator's heavy emphasis on commercial and sales-oriented factors does not always appear to be positively valued. Enator's marketing does not fully comply with the professional identity which characterizes many computer specialists. We have noted that in the project management philosophy course the course leaders/managers felt called upon to stress that "there is nothing wrong with selling" or "making money".

If the marketing situation faced by Enator and similar companies is to be fully understood, it should be noted that attention should not be wholly concentrated on the most complicated problem-solving projects, which are the most difficult to handle both from a buyer and seller perspective. Relatively standardized services are also crucial for the company. Corporate management does not only take on projects in accordance with a strict interpretation of the business concept, but is in fact fully oriented towards the achievement of the basis for making profits in its business: a high level of debiting, both in the short term and in the long term.

The case study also enables us to study the internal marketing phenomenon. To a certain extent, the corporate culture may be regarded as a question of internal marketing since it involves the transmission and selling of a positive basic attitude in relation to the company which is also supposed to permeate consultants' external relationships. If we formulate the corporate culture as an expression of market relations, the effect is to place considerable stress on internal marketing, although not necessarily to the extent which, for example, Grönroos (1983) does by allowing internal marketing to function as a frame of reference for all (internal) management. In this chapter, I have proposed a more narrow approach in which the concept of internal marketing applies to special elements in managerial thinking and action designed to exert a specific influence on the view of the company held by personnel, with the object of getting employees to adopt a more market-oriented approach in relation to customers and the environment. It was noted that, as far as Enator is concerned, there was no need for the crystallization of internal marketing as a special aspect of management strategy at the time when this study was conducted. As Enator expands and a clearer distinction between the centre and the periphery in the group becomes more salient, corporate management may be more inclined to handle personnel in a more market-oriented manner.

In this chapter, it has been noted that clear elements of the internal marketing approach at Enator and the increasing application of the "market" metaphor to conceptualize the firm and its internal relationships may contradict the picture of Enator as "a family" or "a team of buddies".

Notes

[1] This applies to the working time of consultants, which is what the client is purchasing. Of course, the results of the consultant's work – data processing systems – are utilized after the simultaneous production and consumption of the service has taken place.

[2] I prefer the concept of knowledge-intensive to professional services since the issues treated here have rather little to do with whether the services concerned are offered by people who are members of the authorized professions (e.g. physicians, lawyers) or not. The literature uses the concept of professional services, so I choose to follow it to some extent. I use the words knowledge-intensive and professional services interchangably.

[3] This rationale for accepting assignments that clearly deviate from the business is also helpful in avoiding or reducing perceptions of contradictions betwen corporate practices and the business concept.

13 Integration and Contradictions

In Chapters 13 and 14, I will be discussing some broad themes which have been referred to in earlier chapters and which tie up some of the accounts and analyses which have already been presented. These two final chapters do not represent a conventional conclusion; conclusions have already been drawn in connection with the various themes dealt with in previous chapters and there is no reason to repeat them here.

The primary focus of Chapter 13 is on the fundamental nature of the company. How is Enator to be understood as a company in a deeper sense? The development perspective is important in this context, and historical changes need to be taken into account. Another theme involves uniformity and the integration of the various parts of the company. The manner in which various aspects of operations are linked and support each other will be discussed here. In contrast, another theme involves a dialectical perspective on organizations, focusing on contradictions and tensions in the company regarding various dimensions and forces. A full examination of the company's way of working requires that attention is paid both to harmonious circumstances and to basic tensions. Within the framework for the uniformity/harmony and contradiction/tension themes, I will also be looking at the relationship between various types of corporate functions, for example business development, marketing, personnel management, etc.

13.1 Forms for Organizing Exchanges

In recent years, considerable interest has been devoted to examining organizations on the basis of various fundamental forms of exchange relationships. One of the most influential examples has been Ouchi's (1980) classification into three types: market, bureaucracy and clan. In this context, the market is regarded as an organizational form: a way of arranging exchanges. The bureaucracy refers to employment and hierarchical relations in a formal organization as a means of organizing economic exchanges. This classification is partly inspired by Williamson's theory of transaction costs, that is to say costs which arise in connection with the actual economic exchange. (See e.g. Williamson, 1985; Williamson and Ouchi, 1981.) The cost of drawing up a contract, the cost of supervising fulfilment of the contract and the cost of dealing with any deviation from the contract are all examples of transaction costs. Transaction costs have a strong influence on the choice between "the market" and "the hierarchy", that is to say whether a given exchange relationship takes the form of a market-oriented agreement between the buyer and the seller or whether an exchange relationship takes the form of employment in the service of the entity which pays for the work input/or product. (This line of argumentation may be applied at various levels, ranging from employment/market exchanges with a particular labour force to incorporation/market relationships between the supplier and the producer, that is to say vertical integration of various stages within the framework of a company [group] or various value-added phases carried out by units which are formally independent of each other.)

The perfect market has the obvious economic advantage that it can offer the most advantageous exchange option between two interested parties. However, in many cases the transaction costs are so high that the bureaucracy is to be preferred. (In this section, the terms bureaucracy, hierarchy and formal organization are employed synonymously – in accordance, for example, with Ouchi and Williamson's usage.) In the employment situation, this means that the contract is incomplete, in the sense that the exact content of the employee's performance in exchange for his/her pay is not specified. The employee's achievements are determined by the employer's instructions. The advantage of an unspecified contract is that it is not necessary to determine in detail in advance what the employment relationship involves. This makes it possible to avoid the overhead costs involved in defining in detail everything that the buyer wishes to have carried out. Instead of a thousand pages of market contract, an individual is simply employed and his or her duties consist of being at the employer's disposal until employment ceases.

It is assumed that the market relationship is effective when performance is unambiguous, which means that it is easy to deal with opportunistic behaviour or conflicting objectives. Conflicts may be solved by agreement or by replacing the market partner. Transaction costs are not particularly high in this situation. In many exchanges of complex, ambiguous products/services between economically independent entities, that is to say fundamentally in a market, the market relationship is weakened and contacts between buyer and seller are frequent, close and organized to some extent. As indicated in Chapter 12, the relationship between companies like Enator and their customers is often of this nature. Although basically and formally there is a market relationship, the organizational form is also important in this context. The development and stabilization of inter-organizational relationships are crucial.

The bureaucracy relationship is effective where there is a high degree of ambiguity concerning performance and where elements of opportunism and goal conflict are not too much of a problem. In other words, the bureaucracy form can handle a relatively high degree of uncertainty about the required performance since there is an opportunity for hierarchical supervision and control of work operations. Thus, direct control over the performance paid for is greater than in a market relationship. Bureaucracy is also based on a reasonable degree of compliance in regard to objectives between the parties involved in the exchange relationship, that is to say the employer and the employee. Successful operations are in the employee's interests, in contrast with a market exchange where the parties involved are not interested in each other's welfare. In principle, a market relationship is a question of achieving an exchange which is as advantageous as possible, in the form of maximum benefit at minimum cost. (This applies to the market as an ideal type. In reality matters may sometimes be rather different.)

Inspired by studies of Japanese companies, Ouchi (1980, 1981) postulated a third organizational form: the clan. A clan is a collective which is characterized by dependency and a sense of affinity between individuals. Individual and collective interests are perceived to overlap each other heavily in the clan, which means that opportunistic behaviour is unusual and that the relationship between input/rewards is relatively unproblematical. Various types of organizations may function as a clan, to a greater or lesser extent. The prerequisites for clan qualities in a collective are that a set of social mechanisms reduces differences between individuals regarding values and orientation, and also generates a strong sense of affinity. According to Ouchi, the clan is a particularly effective organizational form for exchanges if it is difficult to determine performance with any degree of certainty ("high performance ambiguity") and there is a low degree of opportunism and goal congruence. The latter point would appear to be somewhat tautological since, by definition, the clan assumes a low degree of opportunism and shared interests on the part of the individual and the collective. In other words, low opportunism and shared interest are by definition included in the clan concept, and are thus not external conditions facilitating the effectiveness of the clan form.[1]

Ouchi's line of argument may be summarized in the form of the normative regulatory mechanisms and information elements which are central features of the three forms for organizing exchange relationships.

When he refers to "reciprocity", Ouchi is thinking of the virtually universal norm under which people are expected to live up to agreements which they have entered into and promises which they have made. If there

Table 13.1:   Summary of Ouchi's three organizational forms (Ouchi, 1980 p. 137)

Control Form	Normative regulatory mechanism	Information element
Market	Reciprocity	Prices
Bureaucracy	Reciprocity Legitimate authority	Rules
Clan	Reciprocity Common values and beliefs	Traditions

was no reciprocity, exchanges would be almost impossible since such detailed contracts and such extensive control of compliance with the contract would be required that the costs would be almost insurmountable.

Thus, the reciprocity norm is common in organizations, and legitimate authority is also relatively widespread, even if such authority is recognized to a greater or lesser extent in different organizations, while common values and beliefs are relatively unusual in formal organizations, at least to the extent that they constitute a major regulatory mechanism (according to Ouchi, 1980). In Ouchi's view, the lack of common values and beliefs in American and Western society – in other words the rarity of clans – is a problem since this deficiency leads to both psychological, social and economic difficulties, for example in the form of impoverished social relations and lower productivity. Obviously, the clan concept is close to ideas about a common, distinct culture which binds the company's employees together (Wilkins and Ouchi, 1983).

Sjöstrand (1985, 1986, 1992) also tries to develop a theory of the basic forms for human exchanges. Sjöstrand's starting-point is that the traditionally dominant view of economic man as calculatively maximizing utility is limited and grossly oversimplified. Instead he emphasizes man as an interactive and composite being. People have a collection of needs and characteristics which affect economic exchanges. Exchanges cannot be simply reduced to a question of economic utility. Ideas, ideals, and emotional and social ties, etc. are also important. Sjöstrand proposes six forms for human exchanges, four of which will be briefly described here. (Two of Sjöstrand's categories – the movement and the association/federation – are not particularly relevant in the present context and I will not treat them here.) Sjöstrand's four categories which are of interest are the corporation, the market, the clan and the circle. They are illustrated in Table 13.2.

Very roughly, hierarchies are characterized by clear superior-subordinate relationships, while network relationships are characterized by established mutual expectations or links of a non-hierarchical nature. Calculative relationships involve the maximization of economic utility, while gen-

Table 13.2:   Fundamental forms of human exchanges ("institutions"), adapted from
Sjöstrand (1985, 1992)

Dominant form of relationship	Dominant relationship content	
	Calculatiing	Genuine
Hierarchical relationship	Corporation	Clan
Network relationship	Market	Circle

uine relationships denote relationships based on kinship or friendship in
which the ties cover a broad spectrum of interaction which includes elements of an emotional nature. A genuine relationship is broad, deep and
lasting.

Broadly speaking, Sjöstrand's corporate and market concepts correspond to Ouchi's bureaucracy and market forms. However, Sjöstrand criti-
cizes Ouchi's clan concept:

Ouchi's clan concept has led him into a persuasive, indoctrinating approach as regards how trust is established in organizations. Ouchi's clan is more based on
mankind's need for order rather than the need for ideals, friendship, family, kinship, neighbourly relations or other ties. The leading actors in the hierarchy establish 'common' values and establish an order which promises to supply welfare, if it
is accepted by other people (Sjöstrand, 1985, p 227).

The primary difference between Sjöstrand and Ouchi is that Sjöstrand's
clan is concerned with "natural", spontaneously-emerging ties of kinship
and friendship, and culturally determined patterns formed in this tradition,
while Ouchi emphasizes "designed" clans which may be seen in certain
organizations which are rationally structured and which are consciously
influenced by key actors.

In principle, I concur with Sjöstrand's criticism, although "clan-like"
phenomena in organizations in Western countries are probably normally
based on conscious systematic influence of an "indoctrination" type. A
clan concept which applies to a collective which is closely bound together
by kinship ties, and the imperatives which result from this regarding superior and subordinate status and the orientation of action, only has very
limited applicability in understanding modern companies. The exceptions
might, for example, be the maffia and certain limited aspects of family
companies, but often the majority of employees in family companies are
probably excluded from the clan which may be constituted by the propri-
etorial family.

Perhaps the solution to the problem which is implied here – where the
choice lies between an approach which strictly adheres to the depth of the
traditional, strict clan and emphasizes its highly specific characteristics, but

which is of limited relevance (Sjöstrand) and a perspective which has a broader area of application but which trivializes the phenomenon in question to some extent (Ouchi) – is to clearly use the clan as a metaphor. This means that a company (or a group within the company) is compared to a clan – without claiming that the company is a clan or that a clan is necessarily a dominating regulatory mechanism in exchanges between the people of the organization. This enables us to retain the usefulness (range) of the concept while avoiding distortion of the concept. The advantage of the clan metaphor is that an organization has certain attributes which may be described in terms of the concept, for example strong social ties, while at the same time it is obvious that it is not a question of a clan in the literal sense.

Sjöstrand makes a distinction between the clan and the circle. The circle is an institution of network type based on genuine relationships of friendship. The circle conveys personal identity to its members and, according to Sjöstrand, its relations extend beyond trust to confidential and intimate aspects. So far, we can say that the circle overlaps the clan, but the difference lies in the approach to hierarchy. In the circle, there is no hierarchy and thus the circle may be described as a non-hierarchical clan. Alternatively the clan may be regarded as a "hierarchical circle". Because the hierarchy in the context of the clan is conditioned by history and tradition; it has deep roots and this means, in practice, that there is a considerable difference between the clan and the circle. Other possible differences might be that the circle is somewhat more fluid and unstable than the clan and typically involves fewer people.

Sjöstrand employs his four concepts as ideal types, that is to say as theoretical basic constructs or pure forms – which do not normally occur so clearly in "reality". In reality there are also different forms of emergence, in which combinations of these ideal types may be found. Thus, a real company is characterized by calculative and genuine relationships in both hierarchical and network forms. However, the importance of the ideal-type features may vary considerably. Ouchi (1980) also considers that the market, the bureaucracy and the clan can function simultaneously as control and regulatory mechanisms in companies, even if he seems to consider that one method of organizing transactions will normally be dominant.

13.2   A Model for Forms for Arranging Exchanges in Companies

Basing myself on Ouchi and Sjöstrand, I would like to indicate some fundamental characteristics in Enator's functioning. In this connection I will be modifying Ouchi's and Sjöstrand's conceptual apparatus to a certain extent. When I refer to *formal organization* I mean the hierarchical organizational structure with clear relationships between superiors/subordinates and economically calculative exchanges as the basis for action. (Formal organization corresponds to Ouchi's bureaucracy and Sjöstrand's ideal type of company. The term I use is not fully satisfactory, but it is less confusing than Ouchi's and Sjöstrand's concepts in this context.) The term *market* refers to an open, calculative relationship based on a network between impersonal actors. *Clan* refers to a social group with deep, genuine, comprehensive social and emotional ties based on a spirit of comradeship in which certain approaches, ideals and norms are shared. One or more actors dominate and have the greatest influence on the ideals and norms which hold the group together. When I use the term *circle* I refer to a somewhat looser group – a network without tangible hierarchical relationships in which personal relationships are crucial.

These four concepts can be used to build a simple model describing companies and other organizations as indicated in Figure 13.1.

Like Sjöstrand, I assume that at least the most rudimentary features of these four institutions can be found in practically all types of organizations. But there is probably considerable variation. As a rule, the formal organization dominates in companies, that is to say hierarchical, calculative and economically oriented organizational patterns. Elements of the market form can be found, especially in larger companies with profit centres and divisions (Lindkvist, 1989). In this context, it should be noticed that the market refers to internal exchange relationships within the com-

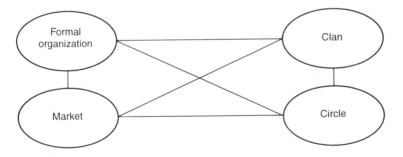

Figure 13.1:   Simple model describing the fundamental aspects of companies

pany. The clan element has some importance in older family companies permeated by tradition, and also in some more youthful enterprises with a special style and intensity. Such companies are often said to have a "strong" corporate culture. Enator belongs to this category. The circle, with its emphasis on equality and strong personal ties, may perhaps be most often found in special groups in organizations at the same hierarchical level rather than within organizations as a whole (except in very small organizations). Circle elements are also present in external or internal organizational networks, for example of a business or professional nature, which extend beyond instrumental aspects and which also contain an element of genuine relationships.

Relations between these four types of relationship may involve both harmony and tension, normally simultaneously. Thus, the six arrows in the diagram depict convergence and integration, but also divergence and conflict. (Compare this with my analysis of organizational structure in corresponding terms at the end of Chapter 6.) I will now attempt to analyze Enator on the basis of this model.

13.3   Enator in Terms of Formal Organization, Market, Circle and Clan

If any of the four organizational principles in the model can be said to carry more weight in Enator's operations, the formal organization would appear to predominate. This conclusion is virtually unavoidable in view of the fact that we are concerned with a relatively large company in which hierarchical exchange relationships based on terms of employment constitute the basis for operations. (It should be noted, however, that formal organization in this sense is not the same thing as formal control since it may constitute the basis for a broader range of control mechanisms, including normative control.) Comparatively speaking, the internal market is thus less crucial as a regulatory mechanism, even if it becomes more important as the company expands. Friendship relationships of various types are important, but are not seriously allowed to interfere with business. There is no doubt that growth and profits are the company's guiding principles. Top management carefully monitors the financial results of subsidiaries and has limited acceptance for poor performances. Turnover, capacity utilization and profit, etc. are easy to measure and constitute crucial information components. Financial evaluation of the various units within the company is relatively simple since each unit is reasonably independent and operates on its own submarkets. The nature of operations means that the financial outcome of measures becomes clear relatively quickly. As Brulin (1987) points out, corporate decentralization is often accompanied by a thorough follow-up and control of financial results exercised at a central level. Although Enator is trying to deemphasize the formal organizational structure and hierarchy to some extent, the company nonetheless has a clearer formal organizational and hierarchical structure than a group of people organized in the form of network. It is quite obvious that there are hierarchical lines extending from top management, subsidiary managers, experienced project managers down to young consultants, just as in virtually all other companies of a certain size. Apart from the formal and organizational reasons for a hierarchical structure, there is also a "natural" justification because employees are at different stages in their professional life cycle (junior, senior, etc.). (Cf. Sveiby and Risling, 1986.)

To some extent, relations between subsidiaries are organized on an internal market basis. Subsidiaries buy and sell consultants from each other, sometimes on a continuous basis with no specification of time or location and sometimes in a forum which resembles a market-place, namely Enator's managing director lunch for Enator Sweden subsidiary managers. Every other week, managers eat lunch together and apart from the general exchange of information and discussion, they buy and sell consultancy services. Subsidiary managers who have more assignments than they can handle internally within their own subsidiary have an opportunity to sell work (rent people), while subsidiary managers with personnel who have surplus capacity can spread the word in the hope that one of their colleagues needs people for an assignment. The subsidiary which has got the assignment receives 10% of the revenue debited to the customer if the consultant concerned is borrowed from another subsidiary. Conversely, a subsidiary with surplus resources receives 90% of the revenue instead of the customary 100%. There is considerable internal debiting at Enator, but relations between subsidiaries function relatively smoothly as a result of this principle, according to interviewees.

However, the background for market relationships is the corporate hierarchy and the formal organization on which operations are based. Subsidiary managers are expected to work in the best interests of the company and not to only optimize their units' results. Relationships between staff are far from market-oriented, particularly at Enator Sweden (see Chapter 7). There is also some control over the buying and selling of consultant services between subsidiaries. Top management sometimes tells subsidiary managers what has to be done in order to achieve a high and even level of capacity utilization of consultant services, which is a factor that has a direct impact on revenue and profits.

The internal market as an organizational principle for exchanges within the company must be compared to elements at Enator that are covered by the circle concept. As already stated, the circle involves non-hierarchical relationships. This means that circle relationships can primarily occur between individuals at roughly the same level even though the formal position is in itself not necessarily decisive. The managing director group at Enator, that is to say top management and subsidiary managers, seems to operate as a circle. The strong sense of affinity within this group was noted in Chapter 7. A further illustration of this affinity may be appropriate at this point. In an interview, Enator's managing director referred to the most recent management conference ("Big-cof"):

I took the whole management group out to Sandhamn. And then we sailed up to visit my parents who live on Arholma island and we stayed at Arholma youth hostel. That's quite a low profile for a conference. We sat out on the old open-air dance-floor and ate crayfish in the evening without any fuss or ceremony. We slept, six to a room, in dormitories. We had some new managing directors along and they thought it was a fantastic experience. They had an opportunity to meet my parents and get a feeling for the family.

A strong spirit of comradeship between subsidiary managers and throughout the Enator management group is an important ingredient in exchange relationships between various parts of the company and in the achievement of synergy effects. Getting a company like Enator to function as an effective unit, despite subsidiaries' relative independence and the loose links between them, is only partly a question of the fact that the formal organization (the company as an ideal type) and its calculative rule-oriented and hierarchically-determined exchange relationships function. Excessively explicit market relationships between different subsidiaries might easily lead to a loss of synergy effects.

Good social relationships pave the way for synergies, since corporate units become more inclined to provide assistance to each other in the form of advice, information, resource back-up, etc. Independence and decentralization can be maintained, while at the same time the relative advantage which subsidiaries may have by utilizing each other can still be enjoyed. One example of this is when older subsidiary managers function as "godfathers" for their younger colleagues. A satisfactory relationship of this kind cannot be primarily based on a maximization of market exchanges or on the execution of orders issued by top management. A genuine interest in helping and being of service is required. As one member of Enator's management who had provided strategic resource back-up for several of Enator's foreign subsidiaries said:

It's important to employ people who you want to work together with, who you don't mind going out and helping or having some fun with.

Circle-like relationships of this kind can be found in many areas at Enator. The clearest example is in the top management group and in the older subsidiaries. Leisure activities in the Enator main office, whose contents are not controlled by top management – even if it was the management that provided the premises, financial contributions etc. – may also be said to be of a circle nature.

But there is another circle worth noting which centres on Enator's (Pronator's) owners. In some service sectors in the Swedish business world, key actors in major companies have relationships in which business and friendship are synthesized. Enator's/Pronator's owners are closely acquainted with the managing directors or owners of a number of prominent Swedish service companies. Clearly, personal relationships are rather crucial in this context, and this also characterizes the entire industry at a somewhat lower level. Personal relationships overlap business relationships. In business terms this is expressed in cross-shareholdings in all directions, consultancy assignments in many different spheres and joint ventures. In addition, many of these key actors sit on the boards of each other's companies.

Enator may also be compared to a clan. I have briefly touched on this in Chapter 8. If, like Sjöstrand, one distinguishes between the circle and the clan on the basis of the hierarchy criteria which typifies the latter, it also becomes possible to detect clan qualities in larger social groups. Large organizations normally have one or more far-reaching types of vertical differentiation, which makes it difficult to refer to circle qualities in this context. Comparing Enator as a whole to a clan means that attention must be focused on the formation of close and intensive social relationships, a community of values and confidential exchanges on a broader social level. It thus becomes a question of tendencies towards genuine relationships which are encouraged or engineered by senior management. It is precisely the importance of top management, corrective action in various situations and various attempts at persuasion on the part of management which indicate the importance of the hierarchical dimension for the clan. Such attempts at persuasion and corrective measures were referred to in Chapter 7 as rites. The structure of the Project Management Philosophy course and its execution illustrate hierarchically determined reproduction of a clan nature at Enator. (However, aspects of management influence on ideas and values which do not involve internal social relationships, but which are more a question of customer relationships and the principles for project operations, for example, have no direct connection with clan qualities.) When my study was conducted, it was a question of traditions which are upheld and consciously transmitted, primarily by key actors at the higher hierarchical levels in the company.

13.4   Integration of Various Organizational Forms

As already mentioned, the four organizational forms may have both a harmonious and a conflicting relationship with each other. In harmony terms, the formal organization, the market, the clan and the circle may jointly pave the way for effective operations as the result of cooperation between a number of essential components in a total arsenal of means for the control and regulation of exchange relationships. In other words, the prerequisites for operations are achieved in terms of hierarchical control and coordination, vertical differentiation, decentralized exchanges of economic benefit, good social relationships, a sense of community, loyalty and involvement in the best interests of the company. A particularly crucial feature is the development of genuine relationships within the framework of the hierarchical and power factors and the overall purposes and objectives of the company. A successful coordination of these attributes involves good social integration, while allowing scope for differentiation. This is considered to be desirable (Lawrence and Lorsch, 1967).

Thus, the four organizational forms supplement each other. In the best possible case, they achieve a balance between management control and the employees' social needs, between the company's requirement of efficient exchange relationships, the sensitivity of operations to willingness on the part of personnel to make an effort and the needs and interests of employees. My impression is that Enator has been successful in achieving a balance of this nature, at least in the circumstances which applied prior to and at the time when my study was conducted. Naturally, favourable external circumstances, in particular a growing market, have facilitated this process.

Of course, this does not mean that there are no tensions. Tension is a built-in feature of operations of this kind (as in organizations in general) and can hardly be eliminated, even with the best possible management resources and under exceptionally favourable conditions. There is a contradiction between hierarchical relationships and relationships based on equality and between calculative exchange relationships and genuine relationships. This is virtually true by definition. In reality, the possibilities of integrating these extreme poles in the course of social relationships will vary. It is not impossible to be both a boss and a friend at the same time, for example – at least not in Sweden where there is a considerable degree of equality in the workplace (Hofstede, 1980). As organizations expand, the possibilities of maintaining tangibly equal relationships between senior management and ordinary employees become more restricted. The former have an increasing work-load to deal with and tend to interact primarily with other management staff. On the whole, the prerequisites for establishing strong ties with employees who are not encountered on a day-to-day basis and who are at different levels in the hierarchy are unfavourable. This also applies to Enator. However, this is not merely a quantitative matter. It is also a question of personality and ability to regulate the hierarchical dimension in interpersonal relationships. As has been treated in Chapters 7 and 8, Enator has made great efforts to be successful in this respect. According to one of my interviewees: Enator does not appoint subsidiary managers who lack the ability to be on friendly terms with their staff and colleagues.

Perhaps it is even more difficult to consistently combine calculative exchange relationships and genuine relationships. The degree of breadth, depth and durability in social relationships is presumably frequently reduced by the primary emphasis on calculative relationships in a corporate context. Ultimately, the basis for the employment of consultants and managers is the contribution they make to profitability, not their intrinsic value as human beings. In Enator's case, despite the strength of social ties in the well-integrated managing director group, it is nonetheless accepted that colleagues have to be dismissed if they are unable to meet performance requirements.

In this kind of business, the prerequisites for combining calculative and genuine aspects are more favourable than in many other companies. Smooth relations at the social level are essential if a project is to be successful. Good social relationships greatly facilitate the achievement of financial objectives. But this does not mean that there are no conflicts or tensions. In some contexts, subsidiaries are competing with each other regarding the boundary lines between different subsidiary submarkets, for example, and there may be disputes about how joint projects are to be manned and run. When it comes to salary negotiations, it may be difficult to combine a spirit of comradeship and a boss-employee relationship in dealings between a consultant and his subsidiary manager. The same applies to efforts to persuade staff to take on unattractive assignments. In a market which is becoming increasingly competitive, conflicts of interest between subsidiaries are likely to occur. This encourages calculative relationships and discourages genuine links. A similar trend may also emerge as consultants and subsidiary managers grow older. It may be more difficult to combine friendship and profitability considerations if individual performance deteriorates or if customers expect computer consultants to be relatively young.

Earlier in this chapter, I referred to certain situations which may be regarded as concrete expressions of the four different organizational forms – situations in which organizational forms as ideal types appear in virtually pure forms, I will now focus on certain situations or action patterns at Enator which express a combination of these organizational forms. The potential conflicts between organizational and regulatory mechanisms are counteracted by realizing these mechanisms in concrete form, often symbolically loaded (rich in expressive content). In other words, different and fundamentally somewhat contradictory organizational forms are integrated in certain situations/action patterns. Several of these forms were described in Chapter 7 and characterized as rites.

The annual general meeting is a good example (see Chapter 7). In Enator's case, the A.G.M. contains tangible elements of all four forms of regulating economic and social exchanges. The purely calculative business aspects are emphasized, of course, at the A.G.M. itself. The focus is on the company as an economic unit and its financial results. At the same time, social qualities are given considerable scope. The various values, sentiments, the company's special style and other features which characterize the company and its staff are communicated. At the same time, it is clear that the leaders of the "clan" are the key actors who set the tone. They have directed the performance and they are the principle actors. All the other participants are passive observers.

A party is held in connection with the A.G.M. The party is primarily for consultants, but board members and some customers are also invited. The spotlight thus switches to Enator as a circle. In this context, the corporate hierarchy and management control are no longer relevant. People stroll around with a glass of wine in one hand and a sandwich in the other, talking to each other. After a little while, a group gathers around the grand piano. The atmosphere is permeated by equality, with everyone on a friendly basis, and this also applies to the Chairman of the Board and the managing director. The hierarchical and calculative aspects of relationships within the company have taken a back-seat, even if they have hardly been forgotten. One exception in this context are the customers who are attending the party. Do Enator personnel talk business with them? But in the relaxed circumstances which prevail, customers are also included in the circle.

The Project Management Philosophy course and the company's morning meetings also serve to integrate the formal organization's and the clan's way of regulating exchanges and social relationships. Hierarchical elements characterize both activities. Course leaders and subsidiary managers are at the centre of events, and they have drawn up the agenda. (This is more clearly marked in the Project Management Philosophy course than at the morning meetings.) It is hardly a question of integrating hierarchy and equality. But one could probably say that there is integration of calculative and genuine relationships. There are efforts being made that indicate there being a greater bond between employee and company that are conventional in modern work life.

The formal organization and the circle are in evidence at certain management conferences. Management conferences which have a significant business content, for example the annual autumn budget conference, differ somewhat from conferences in which the purely social content – and as a result the circle quality – dominates. However, more business-oriented conferences take place under socially favourable circumstances – for example a weekend in Portugal – and it may be assumed that both calculative and genuine relationships enter into the picture.

These action patterns transmit the company's economic and social basis and help to integrate various regulatory mechanisms and to reduce – but hardly eliminate – tensions between hierarchy and equality and between calculative and genuine relationships. Successful management – particularly in companies like Enator – is to some extent a question of regulating these tensions.

13.5   An Integrative Model Describing how Enator Functions

I would now like to discuss certain aspects of the way in which organizational and marketing functions at Enator are linked. (It should be noted that I am now referring to functions, which is not the same thing as the organizational forms for internal exchanges presented above.) I aim to provide an integrated picture of the company in order to build on, and link up further with, the subject matter in the chapters on organizational structure, corporate culture/organizational climate and marketing (Chapters 6, 7 and 12). This section is primarily concerned with harmony and convergence aspects.

As already stated elsewhere, the quality of the product which service companies supply is intrinsically associated with the personal appearance and performance of the producers. The way in which consultants deal with customer personnel directly affects the qualitative content of the service, and what consultants signal when providing the service in question also affects the customer's overall experience of what he/she gains from the service (see Chapter 12). As Schneider (1980, p 55) puts it:

human resources processes and procedures established for customer-contact employees in service organizations have unintentional consequences because they cannot be hidden from the consumer; there is no room for 'quality control' between the employees' behaviour and the customer's 'purchase'. The climate for service 'shows' to those who are served.

At least in the case of Enator projects which are undertaken on the customer's premises – the majority of all consultancy assignments – the customer company is directly exposed to the way consultants work, perhaps over the course of several months or even years. The consultants' approach is obviously affected by a great number of factors, including the organizational climate at Enator. Thus, this climate affects consultants and consequently has an indirect affect on interactions between consultants and the customer's personnel. Ultimately, the organizational climate affects the way in which the project develops, its final technical and functional quality and the customer's perception of this, and also the general pattern of relations between Enator personnel and customer staff and the customer company's general image of Enator. It might be said that every consultancy project produces two final results: *project output* and *customer relations output*. Project output involves the quality experienced by the customer in direct relation to project results. Customer relations output involves mutual personnel and corporate know-how, established network contacts, the customer's image of Enator (and vice versa) and investments in future transactions which are bound up with the project. Thus, customer relations output is a question of the overall prerequisites for further business contacts between customers and consultants as a result of activities connected with the project. Customer relations output is linked to the buyer-seller (client-consultant) relationship which is a normal feature of complex transactions in which mutual dependence is a major component.

Obviously, project output and customer relations output overlap, but apart from the fact that the latter involves wider and more socially-oriented factors, it may also be considered that the two types of output do not work in exactly the same direction. A customer, for example, may be satisfied with a consultant's technical input and the specific work result, but may feel that the consultant in question was not particularly agreeable to work with or perhaps he had the impression that the consultant's competence was limited to the particular type of assignment in question. It is possible for a consultant to do a good job in a functional sense without establishing relationships which extend beyond what is directly involved in the task per se and without becoming acquainted with the customer company, either in breadth or in depth. It is also possible that a particular project has failed, for example, due to changed circumstances or because of other circumstances for which the consultant is not responsible, but that they may have produced a good impression of themselves and the company.

Figure 13.2 presents a model describing a number of major factors underlying consultancy assignments (the production process). The final results of a consultancy assignment in the form of project and customer relations outputs are primarily regarded as a consequence of the interaction between the project group and the customer company's decision makers and contact persons. Four central intra-organizational aspects within the project group which determine the way in which it functions vis-à-vis the customer and project results are identified: the way in which the project is managed and undertaken at a purely technical and functional level, the

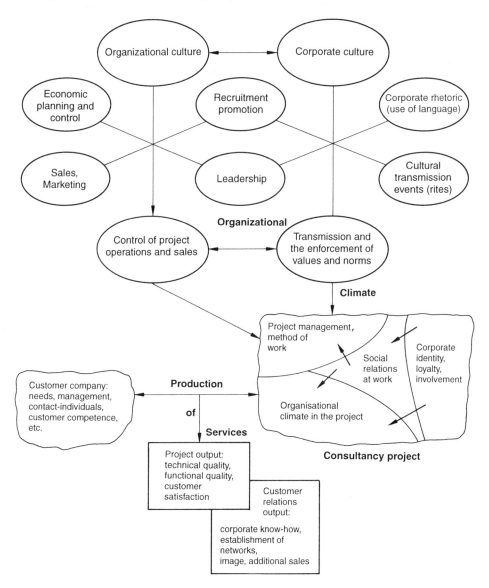

Figure 13.2:   Model describing the functioning of consultancy companies and projects

organizational climate which characterizes the group, the project group's social relationships and the general links between project members and the organization in which they are employed. The latter aspect includes a sense of corporate identity, loyalty and involvement in the company and in the job, etc. A further aspect may be the specific support which the project receives from subsidiary management and other Enator back-up staff.

These factors are expressed directly in concrete terms in project group operations in the method of work and project management style and in the project's (local) organizational climate vis-à-vis the customer company. In their turn, these then affect the social relationships which characterize members of the consultancy project and other consultancy personnel who are directly or indirectly involved. And, once more, this is partly a result of the general attitudes and ties which characterize the personnel in relation to their company and their work.

This covers the concrete work tasks, i.e. the company's material operations or the "primary social practices" (Reed, 1985; see Chapter 9 above). The "primary social practices" are also influenced by "secondary social practices" or various management and integration mechanisms. Two types of such mechanisms may be identified at Enator and at other companies. One type is of a structural nature, while the other involves values, norms and ways of indicating guidelines for definitions of reality (i.e. the corporate culture). Structural control of project operations takes place through the assignments that are acquired, through principles for how projects are to be conducted, and through various management functions for following up the project and exercising quality control. Traditional means of control, such as budgets, marketing plans, sales measures, etc. also come into the picture at this point.

Two types of control have a structural and cultural influence, i.e. affects behaviour as well as mind.[2] These two forms of control are the recruitment of personnel and the ongoing influence of managers/leaders. In the case of recruitment, staff are employed partly on the basis of structural criteria, particularly education, experience and competence, and partly on the basis of social and cultural considerations, where the most important factors are personal characteristics and attitudes. Managers also have a double function in terms of direct control and support, on the one hand, and the transmission of cultural ideas on the other. Managers are supposed to exercise control and to function as partners in a dialogue ("testing out ideas"), but they are also expected to set the tone and transmit and reinforce values and norms (to act as carriers of the culture).

Company rhetoric (use of language) and the events orchestrated for transmission of the culture ("rites") may be seen as purely cultural influences. Managers are involved here, but mainly as transmitters of institutionalized patterns and other employees are also active in this regard. In addition to the effects of corporate culture on recruitment policy and management style, the culture also operates because a certain use of language has been institutionalized in the company – there is frequent reference to creativity, friction, individualism, openness, the right to make a fool of yourself, lack of bureaucracy, fun and profit, etc. Cultural influence is also exercised via specific institutions in the company which, in a relatively pure form, transmit a certain corporate spirit and certain attitudes to personnel.

This corporate spirit has an impact on interactions with customers and is thus of considerable importance from a marketing point of view (Schneider, 1980; Schneider and Bowen, 1993). As far as Enator is concerned, it is not merely a question of a high proportion of staff with direct customer contacts, since the nature of the company's operations means that such staff members not only have a certain contact surface vis-à-vis the customer but in most projects are also largely encompassed and surrounded by the customer company. This is what happens when projects are conducted on the customer's premises and together with customer personnel. In this situation, the local version of Enator's organizational climate as expressed in the project is directly exposed to the customer on a broad front and thus becomes a major component in "customer-experienced quality", which is what ultimately determines Enator's success in the market-place. The success of the type of projects Enator is engaged in are often highly contingent upon the ability to manage the social and communicative aspects of the project work, while the pure technical problems are often less of a problem, according to those interviewed.

Thus, in essential respects the borderlines between Enator and customer companies are weak and diffuse. This may be an advantage or disadvantage, depending on what form the organizational climate takes. It is clear that Enator assumes that "internal organizational" circumstances have a value vis-à-vis customers, and the company tries to exploit this in its marketing in various ways. This is not something which functions purely indirectly as a result of internal social activities which improve the climate, making consultants happier and contributing to their satisfactory functioning vis-à-vis customers; it can also be seen directly when customers participate in Enator's social activities:

We should be able to utilize our more or less well developed social skills as a competitive tool vis-à-vis customers. One of the options is to teach personnel how to arrange successful social meetings so that they, in their turn, can use this knowledge together with customers, in project groups or in other contexts. It might be a question of one-to-one activities with a customer, or it may also be a question of arranging activities such as the inauguration of a building like this, annual general meetings or a subsidiary's five year jubilee, when you invite several customers or all your customers (Subsidiary manager).

Image-oriented activities are another type of link between social activities which primarily benefit the personnel and external relationships. The more spectacular types of social activities, in particular, contribute to Enator's image. One example is the five year jubilee which was celebrated at the Albert Hall in London after the guests had been dancing in the airplane which took them there (some of the seats were removed). Items like this are reported in the mass media and have considerable public relations value for Enator. The company promotes a distinct profile both at the customer level and in the labour market. Presumably, there is a risk that social activities have an excessively decisive influence on the company's image – becoming known as "the party company" may scare off some customers and attract job applicants who have unrealistic expectations. Nonetheless, there is no denying that Enator's social activities have considerable public relations value.

There are thus three types of link between internal, climate-improving social activities and marketing. First because the organizational climate encourages personnel to work well and, in particular, because it transmits a good corporate spirit to customers. Second, because the customer is involved in social activities arranged by the company. Third, because (primarily) the internal social activities which express and reinforce values and ideas, and promote the organizational climate become part of Enator's general image in the market-place. The final point applies chiefly to the more spectacular and readily communicated types of social activities.

Thus, social activities that primarily fulfil a social-integrative and personnel-furthering function may also receive external exposure and be utilized as part of the company's marketing. But this only applies if the social activities function so satisfactorily that it is possible to pull back the curtain and that the external element is not felt to interfere with or influence the quality of activities negatively. For this reason, there is a certain degree of selectivity as regards the relationship between purely internal activities and activities where a demarcation vis-à-vis external contacts does not exist.

13.6   Contradictions and Divergence

As I have indicated earlier, for example in Chapter 6, organizations, like other social forms, are not only characterized by harmony, unity, convergence and integration, but also by tension, antagonism, conflicts and divergence. Contradictions may take place between social groups but also between different aspects, values, functions or objectives seen in the perspective of a social consensus. In other words, contradictions do not necessarily lead to visible social conflicts. Contradictions may emerge between historically established structures and ongoing change processes, between cultural and socio-structural levels, between ideology and practice, or between different types of ideologies and ambiguities which occur as a result of the fundamental complexity of operations, etc. (See e.g. Abravanel, 1983; Benson, 1977; Fombrun, 1986; Martin, 1987; Martin and Meyerson, 1988 and Sköldberg, 1990.)

There is normally only a restricted focus on these aspects in "conventional" organizational theory and business administration. From a functional perspective, conflicts and tensions are often regarded as positive motive forces for development and renewal in companies. It is assumed, for example, that the growth of a company takes place in the form of phases of revolution and evolution, where the former is characterized by contradiction but paves the way for each qualitatively new step in the company's development (Greiner, 1972). New growth and business ideas are also often considered to arise from fruitful tensions within the company or in relations between the company and its external environment (e.g. Normann, 1975; Rhenman, 1974). In this context, tensions and conflicts are regarded as relatively restricted and occurring against a background of balance, harmony and general systems integration, which are considered to be more "normal" characteristics.

How the nature of social reality is conceptualized regarding contradictions and unity is partly a question of which side of the coin is displayed by this reality, but it is also a question of the choice of research perspective. If a dialectical perspective is applied, the antagonisms are fundamental and unavoidable and constitute a central driving force. On the other hand, if a systems approach and/or a consensus perspective is adopted, it will be assumed that balance and compliance between various systems (subsystems) is normal (cf. Burrell and Morgan, 1979). With some slight eclectic bias, it is assumed in this book that both the convergent, integrative aspects of organizations and the tensions and conflicts which manifestly or latently characterize these aspects must be taken into account. Although I have previously primarily emphasized the integrative aspects in this chapter, some basic tensions at Enator will be examined in this section.

Two of Enator's most prominent characteristics are rapid growth, partly on the international arena, and a cohesive spirit and strong links between members of the organization and the company. This implies a fundamental potential area of tension. In the company's earliest years, and indeed also when my study was conducted, the company was characterized by strong socio-emotional ties, particularly in the first established parts of the company and in the managing director group, but also elsewhere and, as a result, in the company in its entirety. Thus, with a little good will the company can be compared to a home, a family, a clan or a circle. These qualities are important, and this means that genuine relationships are crucial for cooperation, motivation, job satisfaction, etc. This influences communicational ability, the level of conflict, personnel turnover, etc. – mainly in a manner which has positive economic effects. Perhaps the typical attitude of personnel towards the company might be described by applying religious metaphors.

A colleague in the business told me when I started to work here that: 'Enator is not a company, it's a religion.'
My wife thinks I'm so involved in my work that she calls the company 'Maranator' (Maranata is a religious revivalist movement in Sweden).

Important factors underlying this attitude appear to be that Enator is a recently established, successful young company, with a low average age of staff, dynamic and powerful leaders, who have institutionalized a distinct set of personnel-oriented ideas and values, a special leadership style, and homogeneous recruitment. The fact that Enator is a relatively large international company – at least in the context of Swedish business – stands in contrast with the strong socio-emotional foundations which have resulted from these factors and from the company's early development. Enator's international status is qualitatively different from the idea of a "family" or "religion" which (still) characterizes the company at the time of my study. Growth and international development detract from the socio-emotional foundations. The socio-emotional basis is weakened because, as the company matures, the founders have less contact with the company and appears to regard it more as a "star" or "cash-cow" for interesting new deals in developing the Pronator Group. Recruitment is becoming increasingly heterogeneous. New employees are no longer primarily friends and the friends of friends. Instead they are likely to be completely unknown people, sometimes from other countries. In addition, existing companies also constitute "employees" as a result of corporate acquisitions. The Pronator Group is geographically located in many different places.

Enator is moving away from being a group of buddies to becoming an international corporate group. Management are optimistically assuming that various national subsidiary groups will emerge outside Sweden. This would appear to mean that the more calculative features of operations will become more central. Economic exchanges and self-interest will become more important, both from the owner side and from the point of view of new employees.

Those who come to Enator ... no longer have the feeling of 'I'm going to give Enator something and we're going to build something together'. New employees have a more egoistic approach to the company. What can they get out of Enator? The emotional ties are not so strong, at least not initially.

The establishment of new companies in other countries and the acquisition of new organizations means that the company spirit and the breadth and depth of relationships within the company is gradually changing. Clan and circle qualities are weakened, while the formal organization and the internal market as organizational and regulatory principles for exchanges become more significant. To use Ouchi's concepts reciprocity and prices become more important as regulatory mechanisms and as informational components, at the expense of shared values, beliefs and traditions. An important trigger factor behind the conflict between Enator's top management and the Norwegian subsidiary was precisely the question of ownership. Enator offered the subsidiary manager 25% of the shares, but the manager wanted to have 50%.

A dramatic formulation of the tension discussed here might be that the most essential social foundations of the company's success are in conflict with the central feature of corporate objectives and strategy: rapid growth, largely on international markets. The social foundations are inevitably affected by rapid expansion and corporate acquisitions and the maintenance of the company's socio-emotional status quo would constitute an obstacle both to growth and to the company's foreign ambitions.[3]

However, at least to some extent, this conflict may be handled by dynamic efforts to establish a group feeling between subsidiary managers and by activities such as the Victoria celebration in which the entire personnel, some 500 strong, participated. From a business point of view, it is also clear that the importance of the corporate socio-emotional basis diminishes once the initial setting-up phase has been completed. The strong involvement which is required in an uncertain entrepreneurial phase is not necessary to the same extent in an established company. In the latter case, there is more demand for planning and "professional management" (bureaucracy). The reporting and presentation of financial results and other indications of performances become important in this context and standardization of financial reporting in the Enator group is required. The fact that Enator forms part of a larger group (Pronator) also means less freedom of action for the company and its subsidiaries in this respect. The strong dependence on the founders as individuals is also reduced. There are better opportunities to offer good pay and other fringe benefits in an established company, and this may compensate for a reduction in close personal links with the original entrepreneurs. Internationalization, for example, means that consultants have an opportunity to work abroad.

The meaning of the "corporate culture" is also changing now that Enator employs several hundred staff and now that new personnel are largely to be found in new subsidiaries, often in other countries. This will be more significant as an explicit management instrument in the light of the decline in the original closely-knit and intense corporate spirit based on personal influence, primarily on the part of the founders, and the special circumstances which characterized the initial phases of the company. In other words, when common values, attitudes and collective emotional ties no longer occur "spontaneously" or "automatically" amongst all staff members, due to increased size and a rapid flow of additional personnel, the "corporate culture" may emerge even more strongly than before as a special concept to guide subsidiary and top management. That is to say: the weaker the natural base for a corporate culture, the greater reason management has for interesting itself as much as possible in systematically trying to influence values, norms, etc. (Alvesson and Berg, 1992, ch. 2). This point is reinforced by a comparison with Kunda's (1992) study of a very large American high tech company founded in the 1950s. As mentioned before this company has considerable similarities with Enator in terms of "corporate culture". It differs in that a vast amount of resources are spent in communicating the culture in carefully pre-planned, standardized ways through a variety of media, including formal presentations, news-letters and videos. The "engineering" element in cultural control is thus much stronger than in Enator. Elements of conscious engineering of values and ideas by key actors have of course characterized Enator from the start, but for some time it was rather closely connected to the personal style of the founders and other managers. The engineering element becomes more salient when leadership becomes replaced by systematic management as the key force behind cultural control.

The corporate culture tends to change its meaning over time in the company. Perhaps its form does not vary very much, but whereas the original – or perhaps embryonic – espoused ideas, values and manifestations of these had a strong emotional loading and constituted a major motive force for action taken by personnel, subsequent developments mean that the culture tends to be a kind of social glue which reduces the distance between the various subsidiaries from a corporate group management perspective and thus fulfils a general social-integrative function. As a result, it ceases to primarily function as an incentive for involvement and action and becomes an instrument to counteract disintegration and divergence in social patterns. This does not mean that normative control becomes less significant, only that it changes meaning and leads to somewhat different outcomes.

Notes

[1]   As shown in Alvesson (1993a) tautologies are rather common in thinking, trying to combine notions of culture and effectivity.

[2]   There is, of course, nothing except physical force that affects behaviour with-
      out first involving the mind. Behaviour (action) is contingent upon the mean-
      ing given to an imperative to act. Nevertheless, certain modes of control are
      less intended to affect feelings and thinking than to affect behaviour, calling
      only for a minimal process of interpretation.
[3]   The situation is a bit more complicated, as rapid growth, during the first years
      of the company, has facilitated a positive work climate and corporate pride.
      Growth may then have mixed effects. With increasing size it will probably
      primarily weaken the corporate socio-emotional basis.

14 Corporate Control via Symbols

The object of this final chapter is to give an overall, summarizing picture of the way Enator works, primarily from a cultural symbolic perspective. I link up with interpretations of symbols which have been made in previous chapters and I also relate the results of this study to a more general understanding of knowledge-intensive companies.

14.1 Structural Sources of Disintegration

As already mentioned, disintegration tendencies are built into the organizational form per se or into the kind of production which characterizes companies which have a weak material core, such as Enator. The weakness of the "substantive" core is partly contingent upon operations consisting of heterogeneous project assignments which are loosely coupled to each other.

Some of the dilemmas that are intrinsic to this kind of work area and which are typical of many knowledge-intensive companies are illustrated in Figure 14.1.

As already indicated, one of the basic requirements in this type of company is a high proportion of debiting of personnel resources. This means that the company in question must have a relatively pragmatic approach to the projects and assignment which it takes on. The fact that projects are often conducted in the field and that customers, assignments and other conditions differ considerably is part of the intrinsic nature of operations. To some extent, growth objectives are a feature of capitalist companies. Owners have expectations and requirements as regards growth. When my study was conducted, Enator's management had definite ambitions in this connection and the idea of growth appeared to be supported by a high proportion of employees. In effect, these themes point at certain crucial aspects of the company's operations from the point of view of efficiency as regards tangible quantitative factors (this is summarized in the left-hand column in Figure 14.1).

On the other hand it is also desirable to have a high level of social cohesion, that is to say that the personnel identify themselves with the com-

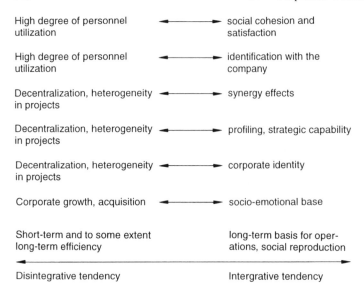

Figure 14.1: Some crucial dilemmas for companies of the Enator type

pany, as well as that there is a certain stability and integration which can provide a basis for the company's identity, profile and image. It is important that there is a strategic capacity for manoeuvring and to have a relatively clear concept of selling on a market. A certain uniformity and homogeneity in methods of work, the nature of assignments, etc. must be achieved if synergy effects are to occur. If operations become excessively diversified, doubts are likely concerning the basis for cooperation and synergy between various consultants, project groups, subsidiaries, etc. and the point of conducting operations in corporate form. (It might be possible however, to imagine a market exchange form instead, in which independent computer consultants cooperated where necessary on temporary projects without having a hierarchical/employment relationship). Further, the company may wish to exploit a socio-emotional base in the form of the identification of staff with the company and a strong sense of belonging to a collective. If such a base is lacking, the personnel are less likely to be loyal and stable. (See Figure 14.1, right-hand column).

The interesting feature is the conflict between these two ambitions (tendencies). In concrete terms, the high proportion of debiting means that the scope for allowing personnel to meet and develop social ties is limited. Customers do not want to pay for expensive consultants sitting at Enator's Head Office and having regular social contact. On the other hand, identification with the company does not occur readily if staff spend long periods

at a customer's place of work. A multiplicity of different projects and assignments of a varying nature counteracts profile, identity and synergy
effects.

On the whole, it can be said that, from a structural point of view, operations of this kind involve clear tendencies towards disintegration and that
the long term base for the company is undermined. Thus, the left-hand
column in Figure 14.1 denotes the company's structural aspects, including
objectives, corporate structure, formal control, concrete methods of work,
etc. Certain structural dimensions also work in the opposite direction – for
example the decentralized development of subsidiaries which, apart from
certain divisive effects, may also mean greater cohesion within subsidiares.

The right-hand column, which represents "non-substantive" aspects
(feelings, perceptions, etc.) is primarily regulated by symbolic means.
Thus, various symbolically-loaded situations, use of language and physical
arrangements, which are deliberately and systematically controlled by
management, have an integrative effect. This includes not merely what is
encompassed by Enator's corporate culture but also a number of other
crucial symbols, for example, the business concept. As a result of the impact and flexibility which characterize symbols, they can counteract tendencies towards structural disintegration, to a greater or lesser extent.
Thus, for example, the quality and the expressive level in an "integration
rite" may partially compensate for the lack of an extensive range of contacts in everyday life in achieving a feeling of social affinity.

I will shortly return to the symbols which are important from an integrative point of view. But first I would like to indicate the dimensions which
are important as a result of the structural prerequisites and which must be
regulated to some extent by symbolic means.

14.2   Some Crucial Dimensions of Corporate Operations

The dimensions which I will be dealing with involve internal factors, relationships with the outside world and the actual exchanges between the
organization and its environment (project work). First I will look at the
internal dimensions.

One of the fundamental problems is achieving a regulation of the frontiers between the company and the outside world (primarily customer
companies) that is both flexible and effective. To accomplish this the company and its staff must be perceived as having special characteristics which
distinguish them from the outside world. According to some authors, the
company must be regarded as a cohesive unit which encompasses various
people, circumstances and factors. In other words, the company must

"have" a clear identity. The corporate identity denotes the organization and the sum of its activities as a whole, clearly distinguishing it in qualitative terms from the outside world in a more or less "objective" sense. I emphasize identity as an expansion of the organizational participants' perception of the company in terms of unity and coherence[1] (Albert and Whetten, 1985).

While the corporate identity primarily denotes the company as an abstraction – separated from and superior to human individuals – the materia and the concrete activities which are included in the company – other themes involve social relationships within the company: cohesion and hierarchy. Every social order is characterized by these two types of relationship (cf. Duncan, 1968).

Social cohesion is a question of the social and affective ties which link people together. A corporate sense of community, where a feeling of community or the collective applies to the company as a whole, is probably not particularly common. Most organizations are likely to have to satisfy themselves with communities within small areas of the company which sometimes adopt a virtually negative approach to management and the owners in the form of worker collectives. At Enator, the sense of a corporate community is one of management's major ambitions and is in fact realized to a considerable extent. The company's social cohesion is of a concrete nature. Thus, in this sense, it is not only a question of ties with the company as a whole or what the company represents (an idea), but rather of a focus on concrete relations between people working at Enator.

A strong sense of the organizational collective can conceivably be combined with a weak corporate identity, or a weak collective feeling coupled with a strong and positive corporate identity in any given organization.[2] In the first case, social ties are strong but the corporate concept is not specific or well developed. In the second case, what the company represents is fully accepted by the personnel without it affecting their mutual relationships. Social cohesion and corporate identity may reinforce each other, of course. This is probably common. Management can try to link the two together to achieve mutual reinforcement. Enator's management style may be described in this manner.

The second fundamental aspect of any given social order is hierarchy. This is a question of the regulation of power and influence and how relationships between superiors and their subordinates are established, maintained and legitimized. One important aspect of a hierarchy is how subordinates are "persuaded" to accept a given hierarchical order. The nature of relations must be based on the "subjectivity" of those involved.

While social cohesion establishes ties between individuals, the hierarchy indicates differences between people. Hierarchical relationships often weaken a sense of community. Community may occur in opposition to the hierarchy, as is the case with a worker collective, for example, in which the dominant class in the social order is totally excluded from this community – sometimes leading to an unsatisfactory situation for a modern manager. However, in some cases a hierarchical situation may reinforce the sense of community, including a sense of community between differing hierarchical levels. For example, an authoritarian or even tyrannical leader may create a community of which he himself is a part, both as a leader and as the dominant member of the collective.

In the case of Enator, the hierarchy and the sense of cohesion work together in a more positive manner. Enator has a relatively strong but also flexible hierarchy. It appears to be able to retreat into the background when this suits its purpose. The sense of community may also operate in a vertical direction. Social cohesion softens up the hierarchy and makes it more flexible. At the same time, the hierarchy also contributes to cohesion. Management's position makes it easier to "conjure up" a sense of community (cf. the clan concept). In the case of Enator, one important aspect of the organizational hierarchy is that, to some extent, it takes the form of managed cohesion.

In more general terms, hierarchy and the structure of authority may easily become diffuse in this type of company, and professional competence and formal hierarchy may work in different directions (Hinings et al., 1991). It thus becomes particularly important to try to handle the hierarchy in a sensitive manner – on the one hand allowing equality and a sense of community to develop and, on the other hand giving managers a strong "position" upon which they can base their actions.

So far, I have described three key dimensions involving the delimitation (identity), integration (cohesion) and (vertical) differentiation (hierarchy) of the organization, all of which are linked to the organization's internal functioning and associated problems. The successful management of these dimensions gives the organization a basis for sticking together, and for the emergence of synergies. It also allows personnel to perceive the execution of their duties in the relevant form as meaningful (i.e. as members of the company Enator rather than as independent consultants). Other fundamental problems are of an external nature and involve relationships with the outside world. However, in between the external and the internal we also have the actual exchange between the company and its environment, that is to say, the actual core of operations in the form of project work.

Compared with the three internal dimensions, project operations are to a greater extent characterized by technical and concrete factors. The scope and need for cultural and symbolic control of ways of relating (thinking, feeling) to the company are greatly reduced. However, this does not mean that structural factors and control instruments of a traditional, i.e. behaviour or output-related nature are sufficient. Symbols also play an important role in this context as guidelines for project operations, particularly in transmitting a standardized but flexible, overall orientation as regards project management throughout the company. When I refer to project operations in this chapter, this is not primarily a question of material and technical characteristics. Instead, I am more concerned with overall perceptions and the principles which guide project work.

In the case of external relationships, I consider that it is fruitful to identify two fundamental themes which are of decisive importance. One theme involves concrete *customer relationships*, that is to say how the company integrates with segments of the outside world with which economic exchanges are conducted (or may be conducted). Hence, this is a question of the regulation of social relationships. The means applied to control such relationships must provide general directives, without being excessively diffuse or ineffective in other respects, and they must also permit flexibility and adaptation to the situation. In this context, symbols are highly appropriate, in contrast, for example, with the formalization of work tasks and procedures, which are of a more unambiguous and rigid character.[3]

The second dimension of an external nature involves how the company is perceived in a wider context. This is a question of the total picture or perceptions of the company held by people from the outside world, in other words its *image* or profile. A company's image contributes to clarifying relations between the company and its environment. Various attempts to control the environment's perception of a company contribute to bridging the perceived gap between the environment and the company. This means that the company becomes well known. The relationship between image and corporate identity involves both similarities and differences. Both image and identity – as topics for managerial action – involve handling and emphasizing the company's special character. However, internally (in terms of identity), this is a question of emphasising distance and contrasts with the environment, while at the external level (in image terms) it is to a large degree a matter of establishing a dialogue with the environment, of creating a basis for interaction and exchanges (cf. Berg and Gagliardi, 1985). While management efforts to regulate ideas about identity tend to favour actions and accounts that maximize the organization's special character, it is important from the image perspective that this special character is adapted in line with the perceptions and values of the environment. Deviation from the environment as regards style, approach, indications, methods, etc. may facilitate the development of a strong identity, but the company may also be perceived as "unconventional", idiosyncratic and unprofessional by the environment.

The six aspects of Enator's operations which have been mentioned – identity, social cohesion, hierarchy, project operations, customer relationships and image – thus constitute central dimensions of significance for

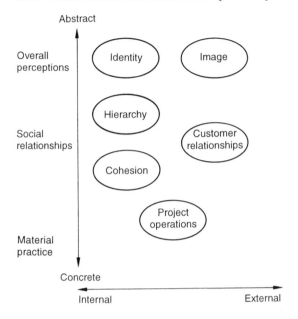

Figure 14.2:   Crucial dimensions for companies of the Enator type

the extent to which the company can manage the tendency towards the disintegration of operations. These aspects are probably important for most or even all types of companies, but as a result of structurally conditioned divergency (loose coupling between highly decentralized work activities), they are particularly critical for operations of the Enator type, i.e. knowledge-intensive companies, especially in the service business. Figure 14.2 summarizes these six dimensions.

In the diagram these dimensions are related to two axis. One axis is concerned with internal/external aspects. It is true that external and internal aspects strongly overlap each other in operations of this type, but the emphasis is clearly in one direction or the other. The other axis illustrates the degree of concretization. Project operations are closer to the material level (what people do), while identity and image are purely mental (abstract) phenomena.

Let us now turn to a number of crucial symbols which were covered in the earlier chapters of this book and see how these relate to the fundamental themes about how the company operates and how it is controlled.

14.3   Key Symbols at Enator

As is the case in the social research of complex phenomena in general, the analysis of symbols offers considerable scope for the independent choice, assessment and arbitrary opinion of the researcher as to what he/she should focus on. It is seldom obvious what should be regarded as symbols and how they should be interpreted. My ambition here is to consider some ten phenomena which may be regarded as important symbols at Enator. Possibly, the criteria for defining such symbols as key symbols may be that "the natives" tell the researcher that X is important, that they react to X in emotional terms rather than with indifference, that X emerges in many different contexts, that X is subject to a considerable amount of investigation (there is considerable interest in its nature) or that restrictions taboos and sanctions surround X (Ortner, 1973).

Various investigators have been seduced to assign implicitly or explicitly the status of key cultural symbol to a bewildering array of phenomena. Anything by definition can be *a symbol*, i.e. *a vehicle for cultural meaning*, and it seems from a survey of the literature that almost anything can be key. I have endeavoured to apply these criteria but without finding that they provide any obvious guidelines as to what are the most essential symbols at Enator. To some extent, the problems is that almost everything may be regarded as a symbol.

One problem is to demarcate symbols in terms of their scope. A certain phenomenon may frequently be regarded as *a single* symbol or as *a set of* symbols in a sequence. The Enator building may be regarded as a single symbol, albeit a complex symbol with considerable impact. Alternatively, the building may be divided into a number of different symbols, for example, the facade, the glass walls, the piano bar, etc. If one prefers the first alternative, the building would undoubtedly be a key symbol. On the other hand, it is not so clear that one of the more restricted material phenomenon which the house encompasses would, per se, fulfil the criteria for a key symbol, described above.

A second problem involves the relationship between the significance of symbols and their representativity with regard to certain cultural patterns. Some symbols have considerable impact, but are rare. Others are less remarkable and less important, per se, and they do not need to meet the above criteria but perhaps nonetheless, they are typical and representative of a certain class of symbols which, in their totality, are important. Perhaps what is culturally important is the sum of individual symbols within a certain class of category rather than individual, separate symbols. Possibly, a focus on individual key symbols, in line with the above criteria, would mean that this factor is ignored.

A third problem is the fact that the local "public sphere" which characterizes many organizations, and particularly companies in which management seriously attempts to exercise control by means of the corporate culture, is largely controlled by dominant actors and groups as regards appropriate expressions of ideas and meanings. Power relationships are an important aspect of the formation of symbols and their impact (Cohen, 1974). It is not automatic, however, that the symbols which dominate the public sphere in a company also exert full impact in groups and situations where the social pressures to conform regarding espoused values are weaker. I will not go into this major problem, but will be content with pointing out that systematic symbolic influence on the part of management may mean that symbols favoured by management such as Victoria are those that are talked about most in various socially prominent contexts and that it may be more difficult to pay sufficient attention to other types of symbols, more significant in everyday life.

A further problem in many cultural studies of modern organization is that such organizations often lack an extensive history. A relatively brief history may mean that layers of meaning are not accumulated in a certain symbolic form and that more recent symbols which are the subject of someone's intentions are often simpler, by their very nature. The lack of a prolonged history or stability as regards symbols may mean that key symbols can change relatively quickly. A top-ten list of symbols at Enator, drawn up for example in accordance with Ortner's criteria referred to above, may vary from one year to another. Speculative social events could emerge and fade away as key symbols rather quickly.

This means that it is difficult to draw up clear indicators of key symbols and to arrive at the right symbols by following a standard procedure. In addition, symbols are far too ambiguous, interwoven and difficult to quantify. In the following, I present eleven phenomena at Enator which I consider may be regarded as key symbols, perhaps primarily in the sense of "keys" to cultural understanding of the company rather than as Enator's most significant symbols, per se. My list is based on the following considerations:

- The advantage of regarding the phenomena (statement, event, etc.) as a symbol of something;
- the relevance of the symbol on the basis of the themes treated in this book (organizational structure, marketing, etc.);
- the significance of the symbol;
- the symbol's representativity of the local cultural patterns which characterize Enator and dominant attempts at influencing symbols in the company.

The eleven symbols are as follows:

• The building
• The business concept
• The project management philosophy course (as a general activity and initiation rite, not all the specific features and elements in the course – these will be dealt with separately since broadly speaking they involve the other ten key symbols)
• Information (about the company as a whole)
• Helicopter view
• Customer perceived quality
• Quarterly conferences
• Victoria
• The Managing Director (as a title/position)
• Big Boss
• Flat organisation

These symbols have been described in previous chapters, and so I will only add a few details regarding information. Information frequently symbolises wisdom, rationality, an overview, security (Feldman and March, 1981). At Enator, the situation is somewhat different. In particular, older employees refer to "getting a lot of information" as something important and of value (Chapter 7). At Enator, information to personnel represents involvement, closeness, confidence, cohesion and – at any rate in the past – excitement. Information from management to consultants has a strong emotional loading which is in rather clear contrast with what I have encountered in other organizational contexts.

In Table 14.1, I have related the eleven symbols to the six crucial dimensions of the company, which I have characterized above. To some extent, all symbols may have a certain relevance for all the dimensions. The meaning of the expression "flat organization" is not just a question of identity and hierarchy. To some extent this symbol also regulates social cohesion, the method of conducting projects (a minor softening-up of traditional ideas about the hierarchical relationship between the project manager and his/her colleagues), customer relationships (a certain tendency for a similar softening-up of the respect of the hierarchy in the customer company) and the corporate image. However, the table gives a hint of which dimensions of operations a given symbol has the greatest significance for. The Enator building, for example, is particularly important for corporate identity, for regulation of social affinity (the generous provision of collective premises and recreation facilities) and its image.

At the same time, it should be noted that various symbols have different degrees of emotional loading and scope, they also vary over time and be-

Table 14.1:   The importance of major organizational symbols and crucial corporate
dimensions at enator

Corporate Dimension	Organizational Symbol					
	Identity	Hierarchy	Cohesion	Project operation	Customer relations	Image
Business concept	X			X	X	X
Enator building	X		X		x	X
Project management philosophy course	X	x	x	X		
Information		x	X			
Helicopter view				X	x	
Customer perceived quality				X	X	
Quarterly conference	x		X			
Victoria	X		X			
Managing Director		X			X	
Big Boss		x	X			
Flat Organization	x	x				

X indicates "considerable" importance, x represents "rather large" importance

tween different individuals and, especially in an organization like Enator,
with many subsidiaries and with personnel who have entered the company
in various phases. It is important to observe variations in the way that
meaning is given to the same phenomenon while the more "average" or
general approaches are often seen as being of the greatest interest to analysis. The ambiguous and flexible nature of symbols mean that they have
no definite, fixed sense. As indicated, for example, in the chapter on the
business concept (Chapter 10) the meaning of symbols may fulfil a number
of different functions. Some of these functions are not covered particularly
well by the symbol concept – for example the analytical function – but,
from the symbolic point of view, rather different meanings may be applied
to the same business concept if people relate to the concept in an ideological, pragmatic, or marketing context.

14.4   Cataloguing Symbols

There are a number of different proposals for cataloguing symbols. Dandridge et al (1980), for example, distinguish between verbal, action and

material symbols. This distinction applies to forms. It is also possible to distinguish various symbolic functions, as Dandridge et al also does. They consider that symbols may serve to regulate emotions; to increase energy (through creating excitement and involvement), reduce energy (reduce tensions) or function in a reproducing, stabilizing manner). Sköldberg (1990) proposes a typology in which he imagines that symbols are cognitive, emotional and/or pragmatic. There are often elements of all three aspects in a given symbol but in most cases one aspect dominates. Sköldberg also distinguishes between the symbol as an expression or a trigger of meaning.

Ortner (1973) makes a fundamental distinction between "summarizing symbols" and "elaborating symbols". The former synthesize, summarize and express the attitudes of a group of members to the culture of which they are a part in an emotionally powerful but, in terms of cognition, not particularly sophisticated manner. This category primarily comprises "holy" symbols in the broadest sense and encompasses objects which express a certain affective attitude and fundamental values. The national flag, the cross, the motor car (for "car-mad young men") may provide examples. While the "summarizing symbols" synthesize and simplify a complex system of ideas and perceptions in a uniform context, the "elaborating" symbols function in the opposite direction. Elaborating symbols serve as instruments to sort out complex and undifferentiated feelings and ideas, making them comprehensible, communicable with others and translatable into concrete action. These symbols achieve their position in the culture due to their ability to organize experiences. They are mainly analytical.

According to Ortner, elaborating symbols may have a clarifying, facilitating effect, either conceptually or with an action orientation. They may facilitate conceptualization or indicate guidelines for social action. Thus they reflect the two fundamental functions of the culture; to provide members with an orientation in life and to suggest strategies, i.e. patterns of actions which comply with culturally acceptable goals and ideals. Symbols with considerable conceptual capacity are termed "root metaphors". One example in a high technologically society might be the machine as a metaphor for social processes in general. Action oriented key symbols are termed "key scenarios". Ortner illustrates this with the American Horatio Alger myth: the poor boy of modest origins with a total belief in the American system, who works very hard and ultimately becomes rich, prosperous and powerful.

Ortner's classification corresponds to Sköldberg's emotional, cognitive and pragmatic symbolic types.

Inspired by these references and by the significant symbols which I have encountered at Enator together with the arguments presented earlier in this chapter about crucial dimensions and dilemmas in this type of company, including the need to regulate boundaries with the environment (identity), the environment's perceptions of the company (image), etc., I will now try to formulate a symbolic typology which is primarily and specifically related to (knowledge-intensive) companies, rather than to the societies anthropologists have traditionally investigated.

14.5 A Symbolic Typology for the Study of Companies

Five different types of symbols are distinguished in this typology. Two of these are fundamentally emotional or affective. Three are mainly clarifying. All symbols, per se, contain both emotional and cognitive elements. However, this typology is concerned with the aspect which is most prominent.

I distinguish between *abstract-affective* and *social-affective* symbols. The characteristic feature of the former type is that they express or transmit the fundamental relationship between an overall concept, idea, ideal, or a totality of which the group in question is part. Abstract-affective symbols thus embody the idea (ideal, totality, etc.) in the conscious emotional world of the collective. In a corporate context, the company (normally) provides this overall concept. The reason why I term this an abstraction is that it is not primarily a question of the company in a material sense, including the people who work in it, the buildings in which operations are carried out or the concrete production which is undertaken. Instead, the company is an overall idea held by the people who work in it, that is to say ideas and feelings connected with the company as a concept. The company cannot be reduced to concrete circumstances but stands at a level "above them". The collective gives the company a deep and emotionally coloured meaning which does not correspond to the total of its "objective", concrete characteristics or with how the company is typically perceived by the outsider.

Thus, a company exists in this case at roughly the same "ontological level" as other abstract categories which function as overall symbols for collectives. This may be a question of religion, nation, a political ideology or a region. Action is often taken in the name of the religion, nation, etc. – the collective of people which accompanies the religion or nation, etc. may be of subordinate importance. In wars, for example, the nation's inhabitants tend to be of secondary importance in relation to the nation as an abstract idea, for which no sacrifices or suffering are considered to be too great. Something similar may also apply to companies. In the best interests of the company – which does not necessarily correspond to the best interests of concrete groups (shareholders, personnel, individuals) – people may be prepared to make considerable efforts and even to commit immoral acts, which are justified in this case, not by egoism, but by the best interests of the company (Schwartz, 1987).

Thus, abstract-affective symbols express what the company represents and the quality of the ties between members of the organization and the company. The dominant feature of the symbols is their emotional character. This may be a question of pride in the company or loyalty to the organization. These abstract-affective symbols are related to the company, per se, as an institution in the sense employed by Selznick (see Chapter 8).

In the case of Enator, the business concept, the corporate building and the Victoria Anniversary may be seen as examples of abstract-affective symbols. In this context, the business concept is regarded as an expression of Enator's unique competence. Sectors of the personnel feel that what makes the company unique and superior to competitors in the computer consulting area is its cohesive business concept and ability to live up to this concept and implement it. The building transmits the companies attitude to its employees. The management philosophy and ties between Enator and its employees are summarized by the piano-bar, glass walls, the sauna, etc. In particular, what is being expressed is a feeling of "home". The Victoria Anniversary also denotes the quality of relations between the personnel and the company. In this case, the company demonstrates its generosity, and also its overall affinity within the Enator group as a whole, across subsidiary and national borders.

In contrast with the abstract-affective aspects, *social-affective symbols* involve concrete social ties and relationships within the company. In this case the company and the corporate entity are not the crucial factors. Instead, the focus is on colleagues and group feelings. This can take various forms in relation to the company. In particular, group feelings and a sense of corporate affinity can overlap in certain activities. In many other cases, social cohesion may be loosely connected to or even independent of the company. Social-affective symbols contribute to creating and expressing the quality of the collective or collectives encompassed by the organization.

One example of this type of symbol at Enator is the quarterly conference. Quarterly conferences take place within the framework of each subsidiary. Almost everyone in the subsidiary participates. The contents of the conference are based primarily on the idea that everybody should enjoy themselves and that they should reinforce the group spirit, thus manifesting group affinity. Personnel denote their involvement by their willingness to devote their spare time to such activities.

Victoria and many other socially oriented corporate activities may also be regarded as social-affective symbols. In comparison to quarterly conferences, the company as a whole permeates the Victoria Anniversary occasion in a more systematic manner. There was a greater measure of management influence, for example on the flight down to Rhodes, the paper antimacassars on the seats were embossed with Enator's name rather than that of the airline.

While the affectively loaded symbols primarily express a certain feeling or attitude as regards a complex of ideas and circumstances, *clarifying symbols* focus the attention and understanding of the environment on certain special lines. They provide orientation and benchmarks. However, this is not a question of traffic signs or other non-ambiguous indications. Such symbols provide general and ambiguous guidelines, with an emphasis on their "persuasive capacity". A symbol appeals to the subjectivity of members of the collective by indicating a cognitive meaning.

I term the first type of clarifying symbol *value-transmitting symbols*, because they provide rules for the evaluative interpretation and understanding of workplace reality. Thus, the symbol condenses aspects which it is important to note and emphasize in a complex world. It provides a form for a certain structure of values by indicating and illustrating what is right, good and desirable and/or what is wrong, harmful and should be avoided. An alternative concept might have been attention-focusing symbols.

Value-transmitting symbols influence mentalities, how one should relate to the environment and indicate certain moral benchmarks. The implications for action are rather weak. Value-transmitting symbols provide an orientation as to how the contexts one is part of can be understood. But the symbols are far too diffuse to function as direct guidelines for action – for better or for worse.

Most of the eleven symbols mentioned above may be regarded as value-transmitting symbols (all symbols involve values, but in many cases this aspect is not so prominent). Symbols such as the Enator building, the business concept and a number of verbal expressions such as "big boss" and "flat organization" are typical of value transmitting (attention-focusing) symbols. The Enator building contains, for example, a large number of symbols which attract attention and influence ideas. Corporate management, for instance, is located on the first floor, near the Reception. Most of the rooms on this floor do not differ that much in terms of size so that room dimensions provide no clear guide as to the position its occupant holds. At the same time, the room and the space available to managers and administrators on this floor are considerably more generously dimensioned than the restricted space available to the tightly packed consultants on the other floors. The location of top management and the comparatively simple premises and fittings tells us something, however – they express certain ideas and values about hierarchy and equality. But the exact implications are somewhat diffuse. These symbols do not provide any clear directives for action.

The same applies, for example, to the expression "big boss". This symbolizes a set of ideas, with an emphasis on informality and relative equality – a slightly ironic attitude to blind faith in titles and formal positions. To the extent that it works, this symbol has the effect of reducing respect for hierarchy – or rather to make people more relaxed about formal status differences in certain situations. However, it is uncertain what this means in concrete terms of behaviour. No doubt it is inappropriate to stand cap-in-hand touching your forelock, but apart from this it is difficult to understand how relationships between "Big Boss" and others are supposed to take place. Such relationships also depend on the situation involved. In certain situations, it is hardly advisable to regard managing directors ironically as "Big Bosses" and it may be perhaps wise to take their formal, hierarchical positions in deadly earnest.

As the label indicates, *action-oriented symbols* have rather clear implications for action. Such symbols provide an indication of where efforts should lead and what concrete, methods are appropriate. However, this is not a question of clear and concrete, detailed instructions. By definition, symbols (as the term is used here) do not function as elements in a handbook or coded signs on a map. They are too ambiguous, general, flexible and dependent on the (inter)subjective meaning which the individual(s) assigns to them. The great advantage of the concept of symbols is, as has been pointed out, in terms of non-rigid social control, precisely their indefinite and flexible nature. (Alternatively reference may be made to signs, indexes or similar terms, see, for example Leach, 1976. It is also possible to refer to the creation of meaning in a general sense.) Nevertheless, action symbols give hints as to the direction of the action.

Like value-transmitting symbols, action-oriented symbols involve a certain focus on attention and the transmission of values, but these qualities are less pronounced than the action implications denoted by the symbol. The content of action-oriented symbols is dominated by a hint of major objectives and of ways in which they can be achieved.

Examples of symbols which have a primarily action-orientation at Enator include customer-perceived quality, the helicopter view and the title of Managing Director. The expression customer-experienced quality indicates, on the one hand, a desirable final outcome – a customer should be satisfied in a broad sense – and, on the other hand, some "strategically" important aspects as to how this state is to be achieved. Action should not solely involve quality in an abstract sense or on the basis of one's own criteria, but instead the focus should be on the customer's perception of quality. To a certain extent, this means that there should be less concentration on doing a good job and more on making the customer feel that a good job has been done – the former then become part of the latter. The helicopter approach has similar qualities for Enator's management and at least for some employees. This metaphor/symbol provides an indication of what (supplementary) perspectives should be employed in carrying out tasks.

The title of managing director has a somewhat different character. The idea of managing directorship expresses, as described in Chapter 6, a more general set of ideas about obligations and rights including responsibility, power, initiative, status and formality which may be seen as expressions for a mixture of social, legal and formal and cultural aspects. Cultural aspects are of special interest in this context. The title of managing director has a general meaning in Swedish society which largely colours the local variant of societal culture which Enator may be said to constitute. However, Enator's special characteristics mean that the managing director of a subsidiary must be understood in a different way than managing directorship in some other context of Swedish business life. The values, attitudes, structural circumstances, etc. which characterize Enator have consequences for the managing director as an organizational symbol.

Managing directorship at Enator denotes expectations as regards action, initiative, responsibility, etc. as far as subsidiary managers are concerned. Managing directorship has different meanings in different corporate contexts, and the difference is particularly clear in internal and external situations. Externally, the formal and leadership aspects are emphasized, but internally these are somewhat toned down.

The action implications of appointing someone as managing director (instead of, for example, having area managers or functional managers at an intermediate level) are considerable, even if there is no precise objective. In particular there is a stress on the importance of having control over matters and of being a dynamic driving force. Amongst other things, this is what is meant when reference is made at Enator to the project manager functioning as "a managing director for the project". This expression clearly indicates that the managing director is regarded as a symbol (cultural category) in contrast with the idea of a managing director as a formal position or a purely social category. It is easy to confuse the two when a symbol is totally "built into" a social/formal category (see Chapter 3 for a discussion of this issue).

I term the last of the five types of symbols which I will discuss the *narrative symbol*. In common with the value-transmitting and action-oriented symbols, the narrative symbol primarily has a clarifying function. The reason why I refer to this category of symbol is because interactions between a company and its environment are crucial for the functioning and "survival" of the company. The "culture" which is encompassed by or which consists of a company (the organization as a local culture) is markedly different from other, perhaps more "natural" (organic) cultures because exchanges with the environment are such a central feature. It is common, per se, that the regulation of relations with the environment and with other cultures (groups) is one aspect of the functioning of all cultural groups (with the exception of those of totally isolated societies), but it is a less crucial aspect of, for example, societal or class cultures (even if these are, of course, far from being closed systems). Companies are special in the sense that the very purpose of the company is to have exchanges with the environment and this means that the regulation of this relationship is of more crucial symbolic and cultural significance than in the case of many other groups. The "cultural traffic"- the transmitting of values ideas and symbols across (often weak) organizational boundaries – is heavy (Alvesson, 1993a). Many knowledge-intensive companies, especially in the service sector, are characterized to a particularly high degree by complex and well developed relationships with groups outside the company (professional communities and/or clients), as a result of the nature of operations.

Various symbolic phenomena – expressions, events, materia – are used as means of communication with the environment. My emphasis, in this context, is on the instrumental aspect. Symbols always communicate. Normally, this communication takes place within a given collective for which the symbols have meaning. The collective is both the transmitter and the receiver, and thus it is a question of "auto-communication" (Broms and Gahmberg, 1983). Leaders and other dominant actors also use symbols for communication with specific target groups, normally people who are part of it the collective or who may be recruited into.

The point of employing the expression "narrative symbol" is rather different. Here, it is more a question of a condensed expression to encompass a complex of perceptions, circumstances and messages which can be transmitted by a symbol. The narrative symbol operates as a signal and an illustration. It indicates a narrative and reveals it. The existence of narrative symbols helps to make it possible for members of a collective to transmit a special message to other people outside the collective. Thus in contrast to the symbols which have been referred to previously, narrative symbols function *between* the collective and some other group (the general public, customers, job applicants, etc.), rather than within the collective.[4]

Narrative symbols have meaning for (the focal) collective involved. The collective's understanding and feelings provide the foundations. However this type of symbol does not primarily increase understanding or summarize a certain attitude present in the collective. This is only a background feature for external communication which dominates the content and function of this type of symbolism. Thus, a certain distance and ability to handle the symbol in instrumental terms is typical, but loyalty and identification with the collective (company) and other emotional aspects are still important in this context. What I am interested in is not pure manipulation of symbols within the framework of a marketing campaign, for example, but rather how ideas, values and ideals are based on broad foundations in a corporate collective and are communicated in symbolic form in various "spontaneous" situation to groups outside the collective.

Typical examples of this at Enator are the business concept and various features of the Enator building. As already mentioned, these phenomena may also be regarded as abstract-affective and value-transmitting symbols does not prevent them from also being regarded as narrative symbols. The various qualities of one and the same symbolic form (for example the Enator building) have different emphasis in different contexts and for different groups. In the Enator building, for example, all passages and other spaces are located so as to avoid right angles (cf. Chapter 7). Various walls and "obstacles" mean that several twists and turns are required if you wish to reach some particular destination. This is not particularly practical. The idea is that it should signal creativity. How much impact this has on the perceptions and functioning of personnel is subject to discussion, but my guess is that creativity – whatever that may be in precise terms – is essentially determined by the capability of personnel and factors such as the nature of tasks, deadlines and other external restrictions. Material messages about creativity have probably little influence on the individual's perceptions and functioning, at least when the person in question has become accustomed to the material structure involved. However, it might be assumed that this material presents certain ideas present amongst Enator personnel and encourages them to transmit the special message illustrated by this material when they meet strangers who come into contact with Enator's architecture and internal decorations for the first time – in the course of visits, by word of mouth or through the mass media. Thus, one important function of the Enator building and its various details is to function as a source of inspiration for communicating and an illustration of the message which management and to some extent other personnel want to transmit. As pointed out in Chapter 7, the material do not function as a pure and unambiguous message, but should instead be seen in terms of organizational symbols which may communicate a special sense via the interpretative patterns available to staff. Thus, if this type of communication is to work in practice, participation on the part of employees is essential. Presumably, this applies particularly in a type of operation of this type in which the content of the product (i.e. the service) is particularly difficult to demonstrate, compared with mass-production service and industrial companies and where the corporate image and the competence of its personnel are almost the only competitive tools (cf. Chapters 7, 12).

Thus, the prerequisites for the operation of narrative symbolism are that it should be supported by the personnel in question as regards attitudes and "commitment" and that the personnel can communicate the message which the symbols encompass, albeit ambiguously. A good narrative symbol is characterized by 1) it arouses the receiver's interest, 2) it encourages a member of the collective to relate to (decipher) it and 3) it is helpful in illustrating and amplifying the message.

14.6   Corporate Dimensions and Types of Symbols

It is now appropriate to relate the types of symbols and the crucial corporate dimensions as previously described in the Chapter to each other. This may be accomplished in the form of a matrix in which the corporate dimension and the type of symbol comprise the two axes. A number of the key symbols at Enator described in this chapter are located in the matrix contained in the Figure 14.3.

It must be emphasized that it is difficult to restrict most symbols to the single type of symbol or to relate them to a single corporate dimension. This means, as I have already implied, that many symbols might be placed in several of the thirty positions contained in the matrix. This is because symbols, by their very nature, are flexible and may fulfil several different functions. They normally also have a combination of various types of content: cognitive, emotional, and pragmatic – even if one of these contents normally proves to be dominant. However, if the emphasis is on the principal content of the symbol and the corporate dimension(s) which it primarily contributes to, it should be possible to locate a number of representative symbols in the matrix. This is the case in Figure 14.3. In a couple of cases I have chosen to associate these symbols with two or more types of symbols or corporate dimensions.

The two dimensions in the matrix are not totally logically independent of each other. On a purely definitional and logical basis, corporate identity and abstract-affective symbols, for example, tend to be interrelated, and this also applies to the two external corporate dimensions (customer relationships and image) and the narrative symbols. In principle, however, the various types of symbols may be relevant for all corporate dimensions and therefore this is more a question of a tendency to overlap between the two dimensions than a matter of absolute, definitional co-relations. For example, narrative symbols (or the narrative functions of symbols) may pave the way for hierarchy and cohesion because they influence initial expectations and the socialization process of new employees. Value-transmitting and action oriented symbols lack definitional or logical links with specific corporate dimensions, even if action oriented symbolism is not clearly linked with identity and image.

Corporate dimension	Symbol type				
	Affective		Clarifying		
	Abstract	Social	Value-transmitting	Action-oriented	Narrative
Identity	Business concept Building		Business concept Building		
Hierarchy			"Flat organization"	Managing Director	
Cohesion	Victoria	Quarterly conference	"Top Manager"		
Principles for work			Business concept "Helicopter view"		
Customer relationships				"Costumer perceived quality"	Business concept
Image					Business concept Building

Figure 14.3:   Matrix describing the relationship between types of symbols and corporate dimensions, illustrating a number of crucial organizational symbols at Enator on the basis of function (corporate dimension) and type of symbol

14.7   Final Comments on the Significance and Symbolism in Management

In conclusion, I would like to repeat and clarify some important aspects of the significance of organizational symbolism for the functioning of the organization.

My choice of a cultural symbolic perspective is not incompatible with the idea that the company's operations in certain regards are best described in substantive and structural terms such as financial objectives, competitive circumstances, customer structure, the labour market situation, computer development, the nature of consultant assignments, etc. (The constructed/enacted nature of these phenomena should, however, be born in mind, cf. Smircich and Stubbart, 1985; Weick, 1979.)

Symbolic aspects are of interest in two different ways; on the one hand in terms of the content associated with different material and structural conditions (e.g. the cultural meanings of budgets, formal structure, etc.), and, on the other hand, as regards the special symbols developed to handle "non-substantive" (cultural, sense-creating) spheres which are undoubtedly an essential aspect of existence in working life and organizations in general and are especially important to consider in order to understand such as Enator. It is clear that "objective" circumstances in an organizational context cannot be comprehended if "intersubjective" aspects (i.e. meaning) are not taken into account. Labour market circumstances, for example, may take highly different forms depending on whether personnel regard their own workplace as an expression for the buy/sell relationship in a utility maximization arena which is called a market or if the workplace is regarded as a social domain, a collective or even a family.

However, this chapter primarily deals with the specific symbols which have been developed at Enator by the management in order to handle the "non-substantive" aspects of activity. (Exceptions are, for example, the symbolic dimension of the managing director's status which might otherwise be regarded as a typical example in the structural category.) Non-substantive aspects encompass expressive-affective dimensions, and also influence and guidance of ideas which are not automatically tightly coupled with or contingent upon concrete and material circumstances.

In operations of this kind, the formal organization can only fulfil to a relatively limited extent central requirements as regards regulation of internal and external relations encompassed by the six corporate dimensions covered above in this chapter. Diffuse borders with the environment, the lack of close, everyday interactions within the organization (Enator) and the complex, organic and heterogeneous nature of operations mean that there is a considerable need for regulation by informal, indirect means. As a result, symbols are of great importance. They are, in themselves, always crucial features of social relations and human existence, but become particularly important for social organization in cases where the formal and material means of regulating boundaries with the environment and internal relationships are weak (Cohen, 1974). This means that the influence of symbols is a decisive feature of corporate management at Enator – and in many other companies where the technical and material circumstances do not determine scope for action to a particularly high degree.

Of course, symbols are not independent of material practice. To some extent, symbols contribute to moulding the latter. However, their greatest significance is as a trigger and expression for ideas and feelings. This is question of a feeling of identity and cohesion, perceptions of what the corporate hierarchy "really" means, how project operations and customer contacts should be regarded and the overall picture of the company which may be appropriately transmitted. Although symbols are closely linked with the world of ideas, their relationship with behaviour is more indirect and weaker. Behaviour at work is also regulated by things other than symbols (as the term is used here).

The collective processes by means of which a group gives a phenomenon a particular meaning is the crucial dimension of symbolism. This cannot be controlled from above! You cannot force symbols down peoples throats. It is possible to oblige people to conform to strict rules involving behaviour restrictions and slogans, but the symbolic outcome means something rather different. Attempts to communicate a particular symbol may result in a completely different meaning being associated with the phenomenon than that intended. Smircich (1983c) provides a good example of this. A manager tried to create unity and cooperation by introducing a wheel symbol into the company. The intended meaning was that employees should "roll along together". But several people in the organization gave the wheel symbol an ironic content – they saw division and confusion in the organization instead of consensus and cooperation. They joked about the wheels going in different directions.

Thus, symbols are difficult to handle from an instrumental point of view. The excellent prerequisites for consensus which characterized Enator at the time of my study as a result of the company's satisfactory position in the past, its recruitment policy and its management style, etc. provide relatively favourable opportunities for management to "sell" special symbols to personnel, for example, to get social gatherings to reinforce and transmit a spirit of affinity within the company and to get personnel to accept verbal symbols such as "the helicopter view", "customer perceived quality", etc. However, employees differ as regards the extent to which they fully accept these symbols (cf. Chapters 7, 13).

The tendencies to divergency which characterize Enator – like other organizations – also exert an influence on organizational symbols. Corporate development can affect organizational symbols in various ways, for example, by weakening their basis or by creating considerable variations within the company in attitudes to symbols. The tenth "Victoria" Anniversary provides an illustration of this. The majority of the employees appear to regard Victoria as an impressive and grand activity which demonstrate what an exciting and generous company they are working for. But there are other attitudes too. One individual who has worked for the company almost since the start regards Victoria as an indication that Enator had developed in the wrong direction:

I think it is a pity when the major, glamorous events get the upper hand and people forget small gestures of mutual appreciation. It's appreciative gestures that really mean something, at any rate as far as I am concerned. I would rather get a pat on the shoulder when I landed an order than being able to travel to Rhodes once a year. I would like that much better. I regard Rhodes as a gimmick while the alternative is an indication of real appreciation.

This quotation illustrates that planned, symbolically loaded activity may be perceived in a way that is quite different from that which was intended. Thus, symbols do not always have a uniform meaning. There is probably greater heterogeneity in attitudes towards symbols than in more stable areas of societies and groups which have a clearer boundary line with their environments. This dimension is neglected by much research into organizational symbols and the degree of consensus, uniformity and clarity which characterizes cultural phenomenon and symbols in organizations is exaggerated (Alvesson, 1993a; Linstead and Grafton-Small, 1992; Martin, 1992; Martin and Meyerson, 1988). Kunda (1992) and Young (1989) are praiseworthy exceptions in terms of studies with empirical depth – describing variation, nuances and ambiguities in relationship to cultural manifestations.

Despite ambiguity and variations in attitudes to symbols and difficulties in fully controlling them, we may nonetheless conclude that various affective and clarifying symbols play an important role in management's method of handling potentially negative effects of structural and substantial circumstances on corporate identity, internal cohesion and the basis for a uniform picture of what the company represents (image). Symbols also contribute to the flexible regulation of contradictions centered on the themes of equality/hierarchy and uniformity/flexibility in the conduct of project operations and the handling of customer relationships. Hence, attempts to emphasize management via symbols constitute a crucial dimension in controlling a company such as Enator.

14.8   Comparison with Other Studies of Knowledge-intensive Companies

I want to briefly relate something of the theme of this book to other literature about knowledge-intensive companies. This has been done in previous chapters, but this is an appropriate point to address the question of the more general relevance of this study in understanding knowledge-intensive companies rather more systematically. It is interesting to note that much of the relevant literature has been published in recent years (early 1990s) and after I completed my empirical study.

The empirical generalizability of average conditions for a certain type of organization or indications of percentages of those within a particular population who share certain characteristics is often of limited interest (Starbuck, 1993). I think this is the case as regards most of the themes on which I have focussed in this book. In fact, case studies do not permit such results, and I do not regard this as a major deficiency. Lack of a basis of strict empirical generalizations does not mean, however, that it is impossible to say something of general theoretical interest. It is then more important to be able to test whether the central dimensions of descriptions in a study, its ideas and concepts, seem to be of relevance and value in understanding at least a number of other objects within the framework of an appropriate overall category, for example, knowledge-intensive companies. The value of a case study is to achieve depth and a certain theoretical and conceptual originality, which means that it is not always possible to make simple comparisons with other research in the same way as when qualitative complexity is reduced by quantification and the researcher operates with abstract variables. However, overall comparisons are normally possible as regards feasibility and the general applicability of results in terms of relevance of ideas, concepts and theories. This means that it is possible to check that a study is not excessively idiosyncratic as regards the nature of the empirical material or the relevance of the interpretations of the study and to ensure that the results of the efforts undertaken have at least a certain broader relevance. In the present case, this is desirable, particularly in the light of my ambition to convey an understanding of knowledge-intensive companies at a more general level. As emphasized in the introduction to this book, I have to some extent deemphasized empirical details in the case study in order to concentrate on a broader argument, analysis and discussion, based on the literature from various fields.

As my study indicates, many other studies of knowledge-intensive companies stress the importance of securing loyalty and commitment. Many authors underline the sensitivity of knowledge-intensive companies to the resignation of key personnel – and in this type of company a large proportion of the personnel are of this nature (Hedberg, 1990; Sveiby and Risling, 1986). Obviously, this problem is accentuated if key personnel also take customers with them, which is mainly an issue in knowledge-intensive service business. As Lindmark (1989) points out, dependence on individuals is largely a question of the possibility of replacing personnel who resign, and this is to some extent a question of how much specific knowledge and how many well-developed contacts they have. Certain well-educated employees possess knowledge and know-how of a general nature and are therefore, in principle, easy to replace, given a not too tight labour market. This applies to most doctors, for example, and to school and university teachers – professional groups which dominate professional bureaucracies. But in many knowledge-intensive companies, key personnel apart from their long period of training, also possess knowledge based on special experience such as knowledge of major customers and the confidence that they inspire with customers, and this makes them hard to replace. Hence, dependence on this category of personnel makes it particularly important to secure loyalty and involvement.

One of the most crucial management tasks at Enator involves creating a climate which means that the company can attract and retain qualified personnel. Financial arrangements such as partnership or shareholding in order to tie in key or even major groups of employees to the company is not uncommon in knowledge-intensive companies, especially professional organizations such as law and accounting firms. Pay scales and other reward systems which are regarded as fair in the long-term may be another method of securing long-term exchange relations (Wilkins and Ouchi, 1983). At Enator, there is less emphasis on this type of relationship because the company has invested heavily in social relationships and activities. Without wishing to go into details of the exact prevalence of variations of combinations of methods of tying in personnel by normative or financial means, there is clear evidence that Enator is not unique. It appears that in many knowledge-intensive companies there are attempts to create environments and attitudes which result in the development of socio-emotional ties amongst employees with each other and to the company (Kanter, 1983). Such workplace environments and ties counteract an interest in more narrow instrumental rewards such as salaries and, to some extent promotion (Alvesson and Lindkvist, 1993). Kunda (1992) and Van Maanen and Kunda (1989) also consider that many employees were characterized by strong emotional ties to their company. However, the variations in attitudes towards the company which I have indicated amongst Enator personnel are more explicit in Kunda's study. Ambivalence and cynicism are more characteristic of Kunda's interviewees than Enator's. These characteristics would appear to be increasing somewhat at Enator, as time passes.

Kunda and Barley (1988) maintain that, in general terms, professional and semi-professional groups may find it more difficult to accept institutional authorities, that the importance of work as a crucial interest in their lives has also declined for this group in recent decades, and that this has contributed to the fact that high involvement in work in this key group can no longer be taken for granted. Instead, corporate managements must take a particular interest in this group of employees. Kunda and Barley consider that this factor has greatly contributed to the popularity of the concept of organizational culture as a hub around which a number of management activities revolve. The idea has thus become, precisely as at Enator, that "top management not only formulates appropriate value systems but somehow 'instils' them in the hearts and minds of those subject to their authority. Management's aim is to eliminate unwanted thoughts and feelings while replacing them with cognitive and emotional orientations that benefit the organization" (p 19). Thus, corporate culture represents the idea of a combination of commitment and rationality.

Weick (1987) also claims that an interest in organizational culture is a response to the need to control a certain type of organization, that is to say organic organizations – companies with strong adhocratic features. Although corporate managers may have good reasons for being interested in cultural patterns in various types of organizations, such patterns are of special importance in companies which can only be controlled to a limited extent via bureaucracy or the authority of a strong leader .

In a study of a major American high technology company, Van Maanen and Kunda (1989) emphasize that for many employees "'culture' replaces 'structure' as an organizing principle and is used both to explain and guide action" (p 72). They consider that the formal organization is not, per se, particularly important. Kunda (1992) maintains, however, that certain elements of bureaucratic control remain in place, even when normative control is predominant. Desirable behaviour is primarily achieved as a result of normative regulations which focus on the individual's experiences and ideas rather on a direct focus on control of behaviour. In this company, which is many times larger than Enator, cultural control is supplemented by bureaucratic and utilitarian control. This is also the case at Enator, although clearly to a lesser extent. In both companies, management rhetoric strongly emphasizes cultural themes, while the existence of bureaucratic control is deemphasized.

Starbuck (1992) also concludes that the formal organization is not particularly dominant in the two knowledge-intensive companies which he studied. Managers exercise control in a non-directive manner and contacts are developed across various formal boundaries. Starbuck also considers that the hierarchy is relatively weak. Similarly Martin and Meyerson (1988) indicate that equality is an important – if not an uncontroversial – aspect of a major high technology company which they studied (see also Martin, 1992). Kanter (1983) reports similar observations. Although Enator is probably unusual as regards the extent to which informalization has been taken and the emphasis on hierarchical relationships – which is partly the result of the fact that Enator is a young, comparitively small Swedish company – this tendency may be also be seen in many other knowledge-intensive companies.

Obviously, communication is always a crucial factor in an organizational context (Deetz, 1992), but communication acquires special importance in companies in which varying circumstances and work in project groups mean that mutual adjustment becomes a decisive coordinative mechanism. Hedberg (1990) emphasizes that "knowledge-intensive firms are to a considerable extent led through ideas and managed by words. Visions, business ideas, symbolism, meaning, speeches, words, and small talk are important building blocks of knowledge-intensive companies" (p 4). Kunda (1992) also reports massive attempts in the company he studied to communicate the right ideals and values – strongly reminiscent of the virtues expressed by Enator management (as in many other companies of this type). A well developed rhetoric, supported by narrative symbolism, is also considered to be crucial in regulating the expectations and perceptions of the environment about the company and its activities. This applies, in particular, to knowledge-intensive service companies. Thus, rhetoric is important for many such company's, both internally and externally (Alvesson, 1993c).

One of the few deviant views which I have encountered, and which runs counter to a few of the findings of my study may be seen in Starbuck's (1992) observation, based on two cases, that knowledge-intensive companies find it difficult to establish and maintain distinct cultures. A third company, a law firm, later studied by Starbuck (1993), was, however, characterized by shared values and ideas. Starbuck considers that the same circumstances which make hierarchical control a problem – autonomy, mobility, professionalization and uncertain revenues – also exercise negative effects on organizational integration and socialization. I have, in fact, also indicated some uncertainty about a specific corporate culture and indicated the relative superficiality and "fragility" which characterize the cultural patterns which denote Enator (Chapter 7). But, at the same time, I would also like to maintain that cultural control – that is to say a management focus on perceptions, values and feelings, and systematic efforts to produce a strong feeling of organization-based community – is a prominent aspect of the company's way of working. It is interesting to note that Starbuck's two examples (Rand Corporation and Arthur D Little) are considerably older than mine, and are also older than most of the examples referred to. Since other examples (e.g. Kanter, 1983; Kunda, 1992; Martin, 1992; Starbuck, 1993) indicate clear similarities with the Enator case as regards the importance – as well as the relative success – of cultural control, the question of historical development may perhaps be raised. Normally, it might be expected that increasing age would imply more distinct cultural patterns within a company (or a section of the company). Perhaps the difference between Starbuck's findings and observations in other literature (including this study) reflects the fact that the professions concerned are more crucial from a cultural point of view in Starbuck's two cases. Possibly, the management style and, underlying this, general circumstances in society in the last decade have changed significantly so that younger and more "modern" companies within the category concerned now indicate a higher degree of cultural homogeneity of the "corporate culture" type.

This point underlines what I maintained in the introductory chapter, namely that the study of knowledge-intensive companies is mainly confined to the study of relatively young companies in a particular epoch in society. In the course of this epoch, corporate culture has also constituted a popular form for management and organization (Barley and Kunda, 1992). It is thus difficult to draw historical conclusions about this type of company. Such companies cannot be understood if historical factors which are connected with positive external conditions, a given labour market situation, management ideas which are fashionable at a given period etc. are not taken into account. But this is the classic dilemma of social scientists. We are studying "moving targets" and it is difficult to arrive at generalizations which resemble natural laws. We should thus be cautious in making sweeping generalizations – they tend to be superficial and abstract and run counter to sensitivity to the context, variation and change. It is more important to arrive at concepts and ideas which may offer understanding at a broader level, but where users of such knowledge themselves decide when and the extent to which the research results provide assistance in understanding phenomena which are of interest (Chapter 4), rather than to achieve strictly empirically based generalizations for a certain category. Thus, going beyond the narrow framework of an empirical case study should take place at the theoretical-conceptual level rather than in empirical terms.

Despite this reservation regarding the possibility and the need for empirical generalizations, I would nonetheless maintain that much of what has emerged in this book should apply to many other knowledge-intensive companies, apart from Enator. Several different case studies and more general comments and reflections also indicate, like my study, the importance of shared values and perceptions, of attempts to deemphasize hierarchies and formal/structural control, of establishing loyalty and commitment with the help of non-instrumental, social and emotional means and of the significance of control via symbols. Thus, what I have termed social-integrative management appears to have a broader relevance in analyzing knowledge-intensive companies. At the same time, it should be noted that the basis for more far-reaching comparisons is somewhat limited. The relatively limited number of case studies of knowledge-intensive companies are primarily concerned with high technology firms and/or have sometimes an orientation which differs from that applied in my study.

Obviously, at a more general level the control of social processes by symbolic means is important for all organizations, even though many of the aspects which I have discussed to do not tell us much about companies which mass produce services or products, for example. Without claiming that this book offers the whole truth about what characterizes all types of knowledge-intensive companies and while recognizing that major aspects – for example the financial side – have not been discussed, my case may nonetheless contribute to an understanding of significant areas of this group of organization. As regards more specific contributions concerning central contradictions in the functioning of the company, especially critical themes (identity, image, hierarchy, etc.), the role of the business concept, and typology of symbols, etc., there is no strong basis for comparison, due to the absence of other studies which examine these questions closely. Deetz (1994), however, as mentioned in Chapter 10, identifies similar aspects of the role of the business concept in a US consultancy organization (despite strong differences in terms of size, history, market situation, etc.). On the whole, I am obliged to rely on the credibility of the interpretations and analysis presented. Since the more comprehensive factors which I have stressed in the case-study company are also referred to in other literature, this suggests that more specific, theoretical and conceptual contributions, partly derived from comparisons with other studies, also have a general theoretical value. Their interpretation potential clearly extends beyond the case and may be considered to be relevant for understanding relatively large areas of contemporary knowledge-intensive companies and similar organizations.

14.9   Conclusions

This relatively long text will soon be coming to a close. Before concluding, however, I would like to say a little about the possible contributions which this book may make to extending our fund of knowledge. Such contributions are normally divided into practical and theoretical aspects. Such a classification may be questioned from two points of view, however. The question of whether social science research can provide a clear practical contribution in a strict sense is open to discussion. By definition, research results tend to be unlikely to result in conclusions which can be directly put into practice. This classification – and the mental configuration which assumes a contradiction between what is practical and what is theoretical – is also problematical in that it implies that the "practical world" operates independently of theory. This is hardly the case in an organizational or corporate management context. To a greater or a lesser extent, everyday life is permeated by more or less well-considered and verbalized theories. Social science theory normally encompasses implications for the understanding of and action in various social situations and vis-à-vis various social phenomena.

Naturally, the present study is no exception and I would imagine, somewhat presumptuously, that the average reader of this book has been able to find items which are relevant to his or her own social action, based on the documentation of practice at Enator, the review of various concepts, theories and research results, my own ideas, analysis, synthesis, and theoretical contributions, etc.

However, the theoretical contributions which it is hoped this book has made are of greater interest than the direct implications for action. I will briefly indicate some possible contributions to knowledge of this nature. One such contribution is, of course, the portrait of Enator. In my opinion, empirical description and interpretation of the company's operation is both of interest per se, as a (unique but revealing) example of a broader social category (knowledge-intensive companies, new and innovative management methods, etc.), and is also useful as a starting point to theoretically analyzing such broader social categories. This latter point means that unique empirical aspects are deemphasized, while characteristics are stressed in the specific case which are of more general interest. In this book, I have decided, for the most part, to limit purely empirical description of the case study and have instead focused on broader, more general themes. A number of theoretical problems and discussions in the literature have been given prominent status and have sometimes been given priority over the case study itself. The underlying idea has been to provide a research contribution which may assist in understanding a certain type of company/organization.

Adhocracy as an organizational form has been given special place in this book. The ambition has been to analyse the workings of this organizational type, primarily as regards (the cultural dimensions of) organizational structure and strategical processes. Particular attention has also been paid to the problem of divergency and the crucial importance of organizational symbols in counteracting disintegration tendencies and the precariousness of corporate identity in the organization, which is organic and instable from a structural point of view. Adhocracy is frequently, but not necessarily, the organizational form which applies in knowledge-intensive companies. Thus, the overlap between adhocracy/the knowledge-intensive company is quite considerable. This book has attempted, however, to contribute to an understanding of (service producing) knowledge-intensive companies, apart from the outcome of an analysis of adhocracy. General management, leadership, and marketing have been important themes in this context.

Some of the attempts to provide contributions made in this book can be seen in the point of intersection between what characterizes a certain type of company/organization and what is of more generally applicable, theoretical interest. This includes, for example, analysis of the relationship between the central "non-substantive" ("intangible") corporate dimensions (corporate identity, social cohesion, image, etc.) and organizational sym-

14   Corporate Control via Symbols

bolism. Another example is the relationship between fundamental forms of organized exchanges (formal hierarchy, the market, the circle, the clan). And this also applies to the supplements and contradictions to the total control of the company implied by various forms of exchanges. These aspects of operations are probably particularly crucial in understanding Enator and other companies which are loosely coupled from a structural point of view, which lack a physical product and where the social content is strong (in contrast to the technical and material content). However, in addition, these aspects may be of considerable relevance to an ability to understand other types of companies, as machine-like manufacturing tends to decrease in significance and organic and service qualities are more salient in an increasing number of organizations.

This book contains two relatively theoretically-oriented contributions which overlap each other to some extent. The first contribution is a question of the critical examination of the existing literature in a number of different areas. I have attempted to discuss a number of prominent ideas about, for example, adhocracy, corporate culture and the marketing of services in a critically-constructive spirit. Secondly, my ambition has been to make a contribution to the usefulness of cultural and symbolic theory in organizational and management research. Some effort has been devoted to studying the opportunities, problems and the obstacles to the use of this overall approach. In particular, I have tried to explore the value of interpreting a number of corporate phenomena as symbols, with the objective of discovering deeper meanings and cultural patterns. This applies for example to the business concept, to which I have tried to problematize conventional understanding thereby indicating a number of different meanings. This has been achieved by regarding the business concept as a crucial organizational symbol.

Obviously, the contributions made by the study must to be ultimately determined by the reader. Thus, these final conclusions should be interpreted as a challenge to the reader to make his/her own assessment as to the extent that my aspirations and ambitions in writing this book have been achieved.

Notes

[1] Another approach to identity is a narrative one, in which identity exists in the "texts" (oral or written) expressing a particular quality of the organization or other relevant subject matter (Czarniawska-Joerges, 1994).

[2] Here I am referring to a positive evaluation of ideas about the company's specific qualities. A company may, of course, "have" a distinct identity (being seen as unique, coherent, stable) which is negatively valued.

When I talk about corporate identity I am not doing this in a reified manner. Identity does not refer to "objective" traits but to how the majority of the personnel understand and relate to the company.

[3]   Many authors emphasize that all human phenomena, including bureaucratic rules, are "symbolic" in the sense that they must be put into a cultural framework in order to be understood (Sköldberg, 1990, Tompkins, 1987). I agree with this insight, but use the concept of symbolism in a more narrow, analytic sense (cf. Chapter 3). It might also be said that when I refer to symbols, I am only concerned with those forms of symbolism which clearly refer to a broader and richer meaning than the objects (action, work, materia) represent, per se. Symbols thus have a complex, ambiguous meaning, not a simple, straightforward one.

[4]   Obviously, some sort of overall common cultural understanding is required if inter-group communication is to be possible. Narrative symbolism assumes and develops local versions of general shared meanings between groups.

References

Abell, D (1980) *Defining the Business: The Starting Point of Strategic Planning.* Englewood Cliffs, NJ: Prentice-Hall.

Abrahamsson, B (1986) *Varför finns organisationer?* Stockholm: Norstedts.

Abravanel, H (1983) Mediatory Myths in the Service of Organizational Ideology, in L Pondy, P Frost, G Morgan and T Dandridge (eds.) *Organizational Symbolism.* Greenwich, CT: JAI Press.

Aldrich, H (1986) *Population Perspectives on Organizations.* Uppsala: Acta Universitatis Upsaliensis.

Allaire, Y and Firsirotu, M (1984a) Theories of Organizational Culture, *Organization Studies,* 5, 193-226.

Allaire, Y and Firsirotu, M (1984b) A Multi-Factor Model of Organizational Culture: Theoretical and Methodological Considerations, Paper, Dept. of Administrative Sciences, University of Quebec at Montreal.

Albert, S and Whetten, D A (1985) Organizational Identity, in B M Staw and L L Cummings (eds.) *Research in Organizational Behaviour, Vol. 7.* Greenwich: JAI Press.

Alvesson, M (1987) *Organization Theory and Technocratic Consciousness.* Berlin/New York: de Gruyter.

Alvesson, M (1990) Organizations: From Substance to Image? *Organization Studies,* 11, 273-294.

Alvesson, M (1991) Budgeten som diskussionstema, Research Report R 1991:6, Dept. of Business Administration, Stockholm University.

Alvesson, M (1993a) *Cultural Perspectives on Organizations.* Cambridge: Cambridge University Press.

Alvesson, M (1993b) The Play of Metaphors, in J Hassard and M Parker (eds.) *Postmodernism and Organizations.* London: Sage.

Alvesson, M (1993c) Organization as Rhetoric. Knowledge-intensive Companies and the Struggle with Ambiguity. *Journal of Management Studies,* 30, 6, 997-1015.

Alvesson, M (1993d) Corporate Culture, Participation and Pseudo-Participation in a Professional Service Company, in W Lafferty and E Rosenstein (eds.) *International Handbook of Participation in Organizations, Vol. 3.* Oxford: Oxford University Press.

Alvesson, M and Berg, P O (1992) *Corporate Culture and Organizational Symbolism.* Berlin/New York: de Gruyter.

Alvesson, M and Lindkvist, L (1993) Transaction Costs, Clans and Corporate Culture. *Journal of Management Studies,* 30, 3, 427-452.

Alvesson, M and Sandkull, B (1988) The Organizational Melting-Pot: An Arena of Different Cultures, *Scandinavian Journal of Management,* 4, 135-145.

Alvesson, M and Sköldberg, K (1995) *Interpretation and Reflexivity.* London: Sage. (Forthcoming)

Alvesson, M and Willmott, H (eds.) (1992) *Critical Management Studies.* London: Sage.

Alvesson, M and Willmott, H (1995) *Making Sense of Management. A Critical Analysis.* London: Sage.

Andriessen, E and Drenth, P (1984) Leadership: Theories and Models, in P Drenth, H Thierry, P Willems and C de Wolff (eds.) *Handbook of Work and Organizational Psychology, Vol 1.* Chichester: Wiley.

Ansoff, I (1978) *Strategic Management.* London: Macmillan.

Ansoff, I (1987) The Emerging Paradigm of Strategic Behavior. *Strategic Management Journal,* 8, 501-515.

Arbnor, I, Borglund, S-E and Liljedahl, T (1980) *Osynligt ockuperad.* Malmö: Liber.

Argyris, C (1964) *Integrating the Individual and the Organisationen.* New York: Wiley.

Ashforth, B (1985) Climate Formation: Issues and Extensions. *Academy of Management Review,* 10, 837-847.

Ashforth, B and Mael, F (1989) Social Identity Theory and the Organization. *Academy of Management Review,* 14, 20-39.

Asplund, J (1970) *Om undran inför samhället.* Lund: Argos.

Asplund, J (1979) *Teorier om framtiden.* Malmö: Liber.

Bagchus, P M and van Dooren, F (1984) The Management of Organizations, in P Drenth, H Thierry, P Willems and C de Wolff (eds.) *Handbook of Work and Organizational Psychology, Vol. 2.* Chichester: Wiley.

Barley, S and Kunda, G (1992) Design and Devotion: Surges of Rational and Normative Ideologies of Control in Managerial Discourse. *Administrative Science Quarterly,* 37, 363-399.

Barney, J (1986) Organizational Culture: Can it Be a Source of Sustained Competitive Advantage? *Academy of Management Review,* 11, 656-665.

Beckérus, Å et al. (1988) *Doktrinskiftet. Nya ideal i svenskt ledarskap.* Stockholm: Svenska Dagbladet.

Bennis, W (1966) The Coming Death of Bureaucracy. *Think,* Nov.-Dec., 30-35.

Benson, J K (1977) Organization: A Dialectical View. *Administrative Science Quarterly,* 22, 1-21.

Berg, P O (1985a) Organization Change as a Symbolic Transformation Process, in P Frost, L Moore, M R Louis, C Lundberg and J Martin (eds.) *Organizational Culture*. Beverly Hills: Sage.

Berg, P O (1985b) Techno-Culture. The Symbolic Framing of Technology in a Volvo Plant. *Scandinavian Journal of Management Studies*, 1, 237-256.

Berg, P O (1986) Symbolic Management of Human Resources. *Human Resource Management*, 25, 557-579.

Berg, P O and Gagliardi, P (1985) Corporate Images: A Symbolic Perspective of the Organization-Environment Interface. Paper presented at the SCOS Conference on Corporate Images, Antibes, June.

Berg, P O and Kreiner, K (1990) Corporate Architecture. Turning Physical Settings into Symbolic Resources, in P Gagliardi (ed.) *Symbols and Artifacts: Views of the Corporate Landscape*. Berlin/New York: de Gruyter.

Berger, P and Luckmann, T (1966) *The Social Construction of Reality: A Treatise on the Sociology of Knowledge*. New York: Doubleday.

Bernstein, R (1983) *Beyond Objectivism and Relativism*. Oxford: Basil Blackwell.

Berry, L (1981) The Employee as Customer. *Journal of Retail Banking*, 1981.

Biggart, N W and Hamilton, G G (1987) An Institutional Theory of Leadership. *Journal of Applied Behavioural Science*, 23, 429-441.

Blackler, F (1993) Knowledge and the Theory of Organizations: Organizations as Activity Systems and the Reframing of Management, *Journal of Management Studies*, 30, 6, 863-884.

Blackler, F (1994) Knowledge, Knowledge Work and Organizations, Working paper, Dept. of Behaviour in Organizations, Lancaster University.

Bonora, E and Revang, Ø (1993) A Framework for Analysing the Storage and Protection of Knowledge in Organizations, in P Lorange, B Chakravarthy, J Roos and A Van de Ven (eds.) *Implementing Strategic Processes*. Oxford: Blackwell.

Bourgeois, L and Brodwin, D (1984) Strategic Implementation: Five Approaches to an Elusive Phenomenon, *Strategic Management Journal*, 5, 141-164.

Bourgeois, W and Pinder, C (1983) Contrasting Philosophical Perspectives in Administrative Science: A Reply to Morgan. *Administrative Science Quarterly*, 28, 608-613.

Bowen, D and Jones, C (1986) Transaction Cost Analysis of Service Organization-Customer Exchange. *Academy of Management Review*, 11, 428-441.

Broady, D (1981) *Den dolda läroplanen*. Järfälla: Symposion.

Broms, H and Gahmberg, H (1983) Communication to Self in Organizations and Cultures. *Administrative Science Quarterly*, 28, 482-495.

Broms, H and Gahmberg, H (1987) *Semiotics of Management.* Helsinki: Helsinki School of Economics.

Brown, R H (1976) Social Theory as Metaphor. *Theory and Society*, 3, 169-197.

Brown, R H (1978) Bureaucracy as Praxis: Toward a Political Phenomenology of Formal Organizations, *Administrative Science Quarterly*, 23, 365-382.

Brulin, G (1987) Motsägelsefull ledning och styrning, in Å Sandberg (ed.) *Ledning för alla?* Stockholm: Center for Working Life.

Brunsson, N (1982) Företagsekonomi – avbildning eller språkbildning?, in N Brunsson (ed.) *Företagsekonomi – sanning eller moral?* Lund: Studentlitteratur.

Brunsson, N (1985) *The Irrational Organization.* London: Wiley.

Bryman, A (1995) Leadership in Organizations, in S Clegg, C Hardy and W Nord (eds.) *Handbook of Organization Studies.* London: Sage.

Burawoy, M (1979) *Manufacturing Consent. Changes in the Labor Process Under Monopoly Capitalism.* Chicago: The University of Chicago Press.

Burrell, G (1992) The Organization of Pleasure, in M Alvesson and H Willmott (eds.) *Critical Management Studies.* London: Sage.

Burrell, G and Morgan, G (1979) *Sociological Paradigms and Organizational Analysis.* London: Heinemann.

Calás, M and Smircich, L (1987) Is the Organization Culture Literature Dominant but Dead? Paper presented at the SCOS International Conference on the Symbolics of Corporate Artifacts, Milan, June.

Chaffee, E (1985) Three Models of Strategy, *Academy of Management Review*, 10, 89-98.

Clifford, J (1986) Introduction: Partial Truths, in J Clifford and G Marcus (eds.) *Writing Culture. The Poetics and Politics of Ethnography.* Los Angeles: University of California Press.

Cohen, A (1974) *Two-Dimensional Man. An Essay on the Anthropology of Power and Symbolism in Complex Society.* London: Routledge and Kegan Paul.

Czarniawska-Joerges, B (1992) *Exploring Complex Organizations.* Newbury Park: Sage.

Czarniawska-Joerges, B (1994) Narratives of Individual and Organizational Identities, in S Deetz (ed.) *Communication Yearbook, Vol. 17*, Thousand Oaks, Ca: Sage.

Daft, R (1983) Symbols in Organizations: A Dual-Content Framework of Analysis, in L Pondy, P Frost, G Morgan and T Dandridge (eds.) *Organizational Symbolism.* Greenwich, CT: JAI Press.

Dandridge, T, Mitroff, I and Joyce, W (1980) Organizational Symbolism: A Topic to Expand Organizational Analysis, *Academy of Management Review*, 5, 77-82.

Davis, S and Lawrence, P (1978) Problems of Matrix Organizations, *Harvard Business Review*, May-June, 131-142.

Deal, T and Kennedy, A (1982) *Corporate Cultures*. Reading: Addison-Wesley.

Deetz, S (1985) Ethical Considerations in Cultural Research in Organizations, in P J Frost, L Moore, M R Louis, C Lundberg and J Martin (eds.), *Organizational Culture*. Newbury Park: Sage.

Deetz, S (1992) *Democracy in an Age of Corporate Colonization: Developments in Communication and the Politics of Everyday Life*. Albany: State University of New York Press.

Deetz, S (1994) Mission, Vision and Control in a Knowledge-Intensive Company. Working paper, Dept of Communication, Rutgers University.

Dervin, B (1990) Illusions of Equality, Reification of Inequality: Problems in Leadership Research. Paper presented at International Communication Association, Dublin, June.

Donaldson, L (1985) *In Defence of Organization Theory. A Reply to Critics*. Cambridge: Cambridge University Press.

Duncan, H (1968) *Symbol and Society*. New York: Oxford University Press.

Edström, A, Norbäck, L-E and Rendahl, J-E (1989) *Förnyelsens ledarskap*. Stockholm: Norstedts.

Ehn, B and Löfgren, O (1982) *Kulturanalys*. Lund: Liber.

Ekstedt, E (1990) Knowledge Renewal and Knowledge Companies, in L Lindmark (ed.) *Kunskap som kritisk resurs*. Umeå: Umeå University.

Ekvall, A (1989) *Affärsidébegreppets innehåll och funktion*, Diss., Dept of Business Administration, Stockholm University.

Ekvall, G (1985) Organisationsklimat. Teori och forskning. *Psykologi i tillämpning*. Lunds Universitet, 3, 1.

Ekvall, G (1986) Företagskultur och organisationsklimat – två skilda begrepp, *Psykolog Tidningen*, 21.

Enis, B and Roering, K (1981) Service Marketing: Different Products, Similar Strategy, in J Donnelly and W George (eds.) *Marketing of Services*. Chicago: American Marketing Association.

Eriksson, A (1986) *Service Kultur Förändring: Ny organisationslära i facklig belysning*. Stockholm: TCO.

Feldman, M and March, J (1981) Information in Organizations as Signal and Symbol, *Administrative Science Quarterly*, 26, 171-186.

Fitzgerald, G (1988) Can Change in Organizational Culture Really be Managed?, *Organizational Dynamics,* 16, 4, 5-15.

Flipo, J-P (1986) Service Firms: Interdependence of External and Internal Marketing Strategies, *European Journal of Marketing*, 20, 8.

Fombrun, C (1986) Structural Dynamics between and within Organizations, *Administrative Science Quarterly*, 31, 403-421.

Frost, P J (1987) Power, Politics, and Influence, in F Jablin, L Putnam, K Roberts and L Porter (eds.). *Handbook of Organizational Communication*. Newbury Park: Sage.

Frost, P J, L Moore, M R Louis, C Lundberg and J Martin (eds.) (1991) *Reframing Organizational Culture*. Newbury Parks: Sage.

Geertz, C (1973) *The Interpretation of Cultures*. New York: Basic Books.

Geijerstam, E and Reitberger, G (1986) *Nya företag! Nytt fack?* Stockholm: Centre for Working Life.

Giddens, A (1979) *Central Problems in Social Theory*. London: Macmillan.

Giddens, A (1982) *Profiles and Critiques in Social Theory*. London: Macmillan.

Gioia, D and Pitre, E (1990) Multiparadigm Perspectives on Theory Building. *Academy of Management Review*, 15, 584-602.

Glaser, B and Strauss, A (1967) *The Discovery of Grounded Theory: Strategies for Qualitative Research*. Chicago: Aldine.

Goffman, E (1960) *Asylums*. New York: Doubleday.

Gray, B, Bougon, M and Donnellon, A (1985) Organizations as Constructions and Deconstructions of Meaning, *Journal of Management*, 11, 2, 83-98.

Greiner, L (1972) Evolution and Revolutions as Organizations Grow, *Harvard Business Review*, July-August, 37-46.

Greiner, L (1983) Senior Executives as Strategic Actors, *New Management*, 1, 2, 11-15.

Grönroos, C (1983) Intern marknadsföring, in J Arndt and A Friman (eds.) *Intern marknadsföring*. Malmö: Liber.

Grönroos, C (1984) *Strategic Management and Marketing in the Service Sector*. Lund: Studentlitteratur.

Grönroos, C (1990) Relationship Approach to Marketing in Service Contexts: The Marketing and Organizational Behavior Interface, *Journal of Business Research*, 20, 3-11.

Guba, E and Lincoln, Y (1994) Competing Paradigms in Qualitative Research, in N Denzin and Y Lincoln (eds.) *Handbook of Qualitative Research*. Thousand Oaks: Sage.

Gummesson, E (1979) The Marketing of Professional Service – An Organizational Dilemma, *European Journal of Marketing*, 13, 5.

Gummesson, E (1990) *Yuppiesnusk eller ledarskapets förnyelse?* Stockholm: SNS.

Gummesson, E (1991) Marketing-Orientation Revisited: The Crucial Role of the Part-Time Marketer, *European Journal of Marketing*, 25, 2, 60-75.

Gummesson, E (1994) Service Management: An Evaluation and the Future, *The International Journal of Service Industry Management*, 5, 1.

Hackman, R, Oldham, G, Janson, R and K Purdy (1975) A New Strategy for Job Enrichment, in B Staw (ed.) *Psychological Foundations of Organizational Behavior*. Santa Monica: Goodyear.

Håkansson, H and Johansson, J (1982) *Analys av industriella affärsförbindelser*. Stockholm: Marknadstekniskt Centrum, MTC-skrift nr 18.

Håkansson, H, Johansson, J and Wootz, B (1977) Influence Tactics in Buyer-Seller Processes. *Industrial Marketing Management*, 5.

Håkansson, H and Snehota, I (1989) No Business is an Island: The Network Concept of Business Strategy. *Scandinavian Journal of Management* 5, 187-200.

Håkansson, H and Östberg, C (1975) Industrial Marketing: An Organizational Problem?, *Industrial Marketing Management*, 4, 2/3, 113-123.

Håkansson, H, Johansson, J and Wootz, B (1981) Påverkanstaktik i köp- och säljprocessen, in J Arndt, C Grönroos and L-G Mattsson (eds.) *Marknadsföring. Nordiska perspektiv*. Lund: Studentlitteratur.

Hallén, L and Wiedersheim-Paul, F (1979) Psychic Distance and Buyer-Seller Interaction, in L Engwall (ed.) *Uppsala Contributions to Business Research*. Uppsala: Acta Universitatis Upsaliensis 1984.

Hannerz, U, Liljeström, R and Löfgren, O (1982) *Kultur och medvetande*. Stockholm: Akademiförlaget.

Harris, B (1981) Strategies for Marketing Professional Services: Current Status and Research Directions, in J Donnelly and W George (eds.) *Marketing of Services*. Chicago: American Marketing Association.

Hatch, M (1993) The Dynamics of Organizational Culture. *Academy of Management Review*. 18, 4, 657-693.

Hedberg, B (1990) Exit, Voice, and Loyalty in Knowledge-Intensive Firms. Paper presented at the 10th Annual International Conference of the Strategic Management Society, Stockholm, September.

Hedberg, B and Jönsson, S (1977) Strategy Formulation as a Discontinuous Process, *International Studies of Management & Organization*, 7, 2, 88-100.

Hinings, C R, Brown, J and Greenwood, R (1991) Change in an Autonomous Professional Organization, *Journal of Management Studies*, 28, 375-389.

Hofstede, G (1980) Motivation, Leadership, and Organization: Do American Theories Apply Abroad?, *Organizational Dynamics*, Summer, 42-63.

Hofstede, G, Jeuijen, B, Ohavy, D and Sanders, G (1990) Measuring Organizational Cultures: A Qualitative and Quantitative Study across Twenty Cases, *Administrative Science Quarterly*, 35, 286-316.

House, R (1977) A 1976 Theory of Charismatic Leadership, in J Hunt and L Larsson (eds.) *Leadership. The Cutting Edge*. Carbondale: Illinois University Press.

Israel, J (1979) *Om relationistisk socialpsykologi*. Gothenburg: Korpen.

Jackson, N and Willmott, H (1987) Beyond Epistemology and Reflective Conversation: Towards Human Relations, *Human Relations*, 40, 6, 361-380.

Jeffcutt, P (1985) Organisation Discourse, *CEBES Journal*, 1, 2, 34-44.

Jeffcutt, P (1993) From Interpretation to Representation, in J Hassard and M Parker (eds.) *Postmodernism and Organizations*. London: Sage.

Jelinik, M, Smircich, L and Hirsch, P (1983) Introduction: A Code of Many Colors, *Administrative Science Quarterly*, 28, 331-338.

Johansson, J and Vahlne, J-E (1977) Företagets internationaliseringsprocess. En modell av kunskapsutveckling och ökande engagemang på utländska marknader, in J Arndt, C Grönroos and L-G Mattsson (eds.) *Marknadsföring. Nordiska perspektiv*. Lund: Studentlitteratur 1981.

Johansson, O L (1990) *Organisationsbegrepp och begreppsmedvetenhet*. Gothenburg: BAS.

Johnsen, E (1985) *Ledningsprocessen*. Lund: Studentlitteratur.

Johnson, G (1987) Rethinking Incrementalism, Paper, Manchester Business School.

Jönsson, S and Lundin, R (1977) Myths and Wishful Thinking as Management Tools, in P Nyström and W Starbuck (eds.) *Prescriptive Models of Organizations*. Amsterdam: North Holland.

Kanter, R M (1977) *Men and Women of the Corporation*. New York: Basic Books.

Kanter, R M (1983) *The Change Masters*. London: Unwin.

Keesing, R (1974) Theories of Culture, *Annual Review of Anthropology*, 3, 73-97.

Kets de Vries, M (1980) *Organizational Paradoxes*. London: Tavistock.

Kilmann, R, Saxton, M, Serpa, R et. al. (1985) *Gaining Control of the Corporate Culture*. San Francisco: Jossey-Bass.

Knight, K (1976) Matrix Organization: A Review, *Journal of Management Studies*, 13, 111-130.

Knights, D and Morgan, G (1991) Corporate Strategy, Organizations, and Subjectivity: A Critique. *Organization Studies*, 12, 251-273.

Knights, D and Willmott, H (1992) Conceptualizing Leadership Processes: A Study of Senior Managers in a Financial Services Company, *Journal of Management Studies*. 29, 761-782.

Knights, D, Murray, F and Willmott, H (1993) Networking as Knowledge Work: A Study of Strategic Interorganizational Development in the Financial Services Industry, *Journal of Management Studies*, 30, 6, 975-995.

Kohn, M (1980) Job Complexity and Adult Personality, in N Smelser and E H Erikson (eds.) *Themes of Work and Love in Adulthood*. Cambridge, MA: Harvard University Press.

Kotler, P (1976) *Marketing Management. Analysis, Planning and Control*. Englewood Cliffs: Prentice-Hall.

Kotler, P and Connor, R (1977) Marketing Professional Services, *Journal of Marketing*, January, 71-76.

Kotter, J P (1982) What General Managers Really Do. *Harvard Business Review*, Nov-Dec, 156-167.

Kotter, J P (1985) *The Leadership Factor*. New York: The Free Press.

Kuhn, T S (1970) *The Structure of Scientific Revolutions*. Chicago: University of Chicago Press.

Kuhn, T S (1977) *The Essential Tension: Selected Studies in Scientific Tradition and Change*. Chicago: University of Chicago Press.

Kunda, G and Barley, S R (1988) Designing Devotion: Corporate Culture and Ideologies of Workplace Control. Paper presented at the American Sociological Association 83rd Annual Meeting, Atlanta, August.

Kunda, G (1992) *Engineering Culture. Control and Commitment in a High-Tech Corporation*. Philadelphia: Temple University Press.

Kvale, S (1989) To Validate is to Question, in S Kvale (ed.) *Issues of Validity in Qualitative Research*. Lund: Studentlitteratur.

Lakoff, G and Johnson, M (1980) *Metaphors We Live By*. Chicago: University of Chicago Press.

Laurent, A (1978) Managerial Subordinacy. *Academy of Management Review*, 3, 220-230.

Lawrence, P and Lorsch, J (1967) Differentiation and Integration in Complex Organizations. *Administrative Science Quarterly*, 12, 1-47.

Leach, E (1968) Ritual, in *Encyclopedia of the Social Sciences*, New York: Collier-McMillan.

Leach, E (1976) *Culture and Communication*. Cambridge: Cambridge University Press.

Leach, E (1982) *Social Anthropology*. Glasgow: Fontana.

Levitt, H (1960) Marketing Myopia, *Harvard Business Review*, Jan.-Feb., 45-56.

Levitt, H (1981) Marketing Intangible Products and Product Intangibles, *Harvard Business Review*, May-June, 94-102.

Lindholm, S (1981) *Vetenskap, verklighet och paradigm*. Stockholm: Awe/Gebers.

Lindkvist, L (1989) Företagsintern styrning och informationsanvändning – en kontraktsansats. Research in Management Series, Report 8903. Dept of Management, Linköping University.

Lindmark, L (1989) Kunskapsföretagens individberoende. En studie av knoppningsföretag i reklambranschen. Paper presented at the Conference 'Kunskap som kritisk resurs', Umeå, June.

Lindström, J (1972) Perspektiv och vetenskapsideal. Avd för vetenskapsteori, Gothenburg University, Report 29.

Linstead, S and Grafton-Small, R (1992) On Reading Organizational Culture, *Organization Studies*, 13, 331-355.

Louis, M R (1980) Surprise and Sense-Making: What Newcomers Experience in Entering Unfamiliar Organizational Settings. *Administrative Science Quarterly*, 25, 226-251.

Louis, M R (1985) An Investigator's Guide to Workplace Culture, in P Frost, L Moore, M R Louis, C Lundberg and J Martin . (eds.) *Organizational Culture*. Beverly Hills: Sage.

Lovelock, C (1981) Why Marketing Management Needs to be Different for Services, in J Donnelly and W George (eds.) *Marketing of Services*. Chicago: American Marketing Association.

Lovelock, C (1983) Classifying Services to Gain Strategic Marketing Insights, *Journal of Marketing*, 47, 9-20.

Lundberg, C (1985) On the Feasibility of Cultural Intervention in Organizations, in P Frost, L Moore, M R Louis, C Lundberg and J Martin (eds.) *Organizational Culture*. Beverly Hills: Sage.

March, J and Olsen, J (1976) *Ambiguity and Choice in Organizations*. Bergen: Universitetsforlaget.

Martin, J (1987) A Black Hole: Ambiguity in Organizational Cultures, Paper presented at the SCOS International Conference on the Symbolics of Corporate Artifacts, Milan.

Martin, J (1992) *The Culture of Organizations. Three Perspectives.* New York: Oxford University Press.

Martin, J and Meyerson, D (1988) Organizational Cultures and the Denial, Channelling and Acknowledgement of Ambiguity, in L R Pondy, R Boland and H Thomas (eds.) *Managing Ambiguity and Change.* New York: Wiley.

Mattsson B (1990) *Ledningsgruppen och dess medlemmar.* Gothenburg: BAS.

Melin, L (1987) Comment to Chapter 4, in A Pettigrew (ed.) *The Management of Strategic Change.* Oxford: Basil Blackwell.

Miller, D and Mintzberg, H (1983) The Case of Configuration, in G Morgan (ed.) *Beyond Method. Strategies for Social Research.* Beverly Hills: Sage.

Mills, P et. al. (1983) Flexiform: A Model for Professional Service Organizations, *Academy of Management Review*, 8, 118-131.

Mills, P and Margulies, N (1980) Toward a Core Typology of Service Organizations, *Academy of Management Review*, 5, 255-265.

Mintzberg, H (1973) Strategy Making in Three Modes, *California Management Review*, Winter, 44-53.

Mintzberg, H (1975) The Manager's Job: Folklore and Fact, *Harvard Business Review*, July-August, 49-61.

Mintzberg, H (1983) *Structure in Fives. Designing Effective Organizations.* Englewood Cliffs: Prentice-Hall.

Mintzberg, H (1990) The Design School: Reconsidering the Basic Premises of Strategic Management, *Strategic Management Journal*, 11, 171-195.

Mintzberg, H and McHugh, A (1985) Strategy Formation in an Adhocracy, *Administrative Science Quarterly*, 30, 160-197.

Mintzberg, H and Waters, J (1985) Of Strategies, Deliberate and Emergent, *Strategic Management Journal*, 6, 3, 257-272.

Mintzberg, H and Waters, J (1990) Does Decisions Get in the Way?, *Organization Studies*, 11, 1-11.

Mintzberg, H, Otis, S, Shamsie, J and Waters, J (1988) Strategy of Design: A Study of "Architects in Co-partnership", in J Grant (ed.) *Strategic Management Frontiers*, Greenwich, Ct.: JAI Press.

Morgan, G (1980) Paradigms, Metaphors, and Puzzle Solving in Organization Theory, *Administrative Science Quarterly,* 25, 605-622.

Morgan, G (1983a) (ed.) *Beyond Method. Strategies for Social Research.* Beverly Hills: Sage.

Morgan, G (1983b) More on Metaphor: Why We Cannot Control Tropes in Administrative Science, *Administrative Science Quarterly*, 28, 601-608.

Morgan, G (1986) *Images of Organization.* Beverly Hills: Sage.

Morgan, G, Frost, P and Pondy, L (1983) Organizational Symbolism, in L Pondy, P Frost, G Morgan and T Dandridge (eds.) *Organizational Symbolism.* Greenwich: JAI Press.

Morgan, G and Smircich, L (1980) The Case for Qualitative Research. *Academy of Management Review.* 5, 491-500.

Moxnes, P (1981) *Ångest och arbetsmiljö – Hur organisationen påverkar personalen.* Stockholm: Natur och Kultur.

Myrdal, G (1968) *Objektivitetsproblemet i samhällsvetenskapen.* Stockholm: Raben & Sjögren.

Nicholls, J (1987) Leadership in Organisations: Meta, Macro and Micro. *European Journal of Management*, 6, 16-25.

Nord, W (1985) Can Organizational Culture be Managed? A Synthesis, in P Frost, L Moore, M R Louis, C Lundberg and J Martin (eds.) *Organizational Culture*. Beverly Hills: Sage.

Normann, R (1975) *Skapande företagsledning*. Stockholm: Bonniers. (English translation: *Management for Growth*. London: Wiley 1977).

Normann, R (1983) *Service Management*. Malmö: Liber. (English translation: *Service Management*. London: Wiley 1984.[1]

Ortner, S (1973) On Key Symbols, *American Anthropologist*, 75, 1338-1346.

Orton, D and Weick, K (1990) Loosely Coupled Systems: A Reconceptualization. *Academy of Management Review*, 15, 203-223.

Østerberg, D (1985) Materiell och praxis, in S Andersson et al., *Mellan människor och ting*. Gothenburg: Korpen.

von Otter, C (1983) Facket och det post-industriella företaget, in *Vägval. Uppsatser om några demokratiproblem*. Stockholm: Brevskolan.

Ouchi, W (1980) Markets, Bureaucracies, and Clans, *Administrative Science Quarterly*, 25, 129-141.

Ouchi, W (1981) *Theory Z: How American Business Can Meet the Japanese Challenge*. Reading, MA: Addison-Wesley.

Pennings, J and Gresov, C (1986) Technoeconomic and Structural Correlates of Organizational Culture: An Integrative Framework, *Organization Studies*, 7, 317-334.

Perrow, C (1986) *Complex Organizations: A Critical Essay*. New York: Random House.

Peters, T (1978) Symbols, Patterns, and Settings: An Optimistic Case for Getting Things Done, *Organizational Dynamics*, 7, 2-23.

Peters, T J and Waterman, R H (1982) *In Search of Excellence*. New York: Harper & Row.

Pettigrew, A (1979) On Studying Organizational Cultures, *Administrative Science Quarterly*, 24, 570-581.

Pettigrew, A (1985) Examining Change in the Long-Term Context of Culture and Politics, in J Pennings et al. (eds.) *Organizational Strategy and Change*. San Francisco: Jossey Bass.

Pfeffer, J (1978) The Ambiguity of Leadership, in M McCall and M Lombardo (eds.) *Leadership: Where Else Can We Go?* Durham: Duke University Press.

Pfeffer, J (1981a) Management as Symbolic Action: The Creation and Maintenance of Organizational Paradigms, in L Cummings and B Staw (eds.) *Research in Organizational Behavior, Vol. 3*. Greenwich: JAI Press.

Pfeffer, J (1981b) *Power in Organizations*. Boston: Pitman.

Pfeffer, J and Salancik, G (1978) *The External Control of Organization: A Resource Dependencies Perspective*. New York: Harper and Row.

Pinder, C C and Bourgeois, V (1982) Controlling Tropes in Administrative Science, *Administrative Science Quarterly*, 27, 641-652.

Pugh, D (1983) Studying Organizational Structure and Process, in G Morgan (ed.) *Beyond Method. Strategies for Social Research.* Beverly Hills: Sage.

Quinn, J B (1978) Strategic Change: Logical Incrementalism, *Sloan Management Review*, Fall, 7-21.

Quinn, J B (1984) Managing Strategies Incrementally, in R Lamb (ed.) *Competitive Strategic Management.* Englewood Cliffs: Prentice-Hall.

Ranson, S, Hinings, C R and Greenwood, R (1980) The Structuring of Organizational Structures, *Administrative Science Quarterly*, 25, 1-17.

Ray, C A (1986) Corporate Culture: The Last Frontier of Control. *Journal of Management Studies*, 23, 287-296.

Reed, M (1985) *Redirections in Organizational Analysis.* London: Tavistock.

Reeser, C (1969) Some Potential Human Problems of the Project Form of Organization, *Academy of Management Journal*, 459-467.

Rhenman, E (1974) *Organisationsproblem och långsiktsplanering.* Stockholm: Bonniers.

Robbins, S (1983) *Organization Theory: The Structure and Design of Organization*, Englewood Cliffs: Prentice-Hall.

Rorty, R (1992) Cosmopolitism without Emancipation, in S Lash and J Friedman (eds.) *Modernity & Identity.* Oxford: Blackwell.

Rosen, M (1985) Breakfast at Spiro's: Dramaturgy and Dominance. *Journal of Management,* 11, 2, 31-48.

Rosen, M (1991) Coming to Terms with the Field: Understanding and Doing Organizational Ethnography. *Journal of Management Studies,* 28, 1-24.

Sackman, S (1992) Culture and Subcultures: An Analysis of Organizational Knowledge. *Administrative Science Quarterly,* 37, 140-161.

Saffold, G (1988) Culture Traits, Strength and Organizational Performance Moving Beyond "Strong Culture", *Academy of Management Review*, 13, 546-558.

Salancik, G and Pfeffer, J (1978) A Social Information Processing Approach to Job Attitudes and Task Design, *Administrative Science Quarterly*, 23, 224-253.

Sandberg, Å (ed.) (1987) *Ledning för alla?* Stockholm: Center for Working Life.

Schein, E (1985) *Organizational Culture and Leadership. A Dynamic View.* San Francisco: Jossey-Bass.

Schneider, B (1980) Service Organizations: Climate is Crucial, *Organizational Dynamics,* Autumn, 52-65.

Schneider, B and Bowen, D (1993) The Service Organization: Human Resources Management is Crucial, *Organizational Dynamics*, 39-52.

Schneider, D (1976) Notes Toward a Theory of Culture, in K Basso and H Selby (eds.) *Meaning in Anthropology*. Albuquerque: University of New Mexico Press.

Schoemaker, P (1993) Strategic Decisions in Organizations: Rational *and* Behavioural Views. *Journal of Management Studies*, 30, 1, 107-129.

Schwartz, H and Davis, S (1981) Matching Corporate Culture and Business Strategy, *Organizational Dynamics*, Summer, 30-48.

Schwartz, H S (1987) Anti-Social Actions of Committed Organizational Participants: An Existential Psychoanalytic Perspective, *Organization Studies*, 8, 327-340.

Schwartzman, H (1993) *Ethnography in Organizations*. Newbury Park: Sage.

Selznick, P (1957) *Leadership in Administration: A Sociological Perspective*. New York: Harper and Row.

Siehl, C and Martin, J (1990) Organizational Culture: A Key to Financial Performance? In B Schneider (ed) *Organizational Culture and Climate*. San Francisco: Jossey-Bass.

Silverman, D (1985) *Qualitative Methodology & Sociology*. Aldershot: Gower.

Silverman, D (1989) Six Rules of Qualitative Research: A Post-Romantic Argument. *Symbolic Interaction*. 12, 2, 25-40.

Singer, M (1968) The Concept of Culture, in *Encyclopedia of the Social Sciences*. New York: Collier-McMillan.

Sjöstrand, S E (1985) *Samhällsorganisation*. Lund: Doxa.

Sjöstrand, S E (1986) The Dual Functions of Organizations, in E Johnsen (ed.) *Trends and Megatrends in the Theory of Management*. Lund: Studentlitteratur.

Sjöstrand, S E (1992) On the Rationale behind "Irrational" Institutions, *Journal of Economic Issues*, 26, 4, 1007-1040.

Sköldberg, K (1990) *Administrationens poetiska logik*. Lund: Studentlitteratur.

Sloterdijk, P (1984) Cynicism – The Twilight of False Consciousness, *New German Critique*, Fall, 33, 190-206.

Smircich, L (1983a) Concepts of Culture and Organizational Analysis, *Administrative Science Quarterly*, 28, 339-358.

Smircich, L (1983b) Studying Organizations as Cultures, in G Morgan (ed.) *Beyond Method Strategies for Social Research*. Beverly Hills: Sage.

Smircich, L (1983c) Organizations as Shared. Meanings, in L Pondy, P Frost, G Morgan and T Dandridge (eds.) *Organizational Symbolism*. Greenwich: JAI Press.

Smircich, L (1985) Is the Concept of Culture a Paradigm for Understanding Organizations and Ourselves?, in P Frost, L Moore, M R Louis, C Lundberg and J Martin (eds.) *Organizational Culture*. Beverly Hills: Sage.

Smircich, L and Calás, M (1987) Organizational Culture: A Critical Assessment, in F Jablin, L Putnam, K Roberts and L Porter (eds.) *Handbook of Organizational Communication*. Beverly Hills: Sage.

Smircich, L and Morgan, G (1982) Leadership: The Management of Meaning, *The Journal of Applied Behavioral Science*, 18, 257-273.

Smircich, L and Stubbart, C (1985) Strategic Management in an Enacted World, *Academy of Management Review*, 10, 724-736.

Starbuck, W (1992) Learning by Knowledge-Intensive Firms. *Journal of Management Studies*, 29, 6, 713-740.

Starbuck, W (1993) Keeping a Butterfly and an Elephant in a House of Cards: The Elements of Exceptional Success, *Journal of Management Studies*, 30, 6, 885-921.

Starrin, B, Larsson, G and Willebrand, K (1984) Upptäckande metodologi, *Sociologisk Forskning*, 3-4 1984, 15-28.

Steier, F (ed.) (1991) *Research and Reflexivity*. Newbury Park: Sage.

Strauss, A and Corbin, J (1990) *Basics of Qualitative Research*. Newbury Park: Sage.

Sveiby, K-E and Risling, A (1986) *Kunskapsföretaget*. Malmö: Liber.

Tompkins, P (1987) Translating Organizational Theory: Symbolism over Substance, in F Jablin, L Putnam, K Roberts and L Porter (eds.) *Handbook of Organizational Communication*. Newbury Park: Sage.

Trice, H and Beyer, J (1984) Studying Organizational Cultures through Rites and Ceremonials, *Academy of Management Review*, 9, 653-669.

Trice, H and Beyer, J (1985) Using Six Organizational Rites to Change Culture, in R Kilmann et al. (ed.) *Gaining Control of the Corporate Culture*. San Francisco: Jossey Bass.

Trice, H and Beyer, J (1989) Cultural Leadership in Organizations. Paper presented at the 4th International Conference on Organizational Symbolism and Corporate Culture, Fontainebleu, June 1989.

Tsoukas, H (1993) Analogical Reasoning and Knowledge Generation in Organization Theory. *Organization Studies*, 14, 323-346.

Turnbull, P and Valla, J-P (1986) Strategic Planning in Industrial Marketing: An Interaction Approach, *European Journal of Marketing*, 20, 7, 5-20.

Van Maanen, J (1978) People Processing: Strategies of Organizational Socialization, *Organizational Dynamics*, Summer, 18-36.

Van Maanen, J (1979) The Fact of Fiction in Organizational Ethnography, *Administrative Science Quarterly*, 24, 539-550.

Van Maanen, J (1988) *Tales of the Field.* Chicago: University of Chicago Press.

Van Maanen, J and Barley, S (1984) Occupational Communities: Culture and Control in Organizations, in B Staw and L Cummings (eds.) *Research in Organizational Behavior, Vol. 6.* Greenwich: JAI Press.

Van Maanen, J and Barley, S (1985) Cultural Organization: Fragments of a Theory, in P Frost, L Moore, M R Louis, C Lundberg and J Martin (eds.) *Organizational Culture.* Beverly Hills: Sage.

Van Maanen, J and Kunda, G (1989) Real Feelings: Emotional Expression and Organizational Culture, in B M Staw and L L Cummings (eds.), *Research in Organizational Behaviour, Vol. 11.* Greenwich: JAI Press.

Van Maanen, J and Schein, E (1979) Towards a Theory of Organizational Socialization, in B Staw (ed.) *Research in Organizational Behavior.* Greenwich, JAI Press.

Veen, P (1984) Characteristics of Organizations, in P Drenth, H Thierry, P Willems and C de Wolff (eds.) *Handbook of Work and Organizational Psychology, Vol. 2.* Chichester: Wiley.

Weber, M (1987) *Ekonomi och samhälle. Förståelsesociologins grunder, del 3.* Lund: Argos.

Weedon, C (1987) *Feminist Practice & Poststructuralist Theory.* Oxford: Basil Blackwell.

Weick, K (1976) Educational Organizations as Loosely Coupled Systems, *Administrative Science Quarterly*, 21, 1-19.

Weick, K (1979) *The Social Psychology of Organizations.* Newbury Park: Sage

Weick, K (1985) The Significance of Corporate Culture, in P Frost, L Moore, M R Louis, C Lundberg and J Martin (eds.) *Organizational Culture.* Beverly Hills: Sage.

Weick, K (1987) Theorizing about Organizational Communication, in F Jablin, L Putnam, K Roberts and L Porter (eds.) *Handbook of Organizational Communication.* Newbury Park: Sage.

Whittington, R (1993) *What is Strategy – and Does It Matter?* London: Routledge.

Whittington, R and Whipp, R (1992) Professional Ideology and Marketing Implementation, *European Journal of Marketing*, 26, 1, 52-63.

Wilkins, A and Dyer, W (1987) Toward a Theory of Culture Change: A Dialectic and Synthesis. Paper presented at the 3rd International conference on Organizational Symbolism and Corporate Culture, Milan, June.

Wilkins, A and Ouchi, W (1983) Efficient Cultures: Exploring the Relationship between Culture and Organizational Performance, *Administrative Science Quarterly,* 28, 468-481.

Wilkins, A and Patterson, K (1985) You Can't Get There From Here: What Will Make Culture-Change Projects Fail, in R Kilmann et al.

(eds.) *Gaining Control of the Corporate Culture*. San Francisco: Jossey-Bass.

Williams, R (1977) *Marxism and Literature*. Oxford: Oxford University Press.

Williamson, O (1985) *The Economic Institutions of Capitalism*. New York: Free Press.

Williamson, O and Ouchi, W (1981) The Markets and Hierarchies and Visible Hand Perspectives, in A Van de Ven and W Joyce (eds.) *Perspectives on Organization Design and Behavior*. New York: Wiley.

Willmott, H (1987) Studying Managerial Work: A Critique and a Proposal. *Journal of Management Studies,* 24, 248-270.

Willmott, H (1993) Strength is Ignorance; Slavery is Freedom: Managing Culture in Modern Organizations. *Journal of Management Studies,* 30, 4, 515-552.

Willmott, H and Alvesson, M (1995) Strategic Management as Domination and Emancipation, in C Stubbart and P Shrivastava (eds.) *Advances in Strategic Management*, Vol. 11, Greenwich: JAI Press.

Wilson, A (1975) *Professional Services and the Market Place*. Stockholm: Marknadstekniskt Centrum, MTC skrift nr 4.

Winch, P (1958) *On the Idea of a Social Science*. London: Routledge and Kegan Paul.

Yukl, G (1989) Managerial Leadership: A Review of Theory and Research. *Journal of Management*, 15, 251-289.

Young, E (1989) On the Naming of the Rose: Interests and Multiple Meaning as Elements of Organizational Culture. *Organization Studies,* 10, 187-206.

Zaleznik, A (1977) Managers and Leaders: Are They Different? *Harvard Business Review*, May-June, 67-68.

Zan, L (1990) Looking for Theories in Strategy Studies. *Scandinavian Journal of Management*, 6, 89-108.

Zeithaml, V, Parasuraman, A and Berry, L (1985) Problems and Strategies in Service Marketing, *Journal of Marketing*, 49, Spring, 33-46.

Zey-Ferrell, M and Aiken, M (1981) *Complex Organizations: Critical Perspectives*. Glenview: Scott, Foresman & Co.

Note

[1]   I have used the original Swedish versions of Normann's two books and translated some quotations. There may be minor differences between the quotations in the present book and in the English versions of Normann's books.